"[Quoting from book, 'The truth about our natures is that the gender binary and hierarchy—the heart of patriarchy—are false and destructively false because they cut us off from loving relationships based on freedom and equality.'] Much more than the memoir of an eminent gay law professor, this title is a seminal treatise on the history of hierarchical patriarchy and the corrosive effect upon both men and women in every stratum of American society...Richards deftly examines the literature of both gay and straight males and females, including Shakespeare, Dickens, Santayana, Melville, James, Woolf, Faulkner, Roth, Baldwin, and many others. The interdisciplinary volume also explores the work of American psychiatrist and student of violence, Dr. James Gilligan, anthropologist Ruth Benedict, and experts of both genders and sexual identities in many other fields who analyze the perpetuation of shame, guilt, and violent ideology through patriarchal repression."

—Kate Robinson, *The US Review of Books*

"*Boys' Secrets and Men's Loves: a Memoir* is a crusading text that argues that women, LGBTQUIA individuals and more enlightened cisgender straight men ought to band together in a valiant bid to salvage democracy under unprecedented assault."

—Joseph S. Peter, *Foreword Reviews*

"The arguments and conclusions are quite compelling particularly for those who have never thought about the patriarchy's effect on men."

—*Kirkus Reviews*

"Mining his experience as a gay, Italian American man raised in post-WWII America, Richards ⋯ ⋯ explore how patriarchy damages boys as they develop into ⋯⋯ y professor's meticulously researched boo ⋯⋯ orks of major literary and cinematic artist ⋯⋯ fluenced him as a young man, helping hi ⋯⋯ ed his "secret self"—his homosexuality—from the ⋯⋯ kable insight, Richards's memoir is a valuable text illuminating the negative impact American patriarchy has had, not only on the development of individuals but on the constitutional framework of society. Readers...will find the analysis fascinating."

—*BlueInk Review* (star review)

"David A.J. Richards tells real-life stories that show how love conquers all…..I loved reading *Boys' Secrets and Men's Loves*."

—Pacific Book Review

"Richards's analysis is dazzling…"

—Booklife Reviews

BOYS' SECRETS AND MEN'S LOVES:

BOYS' SECRETS AND MEN'S LOVES:

A MEMOIR

David A.J. Richards

Library of Congress Control Number:		2019906405
ISBN:	Hardcover	978-1-7960-3728-9
	Softcover	978-1-7960-3727-2
	eBook	978-1-7960-3726-5

Print information available on the last page.

Rev. date: 07/09/2021

To order additional copies of this book, contact:
Xlibris
844-714-8691
www.Xlibris.com
Orders@Xlibris.com
794732

For Phillip Blumberg

CONTENTS

The American ideal of masculinity. This ideal has created cowboys and Indians, good boys and bad guys, punks and studs, tough guys and softies, butch and faggot, black and white. It is an ideal so paralytically infantile that it is virtually forbidden—as an unpatriotic act—that the American boy evolve into the complexity of manhood.

—James Baldwin, "Freaks and the American Ideal of Manhood," *Collected Essays*, pp. 814–29, p. 816.

Midway in our life's journey, I went astray
    from the straight road and woke to find myself
    alone in a dark wood. How shall I say.

What wood that was! I never saw so drear;
    so rank, so arduous a wilderness!
    Its very memory gives a shape to fear;

Death could scarce be more bitter than that place!
    But since it came to good, I will recount
    all that I found revealed there by God's grace.

—Dante Alighieri, *The Divine Comedy*, John Ciardi translation, pp. 16–17

ACKNOWLEDGMENTS

This is the most personal book I have ever written, as it uses my personal life as the basis for its argument, using my own experience as a way into heightened awareness of the experience of many other boys and men, both straight and gay, of a secret self. Such awareness led to empathy for an experience we share as men, and where it leads them.

I was encouraged to do so by my coteacher for some twenty years of a seminar, Resisting Injustice at the New York University School of Law, namely, the developmental psychologist Carol Gilligan. Conversations with her and our students led me into thinking about the initiation of American men into patriarchy, and this book is my exploration of the form of this intiation in my life and my resistance. More recently, I have cotaught a seminar, Retributivism in Criminal Justice Theory and Practice (Shakespeare), with Carol's husband, a psychiatrist, Dr. James Gilligan, and conversations with him have helped me see how broadly shared my experience of initiation has been. This book could not have been written without their love and support.

A book about men's secrets and love was nurtured as well by the love of the man, Donald Levy, with whom I have shared my life in mutual love for now approaching fifty years. His love has made all things possible.

My thanks as well to the love and support over my lifetime of my sister Diane Rita Richards. We share so much, and our support for each other has endured.

Conversations with Drucilla Cornell about her book on Clint Eastwood were invaluable to me, and I am grateful for her support both in the past and now.

Finally, I entered into psychoanalysis a few years ago with a remarkable psychologist and therapist, Phillip Blumberg. Psychoanalysis with Phillip opened up a flood of memories, and we found that one way of understanding my boyhood was my reading as a young man, which led to much of the argument of this book based on the authors who were my closest friends during the years of my greatest loneliness. Phillip is among the most literate and sensitive men I have encountered, and conversations with him about literature and theater and much else shaped the argument of this book in general and in detail.

This book was researched and written during sabbatical leaves and during summers, supported in part by generous research grants from the New York University School of Law Filomen D'Agostino and Max E. Greenberg Faculty Research Fund and by the support of our current dean, Trevor Morrison.

My thanks as well to the advice and help of my extraordinary assistant, Lavinia Barbu, including her preparation of the bibliography.

New York, N.Y., May 28, 2019

INTRODUCTION

The election of Donald Trump raises urgent questions about the future of American democracy. Among those voting for Trump, men were in the majority, and a majority of American men voted for a man who placed our democracy at risk, as many, including Carol Gilligan and myself, have argued.[1] Why were they so vulnerable to his politics? An obvious response is that Trump promised to restore a white patriarchy that had come increasingly under threat, notably from the election of a black man as president and the prospect of his being succeeded by a woman. But why were so many men eager to embrace a racist patriarchy and to put our democracy at threat? A majority of white women who also voted for Trump also calls for explanation, but in this book, I write as a man, and more particularly, a gay man for whom the requisites of patriarchal manhood have always been fraught. More specifically, I write as a man who, in the course of his life and work, has become acutely aware of the harms that patriarchy does to men. Though seemingly in the interests of white, privileged men such as myself, patriarchy exacts a huge cost on men, not only gay as I am but straight men as well—a cost often hidden by men themselves. Among other harms, the most lethal violence is directed by men against

---

[1]   See, on this point, Carol Gilligan and David A. J. Richards, *Darkness Now Visible: Patriarchy's Resurgence and Feminist Resistance* (Cambridge: Cambridge University Press, 2018); Timothy Snyder, *On Tyranny: Twenty Lessons From the Twentieth Century* (New York: Tim Duggan Books, 2017); Timothy Snyder, *The Road to Unfreedom: Russia, Europe, America* (New York: Tim Duggan Books, 2018); Yascha Mounk, *The People vs. Democracy: Why Our Freedom Is in Danger and How to Save It* (Cambridge, Mass.: Harvard University Press, 2018).

men: successful suicides are usually men; the life span of men is shorter than women, due largely to the degree that men disproportionately suffer violence from other men; men are in high-risk professions and occupations; almost all wars are fought by men against men; disproportionate number of prisoners are men; and capital punishment is inflicted largely on men. Why are these harms to men not seen?

In exploring these costs and also how and why they become hidden, I became aware of the links between the initiation into patriarchy and the psychology of trauma. Researchers studying traumatic experiences have noted that the psychic markers of trauma are a loss of voice and of memory. The loss because of its association with shame is held as a secret within the psyche, and it is this secret I wish to explore. This book describes how men harbor a secret self as a way both of registering and resisting the trauma of their initiation into patriarchy.

In entering the realm of boys' secrets and men's loves, both gay and straight, I join reflections on my own struggles with manhood and love with the insights of writers who, across the ages, have illuminated the trauma of patriarchal manhood, although their works have not usually been read in this light. The process of writing this book was thus a process of discovery, spurred by joining autobiographical reflections on my own struggles with patriarchal manhood with earlier works coauthored with Carol Gilligan (Gilligan and Richards, 2008, 2018)[2], and it is with this work I begin.

In 2008, *The Deepening Darkness: Patriarchy, Resistance, and Democracy's Future*[3] sounded an alarm. Writing during the presidency of George W. Bush, Carol Gilligan and I had come to see democracy's future as contingent on resistance to patriarchy, noting the role that concerns about the shaming of manhood played in the interlinked injustices of the war in Iraq and the war on the rights of gays and lesbians. In initiating an unjust war and proposing a constitutional amendment to ban gay marriage, Bush

---

[2]   See Carol Gilligan and David A. J Richards, *The Deepening Darkness: Patriarchy, Resistance, and Democracy's Future* (Cambridge: Cambridge University Press, 2009); Carol Gilligan and David A. J. Richards, *Darkness Now Visible: Patriarchy's Resurgence and Feminist Resistance* (Cambridge: Cambridge University Press, 2018).

[3]   Carol Gilligan and David A. J. Richards, *The Deepening Darkness: Patriarchy's Resurgence and Feminist Resistance* (Cambridge: Cambridge University Press, 2018).

was appealing to a manhood both homophobic and dishonored by the attacks of 9/11. With the election of Obama in 2008 and his reelection in 2012, our fears for the future of American democracy were somewhat allayed. Along with many Americans, we joined with Obama in his hope that despite the setbacks under George W. Bush, the moral arc of the universe did in fact bend toward justice. Yet with Trump's election in 2016, our 2008 book suddenly appeared prophetic. The darkness posed by patriarchy's threat to democracy, the darkness that had been deepening under George W. Bush, was now quite visible. Patriarchy, formerly hiding in democracy, had come unapologetically out into the open.

Patriarchy is an anthropological term denoting families or societies ruled by fathers. It sets up a hierarchy—a rule of priests—in which the priest, the *hieros*, is a father, *pater*. As an order of living, it elevates some men over other men and all men over women. Within the family, it separates fathers from sons (the men from the boys) and places both women and children under a father's authority.[4] We know we are within patriarchy when there is a rigid gender binary (separating the masculine from the feminine, with—contrary to fact—no permissible overlap), and the masculine is always hierarchically above the feminine (irrespective and again, contrary to fact, of any overlap in competences). Trump's politics was so visibly patriarchal because of his embodiment and expression of both this gender binary and hierarchy, under which a woman is *obligated* to give feminine-coded services and is *prohibited* from having or taking masculine-coded goods.[5] Trump's misogyny successfully denigrated Hillary Clinton both for not being properly feminine (Lock her up) and seeking the masculine good of leadership.[6] In my coauthored book with Carol Gilligan, *The Deepening Darkness*, we argued that there are two ways in which patriarchy harms both men and women: first, it makes the free love of equals tragically impossible; and second, it forges a psychology in which men, through moral injuries that impair their sense of competence

---

4   Carol Gilligan and David A. J Richards, *The Deepening Darkness: Patriarchy, Resistance, and Democracy's Future* (Cambridge: Cambridge University Press, 2009), p. 22.

5   On these points, see Kate Manne, *Down Girls: The Logic of Misogyny* (New York: Oxford University Press, 2018), p. 130.

6   On these points, see Id.,_pp. 250–278; Carol Gilligan and David A. J. Richards, *Darkness Now Visible*.

---

and lead to loss of their love, are vulnerable to violence whenever their manhood is questioned, thus women are silenced and do not resist male violence. We develop the idea of patriarchal love laws—laws that determine whom, how, and how much one may love. And we argue that resistance to the love laws (love across the boundaries of race, ethnicity, caste, religion, and gender) empowers both love and empathy that challenge the evils of racism, religious prejudice, sexism, and homophobia.[7]

Many questions have been raised by Americans who found the outcome of the 2016 presidential election shocking. Carol and I address these issues in our 2018 *Darkness Now Visible: Patriarchy's Resurgence and Feminist Resistance*.[8] How could this have happened? Why didn't we see it coming? Why was resistance to Trump's politics so muted? Why was the first woman candidate nominated for the presidency by a major political party so delegitimized and personally denigrated? But the presence of patriarchy in our midst was no longer in question. As Susan Faludi observed in *The Guardian*, "It's almost as if the political culture conjured this 'urmisogynist' to go up against our first feminist political candidate . . . I keep going back to self-pity, and people who aren't suffering as much as they imagine they are . . . That seems to be a really dangerous place to be."[9] Unsurprisingly, women have been in the forefront of many of the resistance movements spurred by Trump's election, including the unprecedently large Women's March following his inauguration as well as the movement that preceded it, Black Lives Matter, initiated by three black women (Alicia Garza, Patrisse Cullops, and Opal Tometi), as well as the #MeToo Movement, and the again unprecedented number of women running for political office. We argue in our book that feminism, properly understood, resists the harms patriarchy inflicts on both women and men and call for coalitions between women and men who take these harms seriously and repair the harms they inflict on our democracy.

---

[7]   I further explore such resistance in David A. J. Richards, *Why Love Leads to Justice*.

[8]   Carol Gilligan and David A. J. Richards, *Darkness Now Visible: Patriarchy's Resurgence and Feminist Resistance* (Cambridge: Cambridge University Press, 2018).

[9]   Quoted in Michelle Dean, "Susan Faludi: the Feminist Writer on Trans Issues, Donald Trump and Masculinity," https://the guardian.com/world/206/jun/17/susan-faludi . . .

In this book, however, my focus is on men and the question, Why so many men saw Trump's election as in their interest? I answer this question in terms of the trauma of men's initiation into manhood, as they are required to separate from and denigrate any parts of their selves regarded as feminine and, indeed, to condemn any threat to the rigid gender binary they have come to regard as in the nature of things. The legacy of trauma is loss of memory and voice, exposing men to a vulnerability to a politics, like Trump's, that mobilizes them to condemn such threats. In effect, men act out the trauma of manhood inflicted on them; its invisibility to them renders them its executioners.

In interrogating the trauma of manhood in the wake of Trump's election, I draw inspiration from the candor of the men who in the fall of 2016, in their final papers for the Resisting Injustice seminar that Carol Gilligan and I have taught for a number of years, wrote stunningly confessional papers revealing their complicity in the persistence of patriarchy and, by implication, in the election of a man whom they themselves had not voted for. The papers were revelatory confessions of the patriarchal pressures of initiation they had, as men, experienced and how, writ large, they explain not only Trump's appeal but the lack of effective resistance. For the men, the pressures, including early bullying and later sometimes brutal fraternity initiations, led, as they put it, to infidelity to their real convictions and passions (their love). It was something they had learned early whenever their interests appeared or were coded as feminine. Unwittingly, or as one put it, without a conscious thought, they had fallen into a pattern that dates back to Abraham's willingness to sacrifice his son, Isaac, to prove his devotion to God.[10] In this book, I examine through autobiographical reflections as well as the insights of writers and filmmakers my own struggles as well as those of other men against pressures to sacrifice what we love for the sake of proving our devotion to a patriarchal order. In doing so, I also explore the secret self that resists such sacrifice and surfaces in ways that call for our attention, especially in this time when men's resistance to patriarchy may be essential for the survival of our democracy.

The secret self I uncover then, in myself in the works of (largely) American male writers, is a loving self—a self harbored within a self or male persona that has taken on the accoutrements of patriarchal manhood,

---

[10] For discussion of and excerpts from these student papers, see Carol Gilligan and David A. J. Richards, *Darkness Now Visible*, pp. 19–27.

in my own case, by attending Harvard and Oxford and becoming a professor of law with an endowed chair while also preserving a voice of resistance.

I address the question of American men resisting patriarchy from the perspective of a gay man whose ethnicity is second-generation Italian American born in East Orange, New Jersey, in 1944 at the end of World War II. Both my sexual orientation and my ethnicity placed me well outside the conventional understanding of American manhood dominant in my youth, and like some other outsiders (I think here of James Joyce and James Baldwin), I never accepted or could accept the conceptions of manhood dominant at that time. My resistance to them is very much my story. I have come to think today that my sense of myself as an outsider throughout my life was a great ethical and intellectual strength for me both in my personal life and my life as a law professor. In the same way, Hannah Arendt came to regard the sense of herself as Jewish as "a conscious pariah" as a strength in her pathbreaking work on anti-Semitism.[11] It not only enabled me to resist irrational forces (American homophobia and racism) that did not regard me as human or fully human but was the basis for producing a body of work in ethics and constitutional law that gave voice to such resistance, uniting with the voices of others, in movements for recognition of basic human rights.[12] My resistance also opened my heart

---

[11]   See, on this point, Michelle Dean, *Sharp: The Women Who Made an Art of Having an Opinion* (New York: Grove Press, 2018), p. 73.

[12]   See David A. J. Richards, *A Theory of Reasons for Action* (Oxford: Clarendon Press, 1971); *The Moral Criticism of Law* (Encino: Dickenson, 1977); *Sex, Drugs, Death and the Law: An Essay on Human Rights and Overcriminalization* (Totowa, NJ: Rowman & Littlefield, 1982); *Toleration and the Constitution* (New York: Oxford University Press, 1986); *Foundations of American Constitutionalism* (New York: Oxford University Press, 1989); *Conscience and the Constitution: History, Theory, and Law of the Reconstruction Amendments* (Princeton: Princeton University Press, 1993); *Women, Gays, and the Constitution: The Grounds for Feminism and Gay Rights in Culture and Law* (Chicago: University of Chicago Press, 1998); *Free Speech and the Politics of Identity* (Oxford: Oxford University Press, 1999); *Identity and the Case for Gay Rights* (Chicago: University of Chicago Press, 1999); *Italian American: The Racializing of an Ethnic Identity* (New York: New York University Press, 1999); *Tragic Manhood and Democracy: Verdi's Voice and the Powers of Musical Art* (Brighton, UK: Sussex Academic Press, 2004); *The Case for Gay Rights: From Bowers to Lawrence and Beyond* (Lawrence: University Press of Kansas, 2005); *Disarming Manhood: Roots of Ethical Resistance in Jesus, Garrison,*

and mind to love another man. It was something I had regarded earlier in my life as unimaginable. How does a man reimagine love, ethics, and law? This book adds to and deepens my body of work by drawing on my sense of self as an outsider to American manhood (in Arendt's sense, "a conscious pariah") to explore the role of American manhood both in enforcing patriarchy and knowing how American men, like myself, have come to resist patriarchy because, drawing on our own experience, it is as much harmful to men as it is to women. We need more testimony from American men about their experience of resistance, dealing honestly with its great challenges and difficulties (in view of the hegemonic strength over American men of patriarchy) as well as with its great benefits both for personal life and for ethical growth and for strengthening and deepening our democracy.

My study here is how men, like myself, nurture this voice of resistance even when they are young, alone, and isolated, as I was as a young man, sixteen to eighteen, and long after (until I was thirty), alone with my secret self (my homosexuality) in a culture that I saw even then as abusively bullying and repressive of what we now call gay voice.[13] How does one make one's way in such a patriarchal culture yet hold on to a voice that resists it? My story is how that voice was nurtured by my relationship to the works of creative men who also resisted, as my secret self found itself not alone, and my relationship to their works tracks my sense over time of how other

---

Tolstoy, Gandhi, King, and Churchill (Athens, Ohio: Swallow Press, 2005); *Patriarchal Religion, Sexuality, and Gender: A Critique of New Natural Law* with Nicholas C. Bamforth (Cambridge: Cambridge University Press, 2008); *The Deepening Darkness: Patriarchy, Resistance, and Democracy's Future* (with Carol Gilligan) (New York: Cambridge University Press, 2009); *The Sodomy Cases: Bowers v. Hardwick and Lawrence v. Texas* (Lawrence: University Press of Kansas 2009); *Fundamentalism in American Religion and Law: Obama's Challenge to Patriarchy's Threat to Democracy* (Cambridge: Cambridge University Press, 2013); *The Rise of Gay Rights and the Fall of the British Empire: Liberal Resistance and the Bloomsbury Group* (New York: Cambridge University Press, 2013); *Resisting Injustice and the Feminist Ethics of Care in the Age of Obama* (New York: Routledge, 2013); *Why Love Leads to Justice: Love Across the Boundaries* (New York: Cambridge University Press, 2016)

13   For a revelatory discussion of how alive this issue remains even today in the experience of gay men, see Guy Branum, "My Gay Voice," *The New York Times,* Sunday, July 29, 2018, p. SR7.

---

men experienced shame over their secret self and found an ethical voice to question the abusive culture that unjustly imposed such shame and thus to see and resist injustice. What riveted me about the works of these men is that they exposed the traumatic initiations they had themselves endured and found an ethical voice arising from their resistance to the demands of patriarchy that unjustly inflicted such harms on both men and women. Nowhere in the culture around me was there any such resisting voice that spoke to me, but the psychological and ethical depth of their works showed me in relational human detail both how men's voices were quashed by the trauma of manhood and how a voice was empowered by resistance. For me, it was a process, and I do mean a process, gradually of coming to see and appreciate one's own traumatic disassociation of mind from body, intellect from sexuality, thought from action, in the experience of others who found a voice through resistance that saw and questioned the disassociation and constructed on that basis a new sense of self through association, including love and empathy. Different creative men and other relationships played different roles at different stages as the disassociation gradually lost its hold on me, and a new construction of a sense of self and personal identity, mind joined to body, thought to action, gradually emerged. New models of self and of community thus grow together dialectically. Dickens (a straight man and victim of shame-filled child abuse) and Henry James (very much a closeted gay man) spoke to me at sixteen to eighteen, Santayana (a less closeted gay man) only later at Harvard College, James Baldwin (black and gay) and James Gilligan (straight) later still, and Philip Roth (straight) only recently. There is a story here of how men, through their shifting sense of self over time and responsive to new cultural forms of resistance to injustice, come to see and resist the codes of masculinity that imprison them, constructing over time a new sense of self and center their lives—their love and work—in an ethical voice that opens their heart and mind to love and empathy that resist injustice. It is my story, a story at bottom of the love of equals (both in personal and ethical life), against all the odds, and it is the story I have come to see of other men not only gay but straight, including, as I argue in chapter 11, ethical and political leaders like Martin Luther King Jr. and Barack Obama.

My argument begins with the relationship of two great American artists, Nathaniel Hawthorne and Herman Melville, and their works of art that most profoundly explore American patriarchy and its disastrous consequences for men's love, works that are for this reason narratives calling for resistance, on which I model my own narrative of resistance (chapter 1). Hawthorne's *The Scarlet Letter* frames the argument of this book, as I begin by investigating its astonishing exploration of the harms patriarchy inflict on good men (Dimmesdale and Chillingworth) and end by comparing Hawthorne's ethical vision of 1850 with that of a contemporary American cinematic artist, Paul Thomas Anderson, dealing with the same theme, in his 2017 movie, *Phantom Thread* (chapter 11). The argument of how patriarchy harms men and the role of women in bringing men to resistance to patriarchy, began by Hawthorne, could not be more alive and contemporary.

But patriarchy itself is a cultural and political form, and any investigation of resistance must meld together a political psychology with a personal psychology. I found the most illuminating way to link the two questions to be the great discovery of the cultural anthropologist Ruth Benedict of the patriarchal shame culture of Japan, the fascistic nation with which we were then at war. What compels me about Benedict is not only her argument but its roots in her own resistance as a lesbian to American patriarchy. She had, I believe, such a creative insight into Japanese patriarchy because she brought to bear on her study of the rather extreme form of shame culture she found in Japan her own experience as an American who once was unhappily married. She came to resist her patriarchal marriage and, in resisting, centered herself in the love of other women for a period, including Margaret Mead. Benedict's astonishing creative voice was able to see Japanese patriarchy because she had, like Virginia Woolf in Britain,[14] come to see, as a lesbian and outsider to American patriarchy, what it was here in America. America might dominantly be a guilt culture (guilt expressing a sense of culpably violating norms of equality and reciprocity), but it had features of a shame culture as well (exposure to humiliation because of failure to live up to cultural ideals of competence as a woman or man), associated with the still-existing forms of American patriarchy in relations between women and men. Benedict had experienced the latter at firsthand, and she brought that experience to bear in understanding the more dominant shame culture of Japan. Building on her work and related work of the psychiatrist James Gilligan, I offer an account of shame vs. guilt cultures, including the transition from one to the other.

---

[14] See, on this point, Carol Gilligan and David A. J. Richards, *The Deepening Darkness*, pp. 213–217.

The role resistance to patriarchy plays in this transition showing how such transitions have taken place both in ancient Greece, reflected in its literature, theater, and philosophy, and in Elizabeth England, in the plays of Shakespeare. I conclude with a discussion linking culture to psychology, namely, drawing on the work of Carol Gilligan, how a patriarchal culture requires a traumatic initiation into a gender binary and hierarchy that is at war with our human natures and how people come to resist through communalizing the trauma sometimes through the experience of artistic voices empowered by such resistance (chapter 2).

The heart of my argument (chapters 3–8) shows I found my way to resistance through finding my own experience in the experience of other men, both straight and gay, whose creative voices, often as artists, were empowered by their own struggles with their abusively traumatic histories as boys and young men.

The novels of Charles Dickens, a straight man, thus spoke to me because his novels center on his own experience of abuse as a boy and young man and how his voice, as an artist and critic of injustice, arose from speaking about and exploring what he and others endured (chapter 3). Dickens wrote out of a secret self—humiliation he endured as a young man and never could speak of during his lifetime—and yet he found a brilliant literary voice for revealing such patterns of abuse endured by both men and women as the roots of profound injustices in private and public life, including the British class system. Thus, according to George Bernard Shaw, "*Little Dorrit* is a more seditious book than *Das Kapital.*"[15]

And during that early period of my life, the novels of Henry James, through their very psychological and ethical complexity in dealing with his own experience of homophobic abuse as a gay boy and man, showed me how a sensitive and ethical gay voice could powerfully expose and resist such abuse in the experience of both men and women (chapter 4). James's secret self, his homosexuality, was my own situation, and yet he showed me how one could find a voice to reveal and explore the abusive patterns that unjustly inflicted moral damage not only on gay men but all men and women who suffer under the demands of patriarchal codes of masculinity and femininity, expressing itself in the betrayal of moral innocence and moral bullying, even terroristic violence. James showed me that the ethical

---

[15] Quoted in Leonard Shengold, *Soul Murder: The Effects of Child Abuse and Deprivations* (New York: Fawcett Columbine, 1989), p. 194.

issue was not only the injustice of homophobia but a larger cultural pattern that damaged ethics itself. This was, for me, revelatory—a new moral and psychological landscape opened before me—a life's work to which I could dedicate myself.

It was when a young man at Harvard College, still alone with my secret self, that the works and art of the philosopher George Santayana spoke to me about how my own passionate interest in moral and political philosophy could nurture my own resisting voice. Santayana, a gay man, had earlier taught at Harvard, experiencing its Puritan homophobia at firsthand, and I came to see both his work at Harvard and his novel, *The Last Puritan*, written after he left to live in Europe, as brilliantly exposing not only how ethically wrong its homophobia was but how psychologically destructive American homophobia was of the young men he taught and loved at Harvard (chapter 5). I was a Harvard man of a later generation and still subject to the same bovine bullying threats from a still Puritan university at least in the period between 1962 and 1968 when I was an undergraduate there. However, someone philosophically profound shared my experience and showed me a path to resistance, including Henry James and Santayana, while living abroad (studying at Oxford for two years). Santayana's path was not to be my path (I saw much more promise in American democratic constitutionalism than he did), but he gave me a way of finding my voice and my own deeply American way. (As a pathbreaking leader in constitutionalism who takes human rights seriously, all my work has been a study of American liberal constitutionalism and critically assessing whether we have been adequate to its mission and promise.) Santayana also gave me a way of understanding how ethically sensitive and damaged men, like him and T. S. Eliot and Ezra Pound, could deal with the moral injury American patriarchy inflicted on them not by resistance but by endorsing, implicitly or explicitly, forms of antidemocratic fascism (itself rooted in patriarchy). It was a path, despite its appeal to me, I would not take.

I am now seventy-five and have now lived through a period of remarkable change in American culture and values, largely in response to the resistance movements, which I joined as a young man, including, of course, the civil rights, antiwar, second-wave feminist, and gay rights movements, in the latter of which I was, among others, an agent of change. During this period, the essays and novels of James Baldwin, a black gay man, spoke to me, as he did to so many others, in an ethical voice exposing the interlinked lies that rationalize both American racism and homophobia—a voice that he found, as an exile from America, in the experience of gay love (resisting the love laws not only by loving and being loved by a man but a white European man, chapter 6). Baldwin found his remarkable ethical voice through resisting the love laws—an experience I shared.

I also found in the life and works of several straight men (James Joyce, Mark Twain, William Faulkner, and Dr. James Gilligan) remarkable creative voices about how young men come to resist patriarchy and thus understand and confront the interlinked evils of religious intolerance, racism, sexism, and homophobia (chapter 7). James Joyce spoke to me about his own secret sexual self in the repressive Catholic Ireland of his youth (like the Catholic culture in which I was brought up), and Mark Twain and William Faulkner explored—the one comically, the other tragically—the secret self of the love men feel for other men, including men of color and how ruthlessly American patriarchy attempts to repress such love. My relationship to James Gilligan has not only been to his works but to teaching and talking with him in a seminar on retributivism in criminal law theory and practice we have cotaught at the New York University School of Law for the past several years. Jim's remarkable ethical voice arose in his own resistance to patriarchal violence, which has made him the most profound analyst of male violence of our time. Through exposing his own traumatized secret self, he has shown how resistance leads to love, including an empathy for men in our prisons Americans find it so easy unjustly to hate. For Jim, such men are as much the unjust victims of American patriarchy as the rest of us.

All these works absorbed me because they took so seriously the traumatic abuse of boys and its consequences for their development as men. But the issues of trauma and voice were crystallized for me when I read and studied the most contemporary novelist I discuss in this work, Philip Roth, a straight man and Jewish, in which both the personal and political consequences of trauma (including the trauma of anti-Semitism) and resisting voice are so powerfully portrayed (chapter 8). It was the philosopher Theodor Adorno, who argued that the most profound injustices sometimes cannot be adequately understood or expressed through argument, and only the arts can give voice to these suppressed voices and experiences.[16] I regard patriarchy as such an injustice—an injustice, because of trauma, men cannot see or acknowledge or take seriously. I myself have come to terms with the problem in my own life in part through the arts, in particular, the many novelists I read as a boy and man, whose work brilliantly clarifies, as Adorno argues art does and should, the trauma of manhood and how men can and do find a voice to repair the damage done them and to resist. Reading Roth made this quite clear to me, but it was powerfully at work in all the artists I had been reading since I was a boy and young man. It is the power of truthful voice in such art—a voice otherwise unavailable in the culture around them—that nourishes a voice of resistance otherwise quashed. That is Adorno's point about the powers of great art, which had such resonance for me, as a young boy and man, as it has had for so many other men and women.

I also discuss such resisting voices of men in the cinematic art of John Ford and Clint Eastwood (chapter 9). Ford is of particular interest to my argument as his secret self (homosexuality) was, so I argue the voice of resisting patriarchy that we find in his art.

It is for this reason that my own voice as a boy and man developed in relationship to the voices of artists, gay and straight, whose journey to love and justice was, to my surprise, mine as well. Patriarchy so divides men from one another as well as men from women that we cannot see what we share. No such division remains more powerful than gay vs. straight. My argument shows the boundary is unreal and that men, gay and straight, share a common trauma—the trauma of manhood—and have so much to learn from and share with one another. What I learned from these artists and the other men and women who filled my life with friendship and love is that the key to resistance is communal voice, sharing both the voice and memory of the trauma. Literature and personal relationships have the healing power they do when men speak from a voice that acknowledges the trauma and, in giving voice to it, breaks its hold on us. That is the story this book tells.

I found this communal voice early in my life when I was most alone through finding that my experience was shared by other men who had been as alone with their trauma as I was with mine. I felt intimately close

---

16   See Theodor W. Adorno, *Aesthetic Theory*, trans. Robert Hullot-Kentor (Minneapolis: University of Minnesota Press, 1997). For further discussion, see chapter 8.

to them. Joseph Conrad in his short story, *The Secret Sharer*, writes of such a young man who has unexpectedly been made captain of a British ship in the Gulf of Siam and feels anxious in his new role and isolated from his crew, wondering, *How far should I turn out faithful to the ideal conception of one's own personality every man sets up for himself secretly?*[17] Ships, as in Melville's novels (see chapter 1), are often metaphors for patriarchy, and the young captain, unlike Melville's Captain Vere, clearly experiences resistance to its claims. The young captain comes to feel closer to another outsider young man, Leggatt—a fugitive from another ship who seeks refuge on the captain's ship from a charge of homicide of a culpably disobedient sailor while Leggatt was acting as first mate during a storm that threatened to destroy the ship. (The homicide may have been in the circumstances justified or excusable.) Leggatt is as alone as the young captain is, and they share a common background (having gone to the same school). The captain experiences Leggatt's lonely plight as his own, "my second self,"[18] secreting him on his ship even from the captain of the other ship seeking the fugitive. He helps Leggatt escape, "a free man striking out for a new destiny."[19] Embedded in patriarchal structures, young men nonetheless find and nurture in themselves a resisting voice, sometimes as I did, by finding a secret sharer in the experiences of other men. One finds oneself not alone but sharing a common struggle of men to be "faithful to the ideal conception of one's own personality every man sets up for himself secretly." My relationship to the men I discuss in this book arose from the discovery that we shared so much secrets as men and that we shared as well a voice that could resist the harms patriarchy inflicted on us all.

An approach of this sort advances much-needed argument about how patriarchy harms all men. It's a problem rooted in men's initiation into patriarchy and their psychological difficulties in resisting its demands, and the catastrophic consequences of the psychological hold patriarchy has on American men. These forms of moral damage not only cripple the love of men but cripple as well their moral empathy. It is shown in the ways men are enlisted mindlessly into deep injustices. I illustrate this latter point in chapter 7 (racialized mass incarceration) and in chapter 10 in men's

---

[17]   Joseph Conrad, *The Secret Sharer*, *Heart of Darkness and The Secret Sharer* (New York: Bantam Dell, 2004), pp. 119–172, at p. 123.

[18]   Joseph Conrad, *The Secret Sharer*, p. 144.

[19]   Joseph Conrad, *The Secret Sharer*, p. 172.

complicity in fighting America's unjust wars, rationalized often by racist appeals to codes of patriarchal manhood at threat. The Vietnam War is in my experience the most notable such experience, but the more recent Iraq War illustrates the same dynamic. The very invisibility of gender in our national public discourse is thus the key to its extraordinary cultural and political power, which has now put democracy itself visibly at threat.

Finally, there is the damage to democracy itself, which I address in chapter 11. Trump's war on immigrants and Muslims illustrates such damage to our values as an immigrant nation committed to constitutionalized values of freedom of religion and conscience, and I connect his America First ideology to earlier attempts by politicians (including Theodore Roosevelt and Woodrow Wilson) who sought to demonize as "hyphenated" Americans my own Italian American family among others and to argue that what our constitutional culture learned and should have learned from that experience is what I call American transnationalism and that our constitution is founded not in ethnicity or religion (or gender or sexual orientation) but in universal human rights.

What many Americans, including Italian Americans like myself, should learn from that history is to refuse the kind of racialized Americanization Trump offers, setting us now against other contemporary immigrants who do not share our ethnicity or our religion. And we should take seriously the features of Trump's presidency that undermine democracy itself, not least his appalling war on a free press. My argument also includes a discussion of moral and political leaders, Martin Luther King Jr. and Barack Obama, whose life and work reflect resistance to patriarchy. I contrast their background and politics to that of Donald Trump. The failure of American men to resist patriarchy, reflected in the election of Donald Trump, now visibly threatens democracy itself. Only feminism, which joins men and women in an alliance resisting patriarchy, can preserve and deepen American democracy, as Carol and I argue in *Darkness Now Visible*. I illustrate this latter point by showing how the narrative of Hawthorne's *The Scarlet Letter*, with which I begin my argument (chapter 1), remains all too contemporary, as shown in Anderson's important recent movie, *The Phantom Thread*. As William Faulkner put the point, "The past is never dead. It's not even past."[20]

---

[20]   William Faulkner, *Requiem for a Nun*, William Faulkner, *Novels 1942–1954*, ed. Joseph Blotner and Noel Polk (New York: The Library of America,1994),

The problem of American patriarchal manhood cannot be responsibly dealt with until men come to see themselves as much harmed as women and join them in resistance. Jessica Valenti recently put this point:

> Men have more cultural and economic power than women, And more often that not, assertions that young men are under siege are more about reinforcing traditional gender gender power dynamics than helping to see how those norms harm boys.
>
> Feminism has been focused on issues of sexual assault, reproductive rights, harassment and more. But issues don't hart women, men do. Until we grapple with how to stop misogynists themselves—starting with ensuring boys don't grow up to be one—women will never be free.[21]

This book is an effort to this end.

The subtitle of Carol and my recent book—patriarchy's resurgence and feminist resistance—evinces the book's concern not only for how and why Trump's politics expresses patriarchy's resurgence but, for the very reason that it made the force of patriarchy in American culture and politics so visible, has given rise to a resistance grounded in resistance to patriarchy. Patriarchy, once an unfashionable idea has become a rallying cry for feminism today.[22] A central claim of our book is that feminism has been marginalized because it has been viewed through a patriarchal frame, setting women against men. Trump's success in our view rests on the way his blatantly patriarchal rhetoric shifted the frame from democracy to patriarchy, viewing feminism through a patriarchal lens. Feminism, however, resists the gender binary and hierarchy (the DNA of patriarchy), which harms men as well as women. It is the most important emancipatory movement of our age because it alone addresses how patriarchy, harming

---

pp. 472–665, p. 535.

[21] Jessica Valenti, "Boys Need Feminists' Help Too," *The New York Times Op-Ed* Thursday July 26, 2018, A27.

[22] See Charlotte Higgins, "The Guardian: The Age of Patriarchy: How an Unfashionable Idea Became a Rallying Cry for Feminism Today," https://www.theguardian.com/news/2018/jun/22/the-age-of patriarchy-...le-idea-became-a rally-cry=for-feminism-tday?CMP+share_btn_link.

---

both men and women, undermines democracy based on free and equal voice.

In this work, I take up and continue the thread of the argument of *Darkness Now Visible,* further exploring the psychology that makes it so difficult for men like me to understand the harm patriarchy inflicts on them and yet how and why some men, many of them American men, resist. Men find it so difficult to acknowledge, let alone resist, patriarchy, because their initiation into a life and psyche defined by the gender binary and hierarchy is traumatic. It requires them to deny and repress a human psyche not confined to patriarchy, including the convictions and love of equals that make us human. Manhood is built upon trauma, which deprives its victims of both voice and memory. Indeed, male identity is so inextricably founded on patriarchy gender stereotypes that any challenge to them shames men, eliciting the kind of repressive fear and anger that Trump successfully mobilized. Yet men sometimes resist.

What I have come to believe is that what men, gay and straight, share is the trauma the dominant patriarchal conception of manhood inflicts on men, which explains why, for men, it is so difficult even to speak, let alone remember, the pressures on them to conform.

If men and women do not make this effort, the vacuum of discussion will be filled by the conventional silencing of the voices of resistance—in particular, men's resistance—and be filled by the reactionary patriarchal forces that have been so dominant in American cultural and political life, as Trump's election now makes so clear, so visible. Such reactionary forces are already now in play not only by men like Trump but by intellectuals who should know better but do not. For example, Harvey C. Mansfield, a Harvard professor of government, had published in 2006 a book, *Manliness,* that responded to the claims of feminism by appealing to a patriarchal value, manliness, that Mansfield associates with the irrationalist individuality of Nietzsche; he acknowledges how problematic this value has been historically (prefiguring fascism) but urges that the just claims of a moderate feminism must make reasonable room for this value.[23] Mansfield's *Manliness*—in its improvisatory aggressive irrationalism— prefigures no one better than Trump himself and, in the wake of the election, understands Trump's victory, as Carol and I do, as grounded in his appeal to patriarchy. Unlike us, however, Mansfield writes of Trump's

---

[23]   Harvey C. Mansfield, *Manliness* (New Haven: Yale University Press, 2006)

presidency not disapprovingly as marking, for Mansfield, the desirable end of "gender-neutrality."[24]

And Jordan Peterson, a psychologist who has taught at Harvard and the University of Toronto, had earlier elaborated a Jungian theory of belief, heavily dependent on patriarchal mythology,[25] and more recently published a best-selling book, *12 Rules for Life: An Antidote to Chaos.*[26] The book, at its end, makes clear the chaos to which the book's bizarre rules (e.g., stand up straight with your shoulders back) are alleged to be antidotes, namely, the feminist critique of patriarchy,[27] and its Terrible Mother.[28] For Peterson, the masculine spirit is under assault. It's obvious.[29] In his world, order is masculine, while chaos is feminine.[30] In his book, Peterson cites as examples of such chaos young men who kill innocent people in shootings at schools and theaters,[31] but as Kate Manne has cogently shown,[32] rather shockingly fails to explore further or acknowledge their real views, shaped by a patriarchal culture that rationalizes their blatantly irrationalist sexism and homophobia (both of which Peterson omits mentioning), their chaos rests precisely on a reactionary patriarchy: "the masculine despair he reinforces and dignifies."[33] As to questioning gender hierarchy, Peterson asserts, citing hierarchy among lobsters, "The people who hold that our culture is an oppressive patriarchy don't want to admit that the current

---

24   See Tunku Baradarajan, "The Weekend Interview with Harvey Mansfield, Manhood in the Age of Trump," *The Wall Street Journal,* Saturday/Sunday March 31–April 1, 2018, A13.

25   Jordan B. Peterson, *Maps of Meaning: The Architecture of Belief* (New York: Routledge, 1999)

26   Jordan B. Peterson, *12 Rules for Life: An Antidote to Chaos* (Toronto: Random House Canada, 2018).

27   See Id., pp. 303–322.

28   Id., p. 322.

29   Nellie Bowles, "The Prophet of the Patriarchs: If an Overdose of Female Is Our Poison, Jordan Peterson Preaches a Masculine Cure," *New York Times,* May 20, 2018, SundayStyles, pp. 1, 7, quoted at p. 1.

30   Id., p. 1.

31   Jordan B. Peterson, *12 Rules for Life: An Antidote to Chaos* (Toronto: Random House Canada, 2018), pp. 147–48.

32   Kate Manne, "Reconsider the Lobster: Jordan Peterson's Failed Antidote for Toxic Masculine Despair," *The Times Literary Supplement,* May 25, 2018, pp. 14–16.

33   Id., p. 16.

hierarchy might be predicated on competence."[34] Of course, neither the gender binary and hierarchy are based today on reasonable measures of competence,[35] and Peterson ultimately appeals not to reason but to patriarchal mythology, which he knows quite well. His followers are drawn to him almost mystically,[36] which is to say by patriarchal psychology (as fascists were once drawn to Mussolini and Hitler). What is remarkable is that this uncritically patriarchal mythology—a mythology that Simone de Beauvoir had subjected in 1949 to such devastating criticism[37] should be so appealing to so many and now.[38] Unsurprisingly, Peterson recently questioned the #MeToo Movement because it allegedly called into question the coed offices because things are deteriorating very rapidly at the moment in terms of the relationships between men and women.[39] For Peterson, as for others,[40] the very raising of the issue of toxic masculinity, as an increasingly obvious threat to both our ethics and politics,[41] is itself a threat, not a long-overdue discussion of issues central to American democracy.

Why? There is a reactionary political psychology at work here, expressed in the subtitle to Peterson's recent book, "an antidote to chaos." It is the psychology that James Gilligan has described as the nihilist response to the skepticisms of modernity about traditional belief systems and ways of life, an irrationalist anger expressed in the political violence

34 Nellie Bowles, "The Prophet of the Patriarchs: If an Overdose of Female Is Our Poison, Jordan Peterson Preaches a Masculine Cure," *New York Times*, May 20, 2018, SundayStyles, pp. 1, 7, quoted at p. 7.

35 See, on this point, Angela Saini, *Inferior: How Science Got Women Wrong—and the New Research That's Rewriting the Story* (Boston: Beacon Press, 2017).

36 See, for examples of his followers, Id., p. 7.

37 See Simone de Beauvoir, *The Second Sex*, trans. Constance Borde and Sheila Malovany-Chevallier (New York: Vintage, 2011; originally published, 1949).

38 See, for example, Ross Douthat, "God and Men and Jordan Peterson," *The New York Times*, Sunday, April 1, 2018, SR9; Kelefa Sanneh, "Sort Yourself Out, Bucko: The Gospel of Jordan Peterson," *The New Yorker*, March 5, 2018, pp. 70–75; Yoram Hazony, "Jordan Peterson and Conservatism's Rebirth," *The Wall Street Journal*, Saturday/Sunday, June 16–17, 2018, A13.

39 Quoted in Michelle Goldberg, "How the Online Left Fuels the Right," *The New York Times*, Sunday, May 13, 2018, p. SR11.

40 See, for an illustrative example, Crispin Sartwell, "Conversion Therapy Isn't the Cure for Toxic Masculinity," *The Wall Street Journal*, June 2–3, 2018, A15.

41 See Carol Gilligan and David A. J. Richards, *Darkness Now Visible*.

of nationalism (fascism), imperialism, totalitarianism, and apocalyptic fundamentalism.[42] One of these traditional belief systems and ways of life is patriarchy, and democratically grounded skepticism about patriarchy has elicited these forms of unjust violence (more on Gilligan's work later) in service of reinstituting patriarchal conceptions now perceived at threat. Both Mansfield and Peterson seek to rationalize, quite unreasonably, such reactionary motives, all too broadly shared among men in America and elsewhere as they rage against now credible threats to their patriarchal privilege. The way to respond is, I believe, to show how and why men themselves come to resist patriarchy, as they come to see how patriarchy harms them as well as women, and join women in resistance in the service of the ethical ideals of democracy itself.

---

[42]   See James Gilligan, "Terrorism, Fundamentalism, and Nihilism: Analyzing the Dilemmas of Modernity," eds. Henri Parens, Alaf Mahfouz, Stuart W. Twemlow, and David E. Sharff, *The Future of Prejudice: Psychoanalysis and the Prevention of Prejudice* (Lanham, Md.: Rowman & Littlefield, 2007), pp. 37–62.

Chapter 1

Melville and Hawthorne on Patriarchal Manhood and Homophobia[43]

That there is a problem in American manhood, which is connected to our patriarchal traditions, is first stated quite clearly and explored profoundly in Nathaniel Hawthorne's *The Scarlet Letter*. It both states the problem and imagines resistance in the voice of a woman condemned for adultery. Hawthorne's masterpiece was published in 1850, and both the book and his relationship to Melville inspired Melville's *Moby-Dick* (published in 1851) and *Billy Budd* (published posthumously in 1924). All these works expose and resist the forces of American patriarchy, albeit in quite different ways. They show us the way American men do and can resist.

I begin my investigation of how and why men come to resist patriarchy with the works and relationship of these two American men, whose works set the stage for the investigations to follow. I begin with the works themselves and then turn to the psychology that underlies, in my view, the creativity of their relationship, for Melville, in particular. Men through love for one another as equals sometimes resist patriarchy, as Hawthorne and Melville clearly did—revealing how it harms not only women, but all men—to the subject of this book.

---

[43] Work on this chapter profited from the advice of Richard Weisberg and Jon-Christian Suggs, for which I am deeply grateful. Conversations with Phillip Blumberg were also indispensable.

1

Hawthorne's *The Scarlet Letter* is, of course, a self-conscious work on and about *patriarchy*, a term he uses repeatedly throughout the novel.[44] We know his sister-in-law, Elizabeth Peabody, was as an abolitionist feminist opposing not only American slavery and racism but sexism, all of which the abolitionist feminists linked to the unjust force of patriarchy in American religion and ethics as well as politics.[45] And *The Scarlet Letter*, which is inspired by the recent death of his beloved mother, brilliantly explores Puritan patriarchal condemnation of the adultery of Hester Prynne leading to the birth of her daughter, Pearl, and the growth of her internal voice of ethical resistance to such patriarchal condemnation, rooted in her love for Pearl and her continuing love for her Puritan minister, Dimmesdale, who cannot and will not acknowledge his love. On this view, which Carol Gilligan first developed, *The Scarlet Letter* is a resistance novel and the resistance to patriarchy, in particular, to unjust patriarchal restraints on women's loving sexual relationships.[46]

Melville's *Moby-Dick* and *Billy Budd* are decidedly not about patriarchal constraints on women (there are few women in the former, none in the latter), but both are about how patriarchy destroys men and how difficult, if not impossible, resistance to patriarchal injustice is for men. Hawthorne makes the same point in *The Scarlet Letter* in the central male characters, Dimmesdale (Hester's minister and lover) and Chillingworth (Hester's husband), both of whom, talented and humane men, have been patriarchally shrunk—the one (Dimmesdale) emotionally dim, the other (Chillingworth) coldly chilly and retributive who, like a psychoanalyst gone mad not only sees Dimmesdale's guilt but exacerbates it. There is something almost homoerotically intense in the relationship of these two men, but in Melville, the homoeroticism among men is, remarkable for this period, more explicit—as in the terms *almost of gay marriage* in the loving relationship of Queequeg and Ishmael in *Moby-Dick* (hugging a fellow male in that matrimonial sort of style)[47] and the twisted repressed

---

44   See Nathaniel Hawthorne, *The Scarlet Letter* (New York: Penguin, 1986), pp. 15, 18, 20, 132, 190.

45   See, for further discussion and elaboration, David A. J. Richards, *Women, Gays, and the Constitution: The Grounds for Feminism and Gay Rights in Culture and Law* (Chicago: University of Chicago Press, 1998).

46   See, for fuller discussion, Carol Gilligan, *The Birth of Pleasure: A New Map of Love* (New York: Vintage, 2003).

47   Herman Melville, *Moby-Dick or, The Whale* (New York: Penguin, 2003), p.

homosexuality of Claggart in *Billy Budd* and the feeling of Captain Vere and Billy for each other. More about this later.

The effects of patriarchy on men is the very center of what arrests our attention in Melville's two masterpieces. *Moby-Dick* is, like *The Scarlet Letter*, an antebellum novel very much framed by the sense, in the early 1850s, of a national tragedy of internecine violence very much in the offing (culminating in the Civil War). The Pequod, a model of the patriarchal ship of state, is led by a monstrous patriarch, Ahab, whose narcissistic rage arises from the insult to his manhood of the loss of a leg to the white whale he was hunting. The novel shows us the lucrative American whaling industry run by Quakers, nonviolent in their religion and politics, but here engaged in a lucrative business that lives off the killing and dismembering not of fish but of mammals, like porpoises and dolphins, which are among the most intelligent of such creatures. In his early novels based on his South Sea adventures, Melville often tried to show the humane features even of cannibals, who horrified American proselytizing clergy,[48] and here, in *Moby-Dick*, he ethically counterpoises to their horror the horror of nonviolent Quakers cannibalizing mammals, a horror shown in vividly remarkable detail. But the center of the novel is not only Ahab's narcissistic rage but the way the men he leads, including Starbuck, who sees the irrationality of the venture, follow him even unto their deaths. As Starbuck sees clearly, Ahab's obsessional object, revenge on the white whale, is utterly irrational, distracting the ship from what its Quaker owners regard as the only rational object of this business—making money off the parts of the whale for which there was a lucrative market. Yet the insult to Ahab's patriarchal manhood, a personal obsession, becomes a political psychology of collective violence that the men of the Pequod, including Starbuck, cannot and will not resist. What Melville shows us is an interlinked personal and political psychology that, under patriarchy, mobilizes irrational political violence, as in the sense in the antebellum American South that any threat to the racist hierarchy of American slavery elicits the violence of civil war with people of color as scapegoats (Ahab may be modeled on Calhoun),[49] or in Hitler's appeal to

---

30; see also pp. 28, 57–58, 60, 62–63, 66–8, 349.

[48] See, on this point, Laurie Robertson-Lorant, *Melville: A Biography* (New York: Clarkson Potter, 1996).p. 140.

[49] Andrew Delbanco, *Melville: His World and Work* (New York: Alfred A.

---

the shame of Versailles that led to the genocidal murder of scapegoats, six million European Jews.[50] What Melville reveals is the scapegoat of insulted patriarchal manhood, a projected emptiness, a white whale, who could be anyone. The more innocent and vulnerable, the better.

The ship, *Bellipotent*, in *Billy Budd* is also a model of the patriarchal state, only here is used as a British military vessel at war with France in the Napoleonic War—a war between two imperialisms: one British, the other French. The contrast drawn here between the patriarchal state of rigid hierarchical order and its alternative is here starkly drawn as Billy, commandeered from his ship, *Rights-of-Man*, to serve on the *Bellipotent* says, "And goodbye to you too, old *Rights-of-Man*,[51]—a terrible breach of naval decorum."[52] Why *terrible*? Even to mention the rights of man, the basis of democracy, in such a context is to provoke terror in the patriarchal order. It is the kind of insult to patriarchal manhood that elicits violence, and Billy is killed. What makes *Billy Budd* so remarkable is that it carries Melville's interest in the effects of patriarchy on men into their psyches, to wit, the psyches of men who are sexually attracted to and sometimes to love men. The text of *Billy Budd* could not be clearer: Billy, the handsome sailor,[53] is loved by everyone, but it is the sexual desire for Billy of the repressed Claggart that is homophobically transformed into violence—a violence that leads to the deaths of both Claggart and Billy. Homophobia experiences homosexual desire as shame, an insult to one's patriarchal manhood, an insulted manhood that elicits violence, as James Gilligan's work so clearly shows.[54] What is of interest in *Billy Budd* is not only exposing such damaging effects of patriarchy on a man like Claggart but its effects on the patriarch of the *Bellipotent*, Captain Vere, a man portrayed in the work as perceptive, scholarly, and humane, surely as humane and learned as Hawthorne's Dimmesdale and Chillingworth. It is Captain Vere who ultimately condemns Billy to death, but his route to this end is not, as with Claggart, so direct. Vere, for whom forms, measured forms

---

Knopf, 2005), pp. 162–66.

50   See, on this analogy, Andrew Delbanco, *Melville*, pp. 174–5.

51   Herman Melville, *Billy Budd, Sailor and Selected Tales*, ed. Robert Milder (Oxford: Oxford University Press, 2009), p. 285.

52   Id., p. 285.

53   Id., p. 286.

54   See James Gilligan, *Violence: Reflections on a National Epidemic* (New York: Vintage, 1997).

are everything,[55] as soon as Billy strikes Claggart dead, he vehemently exclaimed, "Struck dead by an angel of God! Yet the angel must hang!"[56] Yet, as Richard Weisberg has cogently shown, both the procedure and substance of Billy's conviction and death penalty violate the applicable legal norms—norms with which Melville, a former seaman, was well familiar.[57] Even Vere's officers express doubt that Vere is following the proper legal rules and procedure, and they convict and condemn Billy to death at Vere's insistence, concerned otherwise, as Vere puts it, that mutiny would be encouraged.[58] In fact, it is Billy's execution that nearly provokes mutiny among the men who loved him.[59] The compulsion Vere experiences to kill Billy is put by him in two revealing ways: the decision must not rest on "the feminine in man"[60] and must follow "the imperial one"[61] required by law. Appeal to the gender binary shows we are within patriarchy, and the effects of patriarchy on men are evident not only in Claggart but in Vere and even in Billy's acceptance of his death, exclaiming at his death, "God bless, Captain Vere!"[62]

The novella tells us that it is Captain Vere himself who talks privately with Billy about his condemnation to death, but we are not told what was said. Presumably, what was said must explain Billy's blessing of Vere before his death. What we are told, however, is this:

> Captain Vere in end may have developed the passion
> sometimes latent under an exterior stoical or indifferent.
> He was old enough to have been Billy's father. The austere
> devotee of military duty, letting himself melt back into
> what remains primeval in our formalized humanity, may
> in end have Billy to his heart, even as Abraham may have

---

55   Herman Melville, *Billy Budd*, p. 358.
56   Herman Melville, *Billy Budd*, p. 333.
57   See Richard H. Weisberg, *The Failure of the Word: The Protagonist as Lawyer in Modern Fiction* (New Haven: Yale University Press, 1984), pp. 147–159.
58   Herman Melville, *Billy Budd*, pp. 340–45.
59   Herman Melville, *Billy Budd*, p. 356.
60   Id., p. 342.
61   Id., p. 342.
62   Id., p. 353.

caught Isaac on the brink of resolutely offering him up in obedience to the exacting behest.[63]

What the text suggests is that Vere was emotionally engaged by Billy, letting himself melt back into what remains primeval in our formalized humanity, namely, the intimate relationship between father and son. Billy is an orphan, fatherless; and Vere is certainly not Billy's father. But the relationship is here put in the patriarchal terms of the Abraham-Isaac story—in which a father was about to kill his son, as he believed God had ordered. Isaac, however, is not killed, and Billy is killed. Melville, at this point, carries his exposure of the evils of patriarchy as far as he was able, as Vere believes himself compelled, contrary to his feelings and to the skepticism of his fellow officers about the legality of what he does, to condemn the innocent boy to death. Also, the boy, vulnerable to these feelings, embraces his death as he may have believed, through his acceptance of his death, that he was embracing the father he never knew. There is, of course, no real relationship here, but indeed, the breaking of relationship and patriarchy, which kills love, psychologically imposes its will on both Vere and Billy.

Billy Budd was published posthumously long after Melville's death, suggesting that it explored such painfully personal and shameful issues for Melville that he could not publish it in his lifetime. The playwright Eugene O'Neill's insistence that his greatest and most personal play, *Long Day's Journey into Night*, only be played after his death comes to mind as an analogy. Melville's sense of personal pain is, I believe, clearly rooted in his guilt and remorse over the suicide of his eldest son, Malcolm.[64] Melville was as bad a father as he was a husband,[65] and the patriarchal male narcissistic rage, which he exposed earlier in Ahab, is here explored in one of the most intimate of personal relationships under patriarchy. There

---

63 Id., p. 346.

64 See, on this point, Hershel Parker, *Herman Melville: A Biography Volume 2, 1851–1891* (Baltimore:The Johns Hopkins University Press,2002), pp. 642–50.

65 See, on these points, Andrew Delbanco, *Melville: His World and Work* (New York: Alfred A. Knopf, 2005), pp. 180–181, 199–205, 200–202, 275–79; Laurie Robertson-Lorant, *Melville: A Biography*, pp. 295, 370–71, 503–4, 505–9, 509–17; Hershel Parker, *Herman Melville: A Biography Volume 2, 1851–1891*, pp. 628–35, 642–50.

were undoubtedly many other violently abusive husbands and fathers under American patriarchy,[66] but none had the artistic integrity to expose the problem in the way Melville courageously does in his last work in which he overcomes his shame through confessing a sense of a guilt that he had come to believe should be more broadly understood and shared, as both the violent patriarchy of American religion and culture continued to be mindlessly enacted by American men and women.

There is, however, another painful and shameful personal issue that may be implicit in *Billy Budd* and is quite explicit in the opera based on the novella composed by Benjamin Britten to a text, in part, by the British novelist E. M. Forster, namely, repressed homosexuality. [67]

Britten's interest in setting Herman Melville's novella, *Billy Budd,* arose from E. M. Forster's desire to collaborate with Britten on a new opera. "The men were not close, though Britten felt a sense of gratitude toward Forster for introducing him to Crabbe's poetry, repaying him by dedicating his comic opera *Albert Herring* to E. M. Forster in admiration."[68] Britten was much more courageous in dealing with explicit gay themes than Forster, whose gay novel, *Maurice,* written in 1913, was only published after Forster's death. But the men, both gay and in loving relationships (Forster with a policeman and Britten with the singer, Peter Pears), shared a common sensibility about the value of gay love and friendship. Unsurprisingly, it was Britten who proposed *Billy Budd* to Forster.

Billy Budd appealed to Britten as a parable both about how patriarchy destroys love and legitimates imperial violence. Its hero is an honest and handsome sailor who had been impressed into the British navy at the time of the French Revolution. Budd is beloved of everyone who knows him except for John Claggart, the captain at arms. Claggart, a man twisted by homophobia, is sexually attracted to Budd but maliciously decides to destroy him—a counterphobic response to the very idea of gay love, destroying, as homophobia requires, the thing one loves. As the very idea

---

[66]   See, for example, Elaine Showalter, *The Civil Wars of Julia Ward Howe: a Biography* (New York: Simon & Schuster, 2016).

[67]   The analysis that follows (about the collaboration of Britten and Forster) is drawn from David A. J. Richards, *Why Love Leads to Justice: Love Across the Boundaries* (Cambridge: Cambridge University Press, 2015), pp. 65–67.

[68]   Paul Kildea, *Benjamin Britten: A Life in the Twentieth Century* (London: Allen Lane, 2013), p. 324.

of loving the boy leads Claggart to destroy the boy and himself, Claggart falsely accuses Budd of mutiny. Budd, who has a stammer, cannot express his indignation in words and instinctively strikes out at Claggart, killing him. Captain Vere, the scholarly captain of the ship, understands perfectly well Claggart's malice and fully comprehends that Claggart's vindictive attraction to Billy is the real crime.[69] When Claggart dies, however, Vere follows his role as patriarchal captain of the military hierarchy of a ship at war and convenes the required court to follow to the letter the Mutiny Act, which he supposes (wrongly) would condemn Budd to death. Budd is found guilty and hanged. Claggart is buried at sea with full military honors.

Forster began work on a libretto (Eric Crozier, who assisted, was initially skeptical: Who had ever heard of an opera with an all-male cast?).[70] Though he preserved much of Melville's dialogue, Forster's most important change was keeping Vere alive after the events in the novella, making the opera a memory drama in which Vere, now an old man, reflects on his remorse that he performed the role imperial patriarchy required of him and killed a boy he, like others, loved.

The collaboration between Forster and Britten was tempestuous. Some of it was age: Forster was seventy-one and slowing down[71] and Britten was in his midthirties. Forster could not comprehend Britten's fast-pace and full diary.[72] Forster, not a musician, could not appreciate the orchestral colors of the orchestration intended for Forster's setting of Claggart's aria voicing in his motives to destroy Billy (Britten played for him only the piano version). Forster, in a letter to Britten, objected:

> I want *passion*—love constricted, perverted, poisoned, but nevertheless *flowing* down its agonizing channel; a sexual discharge gone evil. Not soggy depression or growling remorse. I seemed [to be] turning from one musical discomfort to another, and was dissastisfied.[73]

---

[69] See id., p. 326.
[70] Id., p. 327.
[71] Id., p. 343.
[72] Id., p. 343.
[73] Quoted at id., p. 346.

Britten was deeply hurt and crippled in his work and sought solace from Pears and others. Except for Auden, Britten had never worked with a librettist as much his artistic equal as Forster, and as for Forster, [n]othing in his previous friendship with Britten prepared him for the composer's single-mindedness.[74] Nonetheless, they continued to collaborate at the highest level of creative accomplishment, as composer and writer, leading to a work that has legitimate claim to being Britten's greatest opera.[75]

What Britten and Forster show us in *Billy Budd,* in which Peter Pears (Britten's lover and a resister to his own family's military background) plays the role of Captain Vere, is nothing less than the structure and psychology of patriarchy through the microcosm of an imperial ship at war with the rights of man. The authority structure of the ship is rigidly organized in terms of the gender binary and hierarchy, and this extends not only to their hierarchically ordered roles on the warship but to the psyches of the officers and men and boys and their lack of real relationship to one another, including the counterphobic violence of both Claggart and Vere who, locked in the patriarchal commands of hierarchy, kill the boy they love. When Billy is publicly executed, after exclaiming (in the opera), "Starry Vere, God bless you," the music explodes. It is a delayed expression of the crew's inarticulate raging indignation, which is then silenced by the officers who feel their authority at threat. The opera ends with Forster's setting of Vere as an old man, realizing that he is as guilty as Claggart for endorsing the death of a boy he loved and who clearly loved him:

> I could have saved him . . . But he has saved me, and blessed me, and the love that passeth understanding has come to me. I was lost on the infinite sea, but I've sighted a sail in the storm . . . There's a land where she'll anchor for ever.[76]

The music swells into an anthem of a world in which loving gay/lesbian relationships are free and equal, a world which Britten and Forster see as coming and celebrate, joined as the great artists they were, in this

---

[74] Id., p. 146.

[75] Id., p. 347.

[76] See libretto, *Billy Budd,* conducted by Benjamin Britten, London c.d., at pp. 69–70.

---

remarkable work that premiered in homophobic Britain in 1951 in prophetic ethical resistance to patriarchy.

The collaboration of Britten and Forster in *Billy Budd* focused as much on the underlying homoerotic relationship not only Claggart to Billy but of Vere to Billy, as Vere quite clearly acknowledges in his final aria in Forster's libretto. Nothing quite so explicit is in the Melville novella, but it seems interpretively not far-fetched that Britten and Forster, concerned as gay artists in the twentieth century to expose and explore the connections of patriarchy to homophobia, should have interpreted the novella as reasonably bearing this interpretation. Is this a reasonable interpretation? Melville wrote most of the novels and short stories for which he is remembered in the 1850s (his last completed novel, *The Confidence-Man*, is published in 1857). In contrast, Melville worked on *Billy Budd* in 1885–91, dying in 1891, and the novella is only published in 1924. Melville's earlier novels certainly touch on issues of love and even sex between men (thus Queequeg and Ishmael) but always indirectly and ironically, even humorously. It is hardly likely that during such a homophobic period in America, when homosexuality barely had a name, Melville could or would have dealt with it in any more explicit way (even Walt Whitman, who was, unlike Melville, certainly gay, denied that his poems were about sex or love between men).[77] Most of the best contemporary biographers of Melville believe that he probably had sex with men and women during his journeys to the South Seas[78] and that he was bisexual.[79] Certainly, he married and had four children. He was, however, an abusive husband and father (his first son commits suicide),[80] and all we know about repressed homosexuality cannot

---

[77] On this point, see David A. J. Richards, *Women, Gays, and the Constitution: The Grounds for Feminism and Gay Rights in Culture and Law* (Chicago: University of Chicago Press, 1998), pp. 29, 303–310.

[78] See, on this point, Hershel Parker, *Herman Melville: A Biography Volume 1, 1829–1851* (Baltimore: The Johns Hopkins University Press, 1996), pp. 207–9, 231, 265, 656–7; Andrew Delbanco, *Melville*, pp. 11, 57.

[79] Laurie Robertson-Lorant, *Melville: A Biography*, pp. 109, 191, 268; but see pp. 617–20.

[80] See, on these points, Andrew Delbanco, *Melville: His World and Work* (New York: Alfred A. Knopf, 2005), pp. 180–181, 199–205, 200–202, 275–79; Laurie Robertson-Lorant, *Melville: A Biography*, pp. 295, 370–71, 503–4, 505–9, 509–17; Hershel Parker, *Herman Melville: A Biography Volume 2, 1851–1891*, pp. 628–35, 642–50.

---

be ruled out as part of the explanation for his tormented and tormenting family life, a connection Andrew Delbanco explicitly makes.[81] If so, *Billy Budd* may be, as Britten and Forster thought it was, a reflection by Melville on the violence, interpersonal and intrapsychic, of the homophobia of repressed homosexuality, which patriarchy enforces.

The question for me is not whether or not Melville exposed the ravages of American patriarchy in *Moby-Dick* and of American patriarchal homophobia in *Billy Budd;* he clearly did. The question, rather, is how psychologically—despite his patriarchal background in a distinguished American family that traced its lineage to heroes of the American Revolution—his creativity came as far as it did in exploring, exposing, and resisting American patriarchy. In my recently published book, *Why Love Leads to Justice,* I argued that the key to such creativity—in both heterosexual and homosexual creative couples—is that falling in sexual love across the boundaries that patriarchy condemns (what Carol Gilligan and I call the love laws), such love frees a voice in the couples that empower them not only to break but to resist the love laws.

What I have come to think about Melville is that, though he and Nathaniel Hawthorne never had a sexual affair, everything we know about Melville's meeting Hawthorne during the period he was working on *Moby-Dick* led to Melville's ecstatically falling in love with a man and very great artist (Hershel Parker, perhaps Melville's greatest biographer, writes that Melville was more than a little febrile—excited intellectually, emotionally, and sexually—sexual arousal being for Melville an integral part of such intensely creative phases).[82] Hawthorne, as a free and equal person and artist, opened Melville's mind and heart to how American patriarchy damaged men and introduced him as well to literary ways of exploring the unconscious;[83] *Moby-Dick* is dedicated to Hawthorne. Whatever experiences of sex or love with men Melville may have had in the South Seas, he had never, as an artist, loved a man as a free man and artist on the terms of freedom and equality that he loved Hawthorne. What Hawthorne had come to mean to Melville is quite explicit in his anonymously published encomium to Hawthorne's genius, as an American

---

[81]   See Andrew Delbanco, *Melville,* pp. 199–205.

[82]   Hershel Parker, *Herman Melville: A Biography Volume 1, 1819–1851,* p. 760.

[83]   See Andrew Delbanco, *Melville,* pp. 126, 148.

Shakespeare, "Hawthorne and His Mosses."[84] Melville, composing anonymously, as a Virginian spending July in Vermont, writes in the heat of a kind of sexual ecstasy:

> I feel that this Hawthorne has dropped germanous seeds into my soul. He expands and deepens down, the more I contemplate him; and further and further, shorts his strong New England roots into the hot soil of my Southern soul.[85]

Melville's article mentions that among the works by Hawthorne, he admires *The Scarlet Letter*,[86] published in 1850 (*Moby-Dick* is published in 1851). As we have seen, Hawthorne's very great novel is a novel that resists patriarchy. Its central protagonist is Hester Prynne, who, through her love for her daughter and continuing love for Dimmesdale, speaks and thinks in a voice that resists patriarchy, a voice conventionally brutally silenced by patriarchy. But the novel also acutely studies two learned and humane men, Dimmesdale and Chillingworth, who are damaged by patriarchy— Dimmesdale, who cannot acknowledge his love, and Chillingworth, who retributively exacerbates Dimmesdale's remorse. Hawthorne's novel is ultimately hopeful and indeed prophetic. If and when Hester Prynne finds a resonance for her resisting voice both in women and in the men she loved, an internal ethical transformation will and did become a political and indeed constitutional transformation.

When Melville met and fell in love with Hawthorne, he found, through the experience of Hawthorne's understanding and support and love, the freeing of a creative voice in himself that could explore how deeply and disastrously patriarchy damages men, which is the subject, as I have argued, of both *Moby-Dick* and *Billy Budd*. Neither work can be regarded as hopeful. Melville's personal relationship to Hawthorne was brief, though they meet later in Britain. Hawthorne's wife, Sofia, who loved Melville's exuberant personality and support of her husband, observed

---

[84]   See Herman Melville, "Hawthorne and His Mosses," in Harrison Hayford, editor, *Herman Melville* (New York: The Library of America, 1984), pp. 1154–1171.

[85]   Id., p. 1167.

[86]   Id., p. 1165.

how different Melville was from her withdrawn husband, who hated even to be touched—"indeed on guard against physically demonstrative men."[87] (Melville was physically demonstrative.) Melville's passion may have homophobically frightened, even panicked Hawthorne, who certainly could not and did not reciprocate his sexual passion. Hawthorne's portrait of the relationship of Coverdale and Hollingsworth in his third novel, *The Blithedale Romance*, probably based on Hawthorne's response to Melville,[88] suggests as much: Coverdale's (Hawthorne's) response to Hollingsworth's (Melville's) expression of passionate love (there is not the man in this wide world, whom I can love as I could you)[89] is abruptly to break with him, forsaking him (as Hollingsworth puts it).[90] Melville certainly did not receive from Hawthorne the kind of continuing love that Hawthorne experienced first from his mother and later from his artistic wife and Britten and Pears experienced in each other as partners in a shared life of love and creative work. Melville's relationship both to his mother and wife was quite different from Hawthorne's. His mother was cold and patriarchally repressive;[91] Melville allegedly told a grandniece that his mother hated him.[92]

Melville's wife, Elizabeth, highly intelligent and well-educated, daughter of Judge Lemuel Shaw, had—in view of his abuse (including a report of throwing her down the stairs)—reason to leave him, as her family in Boston urged her to do so, even planning the escape in some detail.[93] But she chose not to do so, and we know copied his manuscripts for publication and supported his work; her supportive presence in his life may indispensably have sustained him through so much disappointment and loss. Of her love for Melville, there can be no doubt.

But it was Melville's love for Hawthorne and his work—in particular, Hawthorne's remarkable psychological study of the harms patriarchy

---

[87] Laurie Robertson-Lorant, *Melville: A Biography*, p. 254.

[88] See, on this point, Brenda Wineapple, *Hawthorne: A Life* (New York: Random House, 2003), at pp. 227–8.

[89] Nathaniel Hawthorne, "The Blithedale Romance," *Collected Novels* (New York: The Library of America, 1983), pp. 631–848, at p. 749.

[90] "Do not forsake me!" Id.

[91] On this point, see Laurie Robertson-Lorant, *Melville: A Biography*, pp. 48, 52–3, 55

[92] Id., p. 147.

[93] See Hershel Parker, *Herman Melville Volume 2*, pp. 628–31.

---

inflicted on Dimmesdale and Chillingworth—that opened Melville's artistic heart and mind to the astonishing studies of the psychological damage patriarchy inflicted on men that he explores in *Moby-Dick* and that he carries even further in *Billy Budd*. Hawthorne's art in *The Scarlet Letter* centers, however, in Hester Prynne's journey to a stance of resistance to the Puritan patriarchal love laws that condemned her passionate love for Dimmesdale and the product of their union, Pearl, a stance Dimmesdale is unable and unwilling to take (ending in his death). It is, Hawthorne suggests, only when men can join women, who have freed their sexual love from the patriarchal love laws, that men can free themselves as well from the prison of patriarchal masculinity that destroys them. It is astonishing that Hawthorne could carry his analysis of the psychology of patriarchy so far—undoubtedly inspired by his own love for his mother and for his wife—but his focus on redemptive love between women and men did not extend to love between men, implicit perhaps in his panic over Hawthorne's demands and quite explicit in his last novel, *The Marble Faun*, when Kenyon (modeled on Hawthorne) rejects Miriam's suggestion that he might help Donatello:

> I am a man, and between man and man, there is always
> an insuperable gulf. They can never grasp each other's
> hands; and therefore, man never derives any intimate help,
> any heart sustenance, from his brother man, but from
> women—his mother, his sister, or his wife.[94]

In contrast, the search for loving relationships between men—free from patriarchal hierarchy—has plausibly been investigated by Robert Martin as the very heart of Melville's development as an artist.[95] If Martin

---

[94] Nathaniel Hawthorne, "The Marble Faun," *Collected Novels* (New York: The Library of America, 1983), pp. 853–1242, at p. 1089.

[95] See Robert K. Martin, *Hero, Captain, and Stranger: Male Friendship, Social Critique, and Literary Form in the Sea Novels of Herman Melville* (Chapel Hill: The University of North Carolina Press, 1986). For a recent biographical study attributing Melville's inspiration to Sarah Morewood, see Michael Shelden, *Melville in Love: The Secret Life of Herman Melville and the Muse of Moby-Dick* (New York: Harper Collins, 2016). Leading biographers of Melville, including Herschel Parker, dismissed Shelden's thesis as fantasy, "Sarah Morewood was a loose cannon," Mr. Parker says. "But there is

is right, and I believe he is, it may be for this reason that, in contrast to Hawthorne's antiabolitionism as well as racism and even anti-Semitism,[96] Melville's narratives explore love between men across the boundaries of race and religion (e.g., Ishmael and Queequog), narratives that raised ethical questions about American racism and anti-Semitism. And his last great narrative, *Billy Budd*, prefaces the introduction of Billy Budd himself by noting other examples of the experience of the "handsome sailor," including a handsome black sailor,[97] arguably suggesting the injustice to Billy may reflect an injustice to black men quite like that done to Billy (e.g., lynching).[98] These are injustices not on Hawthorne's ethical radar. What Melville's work shows us is how ethically illuminating it can be to extend the critical analysis of patriarchy and resistance to patriarchy to how such resistance arises not only from loving relationships of men to women but of men to men (and also of women to women).[99] It was, nonetheless, Hawthorne's pathbreaking exploration of how patriarchy harms men that set the stage for Melville's further investigations—investigations clearly inspired by his love, however abortive, for Hawthorne.

We can see the initial impact of Hawthorne's *The Scarlet Letter* on Melville in the disastrous novel he published after *Moby-Dick*, *Pierre*.

---

absolutely no evidence that she had any sexual attraction to Melville or that he was attracted to her." Brenda Cronin, "Did Illicit Love Float 'Moby-Dick'?" *The Wall Street Journal*, Friday, May 27, 2016, at D3.

[96] See, on these points, Brenda Wineapple, *Hawthorne: A Life*, pp. 188–9, 199, 241, 322–3, 329–33, 349–50.

[97] See Herman Melville, *Billy Budd*, op. cit., pp. 278–79.

[98] See, on this point, Gregory Jay, "Douglass, Melville, and the Lynching of Billy Budd," eds. Robert S. Levine and Samuel Otter, *Frederick Douglass and Herman Melville: Essays in Relation* (Chapel Hill: The University of North Carolina Press, 2008), pp. 369–395. See also Michael T. Gilmore, "'Speak man!' Billy Budd in the Crucible of Reconstruction," *American Literary History Volume 21*, Number 3, Fall 2009, pp. 492–517; Klaus Benesch, "Melville Black Jack: Billy Budd and the Politics of Race in 19th Century Maritime Life," eds. Joanne M. Braxton and Maria I. Dierich, *Monuments of the Black Atlantic: Slavery and Memory* (Munster: Lit Verlag, 2004), pp. 67–75. See also Jon-Christian Suggs, "Something about the Boy: Law, Ironic Comedy, and the Ideology of Agape in *Billy Budd*" (unpublished paper).

[99] On how and why gay/lesbian loving relationships have led to creative ethical insights into injustice and resistance to injustice, see David A. J. Richards, *Why Love Leads to Injustice*.

Pierre is a well-brought-up young man, the heir to a fortune, whose father had died. The heart of the novel is the love laws, enforced by Pierre's rigidly controlling patriarchal mother, who demands Pierre must only marry someone of whom she approved (thus demanding an arranged marriage). In fact, Pierre is in love with such a woman, but when he learns or rather suspects that his dead father had broken the love laws in adulterously fathering a daughter, he insists on marrying a woman who may or may not be the daughter, abandons the woman he loves, and loses his fortune (his mother's retribution for his disobedience). Pierre and the two women and many others die violently, as patriarchal men seek their revenge. I have no doubt that the novel, which may or may not have concealed homosexual themes,[100] was inspired by Hawthorne's novel (adultery is its central topic) as well as by suspicions. It was never substantiated that Melville's dead father might have had a child out of wedlock.[101] But Melville at least, at this point in his life, is in territory he barely understands, as what in Hawthorne is Hester's resistance to patriarchy is, for Melville in *Pierre,* not resistance, but Pierre's unconsciously acting out, as it were, patriarchy's punishing vengeance—identifying with his father's remorse for his adultery, an irrational guilt in Pierre that punishes both himself and those he claims to love (all die). Where Hawthorne saw hope, Melville, both in *Moby-Dick* and *Pierre,* sees only despair. At this point in his life, Melville is, unlike Hawthorne, still very much a man trapped anxiously within patriarchy, who can see no way out.

What Melville does expose and explore and deepen is Hawthorne's insight that patriarchy is as damaging to men as it is to women. And it is, I believe, through his love for Hawthorne that he found the voice to write the most terrifying study of the damage patriarchy inflicts on men, both in their personal and political lives, in *Moby-Dick.* Melville may, as a man, have more deeply experienced this damage than Hawthorne, but the experience of the love of Hawthorne may have enabled Melville to find a reparative voice that showed us how such damage is inflicted on men and thus enables us to resist this damage. Nothing he had previously written had this Shakespearean power—a power he had found in Hawthorne's work and perhaps more fully realized in this novel than any American

---

[100] See, on this point, Andrew Delbanco, *Melville,* pp. 199–205; James Creech, *Closet Writing/Gay Readings* (Chicago: University of Chicago Press, 1993).
[101] Andrew Delbanco, *Melville,* pp. 187–88.

artist before and since. Love resisting patriarchy, thus inspires, so I have come to believe, courage.

And this legacy from Hawthorne may also have made possible, much later in Melville's life (after he had abandoned his literary career and long after Hawthorne's death), of perhaps the most personal and courageous of Melville's works, *Billy Budd*. At the end of life, unrecognized as the great artist he was and full of regret and remorse, Melville returned to the experience of shipping that always inspired his greatest work, a world of men bound to the rigid hierarchies that patriarchy enforces. And he tells us a tragic love story—the tragedy of Billy and Vere and the tragedy of Melville and his son and his abortive love for the only person Melville may ever have deeply loved, Hawthorne. The story arises from traumatic loss, loss that shows itself in loss of memory and voice.[102] But in the very telling of this terrible story, Melville both remembers and gives voice to the loss, sharing with other men an experience that usually isolates them but can come to understand as all too destructively common under patriarchy. What a psychiatrist like Jonathan Shay came to see as a therapy for combat trauma (men sharing their stories of trauma),[103] Melville achieves through great, imaginative art. In his very telling of this story, he may have told us, as Britten and Forster certainly believed, that there is a way out and that love between men on terms that challenge patriarchal homophobia is not, as Hawthorne believed, impossible, but though fraught with the psychological difficulties arising from men's (including gay men's) internalization of homophobia, possible and even redemptive. Vere sings at the end of their opera:

> The love that passeth understanding has come to me.
> I was lost on the infinite sea, but I've sighted a sail in the
> storm . . . There's a land where she'll anchor for ever.[104]

---

[102] See, on this point, Judith Herman, *Trauma and Recovery* (New York: Basic Books, 1997).

[103] See Jonathan Shay, *Achilles in Vietnam: Combat Trauma and the Undoing of Character* (New York: Scribner, 1994).

[104] See libretto, *Billy Budd*, conducted by Benjamin Britten, London c.d., at pp. 69–70.

CHAPTER 2

Shame and Guilt Cultures

The close connection of theme between Hawthorne and Melville is what they tell us about how patriarchy destroys love: in Hawthorne, the love of Hester and Dimmesdale and in Melville, the love of Budd and Vere. In both cases, the psychological mechanism is shame. Hester, as an adulterous woman breaking the patriarchal love laws, is a bad woman, shamed by wearing *A* as a mark of her shame. The man, Dimmesdale, who had sexually loved Hester, is under patriarchy not shamed by doing so, but her husband, Chillingworth, was shamed, thus his psychological violence against Dimmesdale. In Melville, the issue, gay sexual love, is homophobia—the shaming of a man acting as a woman in sex. In both cases, patriarchy's gender binary and hierarchy place men in control of women or men acting as women, and any breaking of hierarchical control (the free love of equals) is experienced as a humiliation of one's manhood or womanhood, eliciting shame and violence. Women under patriarchy are shamed when they break the love laws that hold them rigidly in subordination to patriarchal men (their fathers, brothers, husbands, sons, etc.). Men are shamed when the women subject to such control break those laws or when they themselves break such laws (men loving outside patriarchy, for example, gay men).

Both Hawthorne and Melville also show us the links of shaming manhood to violence. Hawthorne is acutely conscious, given his Puritan heritage, that Puritans monstrously burned deviant women (who refused to stay in their defined gender roles) as witches, while Melville, in his study of Ahab, of the role of patriarchy in unleashing irrational violence against the innocent scapegoat who allegedly humiliated the manhood of the patriarch, Ahab (anticipating the Southern violence of fighting the Civil War to preserve race-based slavery against a credible threat to their hierarchical control over people of color, men and women). Both artists show us the personal and political power of a patriarchal shame culture, and it is fair to say that they wanted us to see how such shame cultures rest on overriding or marginalizing those parts of their cultures that are guilt cultures, resting on reciprocity and not culpably harming one's equals.

What these works study are the links between political and personal psychology, namely, how patriarchal demands (the political psychology of patriarchy) shape the personal psyche of men and women (personal psychology). In both cases, the mechanism appears to be shame. Patriarchal demands on men and women take the form of exposing deviant men and women to humiliation and shame, and it is because men and women, absorbing those demands into their psyches through initiation, come to regard such deviation as shameful that they express their response through violence against others and themselves. The beginning of wisdom in resisting patriarchy is to see patriarchy and its unjust harms to women and men. Both Hawthorne and Melville are the great artists they are because they show us how patriarchy harms men and women, including its larger political consequences in legitimating injustices to women (burning witches) and, in Melville's case, gay men (also burned at the stake). Both works call for further investigation of the historical development of shame cultures, including how they are enforced and their connections to political violence (including, as we shall see, political fascism).

How and why did America, dominantly a guilt culture, nonetheless embody a patriarchal shame culture in matters of gender and sexuality? To answer this question, we need to understand what shame culture is and how it enforces patriarchy and how such shame culture has persisted in a dominantly guilt culture based on not culpably harming one's equals. The brilliance of *The Scarlet Letter* is to expose this contradiction in the heart of American Puritanism and to show how the unjust demands of the culture of shame may be resisted through the free and equal voice of a woman (appealing to democratic values of equal voice) whose adultery the culture regards as shameful. Hester Prynne thus comes to regard her love for Dimmesdale and her love for their child as not shameful (because based on a responsible love) and indicts Puritan shame culture as inconsistent with its own deep values of the free voice of democratic equals—values that give rise to or should give rise to guilt when one culpably harms one's equals. For Hawthorne, Puritan culture is *guilty* of such wrongs to women.

If we are to understand the psychological power of such resistance, we must understand both the shame culture it challenges and the guilt culture it also challenges as contradictory. We must understand what shame and guilt cultures are and how they enter into the human psyche, in order to understand resistance. Thus, the importance of the question of the initiation of men and women into patriarchy and how they resist when they come to resist (the subject of this book).

I begin by drawing on the pathbreaking work of the cultural anthropologist, Ruth Benedict, who introduced the distinction between shame and guilt cultures and the important, more recent historical work of Zebedai Barbu and James Gilligan, who have plausibly brought the distinction to bear on larger historical developments. In particular, Gilligan has developed an idea of patriarchal political religions to explain the role the shaming of patriarchal manhood, and its attendant violence has played in forms of ethnic nationalism, imperialism, totalitarianism (Hitler's fascism and Stalin's communism), and religious fundamentalism today. I use the insights of Barbu and Gilligan to frame an account of the political psychology of political fascism, including discussion of the pathbreaking work on the authoritarian personality of T. H. Adorno and others and recent elaborations of this view and the brilliant account of the psychology of totalitarianism in Hannah Arendt's towering masterpiece of political psychology, *The Origins of Totalitarianism*. What strikes me and will strike you about the discussion of both Adorno and Arendt is that both views are best explained in terms of what Virginia Woolf would call *patriarchy*, a term not central to either Arendt's or Adorno's accounts. It is time, I believe, explicitly to accord gender the weight it deserves in understanding ourselves and our communities.

I then turn to the question for men in particular of their initiations into patriarchy, the link between political and personal psychology, which I further explore in the following chapters.

The Cultural Anthropology of Ruth Benedict:
Shame Versus Guilt Cultures

Ruth Benedict's work, as a cultural anthropologist, features three notable achievements: her use of cultural anthropology to examine homophobia as an unjust cultural construction like racism and sexism, her brilliant criticism of American and European racism, and her articulation of the distinction between shame and guilt cultures in her remarkable study of Japan, a country she never visited. In all these areas, Benedict's work was pathbreaking and was, as I suggested earlier (Introduction), made possible for her because, in her personal life, she had come to resist the way in which her mother had initiated her into a rigidly patriarchal conception of women's place and role and to resist as well the terms of her patriarchal marriage. The key to her resistance was falling in love with women, like Margaret Mead, with whom she could work as an equal, and later more long-lasting lesbian relationships as well. What she discovered, through her own resistance to the patriarchal conception of women's role she had once accepted, was that free and equal intimate relationships (in this case, between women) released women from the rigid demands of the gender binary and hierarchy. Such resistance, based on free and equal relationships unencumbered by binaries and hierarchies, made it possible for Benedict first to argue, following her teacher Franz Boas, that cultural forms crucially explained differences among cultures and that the primacy accorded race in Western cultures rested not on nature but on cultural racism. Later, in her study of the roots of Japanese political fascism, she made the pathbreaking distinction between shame and guilt cultures in which she identified patriarchy as the cultural tradition that sustained the aggressive violence of shame cultures like Japan. It was only because Benedict had first questioned and resisted patriarchy as an American daughter and wife that she was able to see in Japan the more extreme form of patriarchy and its supporting shame culture that she found there. What made Benedict's work so important in the human sciences was the way in which she linked personal and political psychology, as I now try to show both in her work and in later elaborations of her insights.[105]

---

[105] On the relationship between Margaret Mead and Ruth Benedicts and its consequences in the work of both, see David A. J. Richards, *Why Love Leads to Justice* pp. 189–208.

Benedict's *Patterns of Culture*, published in 1934, sets out her defense of cultural anthropology as an intellectual discipline, focusing on three people: the Zuni, the Dobu, and the Kwakiutl.[106] What made her argument of such importance was not only her emphasis on cultural variation but on the broad cultural themes—Apollonian in the case of the Zuni[107] and Dionysian in the case of the Kwakiutl[108]—that organized each culture's sense of itself and the psychology each culture supported to realize its sense of itself [109] (prefiguring the distinction between shame and guilt cultures she was later to articulate). What is from today's perspective remarkable is that Benedict in 1934 uses the argument she would use to show racism as an unjust cultural construction to suggest that what we today call homophobia has a similar character, taking cultural anthropology into an area her friend and lover, Margaret Mead, did not take. Benedict knew personally the gay psychiatrist, Harry Stack Sullivan, who had tried to develop within psychiatry a more humane understanding of homosexuality than the then dominant view of it as a mental illness.[110] As we become "increasingly culture-conscious,"[111] Benedict suggests that we may want to reformulate our conception of what counts as neurotic, for what we count as disordered may simple reflect a culture where "he is trapped in a repugnant situation, which is reinforced by every contact he makes and which will extend past his mother to his school and his business and his wife."[112] In her concluding chapter, she calls, as Sullivan might have called, for a valid comparative

---

[106] Ruth Benedict, *Patterns of Culture* (Boston: A Mariner Book, 2005—first published, 1934).

[107] See, Id., pp. 238, 242,

[108] See Id., pp. 175, 181.

[109] See, on this point, Ruth Benedict, *Patterns of Culture*, pp. 232–33,

[110] See, for illuminating studies of Sullivan, A. H. Chapman, *Harry Stack Sullivan: The Man and His Work* (New York: G. P. Putnam's Sons, 1976); Helen Swick Perry, *Psychiatrist of America: The Life of Harry Stack Sullivan* (Cambridge, Mass.: The Belknap Press of Harvard University Press, 1982); Naoko Wake, *Private Practices: Harry Stack Sullivan, the Science of Homosexuality, and American Liberalism* (New Brunswick, NJ: Rutgers University Press, 2011); Mark J. Blechner, *Sex Changes: Transformations in Society and Psychoanalysis* (New York: Routledge, 2009).

[111] See Ruth Benedict, *Patterns of Culture*, p. 245.

[112] Id., p. 245.

psychiatry,[113] which takes seriously that what we call abnormals have a legitimate and sometimes valued place in other cultures, whereas, in our culture, abnormals are those who not supported by the institutions of their civilization.[114] Citing the men and women of the Amerindian institution of the berdache (homosexual men living as women, with whom other men sometimes lived)[115] who have an esteemed place in Amerindian cultures, Benedict explicitly argues, on grounds of justice, that our homophobia cannot be justified. We blame homosexuals in a vicious circularity for what our injustice has made of them:

> The invert is exposed to all the conflicts to which aberrants are always exposed. His guilt, his sense of inadequacy, his failures, are consequences of the disrepute, which social tradition visits upon him, and few people can achieve a satisfactory life unsupported by the standards of their own society. The adjustment that society demands of them would strain any man's vitality, and the consequences of this conflict we identity with their homosexuality.[116]

Benedict published *Race and Racism* in 1942 in the midst of World War II.[117] It is a work of a responsible liberal public intellectual of the highest quality and, given its context, of the greatest and most prophetic political importance. Benedict's argument draws together all of Franz Boas's lifelong work on the unjust cultural construction of anti-Semitism and racism and gives it a powerfully argued form to bring the British and Americans, allies in World War II, to a sense of understanding what World War II was about and what victory in that war would and should mean to postwar reconstruction in Britain, the United States, Europe, and Asia. What Benedict shows is that racism has no rational basis, corresponding to no natural fact that justifies unequal treatment. Rather, at some length, Benedict shows how the irrational prejudices of anti-Semitism and racism rose historically through the abridgement of the basic human rights of

---

113 Id., p. 258.
114 Id., p. 258.
115 Id., p. 263.
116 Id., p. 265.
117 Ruth Benedict, *Race and Racism* (London: Routledge & Kegan Paul, 1942).

whole groups of persons and then rationalizing such treatment on the basis of stereotypes whose appeal rests, in a vicious circularity, on the abridgement of basic human rights, including the suppression of any voice that might reasonably challenge such injustice. "[R]acist persecutions replaced religious persecutions in Europe,"[118] only now based on an alleged science of race that was just as irrational because it was supported by the same vicious circularity of dehumanization and violent repression of the voice of reasonable doubt. "It is ironic," she observes, "that it is those very European nations in which anthropometric investigation shows no pure race, which base their claims to superiority on allegation of their pure blood."[119]

It is a brilliant, powerful, and convincing argument. What made it of such importance is that it clarifies what was at stake in the aggressively violent fascism of Germany, Italy, and Japan, namely, aggressive violence rooted in racism, creating scapegoats (the Jews) to rationalize its violence, and hostile to any conception of liberal democracy or basic human rights. The defeat of the fascist powers would be justified in terms of the defeat of their aggressive and mindless racism. The argument is prophetic because its reasonable consequence is that, if Britain and the United States were victorious, they have responsibility to take their own racism seriously—whether the American racism of racial segregation or anti-miscegenation laws, or British imperialism rationalized on racist grounds. Correspondingly, if Europe is to be sensibly reconstructed, it must be on foundations of liberal democracy, at the national and even the European levels. These latter points are not explicitly raised in a book written in 1942, but the implications are clear, and are prophetic of post-war developments, with which we are still struggling.

Finally, in her *The Chrysanthemum and the Sword*,[120] published in 1946, Benedict applies her cultural anthropology to the interpretation of Japan. Benedict had been commissioned by the US government to write a cultural analysis of Japan in June 1944 to help us understand our war-time enemy and how we should deal with them after the war. She never went to Japan, but she consulted written sources, movies, and Japanese Americans.

---

[118] Id., p. 153.

[119] Id., p. 60.

[120] Ruth Benedict, *The Chrysanthemum and the Sword: Patterns of Japanese Culture* (Boston: A Mariner Book, 2005—first published, 1946).

Benedict had long been interested in the role violence plays in shame cultures,[121] and her study of Japan is her fullest and deepest exploration of this question.

In *Patterns of Culture,* Benedict had interpreted the Kwakiutl as a Dionysian culture in which the Kwakiutl reaction to the death of a noble adult was to carry out some plan for getting even, to strike back against a fate that had shamed them.[122] Kwakiutl culture thus encouraged a highly competitive will to power among its people, and any insult, including death of a leader, was experienced as shaming manhood, thus eliciting violence. In her study of Japan, Benedict further developed and elaborated this insight into the idea of shame versus guilt culture and studied Japanese culture as shame culture. Shame is one of the moral emotions central to our sense of ourselves as competent, arising from failures of competence, and expressing itself in the attempt to better exercise our sense of competence and mastery in the future. Guilt, another similarly important moral emotion, arises from failures of moral reciprocity in relationships to other persons, expressing itself in forms of apology and atonement to acknowledge personal culpability and, if feasible, reparation to the victim.[123] All human cultures display both emotions, but in Benedict's view, every culture emphasizes one more than the other. Some cultures rely on shame while others rely on guilt:

> In anthropological studies of different cultures the
> distinction between those that rely heavily on shame and
> those that rely heavily on guilt is an important one. A
> society that inculcates absolute standards of morality and
> relies on men's developing a conscience is a guilt culture by
> definition. Where shame is the major sanction, a man does
> not experience relief when he makes his fault public even
> to a confessor. So long as his bad behavior does not "get

---

[121]   See, on this point, Lois W. Banner, *Intertwined Lives: Margaret Mead, Ruth Benedict, and Their Circle* (New York: Vintage Books, 2003), pp. 204–5.

[122]   See Ruth Benedict, *Patterns of Culture,* p. 239.

[123]   On shame and guilt, see Gerhart Piers and Milton B. Singer, *Shame and Guilt: A Psychoanalytic and Cultural Study* (Springfield, Ill.: Charles C. Thomas, Publisher, 1953).

---

into the world," he need not be troubled, and confession appears to him merely as a way of courting trouble.

> True shame cultures rely on external sanctions for good behavior, not as true guilt cultures so on an internalized conviction of sin. Shame is a reaction to other people's criticism. A man is shamed either by being openly ridiculed and rejected or by fantasying to himself that he has been made ridiculous. In either case it is a potent sanction. But it requires an audience or at least a man's fantasy of an audience. Guilt does not.[124]

From this perspective, the difficulties American had in understanding the Japanese, one of their enemies in World War II, arose from America being a guilt culture and Japan a shame culture.

To understand the kind of shame culture Japan was, Benedict puts great emphasis on the role the gender binary and hierarchy played not only in the individual Japanese family and in social and political life but in shaping the nation's imperial ambitions: "It was necessary for her to fight to establish a hierarchy under Japan, of course, since she alone represented a nation truly hierarchical from top to bottom and hence understood the necessity of taking one's proper place."[125] The Japanese imperial system was a crucial feature of this hierarchy, which explained something otherwise puzzling to democratic Americans, namely, the role of a divinized God Emperor at the top of the hierarchy, "an ecstatic contemplation of a fantasied Good Father untainted by contacts with the world,"[126] an imperial system or so the Japanese came to believe in which succession had been unbroken from ages eternal. Japan was no China with thirty-six different dynasties in recorded history."[127] Rigid hierarchy extended to the family, the emphasis being not to achieve loving-kindness in the family,"[128] but to observe one's duties and obligations. The Japanese said of young children they knew no shame because the system of patriarchal controls had not yet had their

---

[124] Ruth Benedict, *The Chrysanthemum and the Sword*, pp. 222–3.
[125] Id., p. 21.
[126] Id., pp. 125.
[127] Id., p. 127.
[128] Id., p. 124.

effect.[129] Such controls were enforced at school and later in military service by brutal hazing and ridicule.[130] Such breaking of personal relationships gave rise, Benedict argues, to anger at any threat to one's self-esteem, which could take the form of suicide or aggression against others. What saved the Japanese from self-destruction was an ethnic nationalism:

> They embraced nationalistic goals and turned the attack outward again, away from their own breasts. In totalitarian aggression against outside nations they could 'find themselves again' again. They saved themselves from a bad mood and felt a great new strength within them. They could not do it in personal relationships but they believed they could as a conquering nation.[131]

Even the Japanese interpretation of Buddhism, Zen Buddhism, transformed a universalistic religion of loving kindness[132] into a discipline for warriors.[133] Japan's militaristic discipline puzzled Americans by the degree of self-sacrifice required (e.g., suicide when defeated), but the Japanese thought of the matter as meeting the hierarchical duties of manhood, which made the question of self-sacrifice irrelevant.[134]

What Benedict's analysis brilliantly illuminates is the larger question of the violence of patriarchal manhood—what the psychiatrist James Gilligan has recently exposed as the psychological root of violence, namely a shaming of manhood.[135] The experience of shame that leads to violence has, of course, a very different character from the shame involved in achieving competence. The violence is often irrational, corresponding to a perceived threat—loss of faith, dishonor, and an insult to manhood. Men are particularly vulnerable to such shame when, often through a history of traumatically violent abuse of them earlier in their lives, they have

---

129   See, on this point, id., pp. 270, 275.

130   See id., pp. 276–9.

131   Id., p. 169.

132   See, on this point, Richard Gombrich, *What the Buddha Thought* (London: Equinox, 2009).

133   See id., pp. 241–3.

134   See Id. pp. 230–3.

135   See James Gilligan, *Violence: Reflections on a National Epidemic* (New York: Vintage Books, 1996).

identified with the patriarchal conception of manhood of their abuser, identifying with the aggressor. Identification in such cases covers lack of caring relationships or the trauma arising from broken relationships. Such men invest their sense of personal competence in a self-image of patriarchal manhood marked by a strictly observed gender binary and hierarchy (men over women) in which their often fragile sense of manhood requires them strictly to confine themselves to what they take to be their male gender role to be, and the violence is triggered by any insult to this patriarchally defined sense of manhood.

Gilligan, a psychiatrist, follows Piers and Singer[136] in distinguishing the moral emotion of shame from that of guilt along the following lines.[137] Shame is the moral emotion central to our sense of ourselves as competent, arising from failures of competence and expressing itself in the attempt to better exercise our sense of competence and mastery in the future. Guilt, another similarly important moral emotion, arises from failures of moral reciprocity in relationships to other persons, expressing itself in forms of apology and atonement to acknowledge personal culpability and, if feasible, reparation to the victim. Both emotions are, in Gilligan's view, developmentally important. Shame, rooted in the desire for competence, is developmentally earlier, as the child strives to develop a sense of basic competences—walking, for example. Guilt arises from the growing moral sense of the weight to be accorded the interests of others, reflecting the growth of the sense of justice and moral reciprocity.

The importance of shame, as a distinctive moral emotion, was the subject of the sociologist and social philosopher Helen Merrell Lynd's important 1958 book, *On Shame and the Search for Identity*.[138] It deals with the cultural and psychological roots of identity and its dislocations, concepts clearly with important cultural dimensions (as Ruth Benedict, a cultural anthropologist, earlier saw). The focus on shame, as a distinct moral emotion from guilt, was one of the most important developments in

---

[136] Gerhart Piers and Milton B. Singer, *Shame and Guilt: A Psychoanalytic and Cultural Study* (New York: W. W. Norton, 1971).

[137] See James Gilligan, "Shame, Guilt, and Violence," *Social Research Volume 70* No. 4, 2003, pp. 1149–1140

[138] See, for illuminating discussion of the this development, Helen Merrell Lynd, *Shame and the Search for Identity* (London: Routledge, 2014; first published, 1958).

post-Freudian psychology (including psychoanalysis). It is, I think, probable that Freud's exclusive focus on guilt allegedly arising from the Oedipus complex, which Carol Gilligan and I argue in *The Deepening Darkness* arises from his naturalization of patriarchy as human psychology,[139] paradoxically disabled this great observer of human psychology not to see in himself and others the role that shame played as well in human neurosis. It is striking that it was women—Ruth Benedict and Hellen Merrell Lynd, who argued for the importance of shame and explicitly connected it to cultural forms, not to biology or hard-wired evolution (as Freud supposed). And it was a women psychologist, Helen Lewis, who observed that narcissistic neurotic disorders were rooted in shame, not guilt, and that required new forms of therapy.[140] We see here, both in social theory and psychology, how knowledge of the human condition (including both women and men) has been advanced by women's voices resisting the patriarchal models, which dominated the human sciences as they had politics.

Shame was also a central topic in the work of Heinz Kohut, arising from his pathbreaking work on narcissistic personality disorders in the psychology of the self, disorders, based on idealizing self-images, and when threatened, prone to sometimes uncontrollable anger and aggression.[141] "All persons," Kohut observed, "have an important interest in a realistic sense of and self-esteem for the competences central to their sense of self or identity, and the value based on such competences has a cultural dimension, depending on what the culture values." It is developmental injuries to such self-esteem and thus to the self that give rise to grandiosely unrealistic self-images, expressed through aggression at challenge to these self-images.[142] Among the forms of such aggression are those directed

---

[139] See, on this point, Carol Gilligan and David A. J. Richards, *The Deepening Darkness*, pp. 160–190.

[140] See, for an important work in this development, Helen B. Lewis, *Shame and Guilt in Neurosis* (New York: International Universities Press, 1971). For important papers exemplifying this development, see Andrew P. Morrison, *Essential Papers on Narcissism* (New York: New York University Press, 1986).

[141] See Heinz Kohut, *The Analysis of the Self: A Systematic Approach to the Psychoanalytic Treatment of the Personality Disorders* (Chicago: University of Chicago Press, 2009; originally published, 1971); Heinz Kohut, *The Restoration of the Self* (New York: International Universities Press, 1977).

[142] On the roots of such aggression in threats to the self, see Heinz Kohut, *The Restoration of the Self*, pp. 111–133.

by men at women,[143] which Kohut connects to cultural forms, to wit, "patriarchally organized groups."[144]

Kohut is thus pointing to some cultural forms, like patriarchy, which point may be unrealistically to idealize or denigrate aspects of the competences of men and women, and that the experience of humiliation to such culturally supported self-images elicits aggression. The very vulnerability to such shame expresses itself in defensive attitudes and behaviors that mask such shame, as the mark of a loser.[145]

The importance of James Gilligan's work is his discovery that patriarchy—the gender binary and hierarchy—was the basis of the shame culture he found in the psychology of the aggressively violent men he studied in American prisons. Any threat or insult to their sense of patriarchal manhood was experienced as humiliation, eliciting uncontrollable violence. But Gilligan, a gifted psychiatrist and therapist, found something else that was even more important: the vulnerability to violence of these men rested on often appalling developmental injuries to their sense of self as men. That the injuries masked their underlying sense of shame that they were as incompetent—both in their personal and employment lives—as many of them were. Among these injuries were not only traumatic abuse by parents and others but a lack of any of the social and educational advantages that might have made them more competent to advance in the highly competitive society around them. Their vulnerability to uncontrollable violence was the only way they could express their sense of value as men, and there was, Gilligan discovered in his work with them, an inverse psychological relationship between their violence and their voice or, rather, lack of voice. As their voices were supported and strengthened, their vulnerability to violence plummeted.[146]

Further psychological research on the psychology of violent people, directed at both others (homicide) and themselves (suicide), has revealed that the apparently instinctive aggressive violence elicited by humiliation

---

[143] *Id.*, pp. 193–9.

[144] *Id.*, p. 232.

[145] See, for further discussion of the forms of such masking and unmasking, Leon Wurmser, *The Mask of Shame* (Northvale, New Jersey: Jason Aronson, 1984); Leon Wurmser, *The Hidden Dimension: Psychodynamics of Compulsive Drug Use* (Northvale, New Jersey: Jason Aronson, 1995).

[146] See, on all these points, James Gilligan, *Violence.*

arises from developmental injuries that disable people from reflecting on or thinking about why they are thus prompted to violence. The lack of affect regulation is thus tied to a lack of "mentalization" in themselves that forms incompetence that are the object of shame.[147] Therapy for such lack encourages precisely a voice that mentalizes that there is such a gap and understanding and dealing with its psychological destructiveness, the experience of which is what leads one into therapy.

The inverse psychological relationship between patriarchal violence and voice was both confirmed and strengthened in a reform experiment in San Francisco jails.[148] Here, through forms of individual and group therapy and theater work, the prisoners came to sensitize themselves to their own propensities to violence and its roots in trauma and abuse, and they became critics of the patriarchal gender roles they had once assumed to be in the nature of things. When they listened to people who had suffered loss arising from killing people they loved (some of them had killed), some of them experienced an emotion, guilt, that they had used the mask of shame not to acknowledge or feel in themselves. They wept.

What this work shows is both that highly patriarchal shame cultures continue to exist in the United States, and America's high rates of violence should be understood as the consequence of our allowing or encouraging such cultures to exist. But what does this say about the rest of us? We must now investigate an American culture apparently more patriarchal than we and others once assumed, and whether, in light of this, we can understand recent political developments here in terms of historical analogies about the force patriarchy has had in human cultures. Is America more of a shame culture than we and most people have assumed? Isn't that what Trump's electoral victory shows? Doesn't this suggest that American men continue to experience traumatic breaks in relationship as they are initiated, at a quite young age, into patriarchy, and that the legacy of such initiation is

---

[147] See, for an excellent study along these lines, Peter Fonagy, Gyorgy Gergely, Elliot L. Jurist, Mary Target, *Affect Regulation, Mentalization, and the Development of the Self* (New York: Other Press, 2004). See also Rosine Jozef Perelberg, ed., *Psychoanalytic Understanding of Violence and Suicide* (London: Routledge, 1999).

[148] See for discussion of this experiment, Sunny Schwartz and David Boodell, *Dreams from the Monster Factory* (New York: Scribner, 2009).

an acceptance of the gender binary and hierarchy that, when challenged, shames their sense of patriarchal manhood, eliciting violence?

Shame versus Guilt Cultures in Historical Perspective

Ruth Benedict's theory of shame versus guilt cultures was developed as an explanation of one culture—that of Japan. The role of what we call patriarchy—the gender binary and hierarchy—is implicit in her account, suggesting that historically shame cultures are dominantly patriarchal. Later important works of historical psychology by Zevedei Barbu[149] and E. R. Dodds[150] have developed a diachronic dimension of the distinction between shame and guilt cultures. Both study, for example, the development from the dominantly shame culture of *The Iliad* (in which the shaming of manhood and violence are prominent) to the more inward guilt culture reflected in many of the Greek tragedies as well as in the emergence of Socratic philosophy (in which reflection on ethical responsibilities to self and others become central). Barbu prominently uses the rise and decline of patriarchy[151] as an important feature of his historical psychology, as well as the related idea of shame and guilt cultures,[152] both in his account of the development of ancient Greek culture and the development of what he calls British national character.[153] The latter account focuses on the transition from the dominantly religious culture of medieval Britain and the growth of political absolutism, both patriarchal, to the shift to a questioning of the medieval consensus and its hierarchical chains sponsored by the impact of both the Renaissance and Reformation on British culture.

Cross-cultural research indicates that manhood has always been psychologically conflicted and fragile,[154] but the question of psychological

---

[149]   See Zevedei Barbu, *Problems of Historical Psychology* (New York: Grove Press, 1960).

[150]   E. R. Dodds, *The Greeks and the Irrational* (Berkeley: University of California Press, 1959).

[151]   See Zevedei Barbu, *Problems of Historical Psychology*, pp. 7, 52, 60, 83, 91, 92, 95, 98, 110, 119, 120, 123, 179.

[152]   See *Id.*, pp. 96–122.

[153]   See *id.*, pp. 145–218.

[154]   See, on this point, David D. Gilmore, *Manhood in the Making: Cultural Concepts of Masculinity* (New Haven, Conn.: Yale University Press, 1990).

---

fragility takes a different form in cultures like ours (like that of ancient Athens and Britain), which, at certain points in their history, are more democratic though still patriarchal and which are in transition from patriarchy to a more democratic culture.

Zevedei Barbu, in his illuminating book on the historical psychology of this transition in Britain in the seventeenth century, regards the plays of Shakespeare, in particular, as important not only as the great literature they are but as documentary insights into the underlying psychology of the underlying psychological crisis.[155] The psychological focus of Barbu's analysis is the questioning of the previous medieval religious consensus in light of the impact on British cultural and political development of the Renaissance and Reformation. Barbu's focus is on the removal of the constraints on and repressions of thought and feeling in Britain during this period, and he interprets Shakespeare's plays as expressing and exploring the consequences of the new forms of thought and feeling—including not only doubt but erotic and aggressive energies now released and thus now depicted and explored with a depth and psychological complexity not seen since the great period of the ancient Greek theater of Athens.

What interests me here are those plays that reveal and explore doubts about traditional conceptions of patriarchal manhood (*Hamlet*), and the psychological fragility of associated conceptions of heroic manhood (*Macbeth*, *Othello*, and *King Lear*). Of the protagonists in the four plays, only Hamlet is self-consciously not a soldier, but he is rather a university student drenched in the new Renaissance learning of skeptical doubt of Montaigne that Shakespeare either read in the French versions that had been published between 1580 and 1588 or learned of through the essays of William Cornwallis, who acknowledged Montaigne's influence, published in 1600[156] (Florio's English translation of Montaigne was published in 1603;[157] the play, *Hamlet*, dating probably from 1601). Of the essays by

---

[155] See, for Barbu's argument along these lines, Zevedei Barbu, *Problems of Historical Psychology* (New York: Grove Press, 1960), pp. 166–172.

[156] See James Shapiro, *A Year in the Life of William Shakespeare 1599* (New York: HarperPerennial, 2005), pp. 292–97; Ann Thompson and Neil Taylor, ed., *Hamlet: The Arden Shakespeare* rev. ed. (London: Bloomsbury, 2016), pp. 74–75.

[157] See Stephen Greenblatt and Peter G. Platt, *Shakespeare's Montaigne: The Florio Translation of the Essays: A Selection* (New York: New York Review Books, 2014).

Montaigne, skeptical doubt is the subject of the "Apology for Raymond Sebond"[158] and the need for intimate friendship with an equal is the subject of "Of Friendship,"[159] which mourns the death of Montaigne's intimate friend, Etienne de la Boetie (without "the sweet company and society of that man" life is "nothing but smoke, nothing but dark and dreary night").[160] Montaigne carefully omits discussion of his friend's radically liberal views, centering on the rights of free and equal lovers (citing the homosexual lovers, Harmodios and Aristogiton, whose resistance led to Athenian democracy) to refuse to obey tyrannical commands.[161] Hamlet's skeptical doubt extends to the retributive role patriarchy imposes on him in response to the murder of his father by his brother, and the marriage of his mother to his brother. Hamlet thus doubts the verisimilitude of what his father's ghost tells him about his murder and the marriage and tests the ghost's veracity by himself play-acting as insane and stage-managing the acting of a play (part of which he writes), all intended to test the reality of the obligation imposed on him. Hamlet's playing, both in the play and as insane, draws on Erasmus's pathbreaking appeal in *Praise of Folly* to both play and madness as ways of speaking truth to power.[162] Both Hamlet's play-acting and his skepticism comes to extend to lack of trust in the personal attachments of the play not only to the king but to Polonius; his mother, Ophelia; and his former friends, Rosencrantz and Guildenstern—all tainted by the patriarchal authority of the king. Only the friendship of his equal, Horatio, sustains him, again echoing Montaigne. Even when his doubts are resolved, he finds reasons not to seek revenge, leading to the mayhem of the play (the suicide of Ophelia and the deaths of his mother, the king, Polonius, Rosencrantz and Guildenstern, Laertes, and his own death). What makes *Hamlet* so profound and moving

---

158 See Donald M. Frame, translator, *The Complete Essays of Montaigne* (Stanford: Stanford University Press, 1965), pp. 318–457.

159 Id., pp. 135–44.

160 Id., at p. 143.

161 See Etienne De La Boetie, *Anti-Dictator,* trans. Harry Kurz (Mansfield Centre, Ct.: Martino Publishing, 2016), On Harmodios and Aristogiton, see id., p. 28.

162 See Erasmus, *Praise of Folly,* Betty Radice translation (London: Penguin, 1993). On Erasmus's impact on Shakespeare and others during the Renaissance, see Walter Kaiser, *Praisers of Folly* (Cambridge, Mass.: Harvard University Pres, 1963).

---

is that through its great soliloquies, we experience not only Hamlet's doubts but the psychological costs it imposes on him—his isolation from everyone but Horatio (including the loss of university friends, Rosencrantz and Guildenstern, and even the woman he loved), his anger at himself and others (including thoughts of suicide), and his sense of shame, as a man, that he cannot do what other men do so easily. Under the new circumstances of new sources of learning and reflection now available, including the rise of science,[163] the play reveals the fragility of manhood, now doubting patriarchy yet without finding an alternative, confronting moral nihilism.[164] The play portrays such a man, still living within a patriarchy now subject to reasonable doubt, as tragic.

Macbeth, Othello, and Lear are, in contrast, military men, and thus are much more tightly trapped by the demands patriarchy imposes on such men. Macbeth's dilemma is that within patriarchy, he owed allegiance to a good king, but as a patriarchal man, he wants to be first in the gender hierarchy. The latter vulnerability is brilliantly exposed and used by his ambitious wife, Lady Macbeth, as she humiliates him for what she takes to be his unmanly cowardice—a shaming of his manhood, which the play shows and leads us not only to acting against his conscience but so morally damages him that his paranoid suspicions lead him, as king, to the murder of anyone who opposes him or may oppose him, including the innocent wife and children of Macduff. The play reveals a flaw in the hierarchy that patriarchy imposes, namely, that it sets men, sometimes homicidally against one another, destroying ethical thought and feeling.

Othello and *King Lear* expose yet another fragility in patriarchal manhood, namely, that patriarchy, resting on the gender binary and hierarchy, kills love both of a man for a woman and of a father for a daughter. Othello, a man of color and a successful general in service of the Venetian Republic, breaks the love laws by falling in love with and marrying a white woman, Desdemona. But as a highly successful and accomplished patriarchal man (a general, and ruler in Cyprus), his subaltern, Iago, bridles at his lower status in the gender hierarchy. (Lower for two reasons: serving under a black man and, accorded lower status

---

[163] See, on this point, Hans Reichenbach, *The Rise of Scientific Philosophy* (Berkeley, Calif.: University of California Press, 1951).

[164] For a recent argument along these lines, see Rhodri Lewis, *Hamlet and the Vision of Darkness* (Princeton: Princeton University Press, 2017).

than Cassio, a man less deserving.) The play exposes how easily under patriarchy Iago can manipulate Othello into suspecting a sexual infidelity of his wife with Cassio of which she is wholly innocent. Patriarchy, which requires both a rigid gender binary and hierarchy, sets men and women in separate, mutually incommunicable worlds. What Iago knows both about patriarchy and about Othello is that Othello will believe a man but not a woman when it comes to any suspicion of a wife's adultery, the high crime and misdemeanor for a woman under patriarchy.[165] Othello will not listen to Desdemona's denials because under patriarchy, she has no voice; only men have voices, and both Othello and Iago are men. The play thus reveals yet another vulnerability of patriarchal men who cannot see or read the love of those they love or claim to love.

Lear is, in contrast, a king at the top of the gender hierarchy. What the play reveals even in a king—a successful military leader and king—is that he is vulnerable not only to the debilities of age, as all men are, but to the frailty that patriarchy fosters in men, namely, that they cannot distinguish real and unreal love in those closest to them, their daughters. The consequence of this personal frailty is political disaster, putting in charge of his kingdom his two other daughters, Goneril and Regan, who, in fact, hate him and, as it turns out (in vying for the love of Edmund), hate each other, unleashing political violence both on their father and sister and, eventually, one another.

All these plays expose frailties and vulnerabilities in men—injuries patriarchy inflicts on men. The revelation of such frailties is historically prepared, as Barbu argues, by the transition from a more to a less repressive patriarchal culture, unleashing new forms of doubt as well as new thoughts and feelings, including about both personal and political life under patriarchy and the connections between them. The problem of love under patriarchy is thus raised in all four plays—whether the failures of personal love for their lovers of Hamlet and Othello or Lear's failure of love as a father for his daughter or Lady Macbeth's using her husband's love to shame him into murder. None of these plays challenges political patriarchy: Britain under Elizabeth remained an absolute monarchy, even more starkly so under the Stuarts, whose political views and perhaps Shakespeare's

---

[165] At this point, see Carol Gilligan and David A. J. Richards, *The Deepening Darkness*, pp. 2, 41–42, 44–4.

called for hierarchy, "Observe degree, priority, and place."[166] But questions about patriarchy were raised in these and many of Shakespeare's other plays, including the history plays. Jan Kott, in his pathbreaking study of Shakespeare's plays, *Shakespeare Our Contemporary*,[167] analyzed the tragic structure of these plays as reflecting the destructiveness of the "Grand Mechanism"[168]—a mechanism whose cogs are both great lords and hired assassins and a mechanism that forces people to violence, cruelty, and treason, which constantly claim new victims."[169] Commenting on *Richard III*, Kott observes of this and other plays:

> There is no tragedy of history without awareness. Tragedy begins at the point when the king becomes aware of the working of the Grand Mechanism. This can happen when he falls victim to it or when he acts as executioner. These are the points at which Shakespeare carries out his great confrontations, contrasting the moral order with the order of history. Richard III is the mastermind of the Grand Mechanism, with its will and awareness. Here, for the first time, Shakespeare has shown the human face of the Grand Mechanism—a terrifying face in its ugliness and the cruel grimace of its lips. But it's also a fascinating face.[170]

Kott had come to see this "terrifying face" in the totalitarian politics of Stalinism in his native Poland and found in Shakespeare "our contemporary" because the tragedies and histories reveal what he came to see as the destructiveness of political patriarchy both in private and public life. In Britain, the questions raised by these plays prepared the way for the first fundamental questioning of absolute monarchy since democratic Athens. These questions were to culminate in the emergence of

---

[166] See William Shakespeare, "Troilus and Cressida," *Complete Works*, ed. W. J. Craig (London: Oxford University Press, 1966), pp. 667–700, at p. 672, l. 85 (Ulysses).

[167] Jan Kott, *Shakespeare Our Contemporary*, trans. Boleslaw Taborski (New York: W. W. Norton, 1974).

[168] Id., p. 11.

[169] Id., p 38.

[170] Id., p. 41.

arguments for toleration, free speech, and constitutional democracy in the English Civil War and, after the Glorious Revolution, in the development of British democratic constitutionalism—all of which crucially framed both the American Revolution and the Constitution of 1787 and Bill of Rights of 1791.[171]

At times of transition from a more to a less patriarchal culture, the frailties of patriarchal manhood, which exist as long as patriarchy has existed, come more to the surface and are thus subject to doubt and discussion, often preparing the way for democracy or greater democracy. Samuel Beckett's play, *Endgame*,[172] written by him in the wake of World War II after his participation in the French resistance to fascism, reflects in our historical period what Shakespeare's four tragedies reflect in his culture—the sense that the disastrous hold of patriarchy on European cultures had now weakened and that human relationships must now be reconfigured. At the heart of the shift is the sense that patriarchy poisons relationships of all kinds, including the capacity to love and be loved as equals.

Carol Gilligan and my account of these matters in *The Deepening Darkness* argued that a play like *The Oresteia* reflects the transition from a shame to a guilt culture. Also, that part of its brilliance, as part of that guilt culture, is that it both justifies the Athenian democracy as an ethical advance in the control of violence by legal institutions that rest on the proof of personal guilt, but also, on interpretive examination, it

---

[171]　See, on these points, Michael Walzer, *The Revolution of the Saints* (Cambridge, Mass.: Harvard University Press, 1965); ASP Woodhouse, ed., *Puritanism and Liberty* (London: Dent, 1938); Bernard Bailyn, *The Ideological Origins of theAmerican Revolution* (Cambridge, Mass.: Harvard University Press, 1967); Gordon S. Wood, *The Creation of the AmericanRepublic, 1776–1787* (New York: Norton, 1969); Douglass Adair, *Fame and the Founding Fathers* (New York: Norton, 1974); David A. J. Richards, *Toleration and the Constitution* (New York: Oxford University Press, 1986); David A. J. Richards, *Foundations of American Constitutionalism* (New York: Oxford University Press, 1989); David A. J. Richards, *Conscience and the Constitution* (Princeton: Princeton University Press, 1993).

[172]　Samuel Beckett, *Endgame* (New York; Grove Press, 1958).

---

reveals continuing patriarchal assumptions that compromise democracy—a subject that we explore throughout the argument of our earlier book.[173]

The Oresteia, the oldest trilogy in the canon of theatre, celebrates the founding of Athenian democracy. Aeschylus argues for the superiority of the Athenian democracy over autocracies like the rule of kings in Argos and Sparta and Persia because only democracy with its jury system can end the cycle of retributive violence or blood vengeance. In the final play of the trilogy, Athena, the motherless daughter born from the head of Zeus, casts the deciding vote arguing for the acquittal of Orestes (who killed his mother, who killed her husband, and who sacrificed their daughter) on normative grounds: killing a mother is bad but not so bad as killing a father and a king. Because she has no mother, Athena is regarded as more impartial than the Furies, and she persuades them to accept as the price for their admission to the new city of Athens, giving up their anger over the deaths of Klytemnestra and Iphigenia and becoming instead the Eumenides, the kindly minded and the good women of Athens.

The play thus links the founding of democracy with the reinstatement of patriarchy, giving precedence to fathers over mothers, men over women, and silencing women's anger as the condition of their participation. The argument for democracy is deeply flawed along explicitly gendered lines. The normative claim that killing a father is morally worse than killing a mother is not justified but deemed self-evident because it is stated by Apollo. Athenian rationality thus gives way to the will of a patriarchal god. Athena enforces the patriarchal gender binary and hierarchy that elevate reason (masculine) over emotion (feminine) and force the suppression of women's anger in the name of rationality.

Furthermore, the play's alleged solution to the cycle of violence does not solve it at all: violence against women (Agamemnon's sacrifice of his daughter, Iphigenia, and Klytemnestra's killing of Cassandra, Agamemnon's concubine) is overlooked, and the violence of men (the Trojan War and Orestes's killing of his mother) is accepted as in the nature of things. As Athena states explicitly:

---

[173] See Carol Gilligan and David A. J. Richards, *The Deepening Darkness: Patriarchy, Resistance, and Democracy's Future* (New York: Cambridge University Press, 2009), pp. 12–15.

Let our wars
rage on abroad, with all their force, to satisfy
our powerful lust for fame. But as for the bird
that fights at home—my curse on civil war.[174]

Athenian democracy is thus celebrated not because it has solved the problem of male violence (which it has not) but because it his redirected that violence from civil war to imperialistic wars. Athens was, of course, an imperialistic state, which wars, as its greatest historian Thycidides tells us, were often unjust in their ends and means, sometimes including what we would call genocidal murder of the innocent.[175] These wars end in the sheer stupidity of the Peloponnesian War, which Athens lost, leading in time, to the end of the democracy.

We began our 2009 book with the discussion of *The Oresteia* because its argument so brilliantly illustrates how, at the very inception of democracy, its claims to equality were subverted by the forces of patriarchy that were very much alive in Athenian culture. Patriarchy hides in *The Oresteia* in the way the play's superficially plausible rationality at crucial points darkens Athenian political intelligence. Its celebrated aim—ending the cycle of blood vengeance —in fact unleashes not only the suppression of women's voices (as the bad women, Furies, become the good women of Athens, praised, as Pericles put it, for "to be least talked about by men")[176] but also the destructive force of imperialistic wars, which is to say most of the wars in human history.

The root of the problem is the gender-binary, in which reason (masculine) is separated from emotion (feminine). The vaunted rationality of Athenian argument—alleged to distinguish them from barbarian autocracies—hides within it and crucially turns on the gender binary and hierarchy, which darkens and indeed cripples Athenian democratic political intelligence. Our insight rests on our feminism but not the feminism that is itself bound to a gender binary and hierarchy—a feminism that pits women

---

[174] Aeschylus, *The Oresteia,* trans. Robert Fagles (New York: Penguin, 1977), p. 269.

[175] See Thucydides, *History of the Peloponnesian War,* Rex Warner translation (New York: Penguin. 1972) on the unjust murder of innocent Melians, rationalized as not requiring any moral justification, pp. 400–408 (the Melian Dialogue).

[176] *Ibid.,* p. 151.

against men. In our view, the gender binary and hierarchy subvert the capacity to love and to live democratically in both women and men, albeit in different ways. By inflicting moral injury, patriarchy seeds the ground for moral slavery, and feminism, as one of us (Gilligan) has written, is the movement to free democracy from patriarchy.

It is a feature of Greek democratic culture, as of British and American democratic culture, that guilt and shame cultures continue to exist side by side. Both Athens and Britain were democracies, but they were also imperialists. America is democratic but has also engaged in imperialist wars, and like Athens and Britain, its democracy has been marred by racism and sexism—both inconsistent with democracy. As we have seen, both Hawthorne and Melville expose and resist this contradiction in American democracy.

Carol Gilligan and I have taken a distinctive view of how the tensions between democracy and patriarchy should be understood and how they should be resolved. The tension, for us, arises from the normative conception of democracy as resting on free and equal voice while patriarchy's gender binary and hierarchy require the repression of the voices of well over half the human race (women). Our analysis shows that the continuing problem of patriarchy extends not only to our politics, but to our religion, psychology, and literature. Christianity was, we argued, a democratic religion of free and equal voice, but it became more Roman than Christian once Christianity became the established church of the Roman Empire. And the highly patriarchal Roman Empire was taken as the model of many states and empires to follow—all at the cost of democracy and its values of equality and freedom.

We need now to develop a perspective, arising from our conception of the tension between democracy and patriarchy, that will illuminate our current situation.

Political Religions

In light of the distinction between shame and guilt cultures, I turn for illumination of our current situation to relevant work of James Gilligan, Hannah Arendt, T. H. Adorno, and Virginia Woolf.

By political religion,[177] Gilligan means to identify the political ideology that he takes to be central to the political psychology that historically motivated what he takes to be the great evils wrought by nationalism, imperialism, totalitarianism (Hitler's fascism and Stalin's communism), and religious fundamentalism today. For Gilligan, the psychological force of this ideology is that it reinstates a fixed and certain political expression of patriarchy in reaction to the collapse in belief in the conventional sources of patriarchal authority (e.g., patriarchal religion—the death of God), leading to psychologically intolerable forms of moral nihilism. All these political religions are, for Gilligan, in their nature both antidemocratic and antiliberal and have for this reason given expression to the monstrous evils of racism, anti-Semitism, sexism, and homophobia. Gilligan, a leading psychiatrist of violence, analyzes the propensities to aggressive violence of political religions as an expression of the hegemonic shame cultures that typify political religions, covering over and marginalizing the moral emotion of guilt that arises from a sense of culpable harm to other persons, one's equals, rooted in love and humane fellow feeling.

Carol Gilligan and I argued in *The Deepening Darkness* that the political fascism of Mussolini in Italy and Hitler in Germany is best understood as a reactionary political psychology arising from the shaming of patriarchal nationalist manhood after the experience, as defined by Mussolini and Hitler, of the defeats of World War I.[178] Both opposed what they took to be the effeminacy of political liberalism, calling for treating persons as equals. Their rage centered on the attack on patriarchy's gender binary and hierarchy, implicit in democratic liberalism, and their violence targeted as scapegoats those they took to question patriarchy. As an ideology, fascism was empty of serious political theory. Rather, as quoted by Robert O. Paxton, "The fist, asserted a fascist militant in 1920, is the synthesis of our theory."[179] What made Hitler's political fascism so psychologically

---

[177] See James Gilligan, "Terrorism, Nihilism, and Modernity: Analyzing the Dilemmas of Modernity," in Henri Parens and Stuart Twemlow, eds., *The Future of Prejudice: Applications of Psychoanalytic Understanding toward its Prevention* (Lanham, Md.: Rowman & Littlefied, 2006), pp. 37-62.

[178] See Carol Gilligan and David A. J. Richards, *The Deepening Darkness*, pp. 232–238.

[179] Quoted in Robert O. Paxton, *The Anatomy of Fascism* (New York: Vintage Books, 2004), p. 17.

remarkable is that rooted in what he called the shaming of German manhood by the Treaty of Versailles, his sense of sense so resonated with the German people who elected him that it overrode and suppressed the religious and philosophical culture of guilt of German culture, perhaps most brilliantly expressed in the moral philosophy of Immanuel Kant and was, in contrast to Japan, to reassert itself powerfully after the war.[180]

Hitler himself, a deeply narcissistic and shame-ridden man, mobilized Germans, as Captain Ahab did in Melville's *Moby-Dick*, aggressively and genocidally to war on his version of the white whale, the unjust scapegoats of his rage, European Jewry, and Germans, like the mindless crew of Ahab's Pequod, surrendered to him any sense of ethical conscience.[181] If this could happen in one of the most advanced cultures of Europe (populated by the best and the brightest), Gilligan argues it can happen anywhere, and we must understand how vulnerable any people may be to such political religions if they do not take seriously the threat of patriarchy not only to democracy but to ethics itself.

Undoubtedly, the most brilliant psychological analysis of such reactionary politics is Hannah Arendt's *Origins of Totalitarianism*.[182] What Arendt, who had observed the rise of fascism at firsthand as a German student of both Heidegger and Jaspers, found in common in both German fascism and Soviet communism was the antiscientific certitude of, in Hitler's case, racist science and, in Stalin's case, the laws of history, both of which rationalized the patriarchal authority of Hitler and Stalin as a kind of priest-god, uniquely attuned to apodictic scientific and political truth, including whatever murders of the innocent such truth required.[183] It is a feature of this political psychology that, like other forms of patriarchy, it requires the violent suppression of any voice of persons that might reasonably challenge its authority, a challenge all the more threatening because its claims were so unreasonable, both scientifically and ethically. Arendt regarded this feature as central to totalitarian politics:

---

[180]   See, on these points, Ian Buruma, *The Wages of Guilt: Memories of War in Germany and Japan* (New York: New York Review Book, 2015; originally published, 1994).

[181]   See Herman Melville, *Moby-Dick* (New York: Penguin, 1992), pp. 3–35, 174–212, 580–625.

[182]   See Hannah Arendt, *The Origins of Totalitarianism* (Orlando: A Harvest Book, 1976) (originally published 1950).

[183]   See, on these points, id., chapter 11, pp. 341–388.

The ideal subject of totalitarian rule is not the convinced Nazi or the convinced Communist, but people for whom the distinction between fact and fiction (*i.e.,* the reality of experience) and the distinction between true and false (*i.e.,* the standards of thought) no longer exist.[184]

The analogy to Trump's politics is striking (see Gilligan and Richards, *Darkness Now Visible*). Such moral slavery, as I call it, dehumanizes its critics and makes of them sometimes genocidally murdered scapegoats of that gnawing reasonable doubt of its ideology. Thus, the connection of totalitarianism (both fascism and Stalinist communism) to the evils of racism, anti-Semitism, sexism, and homophobia.

There is a comparably illuminating analysis of the underlying psychology of the political religion of fascism in the study by T. W. Adorno and his colleagues of the authoritarian personality.[185] Adorno's work was inspired by the conception of the authoritarian personality introduced by the psychoanalyst, Erich Fromm, to understand how fascism could have arisen from and taken over the German democracy.[186] Like Arendt and Adorno, Fromm—a Jew—had fled his homeland and now tried to make sense of what had happened. Why had Germans come to fear the freedoms of democracy, in particular, its respect for the inalienable right to conscience, ceding ethical judgment to "irrational overestimation and admiration"[187] of a totalitarian leader? Fromm acutely observes the role of gender in Hitler's rhetoric: the satisfaction the masses have in domination.[188] As Hitler puts it, "[L]ike a woman . . . who will submit to the strong man rather than dominate the weakling."[189] There is a psychological disorder here, Fromm argues, a disorder in love: "Love is based on equality and freedom."[190]

Adorno's study, unlike Fromm's, is of the American authoritarian personality. Like Hannah Arendt, Adorno's study does not explicitly

---

[184] Hannah Arendt, *The Origins of Totalitarianism*, p. 474.

[185] T. W. Adorno, Else Frenkel-Brunswick, Daniel J. Levinson R. Nevitt Sanford, *The Authoritarian Personality* (New York: Harper & Row, 1950)

[186] See Erich Fromm, *Escape From Freedom* (New York: Henry Holt, 1965; first published, 1941), pp. 161-63, 167–68.

[187] Id., p. 164.

[188] Id., p. 220.

[189] Quoted at id., p. 220.

[190] Id., p. 159.

use patriarchy in his analysis, but in fact, the F-scale describes, like Fromm's earlier view, what we have called patriarchal psychology—rigid conventionalism, authoritarian submission and aggression, opposition to the subjective, stereotypy, power and toughness, destructiveness and cynicism, projection of dangerous impulses on others, and exaggerated concern with sex (including homophobia).[191] Authoritarian psychology is thus marked by hierarchy (as opposed to equality),[192] by a rigid gender binary and[193] authoritarian moralism,[194] as well as by an intolerance of ambiguity[195] and associated belief in pseudo-science.[196] Bob Altemeyer's more recent confirmation and elaboration of this psychology identifies three features of "right-wing authoritarianism," namely, authoritarian submission, authoritarian aggression, and conventionalism.[197]

What neither Arendt nor Adorno see is how their arguments of political psychology clearly assume and are best understood in terms of the connection between patriarchy and fascism earlier stated by Virginia Woolf in *Three Guineas.*[198] What makes the analysis of *Three Guineas* so astonishing is not only Woolf's pathbreaking analysis of the patriarchal roots of fascist violence but also her larger call for a resistance in which women join with men (resistance to war was, for Woolf, an issue for both men and women, collaboratively). The issue, she argued, was what Josephine Butler called the great principles of justice and equality and liberty. Addressing men, Woolf comments:

---

[191]   See T. W. Adorno, et al., *The Authoritarian Personality,* p. 228. On homophobia, see id., p. 240.

[192]   Id., pp. 413–14

[193]   Id., pp. 428–29.

[194]   *Id.,* p. 458.

[195]   *Id.,* pp. 461–64, 479–82.

[196]   *Id.,* pp. 464–5.

[197]   See Bob Altemeyer, *The Authoritarian Specter* (Cambridge, Mass.: Harvard University Press, 1996), p. 6. For the relationship of Altemeyer's work to Adorno's, see id., pp. 45–47. See also Bob Altemeyer, *Rights-Wing Authoritarianism* (Manitoba, Canada: The University of Manitoba Press, 1981); Bruce E. Hunsberger and Bob Altemeyer, *Atheists: A Groundbreaking Study of America's Nonbelievers* (Amherst, New York: Prometheus Books, 2006).

[198]   Virginia Woolf, *Three Guineas* Jane Marcus edition (Orlando, Florida: Harvest, 2006) (originally published, 1938).

> The words are the same are yours; the claim is the same as yours. The daughters of educated men who were called, to their resentment, "feminists" were in fact the advance guard of your own movement. They were fighting the same enemy that you are fighting and for the same reason. They were fighting the tyranny of the patriarchal state as you are fighting the tyranny of the Fascist state (p. 121).

Neither Arendt nor Adorno, among the very best human scientists of their time, can see, let alone acknowledge, the role gender plays in the phenomena they otherwise investigate so trenchantly. We need to understand how democratic people sometimes espouse what William James called in his own time American stupidity and injustice, arising from what he called an ethical blindness with which we all are afflicted in regard to the feelings of creatures and people different from ourselves.[199] When James wrote, as in the later period of Arendt and Adorno, gender was, as it largely remains today, marginalized in serious intellectual discourse, and he does not investigate the role gender plays in our "blindness."

Woolf sees it because, as her novel *Mrs. Dalloway* makes quite clear, she connects the suicidality of Septimius and the thoughts of suicide of Mrs. Dalloway to the experience of trauma, in Septimius's case to what we would today call post-traumatic stress order, in Mrs. Dalloway's to being a good woman, not following her heart.[200] Woolf had herself been the victim of traumatic sexual abuse by her half brother, which explains her understanding of the issue in both men's and women's experience and why she connects them. The psychological importance of trauma, in understanding the pivotal importance of gender in supporting a range of irrational prejudices, is that patriarchy rests on the infliction of traumatic initiations, and thus the psyches of men and women, morally injured by such initiations, enact the gender binary and hierarchy in their lives— the model for the scapegoating stereotypes that rationalize irrationalist

---

[199] See William James, "On a Certain Blindness in Human Beings," in William James, *Writings 1878–1899* (New York: The Library of America, 1992), pp. 841–60, at p. 841.

[200] See, for further discussion, Carol Gilligan and David A. J. Richards, *The Deepening Darkness*, pp. 213–214.

prejudices (men vs. women, race vs. race, religion vs. religion, straight vs. gay, class vs. class, tribe vs. tribe, etc.). Unreal divisions between thought (male) and emotion (female) feed into unreal hierarchies, attacking, as Arendt saw,[201] the psyche itself. Such mandated divisions and hierarchies are not based in experience but in false authority, thus undermining democracy and, at the worst, rationalizing totalitarianism and genocidal murder of the innocent, as fascist German politics shows so starkly and so unforgettably to people of good will who refuse to deny what reality now shows us. The heart of its darkness is not merely falsifying but killing ethical experience, which rests on empathy for the equal dignity of all persons. And patriarchy is what motors this evil dynamic, this "blindness," in our personal and political lives. It is time for Americans to see and acknowledge that their politics is not now, nor has ever been, immune from this dynamic.[202] It should inspire Americans, always drawn to the authority of our founders, that James Madison, the leading founder, so clearly saw this evil in democratic group psychology, what he called faction, as the central challenge to constructing a constitutional democracy that would respect human rights.[203] It is extraordinary that a form of constitutional originalism, which fails even to see this challenge and its significance, should now, in President Trump's abject admiration for Justice Scalia, be the standard for appointment of justices to the Supreme Court of the United States.[204]

---

[201] See, on this point, Elisabeth Young-Bruehl, *Why Arendt Matters* (New Haven, Conn.: Yale University Press, 2006).

[202] See, for cogent argument on this point, James Q. Whitman, *Hitler's American Model: The United States and the making of Nazi Race Law* (Princeton: Princeton University Press, 2017).

[203] See, for argument on this point, David A. J. Richards, *Foundations of American Constitutionalism* (New York: Oxford University Press, 1989).

[204] For further discussion of this point, see Carol Gilligan and David A. J. Richards, *Darkness Now Visible*, pp. 85–88. See, for supporting historical and textual argument on the critique of originalism, David A. J. Richards, *Foundations of American Constitutionalism* (New York: Oxford University Press, 1989); David A. J. Richards, *Fundamentalism in American Religion and Law: Obama's Challenge to Patriarchy's Threat to Democracy* (Cambridge: Cambridge University Press, 2010).

Initiation into Patriarchy

The Trump election made quite visible how appealing patriarchy remains in our otherwise democratic culture, with which patriarchy is, in fact, in contradiction (ignoring the voices of more than half the human race). Patriarchy, which rests, as we have seen, on an irrationalist shame culture keyed to enforcing the gender binary and hierarchy, draws its power from the degree that threats to patriarchal gender roles elicit a shame that silences voice in both men and women, in effect, silencing the ethical voice of guilt resting on culpable failures to respect the equal voice and dignity of all persons. To understand how patriarchy remains so powerful, we must look more closely at the initiation into patriarchy of both American men and women.

In my experience of teaching with Carol Gilligan, the readings on psychological development led students to reflect on their own experience. Men in the class had experienced a shock of recognition in reading Judy Chu's *When Boys Become Boys*,[205] recalling how they too around the age of five had begun to shield those aspects of themselves that would have led them to be perceived as not a real boy and called girly or gay. Many found a strong resonance in the voices of the adolescent boys in Niobe Way's *Deep Secrets*,[206] where they describe the intimacy and closeness of their friendships with other boys, and yet as Way's research shows, by the end of high school, they no longer have a best friend. Over the four years of high school, many boys come to renounce their desire for emotional closeness with other boys and, in the name of becoming a man, keep their secrets to themselves.

Taken together, Chu and Way's studies illuminate a process of initiation that begins with boys around the ages of four and five and then picks up again in adolescence. Their research shows the costs to boys of a masculinity defined in opposition to and as the opposite of anything perceived as "feminine." For example, to establish their masculinity, the four- and five-year-old boys in Chu's study had formed the "Mean Team"—a team created by the boys and for the boys to prove that they were

[205] Judy Y. Chu, *When Boys Become Boys: Development, Relationships, and Masculinity* (New York: New York University Press, 2014).

[206] Niobe Way, *Deep Secrets: Boys' Friendships and the Crisis of Connection* (Cambridge, Mass.: Harvard University Press, 2011).

in fact boys, not girls. Because girls were perceived by them as being good and nice, the main activity of the Mean Team was, in the words of one of the boys, "to bother people." In her studies of adolescent boys' friendships, Niobe Way documented how in learning how to be more of a man, over 75 percent of the boys, across a range of ethnicity and class, by the end of high school no longer had a best friend, meaning a friend to whom they could tell their deep secrets.

Women in the class had similarly been struck by the resonance they found in the voices of the girls who took part in the Harvard Project studies of girls' development. In particular, many had responded to the frank and fearless voices of girls on the cusp of adolescence—voices that sounded to them at once familiar and surprising. They recalled the pressures they had faced to silence an honest voice for the sake of having relationships, like Neeti, one of the participants in the studies and a top student and school leader—they had buried deep inside themselves "the voice that stands up for what I believe in." Like many of the girls in the Harvard Project studies, the women in our seminar were aware of the costs of saying what they really thought and felt, especially when what they had seen and heard was said not to be happening.[207]

Among the things we found striking in student papers was the division between those written by men and by women (both straight and gay). The men wrote about infidelity: they had been unfaithful to what they loved; the women wrote about silence: they had silenced a voice within themselves. For both, it was an act of betrayal. They had betrayed a part

---

[207] See Carol Gilligan, Janie Victoria Ward, and Jill McLean Taylor, eds., *Mapping the Moral Domain: A Contribution of Women's Thinking to Psychological Theory and Education* (Cambridge, Mass.: Harvard University Press, 1988); Carol Gilligan, Nona Plessner Lyons, and Trudy Hanmer, eds., *Making Connections: The Relational Worlds of Adolescent Girls at Emma Willard School* (Cambridge, Mass.: Harvard University Press, 1990); Carol Gilligan, Annie G. Rogers, and Deborah Tolman (Eds.), Women, Girls, and Psychotherapy: Reframing Resistance (Haworth Press, 1991) Lyn Mikel Brown and Carol Gilligan, *Meeting at the Crossroads: Women's Psychology and Girls' Development* (Cambridge, Mass.: Harvard University Press, 1992 (paperback edition by Ballantine, New York, 1993); Jill McLean Taylor, Carol Gilligan, and Amy Sullivan, *Between Voice and Silence: Women and Girls, Race and Relationship* (Cambridge, Mass.: Harvard University Press, 1995).

of themselves. There was no guise to these descriptions; the papers read like a statement of fact. This had happened; this is how it happened.[208]

In a recent book, Carol Gilligan and Naomi Snider investigate the different impacts of patriarchy on the psychology of women as a way of answering the question: why has patriarchy lasted so long, or as Carol and Naomi put it in the subtitle of a recent paper, why are we still talking about Oedipus?—a tale of male violence and female silence.[209] Drawing on the studies of the Harvard Project on women's psychology and girls' development and the new studies of boys' development and of men and the work with couples that followed in their wake, Gilligan and Snider argue that the earlier timing of boys' initiation into patriarchy (between the ages of four and seven rather than as with girls, at the time of their adolescence) affects the capacity for resistance. The initiation of boys into the codes of patriarchal masculinity at the time when they are entering formal schooling and learning about the way things are means that they are more likely to accept the gender binary and hierarchy as just how things are. Whereas girls being initiated later, when they are more cognitively sophisticated and have had more experience, can see the framework they are entering in becoming young women not as how things are but as the way things are said to be. In fact, it was the awareness among girls of this gap between how things are and how things are said to be that aroused their suspicion and fueled their resistance. When what they were being told about the world, including about women and men, did not ring true to their experience, they had more resources to draw on in, finding ways to stay with what they know.

Girls' later induction into the gender codes and scripts of patriarchal manhood and womanhood thus makes it easier for them to spot their falsity: that is, to see, for example the disparity between the way men and women are and the way they are said to be. It is easier for them to see the framework, to see that they are being asked to shift the framework and to see and to speak in a way that rings false to them but is widely taken to be

---

[208] We discuss these student papers at greater length in our book, Carol Gilligan and David A. J. Richards, *Darkness Now Visible*, Chapter 2.

[209] See Carol Gilligan and Naomi Snider, *Why Does Patriarchy Persist?* (Cambridge, UK: Polity, 2018). See also Carol Gilligan and Naomi Snider, "The Loss of Pleasure, or Why We are Still Talking about Oedipus," *Contemporary Psychoanalysis*, 2017, Vol. 53, No. 2: 173–195.

true, like the notion that men don't care about relationships and women don't know what they think. Summing up the ravages of patriarchy on the human psyche as they affect the lives of women and men, Gilligan and Snider observe that both men and women are pressed into falsity, men into "the pseudo-independence of masculine detachment"[210] and women into "the pseudo-relationships of feminine goodness."

Connecting the developmental studies of Gilligan and her colleagues with John Bowlby's studies of attachment and loss, Carol and Naomi came to a startling discovery: the gender ideals of patriarchal manhood and womanhood correspond to what Bowlby identifies as pathological responses to loss. Pathological in that they compound loss by standing in the way of relationships.

What's more, this observation prompted a further discovery: the initiation into the gender codes of patriarchy subverts the very capacities we rely on in order to live in relationships—that is, our ability to repair the ruptures that are an inescapable part of every day. Relationships are not steady states; in the normal course of things, we move in and out of touch with ourselves and with others, finding and losing and finding again. It is when loss becomes irreparable that love becomes tragic. But when boys in the course of becoming "boys" learn to shield their emotional sensitivity and cover their vulnerability, they become insensitive to the loss of connection or unable to register what they or others are feeling. Within the codes of patriarchal masculinity, the human's need for somebody to "be there for you" as one of the boys in Niobe Way's studies put it, becomes "sissy-like;" that is, being girly or gay. It's not a need that a real boy would acknowledge, or at least not in front of other boys or in public. Thus, the move to repair ruptures in relationships, which requires registering the loss of connection, comes to be seen as unmanly and subjected to shaming.

For girls, it is an honest voice—the voice that says what they are feeling and thinking—that comes to be heard as unseemly. When a girl can't say what she is feeling and thinking without her voice sounding too loud or angry or stupid or rude or without being told she is crazy—that what she sees happening is not really happening—then her ability to repair ruptures in relationships is jeopardized. Her moves to repair in response to losing touch or feeling out of connection become subjected to shaming. Thus, the relational capacities that are essential to love and also integral

---

[210]   Id., p. 21.

to democracy—our ability to live with integrity, in touch with oneself and in connection with others—are at risk in the course of our initiation into the gender codes of patriarchy.

Gilligan and Snider conclude that patriarchy persists because it inflicts a loss of relationship and then renders that loss irreparable. Detachment or seeming independence on the part of men and what Bowlby terms *compulsive caregiving* in women, the selfless caregiving that has been held up as the epitome of feminine goodness, render relationships either seemingly unnecessary for men or as requiring a woman, paradoxically, to give up her desire to be in relationship for the sake of having relationships. For a woman, then it becomes necessary for her not to be herself in order to be someone others want to be with.[211]

The Gilligan-Snider argument thus builds on Gilligan's previous exploration of the psychological consequences of the earlier timing of boys' initiation into patriarchy and the later timing of girls' initiation, including her explanation of why women's voices are essential to resisting patriarchy. Although resistance is in the interest of both women and men, women's participation is crucial because if they don't speak, then it's likely that nobody will speak about the loss of relationship that patriarchy inflicts.

The key discoveries Gilligan and Snider came to arise from the realization that patriarchy, although psychologically unstable (because it falsifies the reality of experience), is held in place because both the pseudo-independence and detachment of patriarchal manhood and the compulsive caregiving and self-silencing of patriarchal womanhood are defenses against the loss of authentic relationship that patriarchy inflicts. What's more, these defenses against loss render the loss of relationship irreparable and hence the stability and the persistence of patriarchy, despite its psychological costs.

So it comes to pass that the losses patriarchy inflicts are not acknowledged, let alone resisted, but accepted as in the very nature of things. The consequence in men is that the shaming of manhood becomes incendiary and can justify violence against those who are perceived as the source of dishonor. In women, shaming leads to the silencing of voice, the very voices that might reasonably challenge the injustice of patriarchal demands. The consequence for both men and women—psychologically locked into patriarchal demands set by the terms of the gender binary

---

[211] Id., p. 21.

and hierarchy—is impairment of their capacity to see, let alone repair the relationships that patriarchy breaks. In effect, our capacity to love and feel empathy across the barriers imposed by the various iterations of the gender binary and hierarchy (the racism, sexism, homophobia, xenophobia, class stratification, anti-Semitism, and so on) is impaired or shattered.

In our teaching of our seminar, Carol and I were surprised and moved by the resonance for several of our male students of the exquisite and sensitive studies of the initiation into patriarchy of young boys (Judith Chu) and older adolescent boys (Niobe Way). Reading the studies of Chu and Way and writing papers about what they found in them—both in their weekly and final papers and in class discussions shared with other students—reminded both students of a voice they remembered in themselves as young and older boys and how that voice had been silenced by demands from other boys and their parents that they now regard as their own initiation into patriarchy. It was a voice they wished to own—a voice they heard in an experience of a psychoanalyst, Donald Moss, discussed in a paper by Carol Gilligan, "Moral Injury and the Ethics of Care" (2014).[212]

In the paper, Carol developed, based on the brilliant study of combat trauma of Vietnam veterans by the psychiatrist Jonathan Shay,[213] a theory of moral injury. Carol argued that like Shay's veterans, the initiation of men and women into patriarchy gave them moral injuries, namely, the stress and trauma of initiation that led to the "betrayal of 'what's right' in a high-stakes situation, where the betrayal was sanctioned by someone in a position of legitimate authority" (p. 91, Gilligan). What riveted our male students was a personal story the psychoanalyst Donald Moss tells, in the epilogue to his *Thirteen Ways of Looking at a Man*, about his experience in first grade. Gilligan wrote (p. 97) the following:

> Every week the children learned a new song and were
> told that at the end of the year, they would each have a
> chance to lead the class in singing their favorite, which
> they were to keep a secret. For Moss, the choice was

---

[212]   Carol Gilligan, "Moral Injury and the Ethic of Care: Reframing the Conversation about Differences," *Journal of Social Philosophy Volume 45* No.1, Spring 2014, pp. 89–106.

[213]   See Jonathan Shay, *Achilles in Vietnam: Combat Trauma and the Undoing of Character* (New York: Scribner, 1994).

clear: "The only song I loved was the lullaby, 'When at Night I Go to Sleep [Fourteen Angels Watch Do Keep]' from *Hansel and Gretel.*" Every night, he would sing it to himself, and like the song said, the angels came, saving him from his night terrors and enabling him to fall asleep. "It was, and would always be, the most beautiful song I had ever heard."

The first graders had learned the song in early autumn, and in late spring, when Moss's turn came, he stood in front of the class. The teacher asked what song he had chosen. Moss recalls this:

> I began to tell her, "It's the lullaby . . ." But immediately, on the corner of my eye, I saw the reaction of the boys in the front row. Their faces were lighting up in shock . . . I knew, knew in a way that was immediate, clear, and certain that what I was about to do, the song I was about to choose, the declaration that I was about to make, represented an enormous, irrevocable error . . . what the boys were teaching me was that I was to know, *and to always have known,* that "When at night I go to sleep' could not be my favorite song, that a lullaby had no place here, that something else was called for. In a flash, in an act of gratitude, not to my angels but to my boys, I change my selection, I smiled at the teacher and told her I was just kidding, told her "I would now lead the class in singing the 'Marines' Hymn' from the halls of Montezuma to the shorts of Tripoli . . ." (italics added).

Moss thus remembers the initiation that Chu observes: the "Marines' Hymn" could still be the song of the Mean

Team formed by the boys she studies. Writing from the vantage point of middle age, Moss says that his book can be thought of as an extended effort to unpack that moment in front of the class and, indirectly, to apologize to the angels from my treachery. He had been unfaithful to them, had renounced them in public, and had continued to do so for many years. The residue was a melancholia, tied to the boy's awareness that,

> What he is really doing in that fateful turning outward is simultaneously preserving and betraying his original love of angels, affirming and denying his new love of boys; after all, now he and the boys are joined together in looking elsewhere for the angels they might have all once had.

Yet in spite of his treachery, the angels are still there.

Patriarchy remains so psychologically powerful for men in particular because their initiation into patriarchy comes so early in their boyhood, as Chu's work makes clear, that they lack the developmental capacities to see, let alone resist it. Carol Gilligan argues that the initiation into patriarchy, involving traumatic breaks in relationship of boys to girls and parts of themselves regarded as "girly," morally injures them in Shays's sense—the stress and trauma of initiation leading to the betrayal of what's right, in a high-stakes situation, where it was sanctioned by someone in a position of legitimate authority. Moss, as a boy, quite clearly knows betraying his "angels" is not right, but he does so because he takes patriarchal authority to require it. Yet, men, like Moss and our students, can not only come to remember such initiations but to question and even resist the impact they had on their lives. The papers of our students showed this. Moral injury is reparable.

The experience of our students, as the young men shared their experiences of trauma arising from their initiations in their conversations and papers, was a form of what Jonathan Shay called new models of healing, which emphasize the communalization of the trauma.[214] In interrogating the trauma of manhood in the wake of Trump's election here, I draw inspiration from the candor of these men who in the fall of 2016, in their final papers for the Resisting Injustice seminar that Carol Gilligan and I coteach, wrote stunningly confessional papers, revealing their complicity in the persistence of patriarchy and, by implication, in the election of a man whom they themselves had not voted for. The papers were revelatory confessions of the patriarchal pressures of initiation they had, as men, experienced and how, writ large, they explain not only Trump's appeal but the lack of effective resistance. For the men, the pressures, including early bullying and later sometimes brutal fraternity initiations, led, as they put it, to infidelity to their real convictions and passions (their love), something they had learned early whenever their interests appeared or were coded as feminine. Unwittingly, or as one put it, "without a conscious thought," they had fallen into a pattern that dates back to Abraham's willingness to sacrifice his son, Isaac, to prove his devotion to God.[215] The marks of trauma are loss of voice and memory, and Jonathan Shay found that healing was possible when trauma victims recovered their voices and memories through sharing with one another experiences they discover were not unique and isolating but that others had had as well. This was the experience of our students as they shared with one another their experiences of their traumatic initiations into patriarchy. Strikingly, Shay links such communalization to the powers of art:

> Combat veterans and American citizenry should meet together face-to-face in daylight, and listen and watch and weep, just as citizen-soldiers of ancient Athens did in the theater at the foot of the Acropolis. We need a modern equivalent of Athenian tragedy. Tragedy brings us to cherish our mortality, to savor and embrace it. Tragedy inclines us to prefer attachment to fragile mortals whom we love, like Odysseus returning from war to his aged wife, Penelope, and to refuse promised immortality.[216]

---

[214] Jonathan Shay, id., p. 194.

[215] For discussion of and excerpts from these student papers, see Carol Gilligan and David A. J. Richards, *Darkness Now Visible*, pp. 19–27.

[216] Id.

We have already seen how artists like Hawthorne and Melville, as well as Shakespeare, offer such modern equivalents, exposing the moral injuries patriarchy inflicts on men. Shakespeare, for example, is, as Kott points out, very much our contemporary because patriarchy remains, as recent political events at home and abroad show, so powerful even in ostensibly democratic cultures, like the United States, Britain, and the nations of the now-embattled European Union. Great artists—Hawthorne, Melville, and Shakespeare among them—communalize the traumas that continue to afflict all of us under patriarchy. It is for this reason that the works of other artists have enabled me among others to communalize the traumas of my own initiation into patriarchy and to find a path to resistance. I begin with how my own story of resistance was illuminated, when I was yet a young closeted gay man, by close reading of the works of such artists, including several gay men, with whom I felt deeply in relationship. Resistance is always, in my experience, collaborative and relational, even when it may not appear to be so.

CHAPTER 3

Charles Dickens on the
Abuse of Children as the Key
to Resisting Injustice

A Young Man Reading Dickens and Late James

I began reading the novels of Charles Dickens and Henry James when I was a young man, sixteen to eighteen years of age, still in high school during the years 1960 to 1962. My sister, with whom I was quite close, had left for Vassar College. I was quite lonely, as alone as I have ever been in that two-year period (I would enter Harvard College in 1962), and my father, responding to my sense of loss, made a point of taking me to Orange Public Library every Saturday to take out books, which I would devour during the week, and return for more the next week. These books filled my imagination, and I discovered I was not as alone as I thought I was.

To give some background, my father was a remarkable man for that historical period both because his marriage to a highly intelligent and spirited and working woman was egalitarian with full voice on both sides and because of his tenderness and playful humor as a father. My mother was intensely serious, loving, and demanding. On Father's Day, as the priest would celebrate an idealized patriarchal fatherhood, my sister and I would burst into gales of laughter; it was so not our world that it was a joke, an Italian American *commedia del'arte* remote from our experience. My father never better expressed his concern and love for me than during this period of my loneliness when we both went to the library each Saturday as father and son. I'm sure he would have preferred that I took more of an interest in athletics (he had been a good athlete before he came down before I was born with kidney stones), but he accepted my interests as my own. ("Children," he said, "must be nurtured to exfoliate"—my word, not his, but the concept is his.) He himself shared my interests, including my interest in the great foreign art movie directors of the period (e.g., Bergman, Fellini, De Sica, Satyajit Ray, Kurosawa, Ozu, Antonioni, Rossellini, Truffaut, Godard, and Bunuel) as well as Hollywood directors like John Ford and, in particular, Alfred Hitchcock, whom he adored. When our Roman Catholic priest asked the congregation to take the vow of the Legion of Decency not to watch some such movies, my parents refused to rise to take the pledge. I learned liberalism from them (neither of them agreed with the church's teaching on contraception and abortion). They were both sympathetic to the civil rights movement, and when my father's brother-in-law indulged anti-Semitic stereotypes, my father insisted to me they were false to his experience of real people who were Jews. We always went to movies as a family every week, and my sister and I continue to go to the movies almost every Sunday with my life partner, Donald Levy. Unlike my mother, my father read novels, though he was probably taken aback by my passion for novel reading of long and complex novels, which included most of the novels of Charles Dickens and many by Henry James. He preferred, as I recall, the historical novels of Gore Vidal.

We were a very close Italian American family, and I loved both my parents and sister, all of whom loved and supported me in my growing intellectual and artistic interests, including a passion for reading and for opera, quite unusual for a boy at that time and already marking me off from other boys as not really one of them. Even Italian American boys of the period had no real interest in opera; the Beatles and others were more alive to them, but certainly not to me. I was captivated by recordings of two operas that I listened to with scores again and again, Mozart's *Marriage of Figaro* and Verdi's *La Traviata*. There was some bullying by other boys, though I have trouble remembering it, which suggests to me trauma (the marks of trauma being loss of memory and voice).

But there was in my experience as a boy nothing like what the psychoanalyst Donald Moss recorded in the previous chapter as the silencing of his love for a certain piece of operatic music because other boys would disapprove. What was the difference? My father was the key;

his example showed me the way to emotional authenticity in such matters. My father, Armand Joseph Richards, had a remarkable operatic voice that his voice teacher thought could lead to a distinguished career in opera. It was a wonderful voice, close to what I had heard in the recordings of Caruso and later heard in the live performances I religiously attended at the Metropolitan Opera in New York, the performance in Italian operas, especially Verdi, sung by Luciano Pavarotti. I loved Verdi and wrote two books trying to explain what moved me in Italian culture, one on resisting racialization[217] and another on Verdi's music and what it showed me about a men and women resisting patriarchy.[218] My father and mother, always experienced by me as passionately and sexually in love as equals, inspired both books. My mother, whose first name was Josephine, always took pride in a first name like that of Verdi's mistress and later wife, Giuseppina.

I should explain that our original name was Ricciardelli, changed to Richards by my grandfather (successful in running a road-building business in Yonkers) as my father explained to me, to deal with what he called the terrible prejudice against Italians in business when we came here at the turn of the twentieth century from Southern Italy. After my partner and I had just visited the hill towns in Southern Italy (outside Naples), where my family came from and where I encountered Ricciardelli relatives, I had asked my father why we left such a beautiful place. He was incredulous—had I no idea of the poverty and lack of opportunity and prejudice against people of the South even in Italy? I suppose I first encountered the prejudice my father mentioned at college; there were no Italian Americans among my roommates or in my classes (there had, in contrast, been many in my high school, though I was, as earlier remarked, an outsider even then—an outsider among outsiders), and even my quite genial college roommates, when I made my background quite clear, engaged in the equivalent of what in Britain was once the genteel anti-Semitism of the British upper classes,[219] only here, genteel racialized prejudice against Italians—including joking insults that would have been unthinkable then

---

[217] David A. J. Richards, *Italian American: The Racializing of an Ethnic Identity* (New York: New York University Press, 1999).

[218] David A. J. Richards, *Tragic Manhood and Democracy: Verdi's Voice and the Powers of Musical Art* (Brighton: Sussex Academic Press, 2004).

[219] See, on this point, Anthony Julius, *Trials of the Diaspora: A History of Anti-Semitism in England* (Oxford: Oxford University Press, 2010).

against other ethnicities and religions. I was shocked and still am that such racialized stereotypes could so falsify the complex Italian American culture and people I knew and loved. Back then, I was silent, as I was about my sexuality.

My father lacked the ambition to pursue an operatic career. (My mother, in view of his remarkable voice, had urged him to pursue one.) He had a distinguished career as a civil engineer with the Army Corps of Engineer, where he achieved the highest civilian rank. When as a young law student, I commuted with my father (whose office was in lower Manhattan) to my summer law office there. I was shocked by the relentless commute he had endured without complaint for so long. And my mother was a pharmacist. In my mother's case, it was very much a choice, and she was good at it (running a hospital pharmacy) as she was at much else (cooking and interior decorating), including investing in the stock market, where she made a fair amount of money for the family. My father, however, continued to sing at home and sometimes in public (at one wedding I recall, stunning the audience), moving both my sister and me to tears with the emotional subtlety and expressiveness of his voice's range—lyric, tender, passionate, always emotionally present, as he was in fact always in my life, including when he learned I was gay and embraced my partner, Donald Levy, among the most moving experiences in my life.

I understood then how much he loved me as the person I was. It was probably very important to a man as relational as my father that when he learned of my sexual orientation, he met and appreciated the person I loved. It was not, for him, an abstract moral question. It was more difficult for my mother, embedded in the patriarchal world of her beloved sisters, always competitive about their children, and I was, at least so it appeared, the only gay son—a failure for which no other achievement could compensate. Or so they thought, and my mother grieved. For a loving Italian American woman so prone to guilt, she must be at fault, and nothing I said could console her. Today, young gay couples have or adopt children, and having children would have made the situation easier for my mother; not having grandchildren was a big part of her grief, as one of my aunts acidly pointed out to me. But that was not a live option for us as a couple, though we knew lesbian couples, even back then, who had children. It was challenging enough for us to sustain and flourish in a relationship neither of us had known before against the lack of support (to say the least) we found around us; and we were both academics, absorbed in our teaching and scholarship (me in law at NYU Law, my partner in philosophy at Brooklyn College). Our love, arising against a world largely hostile to our love, has for this reason always been and still remains romantic.

My closeness to my father and mother and my sister was quite unusual, as I have now come to see. I had no real friendships with other boys, and I am quite sure because it was very early when I recognized both my gay desires and my fear of them, thus my fear of boys whom I desired sexually and my recognition of the American homophobia that my family and my church (Roman Catholicism) and everyone apparently shared. The question of homosexuality came up only twice during my boyhood. First, there was the Kinsey Report on homosexuality among men, which was discussed among members of my extended family, and I registered both their denial and panic. I also recall thinking that *that* was what I was (it had a name) and that my family simply could not deal with it. The feelings must, I thought, go underground. Second, one of my aunts brought the question of my possible homosexuality up with my mother (my interests were not those of other American boys), who raised it with my father, who dismissed the idea. My mother made a point of letting me know about all this; she was always wonderfully honest, sometimes painfully, with me. Nothing thankfully came of it, except confirming to me that my sexual feelings could not, at this point, be acknowledged with the only people I really trusted and loved—my parents and my sister. I think now that my mother's conversation with me was my parents' way of telling me that they and others thought I might be gay. In such a homophobic period, it was their way of saying and denying, a communication to a son they loved about the unspeakable. And denial in that period was as common as the hegemonic homophobia. When I asked my sister, with whom I am close, much later if she had any idea I was gay, she said it never occurred to her, yet it was she who brought to my attention the novels and essays of James Baldwin she had read at Vassar (see chapter 6), works she loved. Denial back then was profound. If my parents were inviting me to speak, I did not. It was, I thought, no one's business but my own. I could not share my feelings with them. Certainly, I could not share it with any friends. I had none. I was alone and afraid.

My mother often observed to me that, in her experience of me growing up, there was a striking shift in my early boyhood. We were always close (her expressive face is always imaginatively with me), and I was often shocked by how well she could read my moods like no one else until I met my life partner much later. But there was a shift in our closeness from transparency to closeness but more veiled and circumspect. The first stage was one of radiant happiness and emotional transparency, both of which she had loved. The second stage was she said a seriousness that puzzled her, and much less transparency. I know exactly what marks the shift for me: the realization of my gay sexual desires, and that my parents could not handle them or help me with them. I believe I must have been seven to eight years old at the time, but this is, of course, a guess. It is the age that makes the best sense of what my mother told me and the shift in my sense of myself and my relationship to my family. My sister has always described our childhood with our parents as her time of greatest happiness, and I never could agree with her because, from my perspective, the experience was full of wonderful things, but there was an ambivalence, indeed a sadness, I always carried with me. Verdi's music dramas, so expressive of the tragedy of patriarchal manhood and womanhood, spoke to me so directly for this reason. It brings me to tears now when I think of it.

Why Dickens?

It is reasonably clear, as I show in the next chapter, why the novels of Henry James, a closeted gay man, spoke to me during this lonely period of my life. But why Charles Dickens? The novels of Dickens, usually immensely long, became an absorbing world for me because Dickens wrote almost always from some child's point of view. George Orwell powerfully made this point:

> No one, at any rate no English writer, has written better about childhood than Dickens. In spite of all the knowledge that has accumulated since, in spite of the fact that children are now comparatively sanely treated, no novelist has shown the same power of entering into the child's point of view. I must have been about nine years old when I first read *David Copperfield*. The mental atmosphere of the opening chapters was so immediately intelligible to me that I vaguely imagined they have been written by a *child*. [In *Great Expectations*] All the isolation of childhood is there. And how accurately he

has recorded the mechanisms of the child's mind, its visualizing tendency, its sensitiveness to certain kinds of impression.[220]

But the children in Dickens, usually young boys but sometimes girls, are often embedded in abusive situations, and Dickens closely centers our attention on the injustice of such abuse and neglect and its connections to larger forms of economic and social injustice in Britain under the impact of the ruthlessly capitalist Industrial Revolution in the early Victorian period. (Dickens died in 1870.) Dickens's artistic voice arose from his own sense of giving voice to the trauma when, as a young man, he was apprenticed by his parents (his mother more insistently than his father) in a job the young boy detested as a humiliation of his gifts—a narrative brilliantly drawn upon in his most autobiographical novel, *David Copperfield*[221] (one of Freud's favorite books[222]). His parents, at that time, were in debtor's prison. Abused, neglected, and orphaned boys and young men are frequent characters in Dickens's creative work,[223] as they are in several of the short stories and novels of Henry James (as we shall see). And there is also his family's imprisonment for debt (his father was financially improvident), which is touched on even in his first comic novel, *Pickwick Papers* (Pickwick, refusing to accept an unjust verdict of guilt for an alleged promise to marry, goes to debtor's prison) as well as in *David Copperfield* (the Micawber family goes to debtor's prison), and then in his late tragic novel, *Little Dorrit,* which centers on a family's experience of imprisonment for debt, a traumatic experience that leads to the moral injury of several of them (their characters are damaged), shown conspicuously when they are released, with the notable exception of Little Dorrit. While my own

---

[220] George Orwell, *A Collection of Essays* (New York: Harvest, 1981; originally published, 1946), p. 60.

[221] See, for fuller discussion, Edgar Johnson, *Charles Dickens: His Tragedy and Triumph Volume 2* (New York: Simon and Schuster, 1952), pp. 677–700; Peter Ackroyd, *Dickens* (New York: HarperCollins, 1990), pp. 566–613.

[222] Jenny Hartley, *Charles Dickens: An Introduction* (Oxford: Oxford University Press, 2016), p. 22.

[223] See, for further discussion, Edgar Johnson, *Charles Dickens: His Tragedy and Triumph_Volumes 1 and 2* (New York: Simon and Schuster, 1952); Peter Ackroyd, *Dickens.* See also Steven Marcus, *Dickens: From Pickwick to Dombey* (New York: W. W. Norton, 1986).

father was certainly not improvident (he was one of the most responsible men of his generation that I met), there was a Pickwickian side to him—theatrically mimicking the pompous and pretentious in Dickensian ways. This was a world quite familiar to me, and yet it had as well its dark side, at least for me, again very Dickensian. He was a father I loved but from whom I hid myself.

The novels of Dickens spoke to my loneliness and even a yet nascent sense of indignation that I had to remain silent, even secretive, about something so deep as my sexuality. For me, this was a breaking of relationship with those I loved and who loved me; and it was, I now believe, personally traumatic. The novels of Dickens, which I devoured, communalized the trauma that I could see were shared with many other children—in particular, boys. It filled the gap in my friendships with actual boys that I earlier mentioned (friendship and love would come much later). No one has better described than Dickens the kind of desolating loneliness I experienced during this period, given expression in David Copperfield's secret agony[224] and the shame I felt in my position[225]—a position in a boot blacking factory (Dickens's own experience, as earlier mentioned). The novel, unusually for Dickens, is written in the personal voice of David (which is Dickens's autobiographical voice): "I had no advice, no counsel, no encouragement, no consolation, no assistance, no support of any kind, from any one, that I can call to mind, as I hope to go to heaven!."[226] Moreover, it was a secret humiliation, of which David could not and would not speak: "That I suffered in secret and that I suffered exquisitely, no one ever knew but I. How much I suffered, it is, as I have said already, utterly beyond my power to tell."[227] Only as an artist of fiction does Dickens find the voice to tell this story, showing his own road to resistance.

The sense of a secret or private self may be common in the experience of men compelled under patriarchy to conceal the parts of themselves that patriarchy condemns not only, as in my case, gay men but men generally who have, like Donald Moss, been bullied not to pursue what they love. And there are many straight and gay. In his important

---

[224] See Charles Dickens, *David Copperfield* rev. ed., ed. Jeremy Tambling (London: Penguin, 2004; first published, 1850), p. 166.

[225] Id.

[226] Id., p. 170.

[227] Id., p. 172.

book, *The Private Self,* the psychiatrist Arnold Modell has explored how common this experience is and how, in psychoanalysis, the nonintrusive analyst may function as a muse-like presence, supporting the analysand in companionable solitude[228]—a presence that enables him or her to see that their supposed "state of self-sufficiency can evolve into a state of companionable solitude"[229] where they give voice to their secret selves. Dickens never publicly spoke or wrote of his humiliation while he lived[230] but, as artists sometime do, found a voice to write fictionally about it and the resonance of his art, for me and so many others, shows how such art may so touch our private selves that we see ourselves in "companionable solitude" with Dickens and others.

Dickens, as a writer, is, of course, also wonderfully entertaining, even hilarious, often in dealing with tragic subject—a mask of humor characteristic of his tragic art. Dickens thus draws upon his ambivalent love for his improvident father in creating, hilariously, Mr. Micawber in *David Copperfield* (whom David meets at the time of his humiliating occupation, to whom "[i]n my forlorn state I became quite attached;"[231] the Micawber family would shortly go to debtor's prison, like Dickens's own family). And even in one of his darkest novels, *Bleak House,* Dickens creates the unforgettable Mrs. Jellyby, who ignores her many unruly children because of her obsession with helping an African country, "the Settlement of Borrioboola Gha."[232] The novels struck me as theatrically operatic (I loved opera), connected, as I experienced them, to the cinematic quality in the plotting of the novels (*Oliver Twist* and *A Christmas Carol,* for example), which has made many of them the subject of sometimes brilliant movies (by directors like David Lean—*Oliver Twist* (1948) and *Great Expectations* (1947)—or the 1951 movie version of *The Christmas Carol,* starring Alastair Sim, whose script closely follows the novel, which reads as a kind of proto-movie script). Perhaps, no great novelist uses cinematic plotting and theatricality and humor in the way Dickens does, which is no

---

228 Arnold H. Modell, *The Private Self* (Cambridge, Mass.: Harvard University Press, 1993), p. 138.
229 Id., p. 138.
230 See Peter Ackroyd, *Dickens,* pp. 96–98.
231 Charles Dickens, *David Copperfield,* p. 173.
232 Charles Dicken, *Bleak House,* ed. Nicola Bradbury (London: Penguin, 1996), p. 216.

doubt part of his enormous popularity and appeal, which masks for many his extraordinary psychological depth (as if only a gloomy seriousness, like that of Dostoevsky, could be psychologically profound, as Dostoevsky's novels certainly are). But there is in Dickens also remarkable psychological observation of the traumas of boys and girls initiated into patriarchy, and the novels over time becomes increasingly, even relentlessly tragic in both subject matter and treatment (culminating in *Dombey and Son, Bleak House, Little Dorrit, Hard Times,* and the heartrending *Great Expectations*). It is his penetrating investigations of the psychology of men and women under Victorian patriarchy that riveted me, including his exposure of the injustices that it legitimated, a resisting voice that spoke to me even then. I discuss the novels from this perspective, dealing with his insights into the psychology of boys and girls under patriarchy, the moral injuries both suffer through violence and coming to resistance through love.

Dickens on the Psychology of Boys and Girls under Patriarchy

I earlier discussed (chapter 2) the developmental views of Carol Gilligan and Naomi Snider. Connecting the developmental studies of Gilligan and her colleagues with John Bowlby's studies of attachment and loss, Carol and Naomi came to a startling discovery: the gender ideals of patriarchal manhood and womanhood correspond to what Bowlby identifies as pathological responses to loss. Pathological in that they compound loss by standing in the way of relationships.[233] Gilligan and Snider conclude that patriarchy persists because it inflicts a loss of relationship and then renders that loss irreparable. Detachment or seeming independence on the part of men and what Bowlby terms *compulsive caregiving* in women, the selfless caregiving that has been held up as the epitome of feminine goodness, render relationships either seemingly unnecessary for men or as requiring a woman, paradoxically, to give up her desire to be in relationship for the sake of having "relationships." For a woman then it becomes necessary for her not to be herself in order to be someone others want to be with. The

---

[233] See Carol Gilligan and Naomi Snider, *Why Does Patriarchy Persist?* (Cambridge, UK: Polity, 2018). See also Carol Gilligan and Naomi Snider, "The Loss of Pleasure, or Why We Are Still Talking about Oedipus," *Contemporary Psychoanalysis,* 2017. Vol. 53, No. 2: 173–195.

consequence in men is that the shaming of manhood becomes incendiary and can justify violence against those who are perceived as the source of dishonor. In women, shaming leads to the silencing of voice, the very voices that might reasonably challenge the injustice of patriarchal demands. The consequence for both men and women—psychologically locked into patriarchal demands set by the terms of the gender binary and hierarchy— is impairment of their capacity to see, let alone repair the relationships that patriarchy breaks. In effect, our capacity to love and feel empathy across the barriers imposed by the various iterations of the gender binary and hierarchy (the racism, sexism, homophobia, xenophobia, class stratification and anti-Semitism, and so on) is impaired or shattered.

Dickens, writing in the early Victorian period, is a remarkably perceptive observer of the gendered psychology of patriarchy Carol and Snider explore, in particular, the psychology of "good" women as caretaking doormats. Dickens shows us two related aspects of these women: their extraordinary capacity for the sacrifice of self in the service of men and their essentialized goodness. What makes the depiction of self-sacrifice so extraordinary is that these young women continue their care of men when the men treat them so abusively: Little Nell endures until her death her grandfather's callous self-absorption in reckless gambling that wrecks such havoc on his granddaughter's pitiable life (*The Old Curiosity Shop*, 1841); Florence Dombey endures her father's patriarchal cruelties to her (including physically assaulting her), and she inexplicably forgives him in a way his estranged wife, Edith, never does (*Dombey and Son*, 1848); and Little Dorrit always tenderly cares for her father and siblings even, after the family's release from debtor's prison into wealth and status, they arrogantly assert their newly found sense of class privilege and condemn and abuse Dorrit for her continuing humane feelings and way of life (*Little Dorrit*, 1865–67). Even when unconventional women extend good care to others, they do so self-sacrifically. For example, the prostitute, Nancy, in *Oliver Twist* (1837–38), alone among her crowd of thieves, shows care for the abused Oliver Twist, raging at and resisting his abuse by Fagin and others at the cost, eventually, of her life).[234] And Edith Dombey in *Dombey and Sons* finally explodes in rage at her coldly abusive husband not because of his coldness to her but because of his abusive treatment of his daughter,

---

[234] See Charles Dickens, *Oliver Twist*, ed. Philip Horne (London: Penguin, 2002, pp. 131–33, 161, 165–70, 332–38.

Florence, herself a doormat who endures without complaint his irrational rage, including physical assault.

Dickens, always the astute observer, shows in Mrs. Jellyby in *Bleak House* (1853) that such feminine caretaking can be excessive, as Mrs. Jellyby disastrously ignores her children for her obsessional interest in an African people. But his satirical eye for such excess works within the framework of the highly gendered psychology of goodness he observed in early Victorian women, and his satirical eye extends as well to the emergence of advocacy of women's rights and men's wrongs as yet another form of abuse of women's properly caretaking roles.[235] Women, within the terms of this gendered psychology, are to be silent about the wrongs done them.

The obverse side of this gendered psychology is that when a woman, like Sally Brass, in *The Old Curiosity Shop* (1841) is more selfishly harmful as a lawyer to others than her brother—the brother seemed to have changed sexes with his sister and to have made over to her any spark of manliness he may have had.[236] Another such woman in Dickens is the domineering Mrs. Bumble in *Oliver Twist*, and Mr. Bumble not unreasonably questions a law that supposes his wife acts under his direction:

> "If the law supposes that," said Mr. Bumble, squeezing his hat emphatically in both hands, "the law is an ass—a idiot. If that is the eye of the law, the law's a bachelor, and the worst I wish the law is, that his eye may be opened by experience—by experience."[237]

And correspondingly, Dickens depicts men in this period as pseudo-independent and careless of and inflicting harm on the interests of others, in the way Gilligan and Snider describe. Such a gendered male psychology shows itself in the breaking of relationships to sisters (Monks in *Oliver Twist*), to wives (Quilp in *The Old Curiosity Shop*), to sons (the

---

[235] See, on this point, Charles Dickens, *Bleak House*, ed. Nicola Bradbury (London: Penguin, 1996), pp. 482–3, 987.

[236] Charles Dickens, *The Old Curiosity Shop*, ed. Norman Page (London: Penguin, 2000), p. 501.

[237] Charles Dickens, *Oliver Twist*, ed. Philip Horne (London: Penguin, 2003), p. 436.

---

fathers Barnaby Rudge and John Chester in *Barnaby Rudge* (1841), and to fathers in *Nicholas Nickleby* and *Our Mutual Friend* (1864–65), as well as grandfathers to grandsons in *Martin Chuzzlewit* (1844), uncles to nephews (*Nicholas Nickleby*, 1839), and fathers to daughters (*Dombey and Son, Little Dorrit*, and *Hard Times*). In these novels, men's capacity for evil is closely connected to a pseudo-independence based on breaking relationships.

Dickens on Moral Injury: Soul Murder

We earlier saw (chapter 2) that Carol Gilligan has argued[238] that the initiation of men and women into patriarchy moral injuries them, namely, the stress and trauma of initiation led to the betrayal of what's right in a high-stakes situation, where the betrayal was sanctioned by someone in a position of legitimate authority (p. 91, Gilligan). As earlier observed, I experienced my own silence about my sexuality as a young man as traumatic, and it took the form of my internalization of the homophobia around me that I only resisted much later (more on this later). Dickens's novels, in the midst of this traumatic period of my life, communalized my experience, as the novels center, quite remarkably, on the experience of boys of abuse and neglect and its consequences.

We are shown such abuse quite starkly in the orphan Oliver Twist's abusive treatment by the beadle Mr. Bumble and others in the orphanage and workhouse, in Smike's sadistic abuse by Wackford Squeers at his school for boys in *Nicholas Nickleby*, and David Coppperfield's abusive treatment by his stepfather, Murdstone, and his sister. But in the later novels, Dickens investigates such abuse as rooted in larger institutions like Dombey's obsession with money-making in *Dombey and Son* or the uncaring and callously inhuman legal system in *Bleak House* or the debtor's prison and ruthless banking system of Mr. Merdle, the master spirit of the age[239] (who commits suicide when his frauds are disclosed) in *Little Dorrit* or the factory system of *Hard Times* (1854) or the prisons (the hulks) and death penalty of the retributive legal system in *Great Expectations* (1861).

---

[238] Carol Gilligan, "Moral Injury and the Ethic of Care: Reframing the Conversation about Differences," *Journal of Social Philosophy Volume 45*, No.1, Spring 2014, pp. 89–106.

[239] Charles Dickens, *Little Dorrit*, eds. Stephen Wall and Ellen Small (Penguin: London, 2003), p. 624.

The moral injury patriarchy inflicts on men is beautifully exemplified in Arthur Clennan in *Little Dorrit*, whom Little Dorrit comes to love and, eventually, marry. In his important book *Soul Murder: The Effects of Childhood Abuse and Deprivation*, the psychiatrist Leonard Shengold discusses Dickens's remarkable insight into the moral injury to abused children in the effects on Arthur Clennan of a cold and demanding father and a fanatically religious and withholding mother enforcing view of a wrathful and retributive God, a woman who in fact is not his natural mother but has concealed this from Arthur.[240] Shengold writes the following:

> In *Little Dorrit*, Dickens examines several instances of emotional deprivations and demonstrates how the "undeveloped heart" can warp the character and inhibit love. It is a novel of terrible accusation—of parents, and of society, and of the capitalist system in mid-nineteenth-century England. According to George Bernard Shaw, *"Little Dorrit* is a more seditious book than *Das Kapital*. *Little Dorrit* contains the great metaphor of the English governmental bureaucracy as the Circumlocution Office, the motto of which is "How Not to Do It." In a masterful sublimation to effective social criticism, Dickens generalizes his parents' "undeveloped heart" and ineffectuality and transfer those qualities on to those who rule England.[241]

Shengold argues that in the novel, Dickens has split himself into a male alter ego and a female one: Arthur Clennan and Little Dorrit, the two main sufferers from lack of love and empathy as children."[242] Reflecting the psychology observed by Gilligan and Snider, the male is pseudo-independent broken and incapable of real connection and the female is compulsively self-sacrificing and caring. The central image throughout the novel is prison (Dickens visited prisons throughout his life) not only the debtor's prison where Little Dorrit's family had been confined

---

[240] See Leonard Shengold, *Soul Murder: The Effects of Child Abuse and Deprivations* (New Yorka; Fawcett Columbine, 1989), pp. 181–208.

[241] Id., p. 194.

[242] Id.

but the psychological and ethical prison in which men and women under patriarchy live. Little Dorrit, who learns the truth of Arthur's background, never tells him, as she regards him as too fragile to bear the truth. The legacy of soul murder thus lives on in the silencing of voice and lack of real relationship covered over by an implausible sentimentality. (Shengold comments the "use of sentimentality to further denial is not uncommon in soul murder victims"[243] like Dickens himself.)

The moral injury this system inflicts on boys and men expresses itself in the killing of moral empathy, shown in the breaking of personal relationships, earlier described. Several of the novels show the role that the love laws play in sustaining this process. It is because Oliver Twist's father is forced to marry a woman he does not love that his sexual relationship to the woman he does love and her resulting child (Oliver) is so condemned, leaving the boy as abused and neglected orphan. And it is the patriarchal refusal of the two fathers in *Barnaby Rudge,* because of religious differences, to allow their children, who are in love, to marry that sets the stage for the novel's violent mayhem (more on this later). And the same patriarchal control of love psychologically motors in *Bleak House* the tragedy of Lady Dedlock, who was forced to abandon the man she loved and their daughter, as it does the separation of the father of Arthur Clennan from the woman he loved and their child and loveless marriage to another in *Little Dorrit.* Same goes with Gradgrind's demand that his daughter marry a man she does not love in *Hard Times* and the attempted control of the patriarchal father over his son (demanding he marry a girl the father capriciously selected) in *Our Mutual Friend* (1865).

With the exception of *Barnaby Rudge,* in which religion is the basis for the strictures of the love laws, what controls the love laws in Dickens is class; and in treating how class privilege dehumanizes other classes, he offers a model for understanding the basis of irrational prejudices generally (including racism, religious intolerance, sexism, and homophobia). In *David Copperfield,* Dickens both shows how these prejudices are passed on from parent to child and their appalling rationalizations. In the novel, Dickens closely examines and compares the different backgrounds of three friends and erstwhile schoolmates—David himself, James Steerworth, and Traddles. Steerworth is older than David and wealthier, handsome and attractive to both men and women, including David; the relationship

---

[243] Id., p. 194.

appears as homoerotic as any such relationship between men in Dickens. Steerworth is, however, rather a bully, insulting Traddles by feminizing him[244] (he later feminizes David himself, "a very Daisy,"[245] but affectionately and homoerotically). When David later is introduced to Steerworth's redoubtable mother and her companion, Rosa Dartle, he learns that, in one of Steerworth's rages as a child, he injured Rosa by throwing a hammer at her, and she still bears a scar. Steerworth and Rosa also discuss the basis of Steerworth's snobbery about lower classes, which he bases on alleged facts: "They are not to be expected to be as sensitive as we are."[246] The same view is expressed by Steerworth's mother when she is confronted by Mr. Peggoty, who, appealing to his love for the innocent, Em'ly, who had been seduced and abandoned by Steerworth, asks that Steerworth marry her. Rejecting the suggestion, Mrs.Steerworth responds, "What is your love to mine? What is your separation to ours?"[247] Indeed, she turns in rage on Peggoty, as if there were no harms to other persons but only in her narcissistic moral solipsism, harm to herself: "My son, who has been the object of my life, to whom its every thought has been devoted, whom I have gratified from a child in every wish, from whom I have had no separate existence since his birth, to take up in a moment with a miserable girl and avoid me? Is this no injury?"[248] David, who knew Steerworth well, observed, "All that I had ever seen in him of an unyielding, willful spirit, I saw in her."[249] Dickens thus shows us how a brutal patriarchal solipsism is imparted intergenerationally from mother to son.

What is the source of this rage, this anger at the goodness of Mr. Peggoty? It is Mrs. Steerworth's patriarchally rooted rage at any criticism, however just of her unjust privilege, the scapegoating so characteristic of irrational prejudice. Dickens thus observes and exposes the psychology of patriarchy, here enforced by a patriarchal woman, and illustrates the larger psychology of irrational prejudice. His observation of such irrationalist violence extends as well to the political psychology of violence (as we shortly see).

---

[244] Charles Dickens, *David Copperfield*, p. 112.

[245] Id., p. 297.

[246] Charles Dickens, *David Copperfield*, p. 303.

[247] Id., p. 476.

[248] Id.

[249] Id., p. 477.

For Dickens, there is an inverse relationship between class privilege and ethical thought and feeling. Little Dorrit's father, a humane man and father when in debtor's prison, becomes, when released and recovering his status and wealth, an ethically shrunk man, who turns on his daughter for her continuing goodness. Perhaps the moving depiction of this inversion is Dickens's late masterpiece, *Great Expectations*. As Pip rises from his background to being a gentleman, he becomes ashamed of the simple goodness of his now-dead sister's husband, Joe Gargery. And yet when Pip is broken and despair, Joe Gargery returns to care for him.

Perhaps the most remarkable personal expression in Dickens of his moral indignation at these dehumanizing class attitudes toward the poor comes in *Bleak House* after the death of the orphan Joe, who was abandoned by all:

> Dead, Your Majesty. Dead, my lords and gentlemen.
> Dead, right reverends and wrong reverends of every order.
> Dead, men and women, born with heavenly compassion
> in your hearts. And dying thus around us, every day.[250]

There is an astute psychological insight here if indeed we, men and women, are born with heavenly compassion in our hearts. Dickens raises the question in a way few artists do, What is it in our patriarchal cultures that divides us in our psychological and ethical prisons and kills empathy?

In *Hard Times*, Dickens came as close as he ever did to identifying and criticizing the moral theory (one that the novel identifies with "utilitarian economists") that, in his view, rationalized such a vacuum of humane ethical thought and feeling. The moral theory is embodied in the teaching of Thomas Gradgrind as a school board superintendant, concerned with facts and numbers, excluding the imagination, in a factory town. Gradgrind brings the theory to bear not only on his teaching at school but on the education of his children—in particular, Louisa and Tom. His marriage to a woman without voice is loveless. The consequence is, in Louisa, a lack of independent moral feeling that leads her to agree to her father's suggestion that she should marry Bounderby, a successful businessman who is much older than she and whom she does not love; the consequence in Tom, whom Louisa blindly adores, is moral psychopathy, as he turns to

---

[250] Charles Dickens, *Bleak House*, p. 734.

robbery and gambling. And Gradgrind misreads Bounderby, who turns out to be a liar and fraud, claiming falsely to be an orphan and denying the existence of his own quite devoted mother. The moral center of the novel is Sissy Jupe, daughter of a circus performer who shows the Gradgrinds the importance of play and imagination in learning how to live in real relationship to other persons.

Many of the novels already discussed deal with the moral injury to women, leading to a silencing of voice and a compulsive caretaking of the sort exemplified by Little Nell, Florence Dombey, and Little Dorrit. But the most perceptive in such investigation come, I believe, in *Dombey and Son* and *Great Expectations*.

Mr. Dombey is Dickens's fullest exploration of the pseudo-independence of a patriarchal men, whose first wife (now dead) had complied completely with his pride in his gender superiority and hierarchy over her. His disastrous second marriage was, however, to a beautiful and intelligent woman who rejected such pretensions, in particular, when his irrationalist patriarchal violence was inflicted mindlessly on his innocent daughter, Florence. Dickens describes Dombey as wearing such patriarchal armor, which "bears with him ever another heavy retribution,"[251] namely, his incapacity to be in relationship, never understanding his wife and thus experiencing her rejection of his claims as shameful, leading to anger and even violence. In fact, he came to hate his wife, and she him. But why did she marry him? Here, the novel explores Edith's anger at her mother who, as Edith puts it, never allowed her to be a child: "I was a woman—artful, designing, mercenary, laying snares for men—before I knew myself."[252] She continues, "There is no slave in market. There is no horse in a fair, so shown and offered and examined and paraded, Mother, as I have been for ten shameful years."[253] The point about patriarchy's moral injury to women, as general feature of women's life under patriarchy, is underscored and counterpoint by a similar confrontation between Alice Marwood and her mother: "the daughter born among poverty and neglect, and she became nurse to it. Nobody taught her, nobody stepped forward to help her, and

---

[251] Charles Dickens, *Dombey and Son*, ed. Andrew Sanders (Penguin: London, 2003), p. 609.

[252] Id., p. 431.

[253] Id., p. 432.

nobody cared for her."[254] Mothers under patriarchy thus inflict its moral injury on their daughters, passing from generation to generation, just as fathers do so with their sons.

On this latter point, correlative with its investigation of the moral injuries to girls and women under patriarchy, *Dombey and Sons* includes as well an extraordinary investigation of the moral injury Dombey inflicts on his young son, Paul, not only in taking away from him a loving nurse (after his mother's death) but in exposing him to the destructive education at the Blimbers, all in service of the father's narcissistic image of what his son must be. Paul dies, and Steven Marcus cogently observes, in his illuminating discussion of the British education of middle class boys closely anatomized in *Dombey and Son*, "Paul is dying of a metaphysical and moral disease: middle-class culture."[255]

Ms. Havisham in *Great Expectations* is perhaps Dickens's most penetrating exploration of how a woman herself, traumatized by a patriarchal man who abandoned her at the altar, is herself in complicity with patriarchy as she works her revenge in shaping the education of an orphan, Estella, who will not be vulnerable, as she was, to falling in love. Rather, Ms. Havisham quite self-consciously educates Estella to play the kind of role that the mother of Edith Dombey trained her daughter to play, namely, marrying only for money and status and not vulnerable as love, as Ms. Havisham was. Once again, Dickens shows how the moral injury patriarchy inflicts on women passes from generation to generation. And then there is poor Pip, drawn into this patriarchal web of loss and deceit, himself further damaged by the way his ambition for wealth and status draws him into this web. His advance in status and wealth leads to an appalling decline in his moral thought and feeling. It is Dickens's most tragic depiction of how patriarchy destroys love (I don't take seriously the alternative "happy" ending that Dickens wrote at the insistence of his friend Foster).

---

[254] Id., p. 530.

[255] Steven Marcus, *Dickens from Pickwick to Dombey* (New York: Simon and Schuster, 1968), p. 329. See, for further investigation by Marcus of his culture and its effects on boys and men, id., pp. 317–29, 340–42, 346.

Dickens on Violence, including Revolutionary Violence

Dickens has, as we have seen, a penetrating understanding of how the moral injuries patriarchy inflicts on men and women support and are supported by deep forms of structural injustice. The personal and political are thus for him closely linked. As we earlier saw, James Gilligan, on the basis of his work with violent criminals, has connected male violence, in particular, to the shaming of patriarchal manhood. Dickens's novels, as part of their focus on the moral injuries patriarchal inflicts on men and also women, correlatively zero in on such violence, both personal and political.

The novels show us personal violence, including assault, murder, fraud, and suicide, from *Oliver Twist* to *Our Mutual Friend*. In *Oliver Twist*, not only are boys like Oliver savagely beaten but Nancy, who has helped Oliver, is brutally murdered by her lover, Bill Sykes. In *Nicholas Nickleby*, boys like Smike are savagely beaten, and Nickleby's uncle, confronted with his complicity with the abuse and death of his son (Smike), commits suicide. In *The Old Curiosity Shop*, Quilp falsely charges Kit with theft leading to his sentence of transportation abroad, and when his knavery comes to light, he commits suicide. In *Martin Chuzzlewit*, Jonas, the son of Martin's uncle, murders Tig. In *Dombey and Son*, Mr. Dombey brutally assaults his own quite innocent daughter. In *Bleak House*, Hortense murders the lawyer, Tulkinghorn, and tries to get Lady Dedlock charged with the murder. In *Little Dorrit*, the highly respected and powerful banker, Mr. Merdle, defrauds his customers, and when it is revealed, he commits suicide. In *Our Mutual Friend*, Bradley Headstone, a teacher, is homicidally jealous when rejected by the woman he loves, and brutally assaults and attempts to murder the man she loves, Wrayburn; and the novel centers on the supposed murder of John Harmon when another was, in fact, killed in his place, and unravelling the mystery of the murder that begins the novel. Many of these novels are structured as murder mysteries, with detectives trying to unravel the truth of murders (*Bleak House, Our Mutual Friend*). Indeed Dickens's last, unfinished novel is explicitly a murder mystery, *The Mystery of Edwin Drood* (1870).

Dickens also investigates the political psychology of revolutionary violence in connection with his deep interests in the depicting and resisting the profound injustices patriarchal Britain inflicted on its most vulnerable citizen. How to resist such injustice? Why not revolution? Two novels of Dickens—*Barnaby Rudge* and *A Tale of Two Cities* (1859)—explore this question: first, the revolutionary violence of the Gordon Riots of 1780 and second, the French Revolution. Dickens refuses in both cases to romanticize violence in political revolution. Even when such revolutions are actuated by real injustices, as in the French Revolution, they themselves rationalize excessive violence and may do more harm than good; the French Revolution does not establish republican government in France but ends in Napoleonic despotism and imperialism, which gave a bad name in Europe to republican democracy for many years to come.

Barnaby Rudge offers one of his most penetrating and darkest investigations of how the moral injuries inflicted by patriarchy, quite unjustly, express themselves in irrationalist political violence. It is Dickens's novel closest to Dostoevsky on the roots of human irrationalism and its expression in terrorism. The stage for the novel's tragedy is set by two rigidly patriarchal fathers, Barnaby Rudge Sr., who, after murdering a friend, abandons his wife and son, Barnaby Rudge, and John Chester, who, after an affair with a woman executed for passing fraudulent checks, abandons his son, Hugh. Barnaby Rudge at least has a loving and devoted mother, but perhaps because of the traumatic circumstances of his birth (the novel is not clear on this point), he is mentally damaged—an idiot.[256] His closest attachment, besides his mother, is to a raven, Grip, who speaks to Barnaby mimetically. Hugh, an orphan, is, however, much more damaged and much more alone, and the novel goes to some length in describing what he has been through, as Mr. Willet (owner of an inn, the Maypole, who hired Hugh to manage his horses, as an hostler) tells his friends:

> "What would my boy Joe have been if I hadn't drawed his faculties out of himself?—Do you mind what I'm a saying of, gentlemen?
> Consequently, then . . . that chap, whose mother was hung when he was a little boy, along with six others, for passing bad notes—and it's a blessed thing to think how many people are hung in batches every six weeks for that, and such like offences, as showing how wide awake our government is. That chap that then turned loose, and he to mind cows and frighten birds away and what not for a few pence to live on, and so got on by degrees to mind

---

[256] Id., p. 208.

horses, and to sleep in course of time in lofts and litter, instead of under haystacks and hedges, till at least he come to be hostler at the Maypole for his board and lodging and an annual trifle. That chap that can't read nor write and has never had much to do with anything but animals and has never lived in any way but like the animals he has lived among, *is* an animal. And," said Mr. Willet, arriving at his logical conclusion, "is to be treated accordingly."[257]

The novel later comments, when a woman rejects him, on how thoroughly savage[258] Hugh could be; and Hugh himself says of liquor it was his only solace: "What else has kept away the cold on bitter nights and driven hunger off in starving times? What else has given me the strength and courage of a man when men would have left me to die a puny child? I should never have had a man's heart but for this. I should have died in a ditch. Where's he who when I was a weak and sickly wretch, with trembling legs and fading sight, bade me cheer up, as this did? I never knew him, not I. I drink to the drink, master."[259] And Hugh speaks of the traumatic experience of his mother's death: "I never knew, nor saw, nor thought about a father. And I was a boy of six—that's not very old—when they hung my mother up at Tyburn for a couple of thousand men to stare at. They might have let her live. She was poor enough." The crowd had no compassion—a dog and I alone had any pity." Being a dog and not having a man's sense, he was sorry.[260]

Barnaby Rudge is not, unlike the French Revolution in *A Tale of Two Cities*, about claims of justice. The Gordon Riots were fascist mob violence, incited by an aristocrat, Lord George Gordon, his fanatic followers, and even members of Parliament (including John Chester, Hugh's natural father), to oppose a parliamentary law to remove some of the unjust limits placed on British Catholics. Its politics was based on a nationalism ground in sectarian religion, and the mobs were largely illiterate, indeed requiring

---

257 Charles Dickens, *Barnaby Rudge,* ed. John Bowen (London: Penguin, 2003), p. 100.

258 Id., p. 178.

259 Id., p. 196.

260 Id., p. 200.

that a new member could neither read nor write.[261] Dickens shows us the roots of fascist violence in an ethnic and religious nationalism based on scapegoating innocent people who are claiming their human rights.

Hugh is one of the most courageous, effective, and violent leaders of the Gordon Riots, acting out his anger at his humiliations as the lowest of the low (an animal, as Mr. Willet paradoxically concludes, reflecting Hugh's dehumanization). He has drawn into the riots the innocent Barnaby Rudge, who has become Hugh's friend (they share abandonment by patriarchal fathers); other leaders include Dennis, the hangman, ironically a great believer in the death penalty, which, incredulously, he suffers. All are condemned to death (only Barnaby is pardoned, and Lord Gordon is later acquitted). At the end, before it is known that Barnaby is pardoned, Hugh passionately pleas for Barnaby's life and responds to a clergyman who called for faith that Hugh's faith was that Barnaby should be spared. His own declaration of faith is a nihilistic attack on the patriarchy that dehumanized him:

> "If this was not faith and strong belief," cried Hugh, raising his right arm aloft and looking upward like a savage prophet whom the near approach of death had filled with inspiration, "where are they! What else should teach me— me, born as I was born and reared as I have been—to hope for any mercy in this hardened, cruel, unrelenting place! Upon these human shambles, I, who never raised this hand in prayer till now, call down the wrath of God! On that black tree, of which I am the ripened fruit, I do invoke the curse of all its victims, past, and present, and to come. On the head of that man, who, in his conscience, owns me for his son, I leave the wish that he may never sicken in his bed of down but die a violent death as I do now and have the night-wind for his only mourner. To this I say, amen, amen!"

Dickens had, as we have seen, developed an increasingly profound and penetrating analysis of the structural injustices that the British

---

[261] Charles Dickens, *Barnaby Rudge*, ed. John Bowen (London: Penguin, 2003), p. 317.

economic, legal, and social system inflicted on the most vulnerable people in Britain. But both *A Tale of Two Cities* and *Barnaby Rudge* are deeply skeptical of revolutionary violence as a way of achieving justice. The point is underscored in *Hard Times* in the response of Stephen Blackpool, who works in Bounderby's factory, to the unjust working conditions in the factory. Blackpool both refuses to join a union to protest working conditions and then condemns Bounderby for not taking seriously the inhuman working conditions in his factory. The consequence is that he is shunned by his fellow workers and fired by Bounderby.[262] Blackpool is skeptical that union activism will do much good yet as an individual he confronts Bounderby with the claims of justice the union endorses. Moral individuality must, for Blackpool, always be preserved from coercive group pressure that threaten such individuality.

I earlier cited George Bernard Shaw's comments that *Little Dorrit* was "more seditious than *Das Kapital.*" Shaw is certainly right that Dickens had as profound an understanding of the injustices of the Industrial Revolution as Marx. But he would not have had, had he known Marx's work, any sympathy with Marx's endorsement of revolutionary violence, including terrorism against a democratic republic.[263] Dickens had a well-informed sense of injustice, but he also closely studied the effects of such injustices, rooted in patriarchal assumptions, on the development of boys and girls, inflicting what I have called moral injury. He closely studied men like Hugh as vulnerable to shame and to violence because, in fact, as James Gilligan points out, they have not justly been accorded the education and care that would render them competent. Lacking a secure sense of self-respect and care from others, they are vulnerable to a shaming of their manhood that elicits violence. Violence is their voice. Dickens is a close student of relational psychology, and he had come to regard the injustices afflicted on Hugh as much more common that many supposed or were prepared to acknowledge, and thus make many, similarly morally injured, vulnerable to shame and irrationalist violence, including political fascism, whose political psychology Dickens quite clearly shows in *Barnaby*

---

[262] See Charles Dickens, *Hard Times,* pp. 140–43, 149.

[263] See, for an illuminating recent investigation of Marx's views, Gareth Stedman Jones, *Karl Marx: Greatness and Illusion* (Cambridge, Mass.: The Belknap Press of Harvard University Press, 2016). For his views on revolutionary violence, see Id., pp. 271, 280–81, 285, 294, 298, 300–2, 307, 310, 311.

Rudge. It is not surprising, from this Dickensian perspective, that Marx's revolutionary politics, calling for a dictatorship of the proletariat,[264] should not have led to political, social, or economic democracy (based on equal voice), but as Arendt showed, totalitarianism, which both fascism and Stalinism exemplify.

If not violence to resist injustice, what?

Dickens on Resisting Voice

All of Dickens's novels may, without exception, be regarded as novels of resistance, but what moved me in them as a boy and young man was that the resisting voice arose in a boy's voice observing how patriarchy morally injured boys and girls and how its consequences supported and did not contest injustice. I've already observed how Dickens's great autobiographical novel, *David Copperfield,* written—unlike most of Dickens's novels—in David's personal (which is Dickens's) voice, most brilliantly illustrates an approach that I believe underlies all his works. His observation, for example, of the honest intelligence and voice of quite young boys is remarkable. The six-year-old Paul Dombey (who will die) thus startles with his truthfulness of his caretaker, Mrs. Pipchin, when he contrasts the real goodness of his sister, Florence, with the lack of comparable virtue in Mrs. Pipchin; Mrs. Pipchin, shocked, does not pursue the matter.[265] And *Nicholas Nickleby,* one of Dickens's most popular novels, is the portrait of a heroic young man and resister, saving Smike from the savage beating of Wackford Squeers and saving his sister from sexual exploitation by depraved aristocrats in complicity with Nickleby's corrupt uncle. But the basis of all Dickens's novels, even when there is no young boy seeing the world afresh or no heroic resister, is the voice of the novels themselves, in which I believe Dickens discovered the only resistance to patriarchy in which he had any confidence, namely, a voice that communalized the trauma he and so many others had endured and wanted truthfully to depict what he had come to see. That is what I mean in calling all Dickens's novels novels of resistance.

It is what the philosopher, Richard Rorty, had in mind when he paid tribute to Dickens as a moral critic who put his penetrating criticisms of

---

[264] See, on this point, Id., pp. 149, 153–4.
[265] Charles Dickens, *Dombey and Son,* pp. 157–58.

injustice not in terms of abstractions but rather concrete cases of particular people ignoring the suffering of other particular people.[266] What is amazing is that the criticism did not repel, but found resonance. Rorty cites Orwell on this point:

> In *Oliver Twist, Hard Times, Bleak House,* and *Little Dorrit*, Dickens attacks English institutions with a ferocity that has never been approached. Yet he managed to do it without making himself hated, and more than this, the very people he attacked have swallowed him so completely that he has become a national institution himself.[267]

Dickens found his way to such resonance through finding a voice as an artist that was a resisting voice that his audience recognized in themselves and their concrete experience, bringing to mind and to moral feeling criticisms they recognized as true and calling for democratic resistance.

David Copperfield, the novel closest to Dickens's experience, shows us his own path to resistance. David's father had died when he was six months old, but his loving, rather childish, mother was devoted to him, as was her servant Peggoty; and he lives happily with them for seven years. Throughout the novel, long after his mother died, the face of his loving mother lives on in David's imagination.[268] This happy period ends when his mother marries Edward Murdstone, who is an abusive husband and stepfather. After his mother's death, Murdstone and his sister send David to the blacking factory, which traumatically humiliates him. David runs away in some distress, is robbed, and feels alone and abandoned, and he searches for his relative, Betsey Trotwood, his dead father's aunt. Betsey had been married to an abusive husband and separated from him. David had never met her, but Betsey had visited his mother before David's birth insisting that the baby must be a girl and named Betsey Trotwood. Infuriated when David is born, Betsey abruptly leaves and never returns. Betsey Trotwood is unusual among Dickens's women because, while a good person, she is no one's doormat. Betsey has a voice and is very much her

---

[266] Richard Rorty, *Essays on Heidegger and Others: Philosophical Papers* (New York: Cambridge University Press, 1991), p. 79.

[267] Quoted at Id.

[268] See Charles Dickens, *David Copperfield*, pp. 36, 121, 133, 144, 186, 283.

---

own person, has herself suffered in a patriarchal marriage (her husband beat her), and lives unconventionally caring for the slightly mad Mr. Dick, who is engaged in a fantastic writing project but is himself generous and perceptive. The turning point in the novel comes when David, abandoned, exhausted, and in a state of nervous breakdown verging on madness, arrives at Betsey's cottage and announces:

> I am David Copperfield of Blunderstone in Suffolk, where you came on the night I was born and saw my dear mama. I have been very unhappy since she died. I have been slighted and taught nothing and thrown upon myself and put to work not for me. It made me run away to you. I was robbed at first setting out and have walked all the way and have never slept in a bed since since I began the journey. Here, my self-support gave way all at once, and with a movement of my hands, I intend to show you my ragged state and call it to witness that I suffered something. I broke into a passion of crying, which I suppose had been pent up within me all the week.[269]

Betsey immediately sees that David is in a state of breakdown, hysterical, and near madness, and after consulting with Mr. Dick, she agrees that they must care for David and do so, taking him into their home. Betsey later meets the Murdstones, brother and sister, and excoriates them for their treatment both of David's mother and David himself. They flee, and Betsey and Mr. Dick—this eccentric woman and man and couple, certainly not in a patriarchal relationship—give David the love, care, and support he desperately needs. What enables David to turn his life around, eventually becoming a writer and finding love, is the love of Betsey Trotwood, who, throughout the rest of the novel, is his supportive adviser and intimate, reading and understanding his thoughts and feelings. David's first marriage is unhappy, and his wife dies, but he then marries his long-term close friend, Agnes, when they realize they are both in love. Agnes encourages him to write. He becomes a successful writer of fiction, and David names one of their five children, a daughter, Betsey Trotwood, after his great-aunt. What the novel shows us is that David, through the

---

[269] Id., p. 201.

love of his mother (her face always with him) and of the highly individual Betsey Trotwood, who had left a patriarchal marriage, had found a way to communalize the consequences of trauma, loss of memory and voice, by finding his voice as an artist to tell what he had endured and how he came to resist, recovering his memory and voice.

It is a story that Dickens tells yet again in his last novel, *Our Mutual Friend*, but it is published in 1865 and *David Copperfield* in 1850, some fifteen years earlier. Dickens had, by this time, entered into a passionate adulterous affair with the actress, Ellen Ternan, and rather brutally and publicly abandoned his wife, with whom he had had ten children. The children apparently aligned their allegiances with their father.[270] It is all very tragically Dickensian, involving the kind of secret life in which consequences Dickens had once studied in *David Copperfield*. Here, however, the secret life is not the humiliation of the blacking factory but an adulterous affair. Adultery is a high crime and misdemeanor under patriarchy. In the highly patriarchal Rome of Caesar Augustus, adultery was regarded as bad as parricide, calling for the same sanguinary penalty, the sack, placing the adulterer or parricide in a sack with ferocious animals and thrown in the Tiber.[271] Victorian England was hardly as patriarchal as that but still patriarchal enough to condemn it. Couples did live adulterously, and at least two of them, George Eliot and Henry Lewes and Harriet Taylor and John Stuart Mill, as I have argued elsewhere,[272] not only broke the love laws (which condemned adultery) but resisted them, leading to extraordinary creative work, including ethical and political creativity. Why? When a loving couple lives outside of and in defiance of patriarchal norms, the relationship itself inspires a creative ethical voice that resists patriarchy itself. Both the novels of George Eliot and the political writings of John Stuart Mill exemplify such empowered creative voice.

I believe the adulterous relationship between Dickens and Ternan led him, as it did George Eliot and John Stuart Mill, to see more deeply into the issues of patriarchy and moral injury that had always preoccupied him, and that the shift in treatment of these themes between *David Copperfield*

---

270 See, for illuminating discussion, Peter Ackroyd, *Dickens* (New York: HarperCollins, 1990), pp. 791–83.

271 See, on this point, Carol Gilligan and David A. J. Richards, *The Deepening Darkness*, pp. 2, 41–52.

272 See David A. J. Richards *Why Love Leads to Justice*, pp. 22–28.

and *Our Mutual Friend* reflects what he had now come to experience and see, an impact seen as well in other later novels.[273] Part of this experience for Dickens was the experience of living outside patriarchy and coming to see his own idealized long-term marriage as personally deeply unhappy. There also was probably also guilt at what he had done, an emotion, when buried and difficult to acknowledge, connected to punishing rage against others and oneself (murder and suicide). His treatment of his wife bespeaks rage. Both themes (murder and suicide) occur in all the novels but more obviously so in the later novels, as their plots center on murder mysteries. *Our Mutual Friend* is certainly one of them, and its two central characters, John Harmon and Bella Wilfer, are among the most surprising and complex in all his novels, in particular, Bella Wilfer, playing the role here that Betsey Trotwood did in the earlier novel.

John Harmon is much more morally damaged than David Copperfield. There is, unlike David, no mother, and his extremely wealthy father, Old Harmon, had abusively treated his son, John Harmon, making it a condition of his son's receiving his money that he marry a mercenary girl, Bella Wilfer, whom Old Harmon capriciously chose. John refuses, and his father's money goes to a couple who worked for his father, the Boffins, and who had observed the abuse of the boy and the damage it had inflicted on him. Upon returning to England from abroad carrying money from sale of his business, John was violently attacked for his money and was believed to be dead; in fact, he had changed clothes with another, who was killed. Harmon takes on several different identities and names in the novel, bespeaking the damage done him both by his father and his attempted murder. In an astonishing long passage in the novel,[274] anticipating the stream of consciousness techniques of Virginia Woolf and James Joyce, Harmon speaks brokenly of his traumatic experiences: "The living-dead man, in thus communing with himself."[275] He moves from one identity to another: John Harmon died and Julius Handford disappeared and John

---

[273] On her possible influence on *Tale of Two Cities*, see Edgar Johnson, *Charles Dickens: His Tragedy and Triumph Volume 2* (New York: Simon and Schuster, 1952), pp. 972-73; on *Great Expectations, Id.*, and on *Our Mutual Friend, Id.*, pp. 1038-41.

[274] Charles Dickens, *Our Mutual Friend*, ed. Adrian Poole (London: Penguin, 1997), pp. 359–67.

[275] Id., p. 367.

Rokesmith was born.[276] The work of the psychiatrist, Leonard Shengold, on soul murder in *Little Dorrit*, earlier discussed, seems on point here. The novel begins with and centers on the trauma of an assault and attempted murder, and as Hanford struggles to make sense of what has happened and responding to it, fragments of his shattered self appear and disappear as multiple selves or identities. Nowhere in Dickens is the experience of trauma so powerfully and painfully explored from within the experience of trauma, reflecting some intimate sense of Dickens's own damaged self to which he could now give voice in a way he had never before. It plays the same role in this novel that the emotional breakdown and exhaustion of David Copperfield plays as he searches for Betsey Trotwood. But Harmon is not searching for a relative but for a lover, and he knows love is not easy but complex and full of ambivalence and requires patience and intelligence.

The process of recovery in *Our Mutual Friend* is not, however, as simple as that sponsored by Betsey in *David Copperfield*. Crucially, Harmon gravitates to the only people who ever showed any care or concern for him, the Boffins, who now have inherited his father's money. Now under the name of John Rokesmith, he works for them as a servant. We learn at the end of the novel and only at the end that the Boffins always knew Rokesmith was Harmon and joined him in the long game Harmon was playing to secure the love of the woman, paradoxically, he had come to love, Bella Wilfer, the mercenary girl he had rejected when his father had ordered him to marry her. The Boffins have invited Bella to live with them, and Bella regards Harmon/Rokesmith as her servant. When Harmon asks her to marry him, she rejects him because she will only marry for money and status.

Bella Wilfer is decidedly not one of Dickens's doormat, self-sacrificing good girls. Like Betsey Trotwood, she has a voice and is spirited. Bella is an unusual female character in Dickens, caught between her mercenary mother and sister and loving father, thus not fixed in her sense of herself. In fact, she's a woman who is also a person. Indeed, she has a self-critical sense of herself as amoral: "I have no more of what they call character, my dear, than a canary bird."[277] She is speaking to Lizzie Hexam, who has suffered multiple injustices: her brother has callously abandoned her; she

---

[276] Id., p. 366.

[277] Charles Dickens, *Our Mutual Friend*, ed. Adrian Poole (London: Penguin, 1997), p. 516,

---

is pursued by a homicidal school master (her brother's teacher) who will not accept her rejection of him; and her father, a criminal and now dead, has been unjustly accused of killing John Harmon and the blame has stigmatized her. Harmon has shown the police that the accusation is false and introduces Lizzie to Bella. It is part of Harmon's long game to win Bella, for talking to and becoming friends with Lizzie opens Bella to the sufferings of other persons. Indeed, Bella is moved to talk with Harmon/ Rokesmith about Lizzie on what she insists and demands must be "on equal terms,"[278] not hierarchically as a servant, as she had treated him in the past. Bella's intimate friendship with Hexam became the unconscious means of bringing[279] Rokesmith/Harmon and Bella together. Both Lizzie's friendship and Harmon's love begin to change Bella—a process of moral growth. When the Boffins, under the impact of their wealth, apparently become miserly and unjustly accuse Harmon, their servant, of wrongdoing, Bella, infuriated, defends him and realizes now that she is in love, though she believes him to be only a servant and without money and status. The Boffins' role in Harmon's long game is finally disclosed. Bella and Harmon marry.

In Dickens, this kind of more egalitarian love, releasing men and women from the traumas of patriarchy, does not always come from caring women but from men as well, as we see in Mr. Boffin. Oliver Twist, so traumatically abused, always holds in his memory that a child at school kissed him; through all the struggles and sufferings of his afterlife, he never once forgot it.[280] And one of the most heartrending moments in *Nicholas Nickleby* is Nickleby's caring love for the traumatized Smike, abandoned by his father (Nicholas's uncle) to the sadism of Squeers, from whom Nickleby saves Smike. Smike, who eventually dies, says to Nickleby, "You are my home—my kind friend—take me with you. Pray."[281] And the comparably heartrending moment in *Great Expectations* is when it is Joe Gargery, whom Pip had disdained as he became a gentleman, who cares for him after his breakdown.

The theme of a servant or ostensible servant—low or lowest in the patriarchal order—extending caring love to a master's moral injuries

[278] Id., p. 510.
[279] Id., p. 509.
[280] Charles Dickens, *Oliver Twist*, p. 57.
[281] Charles Dickens, *Nicholas Nickleby*, p. 162.

appears in Dickens's last novel, *Our Mutual Friend*, and his first, *Pickwick Papers*. Pickwick, though a mature, wealthy, older man and clearly high in the patriarchal order of things, is described as a kind of child possessing "juvenility of spirit."[282] What saves him from his more disastrous mistakes is the loving care of his servant, Sam Weller. Before taking on Weller as his servant, Pickwick is portrayed as lonely, reading a depressing manuscript of a madman.[283] Referencing *Don Quixote*, Weller is a caring Sancho Panza to Pickwick's Quixote:

> Mr. Pickwick was a philosopher, but philosophers are only men in armor after all. The shaft had reached him, penetrated through his philosophical harness, to his very heart. He hurled the inkstand madly forward and followed it up himself. But Mr. Jingle had disappeared, and he found himself in the arms of Sam.[284]

And in *Martin Chuzzlewit*, Martin, who never knew his parents and was abusively raised by his wealthy patriarchal grandfather,[285] is an arrogant young man of his class, who impetuously goes to America to make his fortune. He is foolishly drawn to what he thinks is a utopian community but is nothing of the sort, and he falls ill and is near death. His servant, Mark Tapley, not only saves his life by his loving care but, through his care and concern, morally transforms Martin from a prig into a moral person.[286]

What makes *Our Mutual Friend* for me the most powerful exploration of the journey of an abused/neglected boy into resistance to patriarchy is that it depicts the resistance as requiring not only nonviolent voice depicting the injustices patriarchy inflicts on the most vulnerable, the voice of Dickens the artist, but a voice that extends to intimate life as well. *Our Mutual Friend* is a novel portraying, in the traumatized John Harmon, a journey that resists the corruption of money and status not only of public

[282] Charles Dickens, *Pickwick Papers*, ed. Mark Wormald (London: Penguin, 2003; first published, 1836–37), p. 753.

[283] Id., pp. 149–56.

[284] Id., p. 142.

[285] See, on this point, Charles Dickens, *Martin Chuzzlewit*, ed. Patricia Ingham (London: Penguin, 1999; first published, 1843–44), pp. 100–1, 731.

[286] See Charles Dickens, *Martin Chuzzlewit*, ed. Patricia Ingham (London: Penguin, 1999; first published, 1843–44), pp. 495–99, 687–8, 500.

life but intimate life as well. It is the novel closest to my own experience as a young closeted gay man. I certainly knew the care and concern of good people, my Boffins (my mother and father), and thus was better positioned than the abused, neglected boys in Dickens to resist. But I was alone with my desire for sexual love, which was traumatic for me. I knew my parents thought I would want conventional patriarchal married life and would use my education and ambition to pursue wealth and status as ends in themselves. I wanted neither, and I see now why Dickens spoke to me, why *Our Mutual Friend* seems to me now so much more profound than *David Copperfield*. If I were to find the love for an equal I craved, it would require both finding my own voice (*David Copperfield*) and a long game to find the person I loved (*Our Mutual Friend*). It would be many years before I was able to find either, but the novels of Dickens filled my imagination with the sense that I was not alone. And love, when I found it, would empower a voice exploring and making claims of justice.

CHAPTER 4

Henry James on American Patriarchy and Resistance

A Young Man Reading Late James

What I had were secrets, or a secret, that I could not share with anyone. What drew me to the novels of Henry James—in particular, the last three great novels, *The Ambassadors, The Wings of the Dove,* and *The Golden Bowl*—was my sense that James and I were in the same world, and that his art, more exactly and precisely than any other art I then encountered, showed with astonishing sensitivity the moral insights that one trapped in such a world could nonetheless have and express. These are not novels of action, since nothing much happens, nor are they full of wonderfully believable eccentrics and hilarious situations and harrowing social injustices, as in Dickens, whose works I also devoured during this period. What attracted me to these novels of James is that there were essentially about intimate personal life and families, which was and had been my life until that point. I was fascinated by what could be said by a great artist like James about what could not be said among people close or ostensibly close to one another.

In his remarkable novel, *The Master,* the novelist, Colm Tóibín, shows us the world of Henry James based on the part of him he guarded most fiercely—his hidden self,[287] his homosexuality, and his being Irish, and

---

[287] Colm Tóibín, *The Master* (New York: Scribner, 2004), p. 108.

how it connects to the moral insights of his art. In one scene, for example, in which James is visiting Ireland and staying with British nobility (he was already regarded as a high-status presence at dinners), the question of himself being Irish is raised by a rather spiteful guest and James sees the sneer on Lady Wolseley's face when Webster had mentioned Bailieborough,[288] from which the James family come. The sneer is unforgettable, bespeaking British racism, not lost on James.

Tóibín has not only closely studied James's life and art but, himself gay and Irish and a gifted novelist, reveals how James, clearly a gay man, becomes an artist finding his voice around the question of secrets and moral betrayal and dealing with both ethically.[289] For a remarkable recent exhibit in New York City at the Morgan Library on Henry James and American painting, Tóibín wrote an illuminating essay not only on James's relationship to various painters (including another gay artist, John Singer Sargent) but how several of his novels were modeled on his relationships to various of these artists—some of whom were close friends.[290] Everything in James is built from his close observation of personal relationships, and he was an astute observer, in particular, of the underworld of the unspoken and unspeakable.

When I read the late novels of James, it was 1960–62 and I was sixteen to eighteen years old. Leon Edel had only published the first volume of his magisterial multivolume biography of James in 1953 (the two next volumes would be published in 1962 and the last two volumes in 1969 and 1972). In these volumes, James's repressed homosexuality plays a dominant role in one of the best psychoanalytic studies of a great artist ever published,[291] and

---

[288] Id., p. 35.

[289] For an illuminating study of James's sexuality, see Hugh Stevens, *Henry James and Sexuality* (Cambridge: Cambridge University Press, 1998).

[290] See Colm Tóibín, "Henry James: Shadow and Substance," Colm Tóibín, Marc Simpson, Declan Kiely, *Henry James and American Painting* (University Park, Pa.: Pennsylvania State University Press, 2017), pp. 1–47.

[291] See Leon Edel, *Henry James: The Untried Years: 1843–1870* (New York: Avon, 1953); *Henry James: The Conquest of London: 1870–1881* (New York: Avon, 1962); *Henry James: The Middle Years: 1882–1895* (New York: Avon 1962); *Henry James: The Treacherous Years: 1895–1901* (New York: Avon, 1969); *Henry James: The Master: 1901–1916* (New York: Avon, 1972). For recent commentary on Edel's struggle with James's family to secure access to his papers and exclude others interested in James, see Michael Anesko,

I knew at least of the first volume, though I only read the Edel biography in its entirety years later (in fact, within the past five years). So I certainly knew even then that homosexuality was in fact in the background of James's fictional art, and it was clear to me in reading him that he wrote from an experience I also had, namely, of having "a hidden self" he could not disclose to the family he loved.

I knew enough from reading the novels that James and I, myself at sixteen to eighteen years of age, shared the same "hidden self"—homosexuality on which we could not and would not act, and yet also had a demanding, very American and even Puritan ethical conscience. It was not at all clear to me then (at age sixteen to eighteen, living with my parents in Orange, New Jersey) how I could square my erotic preferences with my sense of ethics, let alone with my love for my mother and father, probably the more important motive at that point in my life. But reading James was discovering the close, good friend I then needed, whose voice spoke to me about my own loneliness and sensitivity, which had been his loneliness and sensitivity in a family he ostensibly loved, and had found a voice and a way out with exquisite ethical awareness and insight into human relationships structured around unspeakable secrets. Why did his most complex and demanding late works so compel me?

There is at the heart of my feeling for these novels the moral innocence of its main very American leading protagonists—whether the man Lambert Strether in *The Ambassadors*[292] or the women Milly Theale in *Wings of the Dove*[293] or Maggie Verver in *The Golden Bowl*.[294] And there is the ethical dilemma at the heart of the moral drama of each of the novels as each of these American innocents confront European duplicity.

Strether, commissioned by his wealthy fiancée, Mrs. Newsome, to rescue her son, Chad, from the clutches of a fallen woman in Paris, comes to doubt the premises of his mission both through conversations with a spirited woman he meets in Paris, Maria Gostrey, and through

---

Monopolizing the Master: Henry James and the Politics of Modern Literary Scholarship (Stanford: Stanford University Press, 2012).

[292] Henry James, *The Ambassadors, Novels 1903–1911*, ed. Ross Posnock (New York: The Library of America, 2010), pp. 1–430.

[293] Henry James, *The Wings of the Dove, Novels 1901–1902*, ed. Leo Bersani (New York: The Library of America, 2006).

[294] Henry James, *The Golden Bowl, Novels 1903–1911*, pp. 433–982.

---

experiencing the maturation and happiness of Chad and the qualities of the married woman, Marie de Vionnet, to whom he is attached. Chad and Marie duplicitously concealed the nature of their relationship from Strether, but when he sees clearly that they are a sexual couple in love, he nonetheless advises Chad to stay with her and, though Maria Gostrey practically proposes to him, he returns to the United States.

Milly Theale, a wealthy but sickly American heiress, had met in America a Londoner, Merton Densher, with whom she fell in love but never told him. Merton was in love with and engaged to another Londoner, Kate Croy, but their poverty leads them to wait until marriage; no one knows of their engagement. When Milly comes to London, she and Kate become friends, and on the basis of Milly's consultation with a London physician, Kate becomes convinced that Milly is dying, which she is. When Merton returns to London and encounters Milly once again, Kate urges him to pay closer attention to Milly, though Merton doesn't know why. In Venice, where Milly and the others go, Kate explains her plan to Merton that he should marry Milly and, after she dies, receive her money. Then she and Merton can marry. Merton agrees but only if Kate and he have premarital sex, which they do. Milly learns of Kate's plan from another suitor and breaks off her relationship with Densher, but notwithstanding the deception, she leaves Densher a substantial amount of money. After Milly's death, Densher tells Kate he will not accept the money and will only marry her if she also refuses the bequest; if she wants the bequest, Densher will transfer it to her. The novel ends as the couple breaks up, with Kate exclaiming at the end, "We shall never be again as we were."[295]

In *The Golden Bowl*, Maggie Verver and her father, Adam, a very wealthy man, live in Europe so Adam, with Maggie's help, may acquire various European art works for display in a projected American museum, which Adam plans to open. Maggie had a childhood friend, Charlotte Stent. Unknown to Maggie and her father, Charlotte had met and fallen in love with Prince Amerigo, impoverished Italian nobility, and they had an affair. Because of their poverty, the lovers agreed not to marry and separate. Amerigo and Maggie had met and fallen in love, and they plan to marry in London, and there they meet Charlotte, who has come to attend the wedding; Maggie does not know of their prior relationship. Amerigo and Charlotte go to a London shop to buy a wedding present,

---

[295] Henry James, *The Wings of the Dove*, op. cit., p. 689.

and Charlotte fixes on a golden bowl but, Amerigo, seeing flaws in the bowl, refuses to buy it. After Amerigo and Maggie marry and have a child, a boy, Maggie, concerned at her father's loneliness, urges him to marry Charlotte, which he does. The two couples spend much time together. Because Maggie is so absorbed in her father's interests, Amerigo and Charlotte are thrown together and have an adulterous affair. Maggie comes to have reason to suspect the affair and goes to the same London shop where Amerigo and Charlotte had contemplated buying the golden bowl. Maggie buys it, but when the owner of the shop comes to her home to point out to her the bowl's flaws, he sees a photograph of Amerigo and Charlotte and remembers them as the couple who had come to his shop possibly to buy the same bowl and who the owner perceives, from their conversation, as intimates. Maggie now knows that Charlotte and Amerigo knew each other as lovers before her marriage and confronts him with his infidelity. Without ever confronting Charlotte with her betrayal of her friend, Maggie persuades her father to return to America with Charlotte. Neither her father nor Charlotte ever speak about or acknowledge what motivates Maggie, but they agree to go. Adam and Charlotte return to America. Amerigo, coming to appreciate his wife's discretion and wisdom, says to Maggie, "I see nothing but *you*,"[296] and embraces her.

In her perceptive essay on *The Golden Bowl*, Martha Nussbaum trenchantly observes that both Adam Verver and his daughter, Maggie, are not only collectors of fine art but bring the same aesthetic attitude to people: Maggie collects an Italian prince, Amerigo, and Adam a beautiful American girl, Charlotte. Both Amerigo and Charlotte are impecunious, which may explain both their vulnerability to being collected by the wealthy father and daughter, but it also explain their vulnerability to reigniting their sexual love for each other. Nussbaum also emphasizes Maggie's desire to be and to do good, which explains her dismay on learning of her moral betrayal by both her husband and best friend. Maggie comes to realize, however, if she is to come into any kind of real relationship to her husband, she must not only confront him with the knowledge of how morally flawed he is but that she herself must overcome her aesthetic objectification of the prince and her friend and relate to them as the flawed people they are, which requires her to confront as well her own flawed objectification of her lovers and friends. In not speaking to Charlotte or to her father about

---

[296]   Henry James, *The Ambassadors, op. cit.,* p. 982.

what she is doing, she experiences herself "guilt, pity, and dread of them"[297] (her father and Charlotte). It is perhaps for the first time in her life and, as Nussbaum suggests, Maggie becomes for this reason human.[298]

Why did the moral drama of Strether, Milly, and Maggie—all American innocents abroad—so engage my imagination? James, like me at least at ages sixteen to eighteen, did not and would not act on, let alone acknowledge, gay desires, and thus had the experience of moral innocence, or at least James's art helped me see my experience as one of moral innocence. After all, I had not and would not act on my gay desires for some time, and I had no one, absolutely no one, with whom I could even discuss, let alone acknowledge, my desires. I also saw clearly the moral panic about homosexuality that even my loving parents shared with others in my extended family even at the thought that male homosexuality was as common in the experience of American men as the Kinsey study showed; of course, they denied it could be true. So there I was, alone with powerful sexual desires that would remain masturbatory for some time, and I knew my church condemned even masturbation. I was quite religious in my earlier life (at one point, wanting to enter the priesthood, before my mother stopped me), and I relentlessly went to confession every week to confess the only sin that interested me, and the priests would always ask whether I did it with someone else, which I had not, and they would dismiss me as not of much interest to them with the requisite penance.

However, by the time I was sixteen, my religious period had abruptly ended (I didn't fully realize this until I entered Harvard College), and I regarded masturbation as a harmless pleasure and no longer regarded that pleasure as sinful. So reading James gave me a name for my state, my hidden self, and suggested to me that that Americans, or at least the Americans that he wrote about in this three late novels (Strether, Millie, and Maggie) were morally innocent and that not only me but my family was morally innocent, yet as Americans, flawed because not able to understand the complexities of our ethical and psychological human natures, and therefore vulnerable to betrayal. I could not speak to them of my sexual feelings for

---

[297] Id., p. 982.
[298] See Martha Nussbaum, "Flawed Crystals: James's *The Golden Bowl* and Literature as Moral Philosophy," *Love's Knowledge: Essays on Philosophy and Literature* (New York: Oxford University Press, 1990), pp. 125–147. I am grateful to Carol Gilligan for bringing this essay to my attention.

men about which I was ashamed, but my betrayal was necessary to protect my hidden self until I was ready to explore or develop on my own terms. And they betrayed me because they give me no way of even acknowledging or speaking about such intimate matters, but they rather perpetuated a silence that left me quite helplessly alone. Our innocence (mine and theirs) as Americans was not a strength but a vulnerability.

Morally innocent but in a way I did not then fully understand, trapped, these novels also gave me a sense of how Americans in particular, coming from a dominantly Puritan moral and religious culture, could be culturally trapped, so again, I was not alone. For one thing, the ethical criticism of this culture may be the central theme of James's fiction, and it was the ethical impulse in James that, I think, really absorbed me, worked out, as I shall later show, with such remarkable moral and psychological complexity. In her study of Henry James, Rebecca West observes, comparing the brothers William and Henry James: "Each of them grew up to write fiction as though it were philosophy and the other to write philosophy as though it were fiction, at a very early age."[299] Henry James would have had no patience with the kind of abstract moral and political philosophy I would spend my college and graduate school life studying, but he was one of the most acute ethical critics of his period of the then dominant American Puritan patriarchal sexual morality of his period, and such ethical criticism was to be the heart of all my later work, as a philosopher and law professor. Rebecca West is quite right on this point: Henry James was a philosopher in some ways much more ethically radical, at least in matters of gender and sexuality, than his brother. For this reason, it always seemed to me that T. S. Eliot's incredibly stupid remark that James "had a mind so fine that no idea could violate it"[300] revealed how invisible James's ethically radical view were to more patriarchal men like Eliot (more on Eliot in chapter 5) and how trapped Eliot's intelligence was by the patriarchal blinkers through which he saw his life and work.

So I came to James before I came to philosophy, and saw in his work the kind of acute and beautifully observed ethical criticism of conventions that unjustly afflicted the morally innocent, and I found in his art a place and dignity for the moral philosophy I would later study and elaborate and that he practiced before me.

---

[299] Rebecca West, *Henry James* (New York: Henry Holt, 1916), p. 11.
[300] Quoted in Michael Anesto, *Monopolizing the Master,* at p. 117.

James on Gays and Women under Patriarchy

The dominant moral culture of America, for Hawthorne and Melville as for William and Henry James, was Puritanism, albeit a Puritanism that had been liberalized over time.[301] Both Hawthorne and Melville's art, as we have seen (chapter 1), certainly exposed to ethical examination and criticism the patriarchal structures of religious and political authority that American Puritanism had assumed to be axiomatic. Hawthorne had posed his criticism in *The Scarlet Letter* through the ethical reflections of Hester Prynne:

> The world's law was no law for her mind. It was an age in which the human intellect, newly emancipated, had taken a more active and a wider range than for many centuries before. Men of the sword had overthrown nobles and kings. Men bolder than these had overthrown and rearranged—not actually but within the sphere of theory, which was their most real abode—the whole system of ancient prejudice, wherewith was linked much of ancient principle. Hester Prynne imbibed this spirit.[302]

Why, in the spirit of such criticism, would not the same apply to Puritanism's patriarchal constraints on women's freedom as Hester muses?

> As a first step, the whole system of society is to be torn down and built up anew. Then the very nature of the opposite sex, or its long hereditary habit, which has become like nature, is to be essentially modified before woman can be allowed to assume what seems a fair and suitable position.[303]

---

[301] See, on this development, Perry Miller, *The New England Mind: The Seventeenth Century* (Cambridge, Mass.: Belknap Press of Harvard University Press, 1939); Perry Miller, *The New England Mind: From Colony to Province* (Cambridge, Mass.: Belknap Press of Harvard University Press, 1953); Perry Miller, *The Life of the Mind in America* (New York: Harcourt, Brace & World, 1965).

[302] Nathaniel Hawthorne, *The Scarlet Letter,* p. 143.

[303] Id., p. 144.

The novels of Henry James that I read were very much in this ethical tradition. James deeply admired Hawthorne's art, and I believe its hidden world of Puritan guilt and shame, or which Hawthorne was so critical, was one of the inspirations of his own art, with which it is continuous. (James does not apparently acknowledge Melville as an influence.) In his long essay on Hawthorne, James contrasts "the coldness, the thinness, the blankness" of the America of Hawthorne's novels, in contrast to the "denser, richer, warmer European spectacle" with its accumulation of history and custom, such a complexity of manners and types and what its impact would have been on Hawthorne's work if he were a young Englishman or a young Frenchman of the same degree of genius.[304] James, of course, is thinking of himself—how important it was to his development of James's art that he lived in and loved European culture. But the nerve of James's art was, like Hawthorne, a critique of patriarchy, made more vivid by the confrontation of Americans and Europeans.

I had become even at ages sixteen to eighteen quite skeptical of the traditional patriarchal authority of the Catholic church (in this, I followed the lead of my parents) and was already well on my way to a more Protestant understanding of the role of the right of personal conscience in both ethics and politics, an understanding at the center, as I would later learn and argue of the rights-based tradition of American constitutionalism.[305] And I would shortly attend the American Puritan university historically par excellence, Harvard.

Though I did not know it when I first read James in my early manhood, we shared something else, namely, close family ties. Like James, I was enmeshed in close relationships to a family (my father and mother and sister) whose continuing love required my silence, and thus the sacrifice of essential parts of myself in the name of love. I am sure I could not, at the time, have consciously understood either myself or my family as betraying our love (though unconsciously, I now see I was angry, even indignant, covered by silence and reticence), but I am also sure now that it was the inchoate sense of such betrayal that made James's late novels so revelatory for me. There was betrayal at the heart of our love, and I sensed even then

---

[304] Henry James, "Nathaniel Hawthorne," *Literary Criticism*, ed. Leon Edel (New York: The Library of America, 1984), pp. 317–457, p. 541.

[305] See David A. J. Richards, *Toleration and the Constitution* (New York: Oxford University Press, 1986).

that I had to find, as James did, an ethical way out of a world based on such betrayal. I was innocent, but I found myself drawn into a web of love that called for betrayal as the condition of love, as Chad and Marie did in *The Ambassadors,* as Kate and Drensher did in *Wings of the Dove,* and Amerigo and Charlotte did in *The Golden Bowl.* The innocents in all three novels—Strether, Milly, and Maggie—do not themselves betray, but they are betrayed. But they respond to betrayal, having learned something about what love is in a certain time and place and culture and also having grown ethically. Strether no longer accepts the moral premises of Mrs. Newsome's statement of his mission to save Chad and saves Chad in his own terms, Milly responds to betrayal with a largeness of heart and mind that brings Densher to a sense of the unacceptable ethical price of his love for Kate, and Maggie grows through the experience of betrayal by her husband and best friend into a larger ethical intelligence, which both holds her husband and friend accountable and yet preserves relationships.

All of them engage in ethical self-sacrifice: Strether returns to an America he now knows does not understand love and inflicts a loss of love on himself though he saves Chad, Milly dies though she saves Densher from the ethically morass into which Kate had led him, and Maggie loses the father she loved and the friend she cherished, though she becomes more the equal and loving companion of her husband. I think I thought of my love for my family as requiring a comparable ethical self-sacrifice. Their love or retaining their love was worth it. Breaking with them was, for me, unthinkable. Whatever I did, staying in relationship with them was a fixed point in my life. What I did not realize until much later is that my being gay would be easier for them than I earlier and fearfully thought, for they loved me.

So reading these three novels led me to a sense that my moral innocence was more broadly shared by other American men and women, and also how, though innocent, our dominant moral and political culture trapped us by not according us any voice to question its demands. Henry James spoke to me because through his art he had found and developed a voice that broke the silence of those most directly trapped by those demands, namely, women. James was one of many gay men (think of Tennessee Williams) who found his voice as a gay man through creating vibrant, complex, intelligent, and alive women (think of Blanche DuBois in *A Streetcar Named Desire*) who shared an experience he had had, namely, trapped in patriarchal conceptions of one's nature, place, and role, including sexuality (for gay men, unspeakability). Nathaniel Hawthorne, a straight man, had done the same when he created and gave a voice to Hester Prynne, but as we saw in chapter 1, Hawthorne certainly saw how patriarchy deformed men (Dimmesdale and Chillingworth), though he did not, unlike Melville, explore how resisting patriarchy might make possible not only love between men and women but between men and men. James, like Melville, does so, or at least, so I argue below.

James's feeling for women—reflected in the three late novels as well as his earlier masterpiece, *Portrait of a Lady*,[306] and his extraordinary study of the development of a resilient young girl against terrible parental odds, *What Maisie Knew*[307]—exposed him to some remarkable homophobic criticism by no less than Theodore Roosevelt himself, referring to Henry James as that "little emasculated mass of inanity."[308] The role of irrationalist appeals to gender, provoking Americans into an imperialistic war, is shockingly visible in the Spanish-American and Philippine-American wars in which Theodore Roosevelt's conflicted psychology of manhood, as an American leader and provocateur, played so pivotal a role, as many scholars have cogently observed.[309] Roosevelt had had to struggle to conform to then dominant conceptions of manhood; when he first appeared as a legislator in the New York Assembly, both his clothes and manner and voice led "the newcomer [to] quickly become known as 'Oscar Wilde,' after the famous fop who, coincidentally, had arrived in America earlier the same

---

[306] Henry James, *The Portrait of a Lady*, *Novels 1881–1886*, ed. William T. Stafford (New York: The Library of America, 1985), pp. 191–800.

[307] Henry James, *What Maisie Knew*, *Novels 1896–1899*, ed. Myra Jehlen (New York: The Library of America, 2003), pp. 395–650.

[308] Quoted in Edmund Morris, *The Rise of Theodore Roosevelt* (New York: Random House, 1979), at p. 425.

[309] See, for example, Gail Bederman, *Manliness and Civilization* (Chicago: University of Chicago Press, 1995), pp. 170–215; Kristin L. Hoganson, *Fighting for American Manhood: How Gender Politics Provoked the Spanish-American and Philippine-American Wars* (New Haven: Yale University Press, 1998); Stephen Kinzer, *The True Flag: Theodore Roosevelt, Mark Twain, and the Birth of American Empire* (New York: Henry Holt, 2017); Kim Townsend, *Manhood at Harvard: William James and Others* (New York: W. W. Norton, 1996), pp. 256–86; Edward J. Renehan Jr., *The Lion's Pride: Theodore Roosevelt and His Family in Peace and War* (New York: Oxford University Press, 1998).

day"[310]; after the traumatic deaths of both his beloved mother and wife at roughly the same time, he recovered his always fragile sense of manly self by a physically demanding period of hunting and riding in the American West,[311] about which he would later publish a multivolume study, *The Winning of the West*. [312] Roosevelt had no patience and indeed turned violently on any man with "a certain feminine reticence," which included, evidently, both Henry Adams, the historian, and Henry James, the artist.[313]

Henry James had been born and raised in America in which such homophobic denigration of a gay man and artist came not only from on presidential high but early in his life, from within his own complex family, which clarifies, I believe, how and why James both turned to writing fiction and left America to live abroad in order to pursue his sense of vocation as both an artist and moralist. The sense of a very sharp gender binary and hierarchy was evidently surprisingly strong not only in American culture generally but in the otherwise enlightened and progressive James family in particular. The patriarch of the James family of Henry James Sr., whose inherited wealth released him from any conventionally American work life to pursue, with his five children and wife and wife's sister (Aunt Kate) in tow, his search for divine ethical truth in travels throughout Europe and shifting homes in the United States. The father had as a boy been severely injured in a fire and endured the trauma of having his leg amputed, and would walk on a false leg all this life. And his relentless search for ultimate ethical truth culminated in a kind of nervous breakdown (called by him a "vastation"). Both his sons, William and Henry, have in their background this traumatizing, sometimes irrational force. The father interpreted his breakdown as showing him the truth of Swedenborgianism,[314] writing several unreadable books trying to explain its truth and, above all its transformative universal ethical appeal.[315] Henry James Sr. believed,

---

[310]   Edmund Morris, *The Rise of Theodore Roosevelt* (New York: Random House, 1979), p. 144.

[311]   Id., pp. 229–34, pp. 264–276.

[312]   See id., pp. 474–48, 484.

[313]   Id., p. 425 (footnotes omitted).

[314]   See, on William James Sr. as a father, Robert D.Richardson, *William James in the Maelstrom of American Modernism: A Biography* (Boston: Mariner, 2006), pp. 28–33.

[315]   See Henry James, *The Nature of Evil: Considers in a Letter to the Rev. Edward Beecher, D. D._*(New York: D. Appleton and Company, 1855); Henry James,

---

above all, in radical religious freedom and in strenuous argument with the best minds of his time (Emerson was a friend), including his children; he and William argued constantly; Henry was silent, observing. Of his father's aggressive style of speech, William James observed to his brother, Henry: "He is so little restrained by conventional considerations that if you or I or Mama were to die to night he would send off a contribution to the *Daily Advertiser* to morrow tearing us to pieces."[316] The father's ethical universalism did not, however, extend to women, whose nature he interpreted in terms of a particularly rigid view of the patriarchal gender binary and hierarchy of the period, men (rational and strong), women (emotional and spiritual door mats):

> The fundamental law of all true creation or prolification [sic] is marriage, and marriage never takes place between equals, but on the contrary invariably exacts a hierarchical distribution of the parties to it, the wife deriving rank from the husband . . . *The desire of the wife is to the husband, and he shall rule over her.*[317]

It is not surprising that his one highly intelligent and spirited daughter, Alice, the youngest child with three quarrelsome and mocking brothers and one more supportive (Henry) should have been psychologically damaged, retreating into permanent convalescent illness. Henry James was much the closest brother to her, and she spent the last years of her life in Britain near him, taken care of by her intimate friend, Katherine Loring, in "a Boston marriage."[318] "What bound Henry and Alice together was a different kind

---

Sr., *Substance and Shadow: Or, Morality and Religion in Their Relation to Life: An Essay Upon the Physics of Creation* (Boston: Ticknor and Fields, 1863). The theory of love in *Substance and Shadow,* namely that love "must be reserved only what intrinsically is most bitterly hostile and negative to itself" is embraced by Charles Saunders Peirce in "Evolutionary Love," *The Monist Volume 3*, No. 2. (January, 1893), pp. 176–200, at p. 177. For William James's defense of his father and his views, see William James, *The Literary Remains of the Late Henry James* (Boston: James R. Osgood and Company, 1885).

316 Quoted in Michael Anesko, *Monopolizing the Master*, at p. 19.

317 Henry James, *Substance and Shadow*, at p. 498.

318 See Jean Strouse, *Alice James: A Biiography* (New York: New York Review Books, 2011). On the relationship between Alice and Katherine, see id., pp.

of exclusion and a profound mutual understanding. Henry had withdrawn early from the competitive masculine fray to a safe inner world, taking the part of the docile, easy, "good" James child. The novelist then took the place that might have been filled by the only girl in another family. As his mother's "angel," the watcher in the family drama, he freed himself to see and learn, preempting the role of creative receptor often occupied in the nineteenth century by women to whom avenues for other kinds of activities were closed."[319]

The consequence of Henry James Jr.'s ongoing spiritual quest was that his children were not conventionally educated, but they had tutors as they traveled around Europe and back to America. All the children were, in fact, well educated and quite cosmopolitan (in particular, both William, who studied in Germany, and Henry, who ended up living in France, Italy, and finally Britain). William, the eldest, was clearly the main object of the father's attention, who discouraged his son from his real gift and sense of vocation as a painter; William, prone throughout his later life to moods of elation and depression, turned to medicine at Harvard, and then psychology and finally, philosophy, all subjects in which he struggled to find the ethical truth that his father also had sought, including a serious interest in spiritualism and a defense of religious belief. William James invented American psychology as a discipline, and invented as well a philosophy, pragmatism, and was, consistent with his father's radical abolitionism, a public intellectual voice for American liberalism, contesting both America's imperialist wars with Spain and the practice of the lynching of American blacks.[320]

William and Henry James were brought up together (one year apart in age), but unsurprisingly, they responded in quite different ways to their father's demands and dominance. William sought somehow to find himself in his father's undisciplined search for universal ethical truth and a model of dominant-aggressive manhood.[321] In contrast, his younger brother was regarded within the family as an "angel," quiet and listening and compliant. His artistic interests were nurtured by both his mother and aunt—the

---

200, 241–42.

[319] Id., p. 49.

[320] See, on all these points, Robert D. Richardson, *William James in the Maelstrom of American Modernism.*

[321] See William James, *The Literary Remains of the Late Henry James.*

---

great love of his early life. His brother unsurprisingly turned on Henry, refusing to play with him, with the remark, "I play with boys who curse and swear!'" The words obviously meant a lot to Henry, as he remembers them in his autobiography and yet denies he was an actively rebuffed suitor because, as he puts it, "Such aggressions were so little in order for me." This meant that by this time he had already withdrawn from seeking intimate closeness with his brother, whom he regarded, consistent with the gender binary, as his superior because of his manly manner and interests over Henry's more feminine interests.[322] Leon Edel, commenting on this incident, observes, "This had certainly been one way of calling him Angela rather than Angel. What is involved here may not be so much a relegation of Henry to a feminine role as to a kind of second-class citizenship."[323] To me, the interlinked homophobia and sexism are obvious.

Along these lines, there is a revelatory letter sent from William to Henry when the latter was thinking of returning to the United States:

> This is your dilemma. The congeniality of Europe on the one hand plus the difficulty of making an entire living out of original writing and its abnormality as a matter of mental hygiene—the dreariness of American conditions of life plus a mechanical routine occupation possible to be obtained, which from day to day is *done* when 'tis done, mixed up with the writing into which you distil your essence.[324]

Edel observes, "William was saying that Henry could not support himself by his writing and would be wise to take a job when he came home—something Henry had long ago determined not to do, but there was also the general fact, recognized by Henry, that in America, more than elsewhere at the time, to be a writer was to accept the way of loneliness and isolation, and William implied that writing wasn't quite an active, manly,

---

[322] Quoted in Henry James, *Autobiographies,* ed. Philip Horne (New York: The Library of America, 2016), p. 158. On William referring to his brother as "the angel," see Leon Edel, *Henry James: The Conquest of London: 1870–1881,* p. 147.

[323] Leon Edel, id., p. 386.

[324] Quoted in id., p. 157.

healthy way of existence."[325] William summed up by telling Henry, "If you are not prepared to face a three-year slough of despond, you will do well to remain abroad."[326] "It is," Edel observes, "perhaps difficult for parents and brothers to be aware that there is a genius in their midst."[327]

Difficult is not quite the word for what the letter shows us of how William and probably his father, Henry Sr., thought of Henry and the kinds of pressures and even bullying to which he was likely subject. It is no accident, I believe, but integral to James's ethical and psychological genius, as an artist, that his works pose not only critical ethical questions about then dominant views of gender and sexuality but psychologically reveal patterns of abuse in the childhoods of both girls and boys. I believe he had experienced such abuse at firsthand clearly from his admired elder brother, William, and probably from others. Consider William's quite sexist, even homophobic, denigration of Henry's personality and interests in his boyhood, now adding in the above-discussed letter, in the terms of the medicine and psychology of the period, "abnormality as a matter of mental hygiene," essentially pathologizing Henry's life and interests.

My own experience in a close family was the same in one respect but different in most others. It was the same to the extent I was alone with my sexuality, not to be discussed with those I loved. I withdrew to a kind of cunning and concealment in my relationships to my parents and sister, so they clearly did not know me in the way they supposed. I believe James was in the same situation, but it was clearly different and worse in the sense that his family (his parents, Aunt Kate, and three brothers and sister) were drenched in the patriarchal father's contradictory embrace of universal ethical brotherhood and quite rigid sexism.

As I earlier observed, the issue of homosexuality had certainly come up during my childhood, but little was made of it, other than my clear understanding of adult moral panic about the question. More importantly, both the relationship of my parents and their relationship to their children was remarkably free of the gender stereotypes of the period. The marriage itself was quite egalitarian and fully voiced on both sides, and my parents insisted that the relationship of me and my sister should be conducted on similar egalitarian terms; it was because of this that my sister was,

---

[325] Id.
[326] Id.
[327] Id.

during my childhood, my closest friend, and her going to Vassar was so devastating to me. I don't recall ever experiencing from my family any denigration of my unconventional interests as an American boy (in reading, opera, and the arts) as in any way problematic (quite the opposite), perhaps because my interests were connected, in the view of my parents, to my unusual excellence as a student, culminating in my admission to Harvard College. Neither of my parents fit the conventional gender binary as a woman or a man (my mother was highly rational, serious, and driving, yet caring, relational, and tender as a mother, while my father was intelligent, humorous, caring, and musical), and there was nothing, in fact, like a hierarchy between them, or at least that was how I and my sister, who knew them most intimately, experienced their relationship. Strangely enough, if I experienced any patriarchal control from my parents, it was from my mother, not my father. It was my father who urged me to be patient with her difficulties in dealing with, as I grew older, my resistance to her relentless demands. Underlying her apparent strength, he told me that there was a frailty fearing loss of love, and I should be sensitive to her vulnerabilities; and of her love for me, I never had any doubt. I was learning from my father the required sensitivity to these vulnerabilities in one's parents and to anyone one loved. So if I was subject to bullying at school over gender issues, I could always withdraw to the safety and support of my family. This explains, I think, why they meant so much to me. It also explains why the dominant gender stereotypes of the period made so little sense to me or had so little hold on me except, of course, for my homosexuality—my secret self.

Henry James also had a secret self and expressed itself in literary interests nurtured in close relationships to his supportive mother and Aunt Kate, the love of his early life. Notably, his father, who quashed William's vocation for painting (he had, evidently, a real gift), apparently left Henry alone as he developed his early interests, trying his hand at writing fiction. These interests would have been regarded by William and by Henry Sr. as not, for an American man at least, masculine (as William's letter to his brother makes clear), which is one of the reasons William supports his brother living abroad. But there were other reasons, most importantly, Henry's *need* not to be under the patriarchal thumb of his father and brother. Henry could not have developed the artistic voice he did if he had remained in a family or, for that matter, a country in which patriarchal assumptions were so hegemonic over both private and public life, including the lives of the women in the family he loved and the women outside his family he loved (Minnie Temple, his beloved cousin who died early of tuberculosis, the model for Isabel Archer in *Portrait of a Lady*) and including himself as a gay man, like Tennessee Williams, with deep feeling for the plight of women under patriarchy.

Henry saw his own plight in that of women and made that plight, women's and his own, the subject of his art in a way that was unthinkable for both his father and brother, namely, to think, as Hester Prynne did, outside the box of patriarchy and to question it ethically. For James, this required living abroad in countries less homophobic than the United States, and his art accordingly often centered on American moral innocents abroad, finding in the comparison the basis for his ethical and psychological art. Henry knew, as a gay man, that he was as much outside of and afflicted by patriarchy as Hester was and that, like Hester, the condemnation by his own brother of his gender-bending could be an ethical strength. Like Hester as well, Henry understood the violence inflicted on those breaking the love laws and, for this reason, did not, unlike Oscar Wilde, act on his sexual passions. All the evidence suggests that he loved several young men and loved their company, showing in his conversations with and letters to them his devastating sharpness of wit, his extravagant inventions of intimacy, and his Rabelaisian powers of innuendo.[328] Further intimacy was not for James possible, but he discovered, as he matured into his fuller artistic powers, enough confidence in his love for men that he found a voice, like Hester's, that both exposes and resists the patriarchal love laws. To this extent, Hugh Stevens seems to be me quite right: James is and should be regarded as a gay artist.[329] Art may have played the central role in James's life that it did in the life and sense of vocation of another, less closeted, more sexually active gay artist, Marcel Proust, who had "learned his life's lesson: the price the searcher for lost truth must pay is steep, even extortionate, but it is worth paying. Art alone can bridge the gaps between the intermittences of the heart. 'The true life, life at last discovered and illuminated, the only life really lived is that of the artist.'"[330]

---

[328] See Michael Anesko, *Monopolizing the Master,* at p.55. For a fuller treatment of James's sexuality, see Hugh Stevens, *Henry James and Sexuality.*

[329] See Hugh Sevens, *Henry James and Sexuality.*

[330] Peter Gay, *Modernism: The Lure of Heresy From Baudelaire to Beckett and Beyond* (New York: W. W. Norton, 2008), pp. 210–211.

Thankfully, in contrast to James, I had come from a different family with a very different father and mother and sister. My loving relationship to this egalitarian and expressive man made love for men (when I was ready for it) natural for me, and certainly not the psychological minefield it apparently was for James.

Henry was, for this reason, in a much more difficult psychological place in his relationship to his family than I was. James family life was dominated by the almost irrationalist patriarchal authority of Henry Sr., which penetrated and traumatized the psyche of everyone close to him, in particular, his vulnerable children. Henry's sense of a secret self was thus closely connected to never again being in the position of the helpless child he was in the James's family, a position he thought everyone was in his family under the authority of the patriarchal father. Preserving himself from that kind of domination so damaged his sense of trust that he so centered his sense of himself in an inviolable secret self that made intimacy for James possible only in very special circumstances and always vulnerable to misunderstanding, and intimate love for a man, as we understand it today, evidently impossible. Colm Tóibín treats this aspect of James with great sensitivity in *The Master*, as he recreates James's relationship to his steadfast and self-contained and secret best friend,[331]— the novelist, Constance Fenimore Woolson, who commits suicide. James did not, however, want their friendship to be known to others, and when Constance began disclosing things, which compromised James's control over his privacy, "he felt a powerlessness that he had not felt since he was a child"[332] and withdrew from the relationship, as he felt Constance was exposing a secret between them that was only for them and not to be disclosed to anyone else.[333] Henry James wanted to be seen intimately by no one, which explains his difference from Oscar Wilde, a gay man who wanted to be seen and celebrated by everyone and paid a terrible and terrifying price for disclosure in homophobic Britain.[334]

---

[331] Colm Tóibín, *The Master*, p. 216.

[332] Colm Tóibín, *The Master*, p. 236.

[333] See, for fuller discussion of the relationship, including his response to her suicide, *id.*, pp. 210-255

[334] On James's response to Wilde's conviction and imprisonment, see Leon Edel, *Henry James: The Treacherous Years 1895–1901*, pp. 128–30.

But in his art, James could play with revealing or drawing upon tantalizing pieces of his secret self. But here, disclosure was always in his control (Woolson had compromised his control), which explains why working relentlessly at his art, often so inward, psychologically and ethically complex, and intimate, *was* his intimate life. In his great statement of vocation, "The Art of Fiction," James objected to "the moral timidity of the usual English novelist," expressly denying that such timidity could be regarded as moral in a novel for adults: "There are certain things, which it is generally agreed not to discuss, not even to mention before young people. That is very well, but the absence of discussion is not a symptom of the moral passion."[335] The moral passion of art, for James, means going deeper into precisely the issues "not to discuss, not even to mention." And one of those issues he mentions is tracing the development of the moral consciousness of a child,[336] reminding the reader, "I have been a child in fact."[337]

James reveals pieces of his secret self throughout his works but with special poignancy when he gives voice to what it is like to be a child in an abusive family. I've already mentioned James's remarkable study of a resilient young girl, Maisie, in *What Maisie Knew*. Maisie is caught between warring, careless, and now divorced parents; two young caretakers who fall in love in caring for Maisie and then, as the price of continuing their relationship, abandon her; and another rather Puritanical older women caretaker, who demands of the young child that she must abandon the immoral young couple (who would like to care for the child as a couple), though the child has come to love the young man and wants him alone as her caretaker. The novel reads this web of conflicting relationships and claims and love from Maisie's highly intelligent perspective, looking for the attention and care, which all children need, but placed here in choosing or having imposed on herself a range of alternatives, all of which are problematic or are made to seem so. Only James, with his own background of an abusive patriarchal family could in this period create so lively and engaging a young woman as

---

[335] Henry James, "The Art of Fiction," *Literary Criticism*, ed. Leon Edel (New York: The Library of America, 1984), pp. 44–65, at p. 63. On James's love of less inhibited French fiction, see Peter Brooks, *Henry James Goes to Paris* (Princeton: Prince University Press, 2007).

[336] Henry James, "The Art of Fiction," op.cit., p. 61.

[337] Id., p. 62.

Maisie and suggest, even though she is unjustly separated from the young people she loved by the moralism of a caretaker she cannot understand, and she questions if she will survive and perhaps prosper. James sees young women as more resilient than young men, as his studies of abused boys make clear.

James on Abused Boys

The two short stories dealing with the abuse of boys—both quite close to his own experience and his secret self—are not so sanguine: in the case of both stories, "The Author of Beltraffio"[338] and *The Turn of the Screw*, the boys die. The idea for the first story came from what the critic, Edmund Gosse, had told James about the life of the historian of the Italian Renaissance, John Addington Symonds, whom James met only once. Symonds had married and had children but was a sexually active gay man (in Venice) and wrote at least two books, both of which James had read, one taking same-sex relations in the ancient world as a model (*A Problem in Greek Ethics*, 1883) and the other refuting modern prejudice against homosexuality on the basis of current medical knowledge (*A Problem in Modern Ethics*, 1891). Gosse told James Symonds' works shocked his wife, but no one dies. James's story focuses on the wife of a novelist, Mark Ambient, visited by an admiring American, who tells the story. Ambient's works are about Pagan Mediterranean culture—works that his wife detests. She tries to keep their son, Dolcino, away from his father. The narrator persuades Mrs. Ambien to read the proofs of her husband's new work, and she takes the book with her into the boy's sick room; she is so distressed by the story that she lets the boy die rather than submit him to the husband's care.[339] Here, James gives voice to the psychological damage that homophobia wrecks on a mother, in effect, a fear so great that she wills the death of her son.

---

[338] See Henry James, "The Author of Beltraffio," *Complete Stories 1874–1884*, ed. William I. Vance (New York: The Library of America, 1990), pp. 865–910.

[339] For illuminating discussion of the background of this story, see Michael Gorra, *Portrait of a Novel: Henry James and the Making of an American Masterpiece* (New York: Liverwright, 2012), pp. 82–86.

There is also an increasingly distressed woman, a governess, at the center of the narrative of James's *The Turn of the Screw*.[340] Two children, a boy and a girl, are left in the care of the governess in a country home by their legal guardian, who instructs the governess not to bother him with questions about the care of the children. The governess learns that the previous caretakers of the children are now dead—that the man and woman had had an affair—and come to believe that the man, Peter Quint, may also have abused the children. The governess sees the ghost of Peter Quint (no one else does), and in insisting that the young man, Miles, must separate from Quint, the boy dies. The story is written entirely from the governess's point of view and shows, once again, what James saw in how his own family's fear of his own gender-bending ways, including his brother's homophobia, could so forge irrational fears in others that they are drawn into them, including the terror of a vulnerable child ending in death.[341] The story is one of James's most revealing revelations of the feelings of abuse he may have suffered as a boy, as the governess refers to Miles, at one point, as an angel[342]—a term that had been used by James's mother to describe her favorite child. It is a terrifying story, showing us the terrors James felt as a child in the family he knew he had to flee.

Yet another short story, "Owen Wingrave,"[343] explores the crippling effects of a patriarchal family like his own—demanding that children follow in the steps demanded by their fathers—on the psychology of a young man, Owen Wingrave, who resists his family's demands that he follow in the footsteps of all the other men in his family who have served in Britain's wars. Wingrave's resistance takes the form of pacifism that his family, including his grandfather Sir Philip (who would disown him), rejects. Even his fiancée turns on him, calling him a coward, and goads him to sleep in a haunted room in the family house, where one of his

---

[340] See Henry James, *The Turn of the Screw, Complete Stories 1892–1898*, eds. David Bromwich and John Hollander (New York: The Library of America, 1996), pp. 635–740.

[341] For a reading of the short story alone these lines, see Leon Edel, *Henry James: The Treacherous Years: 1895–1901*, pp. 203–208.

[342] See Henry James, *The Turn of the Screw*, p. 657.

[343] See Henry James, *Owen Wingrave, Complete Stories 1892–1898*, eds. David Bromwich and John Hollander (New York: The Library of America, 1996), pp. 256–290.

ancestors had killed a son who, like Owen, rebelled. Owen sleeps in the room and is found dead in the morning.[344]

Pacifism is an unusual topic in James's work as are controversial political issues more generally. But as we shall later see, at least two of James's other works—*The Bostonians*[345] and *Princess Casamassima*[346]—both remarkable in different ways, deal with topics as controversial in James's period—feminism and terrorism, as they remain today. As in the other political works we shall discuss, James's interest in pacifism is both to give fair voice to its ethical claims (as Owen Wingrave does in the novella, challenging, in effect, the role of militarism in British imperialism) but also to show us, as he does elsewhere, the ways in which highly patriarchal family structures, like his own, make resistance, even on good ethical grounds not only difficult but psychologically deadly. I take completely seriously James's very real concern for the psychological difficulties of such resistance for men, as he draws yet again on the experience of his own domineering father, finding in Owen's plight a way, yet again, of letting us see how and why he withdrew into his secret self, never confronting his family, as Owen does his with his own convictions. There is, however, something quite brave, even courageous, in even dealing with such material in a period of British imperialism when Kipling's paeans to racist imperialist British manhood were celebrated in the United States (his poem, "The White Man's Burden," subtitled "The United States and the Philippine Islands," was published in 1899 expressly to urge Americans on following the example of Britain to their patriarchal duties of imperialist racism in fighting the Spanish American and Philippine American Wars[347]).

Where did James, an American writing in Britain, get such courage? James was not only an outsider to American patriarchy (thus his secret self) but, as an American of Irish ethnicity, an outsider to British patriarchy

---

[344] See, on this story, Leon Edel, *Henry James: The Treacherous Years: 1895–1901*, pp. 103–106.

[345] Henry James, *The Bostonians, Novels 1881–1886*, ed. William T. Stafford (New York: The Library of America, 1985), pp. 801–1220.

[346] Henry James, *The Princess Casamassima, Novels 1880–1890*, ed. Daniel Mark Fogel (New York: The Library of America, 1989), pp. 1–554.

[347] See Rudyard Kipling, "The White Man's Burden," *The Collected Poems of Rudyard Kipling* (London: Wordsworth, 1994). See also Rudyard Kipling, *Something of Myself and Other Autobiographical Writings* (Cambridge: Cambridge University Press, 2013).

as well. I believe, though he came to love and indeed flourish in Britain's form of liberal democracy (he becomes a British citizen during World War I), he shows us Britain's ethical darkness, its imperialism and racism, and how the initiation of British boys into patriarchy was so destructive, both personally and politically.

Certainly, James's courageous example inspired the pathbreaking work of a later great gay artist, the composer Benjamin Britten, who wrote two important operas based respectively, on *The Turn of the Screw* and *Owen Wingrave*.[348] *The Turn of the Screw* (1954) is a remarkable, poignant work innovating voice and music (including pentatonic scales and celesta)[349] expressing the psychic confusion, disassociation, and loss of a sense of the real and imagined of an abused boy, exacerbated by a homophobic culture that refuses to acknowledge let alone take seriously such abuse or how to deal with the damage it inflicts. It is a work that, unsurprisingly, Britten (preoccupied from boyhood with the patriarchal violence inflicted on boys) called "nearest to me."[350] And in *Owen Wingrave* (1970), Owen, who wants to break the long-standing patriarchal family tradition of serving in the military, is opposed by his family and fiancée. The oldest male member of the family, General Sir Philip Wingrave, is played by Britten's lover, Peter Pears (also the opera's narrator), who, in fact, had, like Owen, broken with his family tradition of imperialistic military service but, unlike Owen, had the support of the person he loved. Owen locks himself in an allegedly haunted room where an ancestor killed a boy and himself is found dead in the morning. In each case, innocent boys or young men are destroyed by a patriarchal culture that will not see or acknowledge the culture's unjust demands on the vulnerable and the innocent.

Britten was a pacifist, and would go on musically to explore the patriarchal sacrifice of young men in war the *War Requiem* (1961), the most musically well-articulated, powerful, and ambitious expression of the

---

[348] See, for further discussion of Britten's operas as resisting British patriarchy and homophobia, including the roots of his art in his loving relationship with the singer Peter Pears, David A. J. Richards, *Why Love Leads to Justice: Love Across the Boundaries* (New York: Cambridge University Press, 2016), pp. 31–72.

[349] See, for illuminating discussion, Humphrey Carpenter, *Benjamin Britten: a Biography* (New York: Charles Scribner's Sons, 1992), pp. 337–340.

[350] Quoted in Neil Powell, *Benjamin Britten: A Life for Music* (New York: Henry Holt and Company, 2013), at p. 327.

pacifism of Britten and his lover, Peter Pears. *The War Requiem* prominently uses the antiwar poetry of Wilfrid Owen, who was killed fighting in World War I, and its conception called for soloists from three of the leading nations of World War II: Great Britain (Peter Pears), Germany (Dietrich Fischer-Dieskau), and the Soviet Union (Galina Vishnevskaya).[351] Fischer-Dieskau had, in fact, fought on the German side in that war. The emotional cornerstone of the work are settings of two Owen poems, sung by the tenor, Peter Pears, and the baritone, Fischer-Dieskau. The first is the Owen poem, "The Parable of the Old Man and the Young," which the work sets in the original Owen version, based on the Abraham-Isaac narrative in which Abraham is about to sacrifice his son, as God commanded, and is then stopped by an angel, but in Owen's version, "the old man would not so but slew his son / And half the seed of Europe, one by one."[352] The other is a redacted version of Owen's poem, "Strange Meeting"[353] about two soldiers, British and German, who meet after death. They realize they killed each other and realize the futility and loss thus endured, "The pity of war / Let us sleep now."[354]

Britten and Pears make their artistic case for pacifism in a work of both thunderous indignation and piercing pity, which gives some sense of what lay behind their lifelong pacifism. There was the searing sense of many Britons after World War I that Britain had sacrificed young men in a war unjust in its ends and means and catastrophic in its consequences (World War II). The Owen poem about Abraham and Isaac is the vehicle to express their indignation at war that severs intimate connections. And the musical setting of Owen's "Strange Meeting," which ends the work, embraces in an inclusive pity both the British (Pears) and German (Fischer-Dieskau)

---

[351] Because of opposition from the Soviet bureaucracy, Vishnevskaya was unable to sing at the premiere of the work at Coventry Cathedral, which had been bombed by the Germans during the war; but, the three voices for whom the work was written are heard on the recording of the *War Requiem*, Benjamin Britten conducting, on the London label and available on CD, recorded in Kingsway Hall, London, January 1963.

[352] See Wilfrid Owen, *The Collected Poems of Wilfred Owen*, ed. C. D. Lewis (New York: New Directions Book, 1963) first published, 1920), p. 42.

[353] For Owen's full version, see id., pp. 35–6.

[354] The redacted version omits some lines from the original, and adds two lines near the end. . For the full redacted version, see libretto to Benjamin Britten, *War Requiem*, conducted by Benjamin Britten, London, at pp. 50 and 52.

---

soldiers, whom patriarchy has divided from their common plight and common humanity.

James on Women's Plight: *Washington Square* and *Portrait of a Lady*

James's secret self had, as we have seen, been nurtured in close relationships to his mother and Aunt Kate, and he had close relationships to women throughout his life. There is little doubt that, in view of his father's and brother's homophobia, James saw his own plight as a gay man, his secret self, in the plight of women, in particular, patriarchal control of women's choices in matters of love and marriage. It is the subject of two important novels: *Washington Square* and *Portrait of a Lady*.

James writes *Washington Square*[355] very much out of his own experience. A wealthy New York doctor (modeled on his brother, William) has a daughter, Catherine Sloper, a romantic imaginative girl, "a rather plain and unpretentious girl," as Edel observes.[356] She falls in love with a handsome impecunious young man, Morris Townsend. The novel gives a brilliant picture of a father's clumsiness in dealing with his daughter's love and his crude failure to spare her feelings. He is a successful medical man and also a martinet, and his skills in diagnosis and doctoring seem to have ill-equipped him for the simple task of attending to his daughter's heart.[357] Dr. Sloper, having talked with Morris's honest sister, has good reason to believe that Morris is a gold digger and tells his daughter she will not inherit his substantial estate if she marries him. Catherine decides to elope with Morris nonetheless, but when she tells him she will no longer be a rich heiress, he abandons her. Years later, after her father's death, Catherine spurns her lover. Henry's sympathies are clearly with the daughter. And in terms of his recent life, she is an image of himself as victim of his brother's—and America's—failure to understand either his feelings or his career.[358]

---

[355] Henry James, *Washington Square, Novels 1881–1886*, ed. William T. Stafford (New York: The Library of America, 1985), pp. 1–190.

[356] Leon Edel, *Henry James: The Conquest of London: 1870–1881*, p. 398.

[357] Id., p. 398.

[358] Id., p. 399.

The protagonist in *Portrait of a Lady,* Isabel Archer, one of Henry James's most unforgettable characters, is certainly not "plain and unpretentious," nor does she face anything like the crude patriarchal father that Catherine Sloper both loves and comes to resist. Isabel is not only beautiful but highly intelligent and willful, certainly as inexperienced, even as naive, as Catherine, but facing altogether more subtle patriarchal forces and, like Catherine, a disastrous choice of both a lover and, in Isabel's case, a husband. The extraordinary power of this long and complex novel, in which James achieves one of the high points of his artistic achievement, is how deeply and sympathetically he enters into Isabel's psyche. It is as if he is working out through her, as an alter ego, the perilous search for an enduring love that would, at once, marry imaginative artistic and erotic passion to the responsible exercise of ethical freedom, as thoughtful Americans in the Puritan tradition, like James, were coming to understand ethical freedom—based on what remains valuable in that tradition, yet because of its patriarchal assumptions, critically deficient and morally problematic. James later described his ambition in writing this novel: "Place the center of the subject in the young woman's own consciousness."[359] It was, in fact, very much his own, thus the novel's revelatory and unidealized intimacy.

What is remarkable in the novel is how seriously James, a gay man who writes from the experience of his secret self so damaged by patriarchy, takes both dimensions of Isabel's quest—both erotic, imaginative passion and ethical responsibility. Perhaps, only George Eliot, whose work James admired, created comparable real women in which sexual love and a sense of ethics were taken as seriously, usually, as in James, to disastrous effect (e.g., Maggie Tulliver in *Mill on the Floss* or Dorothea Brooke in *Middlemarch* or Gwendolyn Harleath in *Daniel Deronda*).[360]

James's model for Isabel, like so many of his other novels, is based on his close relationships to people he knew so well and sometimes loved, in this case, to his beloved cousin, Minnie Temple, who died prematurely of tuberculosis. "[James] was to confess that he had actually thought of

---

[359] Henry James, "The Portrait of a Lady in Prefaces to the New York Edition," in Henry James, *Literary Criticism,* ed. Leo Edel (New York: The Library of America, 1984), pp. 1070–1085, at p. 1079.

[360] See, for a revelatory recent exploration of George Eliot's life and art, Philip Davis, *The Transferred Life of George Eliot* (Oxford: Oxford University Press, 2017).

Minnie in creating the eager imagination and the intellectual shortcomings of his heroine. Death had deprived her of the trials—and the joys—of maturity. Henry, as artist, could imagine and 'complete' that which had been left undone. Nevertheless, if Isabel has something of Henry's cousin in her makeup, she has much of Henry himself."[361] Minnie had never traveled to Europe, but James imagines how her life would have gone if, like him, she had lived in Europe and had achieved independence from family (as James had from the success of his writing).

In James's narrative, Isabel is brought to Europe by her wealthy aunt and achieves financial independence, becoming an heiress when her cousin, the sickly Ralph Touchett, the son of her aunt, persuades his wealthy father to leave his estate to Isabel. Isabel does not know of Ralph's role in arranging the bequest, nor of his motives, according her a freedom that will enable this remarkable woman, whom he loves, to do with her life what she pleases—a freedom that, as Ralph later realizes, has been used disastrously. Both Ralph's role (concealed from Isabel) and the later structure of the narrative are patriarchally structured: Isabel's freedom is essentially a freedom to decide whom she will marry, and controlling men manipulate her choices. In addition to Ralph, there are three other men among whom she chooses: Caspar Goodwood, an American successful businessman who had earlier proposed to her in America and pursues her throughout the novel and to whom Isabel is sexually attracted but finds his forceful masculinity repelling; a wealthy British lord, Warburton, an enlightened, if somewhat dull, British liberal who would have given Isabel even greater wealth and much greater status; and Gilbert Osmond, an American transplanted to Italy, where he has become a highly refined but impecunious aesthete (his first wife had died, and he has a child, Pansy, not, as it turns out, the child of his wife but the offspring of a love affair he had with Madame Merle, an accomplished pianist who becomes a friend of Isabel's).

Isabel is the victim of two deceptions and manipulations—that of Ralph, who conceals from her his role and reasons for making her an heiress and that of Osmond and Madame Merle, who conceal their earlier sexual liaison from Isabel and conspire that Osmond should so ingratiate himself to Isabel that she will fall in love and marry him, bringing him her fortune to save him from indigency and enable him to live the life of artistic

---

[361] Leon Edel, *Henry James: The Conquest of London: 1870–1881*, p. 422.

refinement he seeks, and thus enable Pansy, the daughter of Osmond and Madame Merle, to marry the kind of man Osmond wants her to marry. In fact, Pansy has fallen in love with another young man, and the father, once married to Isabel, ferociously exercises his patriarchal privileges to separate them, indeed placing Pansy with nuns for appropriate care more consistent with her father's aims for her.

The novel falls into two parts: first, the narrative up to Isabel's marriage to Osmond and second, several years after the marriage. Isabel has lost a child in childbirth and has come to realize her mistake in marrying Osmond—a marriage against which all her friends, including Ralph, had warned her. She also eventually learns, from Osmond's estranged sister, of Osmond's and Madame Merle's affair, of Pansy their child, and of their plan for Osmond's marriage to the wealthy American heiress. When she learns that Ralph Touchett is dying, Isabel leaves her husband and returns to Britain to minister to Ralph, as he is dying, and to finally learn the role he played in her becoming an heiress. After Ralph's death and Caspar Goodwood's passionate embrace of her from which she flees, Isabel returns to Italy.

The artistic high point of the novel is its justly famous forty-second chapter. Isabel does not yet know of the truth of Osmond's affair with Madame Merle but had earlier come into a room finding them in intimate conversation—an image that haunts her. But her husband has just come to talk with her insisting that she encourage Lord Warburton to marry Pansy, to whom Warburton is attracted, though Pansy loves another. Isabel spends the evening thinking about the significance of what her husband has just told her. Nothing happens, but psychologically, everything happens.[362]

Something had happened between husband and wife, something that revealed to Isabel "her deep distrust of her husband, and this was what darkened the world.[363] She knew of no wrong that he had done. He was not violent; he was not cruel. She simply believed that he hated her."[364] What had happened? During their courtship, when his artistic interests and sensitivities so moved her, "[s]he had effaced herself and had made

---

[362] See, for an illuminating account of the novel and James's work on the novel, Michael Gorra, *Portrait of a Novel.*

[363] Henry James, *The Portrait of a Lady*, p. 629, *Novels 1881–1886,* ed. William T. Stafford (New York: The Library of America, 1985).

[364] Id., p. 630.

---

herself small, pretending there was less of herself than there really was. It was because she had been under the extraordinary charm that he, on his side, had taken pains to put forth. He was not changed; he had not disguised himself, during the year of his courtship, any more than her. But she had seen only half his nature then, as one saw the disk of the moon when it was partly masked by the shadow of the earth. She saw the full moon now; she saw the whole man."[365] When they were courting, Osmond had told her "she was the most imaginative women he had known," and for her part, "[t]here was an indefinable beauty about him—in his situation, in his mind, in his face. She had felt at the same time that he was helpless and ineffectual, but the feeling had taken the form of a tenderness, which was the very flower of respect."[366] She had married him in part "in order to do something finely appreciable with her money" but also because of "a sense of the earnestness of his affection and a delight in her personal qualities. He was better than anyone else."[367] Now, however, she realized "the magnitude of *his* deception. It has been like the bell that was to ring up the curtain upon the real drama of their lives. He said to her one day that she had too many ideas and that she must get rid of them."[368] "He really meant it; he would have liked her to have nothing of her own but her pretty appearance. She knew she had too many ideas; she had more even than he supposed, many more than she had expressed to him when he asked her to marry him. Yes, she *had* been hypocritical; she liked him so much. She had too many ideas for her self, but that was just what one married for, to share them with someone else."[369]

Now she found that her husband had no interest in the life of the mind, nor respect for freedom of mind—"u]nder all his culture, his cleverness, his amenity, under his good nature, his facility, his knowledge of life, his egotism lay hidden like a serpent in a bank of flowers."[370] The Osmond she had come to see did not live in the kind of aristocratic world she respected. "Her notion of the aristocratic life was simply the union of great knowledge with great liberty—the knowledge would give on a sense of duty and the

---

[365] Id.
[366] Id., p. 631.
[367] Id., p. 632.
[368] Id.
[369] Id., pp. 632–633.
[370] Id., p. 634.

liberty a sense of enjoyment. But for Osmond, it was altogether a thing of forms, a conscious, calculated attitude, an immense esteem for tradition."[371] "When Isabel saw this rigid system closing about her, draped though it was in pictured tapestries, that sense of darkness and suffocation took possession of her; she seemed to be shut up with an odor of mold and decay."[372] When Isabel resisted and spoke to Osmond of her belief in and need of freedom, "she could see that he was ineffably ashamed of her. The real offence, as she ultimately perceived, was her having a mind of her own. She was not a daughter of the Puritans, but for that, she believed in such a thing as purity."[373] Osmond had come to hate her because he now realized Isabel had and valued a free mind that rebelled at the patriarchal forms that Osmond mindlessly worshipped. The crisis point in the marriage had come when Osmond pressured Isabel to enforce his patriarchal demands on whom his daughter Pansy should marry, a man she did not love. It was at this point that Isabel, resisting his demands and the patriarchal conception of women's roles that motivated those demands, echoes, in her lonely and despairing ruminations, the reflections of Hawthorne's Hester Prynne.

In this remarkable chapter (42), James anticipates and exemplifies the stream of consciousness his brother, the psychologist William James, was to discuss a few years later.[374] But he goes beyond his brother in exemplifying as well the force of the unconscious in human motivation—an idea that his brother would criticize at some, rather unpersuasive length,[375] and the role free association would and does play in revealing unconscious motives. Isabel is free associating, long before Freud, among others, had given it a name,[376] and she reveals to herself thoughts and feelings she could not

---

[371] Id., p. 635.

[372] Id., pp. 635–636.

[373] Id., p. 636.

[374] See, on this point, Michael Gorra, *Portrait of a Novel*, pp. 234–35.

[375] See William James, *The Principles of Psychology Volume 1* (New York: Dover, 2015; originally published, 1890), pp. 162–176, 202–213, 379–80, 383–93, 489, 503–4. For criticism of James's arguments, see Donald Levy, *Freud Among the Philosophers: The Psychoanalytic Unconscious and Its Philosophical Critics* (New Haven: Yale University Press, 1996), pp. 64–82, 167–168.

[376] On the development of the ideas of the unconscious and free association, see Henry F. Ellenberger, *The Discovery of the Unconscious: The History and Evolution of Dynamic Psychiatry* (New York: BasicBooks, 1970).

previously acknowledge or, in psychoanalytic parlance, had repressed.[377] They now flood into her thoughts—previously unacceptable thoughts for a good woman, namely, that her husband hates her and is ashamed of her and that her psyche calls for and demands resistance. And then there is the conversation of Osmond and Madame Merle that she observed prior to her meeting with her husband. There is an unconscious thought she has about that as well, though it will only be brought to consciousness later when the duplicities of Madame Merle and Osmond confront Isabel inescapably.

In this novel, Henry James reveals, once again, his own secret self—the sensual, romantic, and erotic attractions of European culture (in particular, Italy, France, and Britain) and how he had found in himself a voice—one that he usually silenced, both to express desire and to be skeptical in a homophobic culture, whether a deep love, uniting passion with moral intelligence, could be and was possible. If it was not possible for Isabel Archer with all her intelligence and advantages, how could it be possible for any person, let alone Henry James, a gay son damaged by a patriarchal family and finding it so difficult to resist? Isn't that what James wants to share with us through *The Portrait of a Lady* or, should we say, *Portrait of an Artist?* It is that autobiographically intimate.

But there is also, as always with James, the ethical dimension, quite clearly stated in Isabel's free associations. Even her passion for Osmond apparently had, in her mind, an ethical dimension. He was, she then believed, poor and artistic and "better than anyone else," and she would save him, a man she loved and respected, raising him up to her level through her wealth. And there is her confession that she diminished and silenced herself as a way of expressing her love for Osmond, suggesting accommodation to the terms of inequality in patriarchal marriages, an accommodation she comes both to see and regret, for, like James, she had a secret self that she would not show her lover. Apparently, Osmond was also not sexually attractive to Isabel, at least in the terms Caspar Goodwood was. Is James acknowledging, as far as he was able, a fear of a certain dominating, attractive sexuality? But there is also the question that puzzles all readers of the novel: why does Isabel, after Ralph Touchett dies (the only man in the novel she comes to realize she loved in the heartrending

---

[377] I am indebted for these thoughts and references on Freud and James to conversations with Donald Levy. See, for further discussion, Donald Levy, *Freud Among the Philosophers.*

scene of his death) return to Italy? I think James has given us the answer in Isabel's long free association, her ethical resistance to Osmond's cold, unfeeling demand that Pansy break with the man she loves, placing her in the arms of the patriarchal Catholic church, where her duty as a good Catholic woman, obedient to her father, will be inculcated. Isabel, who already has shown an impulse to ethical self-sacrifice (marrying Osmond), returns to save Pansy from a man Isabel now believes she can resist and effectively resist. If I am right about this, Isabel is acting out of her own realization of her ethical convictions as a free woman who has come to see, in her husband, patriarchy at its intimate best and worst and now must act and resist. Her marriage is a disaster, and she does not return for Osmond. The key is her sense of the damage she may, inadvertently—in her war with Osmond, have done Pansy, and now she sees clearly that this innocent girl is completely in thrall to the patriarchal ambitions of her father and Madame Merle, her mother. Isabel, not the mother of Pansy but more caring than either of her natural parents, returns to resist. Is James, the victim of a patriarchal family, questioning, yet again, abusive parenting? If so, Isabel is, for James, an ethical heroine, resisting Italian Catholic patriarchy. You can see why such resistance would move me, an Italian American man, increasingly skeptical of the patriarchal Christianity into which I was born.

John Banville, in his recent novel *Mrs. Osmond,* attempts to complete the novel after Isabel returns to Italy.[378] He reads Isabel's return, as I do, as based on her care for Pansy. However, Pansy, on Banville's reading, has been corrupted beyond redemption, and Isabel discovers Osmond and Madame Merle had been guilty of a yet worse immorality than their deception of her (namely, exposing Osmond's first wife to likely death by sending her to a city rife with typhoid fever). She settles money and property on Osmond as a basis for separation and confronts him and Merle, as retribution with the extent of their wrongdoing, and leaves them to their own devices. Isabel returns to London, possibly dedicating herself to women's rights, the topic of one of James's political novels.

---

[378] John Banville, *Mrs. Osmond* (New York: Alfred A. Knopf, 2017).

James on Resistance: *The Bostonians*

My reading of *Portrait of a Lady* as a resistance narrative leads me to a comparable reading of the two novels that he wrote directly after *Portrait,* his two most explicitly political novels, *The Bostonians* and *Princess Casamassima.* I am moved to this reading by the resonance each novel had for me when I reread them recently after rereading *Portrait.* Just as in *Portrait,* James gives intimate voice to his secret self through his alter ego, Isabel Archer, as she comes to resist patriarchy. So in *The Bostonians* and *Princess Casamassima,* James gives voice also to his secret self in more explicitly political characters: the radical Bostonian, politically active feminist Olive Chancellor and the little London book-binder, Hyacinth Robinson, drawn into active complicity with terrorism. Olive is the only explicitly gay character in James's fiction, and her feminism is psychologically linked in the novel to her lesbian passion, disastrous as it turns out, for a young woman, Verena Tarrant. Hyacinth's sexuality is, like James's, more covert, repressed as James's was, and the novel brilliantly explores this damaged young man (as usual in James, the product of abusively careless parents) drawn by his love for a young man and passionate idealization of a woman (the princess) into radical politics and terror, again disastrously (Hyacinth commits suicide rather than kill another, as his terrorist friends require). Both novels, in their different ways, explore, as bravely as James was ever to allow himself, the complex psychological and ethical dynamics of gay sexual passion in homophobic cultures and how those cultures make resistance so psychologically fraught and sometimes tragic. I myself find the experience of loss of both Verena and Hyacinth unbearably moving, as both—so passionately in love—realize they have never been loved, and that their ethical impulses have not, as they had hoped, married their sexual passions but destroyed them.

James himself came to regard *The Bostonians* as unsuccessful, excluding the novel from the New York edition. He confessed to William, "I should have been more rapid and had a lighter hand." His readers of that time would have agreed heartily.[379] Several, including his aunt Kate and his brother William, thought Miss Birdseye, a character in the novel, had unjustly "lampooned a much-respected Boston reformer, Miss Elizabeth Peabody, the elderly sister-in-law of Hawthorne, whose good works and

---

[379]   Leon Edel, *Henry James: The Middle Years: 1882–1895,* p. 138.

crusading zeal were famous."[380] And the British militant suffragette, Mary Wood, who in 1914 took a hatchet to Sargent's extraordinary portrait of James, may have been motivated by a similar aggrieved response.[381] I agree neither with James, his contemporary readers, nor with Edel, who is critical of the novel.[382] James allowed himself in *The Bostonians* to explore, as frankly as he was ever to do so, the psychological and ethical tensions between Boston's radical ethical culture (its radical abolitionism, for example) and its repressive sexism and homophobia. It is the novel in which he most directly engages with the contradictions he experienced as the child of Henry James Sr.—his father's relentless search for universal ethical truth as the essence of what is legitimate in religion (a search allied to that of his friend, Emerson), and his patriarchal rigidity—extreme sexism and homophobia. It was in this family with this domineering presence, dragging his wife, aunts, and five children hither and yon in his relentless search for ethical truth, that Henry James with his secret self experienced at firsthand not only his father's homophobia but that of his beloved brother, William.

Both Henry's turn to writing fiction and his leaving America for Europe were acts of resistance to the patriarchal tyrannies of both his father and brother. Henry creates and explores the psyche of Isabel Archer in *Portrait of a Lady*, as a way of exploring both the ethical and psychological pitfalls of such resistance when love is patriarchally defined. It is that terrible and terrifying truth that Isabel comes to see in her free associations in chapter 42 of *Portrait*, namely, her choice among lovers were never really based on freedom and equality, as she supposed (once she was an heiress) but subject to manipulation by her close and well-meaning friend, Ralph Touchett, and by the duplicities of Osmond and Madame Merle. When she comes to see that her patriarchal husband objectifies her, she finally resists, leaving him and returning, in my view, to resist his patriarchal demands on his innocent and vulnerable daughter, Pansy, whom Isabel, herself childless, has grown to love.

James carries his investigation into patriarchy and resistance into what must have been for him more personally difficult waters when he starkly

---

[380] Id., p. 142.

[381] On this episode, see Colm Tóibín, "Shadow and Substance," op. cit., pp. 43–44. The painting was repaired.

[382] Leon Edel, *Henry James: The Middle Years: 1882–1895*, pp. 138–39.

divides his father's contradictory psychology into two characters: the ethical abolitionist (strikingly, a woman, Olive Chancellor) and the patriarchal sexist (the Southerner, Basil Ransom). The novel poses its drama in a love triangle—Olive Chancellor loves Verena Tarrant, and their arrangement is interrupted by a handsome Southerner, Basil Ransom, who fought for the South in the Civil War and had now come North to advance his career and fell in love with Verena and she with him. It is quite unsurprising that James, who experienced at firsthand the contradictions in a father's vaunted search for ethical truth and his sexism and homophobia, should have created in Olive Chancellor a character who carries Bostonian radical abolitionism beyond race to gender but whose feminism is as much based on woman's hierarchical superiority over men as his father's sexism was based on the hierarchy of men over women. (Miss Birdseye is, by comparison, gentle and humane to all, including Ransom. Another feminist character in the novel, a woman physician, Dr. Prance, tells Ransom, "There is room for improvement in both sexes,"[383] perceiving patriarchy as a harm to both sexes.) Chancellor never imagines that patriarchy itself is an injury to both men and women, and her ethical impulses are thus themselves patriarchal, which takes the paradoxical form of domineering the young woman she comes to love. Olive's love for Verena is as distorted, indeed blinded, by patriarchy as Isabel's love for Osmond.

What makes the novel psychologically and ethically remarkable is the way James explores the matter of voice in resistance. Olive, the radical abolitionist, lacks the kind of voice effectively to communicate her ethical feminism, and immediately recognizes, when she hears Verena speak, the voice the movement needs. Her passion for Verena arises from her sense that under her tutelage (living with her), Verena's voice may be rendered more powerful, intelligent, and resonant. In fact, however, Verena is the product of two of James's usual careless and uncaring parents, who have used Verena's beauty and voice theatrically to advance their own careers in abolitionist Boston, but her voice is a kind of ventriloquism by and for her parents, and later, Olive tragically fails to see whom Verena understandably values and may even, in some sense, love. They are happy to have Olive more or less adopt Verena, because it will advance their ends (another of James's abusive parents). Verena, in fact, does not speak from conviction

---

[383] See Henry James, *The Bostonians, Novels 1881–1886*, ed. William T. Stafford (New York: The Library of America, 1985), pp. 801–1,220, at p. 838.

but has cultivated a voice she knows moves people, but it is certainly nothing like her real voice, which is largely silent until she meets Basil Ransom. Basil Ransom reads Verena correctly as a quite conventional young woman with the usual desires such women have and woos and wins her because he is right about her.

The psychological crux of the novel is that both Ransom and Olive are both patriarchally controlling of Verena, though ethically they are on opposing ethical sides: Ransom has begun writing reactionary literature defending, one surmises, traditional Southern patriarchal and racist values, and Olive is in the radical abolitionist tradition, which condemned American patriarchy and the racism and sexism that it rationalized. There is, however, the difference between them that Ransom and Verena both live within patriarchy, and Ransom reads Verena much as the quite conventional woman she is (pleasing her parents and Olive by becoming their "preposterous puppet" instead of "standing forth in her freedom as well as in her loveliness!")[384] and loves her for the woman she, in fact, is. Understandably, she falls in love with him. As in contrast, Olive passionately espouses a feminism hostile to patriarchy, but her interpretation of feminism centers on harms to women alone and men as the perpetrators of these harms in contrast to Hawthorne's and Melville's view that patriarchy harms both men and women. It is for this reason that Olive does not question patriarchy and its role in repressing voice but, in her relationship to Verena, reenacts it. Verena is much more Olive's victim than she is Ransom's, who at least listens to Verena's voice. You can see why she falls in love with him.

There is also the matter of Olive's lesbianism, which never in the novel takes an overt sexual form, very much part of James's experience in light of his sister, Alice's, relationship to Katherine Loring.[385] Apparently, Olive's ethical feminism is disassociated from any sense of human sexuality, her own and others, thus she cannot or will not see Verena's falling sexually in love with a patriarchal man as anything but betrayal. Yet when Verena chooses Ransom, James is very clear that life with this man may well be one of shedding tears as she does when she abandons Olive before a great inaugural feminist speech Verena is to give: "It is to be feared that with this union, so far from brilliant, into which she was about to enter, these

---

384 Henry James, *The Bostonians*, p. 1114.
385 See Jean Strouse, *Alice James: A Biography*, pp. 244–245.

were not the last she was destined to shed."[386] Verena is caught between two patriarchies and chooses the one conventional for women of that time.

But the tragic center of the novel is for me Olive Chancellor, as, like Isabel Archer, she suffers the dual betrayals of love and ethics: Verena did not love her as Olive wanted to be loved, and Verena did not share Olive's abolitionist feminist convictions (as Osmond, a patriarchal man, did not share Isabel's). Her confusion and rage and loss—always rooted in integrity—are heart breaking, and James wants us to see and feel both her ethical integrity and her broken heart. His feeling for her suggests he sees through her how much his patriarchal father had distorted ethics and made, for his vulnerable and perceptive son with his secret self, love something distorted by domination and fear. Olive's tragedy is, for James, his father's and his family's, and thus carried in James's psyche as a cautionary warning: under patriarchy, love at your peril. Against this background, it is not unsurprising that James should have been notorious among his friends for his love of gossip and endless sexual curiosity, observing closely the amours of others (sometimes even assisting, as in the bisexual Morton Fullerton's sexual affair with James's close friend, the novelist Edith Wharton),[387] sometimes even flirting with and perhaps kissing young men he came to love but going no further.[388]

James on Trauma and Terrorism: *Princess Casamassima*

The protagonist of *Princess Casamassima*, Hyacinth Robinson, is, in my view, the most explicitly repressed male homosexual character in James's fiction, and for this reason, James, writing from his secret self, goes to great pains in the novel to distinguish Hyacinth from the relatively privileged background and life of Henry James. Hyacinth is the illegitimate son of Lord Frederick Purvis, murdered by his French mother, Florentine Vivier, whom the son met only once in the infirmary of Milbank Prison before she died (not knowing she was his mother). He is brought up by a friend of his mother's, Miss Pynsent, assisted by Mr. Vetch, a violinist, who constitute

---

386 Henry James, *The Bostonians, Novels 1881–1886*, ed. William T. Stafford (New York: The Library of America, 1985), p. 1,219.

387 See, on this point, R. W. B. Lewis, *Edith Wharton: A Biography* (New York: Fromm International, 1985), pp. 183–232.

388 See Hugh Stevens, *Henry James and Sexuality*, pp. 167–68.

a parental pair, advising, admonishing, and helping.[389] James, who had lived in London, here explores a world of poverty and disadvantage he did not know at first hand, but had clearly closely observed and regarded as unjust. It is James's most Dickensian novel and a tribute to Dickens, a novelist James loved.

So with all these differences between Hyacinth Robinson and Henry James, where are the similarities? There is Hyacinth's repressed homosexuality not only marked in the novel by his name (Hyacinth in Greek mythology was the lover of Apollo) but by his passionate attachment to a young working man and activist on behalf of working men, Paul Muniment, who lives with his loquacious sister, Rosy, clearly modeled on James's sister, Alice James. But there is also that Hyacinth is an artist (our little hero's being a genuine artist),[390] albeit constrained by circumstances to be a book binder, and James's struggle to become an artist was central to his life. Most importantly, James brought to his fiction his own sense of being brought up in an abusive family dominated by his patriarchal father, thus as in a sense, an orphan, and James imagined and created Hyacinth, clearly an orphan, as a way of showing developmentally the effects on the psyche of a child, who is an artist, of the trauma of learning not only of careless and uncaring parents but the murderous violence of his mother against his father. Hyacinth only meets his mother once and is not told she is his mother, and he only learns later about his origin, which haunts the rest of his life, in particular, the injustice of his noble father's treatment of his mother and his mother's rage and vengeful murder ending in prison. His mother and father are real to him, but they were never real parents, and James brilliantly explores the effects of such absence and traumatic loss on later attachments.

There are two such attachments in the working classes, Paul Muniment, and a childhood friend, Millicent Henning, a practical and level-headed cockney whom some readers regard as the most brilliantly realized character in the book.[391]

The pivotal upper-class attachment of Hyacinth is to the Princess Casamassima, a woman of American and Italian parentage who had been given in an arranged married by her family to an Italian prince and

---

[389] Leon Edel, *Henry James: The Middle Years 1882–1895*, p. 205.

[390] Henry James, *Princess Casamassima*, p. 360.

[391] See id., p. 190.

who, as she tells Hyacinth, had been humiliated, outraged, and tortured by them—by the prince and the prince's family—and thus identified with the numerous class who could be put on tolerable footing only by a revolution.[392] The princess is drawn to support revolution and terrorism rather than works of practical aid to the poor, as in the novel, is Aurora Languish. Hyacinth, with the festering sense of the injustice inflicted by his noble father, is drawn into the princess's revolutionary world by her and his friend, Paul Muniment. The princess and Muniment become lovers, leaving Hyacinth out in the cold. Hyacinth has now committed himself to Diedrich Hoffendahl (a kind of patriarchal father figure in the absence of a real father and mother and the trauma they inflicted on their child), the master of terror, and agreed to kill a duke.

Between his commitment to the cause and his being given a gun, Hyacinth has reconsidered. Having received a small inheritance from the dressmaker who brought him up, he traveled to Paris and Venice and been so impressed with the values of such civilizations that he lost his revolutionary ardor. Abandoned by the princess and Muniment, Hyacinth is quite alone and realizes that in killing the Duke, he would be repeating his mother's murder of his father. He turns the gun on himself, committing suicide.

James may very well have thought of himself, like Hyacinth, as the victim of injustice, even trauma. But he had also found his artistic voice and gave voice through it, as my discussion of his novels shows, to his experience—writing from his hidden self and yet finding ways through his novels and short stories to reveal aspects of his hidden self and the problems of love and ethical responsibility that he came to think were more broadly shared and should be discussed and explored. James found Hyacinth such an illuminating alter ego for his art because he could explore what happens when injustice, including abusive upbringing, silences voice or disables an intelligent artistic man like Hyacinth from finding his voice. To that extent, James in this remarkable novel shows us what we saw in chapter 2 in James Gilligan's work on violent criminals, namely, that traumatic injustices can so damage people that the lack the competence to realize a sense of worth and are thus vulnerable to shaming of their manhood and propensities to violence. In those subject to such injustice, the propensity to violence

---

[392] See Henry James, *The Princess Casamassima, Novels 1886–1890*, ed. Daniel Mark Fogel (New York: The Library of America, 1989), p. 206.

is directed against others or oneself. Hyacinth's suicide, once he decides injustice should not be resisted through killing, experiences worthlessness, abandoned by those he loved, that expresses itself in violence against the self. So in this novel, James continues to explore both the psychology and ethics of resistance to injustice and suggests as well how and why terrorism can become a political religion, as it does for Princess Casamassima, as her humiliation expresses itself in terroristic violence.

None of James's novels that deal with abusive parents goes as far or as deep as *Princess Casamassima,* drawing, more directly than any of his other works, on what he experienced as a child in the patriarchal domination of his father—his irrational outbursts and bullying that James as a child would, I believe, have perceived as violence. Of all the men I study in this book, only James Gilligan comes from a family with a patriarchal father more violent than James's (see chapter 7), but I believe James's experience as a child may have been experienced by him in the same way. How else can we understand how far this novel goes in exposing the psyche of Hyacinth, who is so damaged by the violence and abandonment of his parents, so ignored and abandoned by the people he comes to love or thinks he loves? As we shall see, Jim Gilligan found a way out from this world, but he dedicated his life to showing us this world and our responsibility to helping those afflicted to find their way out. James cannot go this far in *Princess Casmassima,* but he goes surely quite far. Hyacinth is, as James tells us, an artist who has not had the fair opportunity to embrace his vocation as an artist. The injustice is his tragedy, and perhaps James, in the most ethically progressive of his novels, is insisting that we see our unjust complicity with such injustice.

CHAPTER 5

George Santayana on Resisting Homophobia

I entered Harvard College in 1962 and began my intense interest in moral and political philosophy, taking courses and seminars from John Rawls, who supervised my senior thesis and continuing my studies at Oxford University in 1966 to 1968 first under H. L. A. Hart and then G. J. Warnock, writing my doctoral thesis, "A Theory of Reasons for Action," which was published by Oxford University Press in 1971. (I was then at Harvard Law School, 1968–1971.) It was while at Harvard College that I first read George Santayana, in particular, his multivolume, *The Life of Reason*. George Santayana and his work fascinated me because even back then, his homosexuality was well known among Harvard undergraduates. I recall a dinner at Kirkland House, where I lived, where a Harvard philosophy professor, Henry David Aiken, who apparently knew Santayana or of Santayana, told homophobic jokes about Santayana touching desirable Harvard men under the table. Even then, I was not amused. Harvard College, founded by Puritans, was, even in 1962 to 1968, rather behind the curve in discussing homosexuality, and I was a bit shocked when I returned to Harvard in 1968 to study law and taught a section in legal philosophy at the college (taught by Professor Charles Fried at the Harvard School of Law) that students quite openly discussed their own homosexuality and, to my discomfiture, asked me about my own sexuality. By that time, I had worked out my own views on moral and political philosophy, inspired by John Rawls and his reconstruction of the moral philosophy of Immanuel

Kant, and no longer regarded homosexual sex as wrong. I had satisfied my own ethical conscience but was not yet ready to live a gay life. I would make arguments for gay rights only later after I had fallen in love with my life partner and lived more truthfully in relationship to my parents and sister (the issues were, for me, one).

Reading George Santayana while I was an undergraduate meant as much to me as reading late Henry James had meant to me when I was sixteen to eighteen. My studies with John Rawls, now regarded as the leading moral and political philosopher of his generation, had led to the close study of the great philosophers of the Western tradition (Rawls was remarkable back then for wedding the contemporary study of normative philosophy to interest in the history of philosophy). The study was quite abstract, as philosophical argument usually is, and did not engage my secret self until Rawls himself, in a memorable discussion I had with him during my senior year, questioned the traditional condemnation of homosexuality as anachronistic and unjust. The modern philosopher during that period who did more personally engage my secret self and my burgeoning interest in philosophy was George Santayana.

I knew even then that Santayana was gay and, though born in Spain, lived his early life in the Boston area and had studied at Harvard with William James, who admired and supported Santayana. *The Life of Reason* secured him tenure in the Harvard Philosophy Department though the then president of the university had made homophobic aspersions on Santayana's qualifications. Santayana left Harvard and spent the rest of his life in Europe, finally settling in Rome, Italy. My interest in Santayana, like my earlier interest in Henry James, was a way of exploring own sense of being an outsider, being gay and Italian American (Santayana was gay and Spanish), and also now drenched, as both James and Santayana had been, in the high Puritan culture of Boston and Cambridge, Massachusetts. For all these reasons, Santayana's life and work spoke to me, including why, like him and James, I increasingly felt I had to live abroad for several years though that would mean for me loneliness, separated from my beloved father, mother, and sister. How, I wondered, had Santayana made sense philosophically of his sexual orientation and his Latin ethnicity, and how might his struggle illuminate mine and others? What had he come to see about American homophobic Puritanism, which he grew to hate and drove him, eventually, abroad? As it turned out, our journeys were quite different and much of the difference connects, as I explain below, on our very different families and on the American culture of the civil rights movement and anti-Vietnam War resistance (the 1960s) which moved and nurtured me, as it did so many others of my generation. Santayana came to his philosophical maturity in a very different America and a very different Harvard College.

Santayana's *The Life of Reason*

My interest in Santayana's work during my undergraduate years centered on *The Life of Reason*,[393] a masterpiece of historically informed contemporary philosophy, beautifully written and well argued, in which, unlike most philosophy I then studied, Santayana's personal voice—ironic and playful—was quite clear. His sense that earlier philosophers (Socrates and Plato, in particular) had shown us how to lead a rational life; his naturalistic atheism and belief in science as the only road to empirical truth and condemnation of the role religion had played in supporting intolerance and fanaticism, thus his admiration for Spinoza, his liberalism (albeit more aristocratic than egalitarian),[394] and as a subsidiary theme, his ongoing criticism of the evil of repressing sexual interests and passions on wholly irrational grounds. As I was myself gay with my still secret self and struggling with my Catholic homophobia as a Latin man, both his writing about what I read as gay sexual feeling and his attack on religion (which I read as Catholicism) riveted me. I was otherwise quite alone.

His writing on what I read as gay sexual attraction amazed me: "Each feels in a generic way the presence and attraction of his fellows. He vibrates to their touch, he dreams of their image, he is restless and wistful if

---

[393] See George Santayana, *The Life of Reason Volume 1: Reason in Common Sense* (New York: Dover, 1980, originally published, 1905); *The Life of Reason Volume 2: Reason in Society* (New York: Dover, 1980, originally published, 1905); George Santayana, *The Life of Reason Volume 3: Reason in Religion* (New York: Collier, 1962, originalliy published, 1905); George Santayana, *The Life of Reason Volume 4: Reason in Art* (New York: Dover, 1982, originally published 1905); George Santayana, *The Life of Reason Volume 5: Reason in Science* (New York: Dover, 1983, originally published, 1906).

[394] See, on this point, George Santayana, *The Life of Reason Volume 2: Reason in Society_*(New York: Dover, 1980, originally published, 1905), pp. 97–113, 124–134.

---

alone,[395] and later, its thrill, flutter, and absolute sway over happiness and misery."[396]

I was also moved by his remarks on war: "Internecine war, foreign and civil, brought about the greatest setback, which the Life of Reason has ever suffered. It exterminated the Greek and the Italian aristocracies. To call war the soil of courage and virtue is like calling debauchery the soil of love."[397] We were then in the midst of the Vietnam War.

And his writing about irrationalist moral censure of sexual feeling spoke directly to me about the homophobia I had once regarded as in the nature of things:

> Public opinion will come to condemn what in itself was perfectly innocent. The corruption of a given instinct by others and of others by it becomes the ground for long attempts to suppress or enslave it. With the haste and formalism natural to language and to law, external and arbitrary limits are set to its operation. As no inward adjustment can possibly correspond to these conventional barriers and compartments of life, a war between nature and morality breaks out both in society and in each particular bosom—a war in which every victory is a sorrow and every defeat a dishonor. As one instinct after another becomes furious or disorganized, cowardly or criminal, under these artificial restrictions, the public and private conscience turns against it all its forces, necessarily without much nice discrimination; the frank passions of youth are met with a grimace of horror on all sides, with an insistence on reticence and hypocrisy. Such suppression is favourable to corruption: the fancy with a sort of idiotic ingenuity come to supply the place of experience; and nature is rendered vicious and overlaid with pruriency, artifice, and the love of novelty. Hereupon the authorities that rule in such matters naturally redouble their vigilance

---

[395] George Santayana, *The Life of Reason Volume 2 Reason in Society* (New York: Dover, 1980, originally published, 1905), p. 10.

[396] Ibid., p. 21.

[397] Ibid., pp. 82–83.

---

and exaggerate their reasonable censure; chastity begins to seem essentially holy and perpetual virginity ends by becoming an absolute ideal. Thus the disorder in man's life and disposition, when grown intolerable, leads him to condemn the very elements out of which order might have been constituted, and to mistake his total confusion for his total depravity.[398]

I quote the excerpt in its entirety to give some sense of how it seemed to me then, as it stills seems to me now, a quite exact description and indictment of how homophobia arises and its devastating consequences for the psyche of a young boy or man drawn into its unjust demands. It was, in fact, my psyche or the psyche of my secret self, and Santayana showed me that I was not alone, that someone shared my experience and my outrage, and yet was a good, indeed admirable philosopher.

But there was another aspect of the long argument of *The Life of Reason* that gave me reasons for thinking that the religion that had afflicted me was itself reasonably questionable because, as Santayana argued, it could have only an imaginative, mythological meaning[399] as its claims to truth had been supplanted by science—the only road to truth about the human and material world.[400] In a remarkable letter to his teacher, William James, who had expressed appreciation of the first three volumes of *The Life of Reason* he had read, Santayana bitterly denounces religion and Emerson's failure to acknowledge abuses carried out in its name:

Religion was *found out* more than one hundred years ago, and it seems to me intolerable that we should still be condemned to ignore the fact and to give the parsons and the "idealists" a monopoly of indignation and of contemptuous dogmatism. It is they, not we, that are the pest; and while I wish to be just and to understand people's feelings, wherever they are at all significant, I

---

398 Ibid., pp. 17–18.

399 See George Santayana, *The Life of Reason Volume 3 Reason in Religion* (New York: Collier, 1962, originalliy published, 1905).

400 George Santayana, *The Life of Reason Volume 5 Reason in Science* (New York: Dover, 1983, originally published, 1906).

am deliberately minded to be contemptuous toward what seems to me contemptible and not to have any share in the conspiracy of mock respect by which intellectual ignominy and moral stagnation are kept up in our society. What did Emerson know or care about the passionate insanities and political disasters which religion, for instance, has so often been another name for? He could give that name to his last personal intuition and ignore what it stands for and what it expresses in the world. It is the latter that absorbs me.

I have read practically no review of my book so that I don't know if any one has felt in it something which, I am sure, is there: I mean the *tears*. "Sunt lachrimae rerum, et mentem mortalia tangent." Not that I care to moan over the gods of Greece, turned in the law of gravity, or over the stained-glass cathedrals broken to let in the sunlight and the air. It is not that past that seems to me affecting, entrancing, or pitiful to lose. It is the ideal. It is that vision of perfection that we just catch or for a moment embody in some work of art or in some idealized reality. And it is my adoration of this real and familiar good, this lover often embraced but always elusive, that makes me detest the Absolutes and the dragooned myths for which people try to cancel the passing ideal or to denaturalise it. That's the inhumanity, an impiety, that I can't bear...

I seldom write to any one so frankly as I have here. But I know you are human, and tolerant to anything, however alien, that smells of blood.[401]

Reading Santayana led me to ask a question I could not have asked before reading him: Was there a way to wed personal voice and philosophically cogent criticism of American homophobia? Santayana's work suggested to me there was a way, and it was connected to being an outsider (both a gay man and a Latin), which would lead him to leave America and Harvard in 1912 after living here for some forty years. It was not Santayana's atheism that appealed to me because I thought even back then that there

---

[401] Quoted in John McCormick, *George Santayana: A Biography* (New Brunswick: Transaction, 2008), pp. 183-184.

were liberal strands in Christian thought that might themselves be sound historical and normative grounds for questioning dominant homophobic views of established churches, including Roman Catholicism, and have developed such arguments in a more recent collaborative book with Carol Gilligan, criticizing, among other things, the uncritical role Roman patriarchy played in shaping Christian thought much to its detriment.[402] Erich Auerbach in his great book, *Mimesis,* observes that early Christian thought and practice, through the doctrine of the incarnation, opened up a new ethical sensitivity to the unjust suffering of ordinary people, including slaves and women, and a value placed on the virtue of humility and the experience of the humble, quite unlike pagan Greco-Roman thought, and that was a strand of early Christianity that deeply appealed to me ethically and still does.[403] So Santayaya's love for the Greeks, in particular, and hostility to Christianity as such seemed to me even back then as ethically questionable. But his philosophical criticism of religion suggested to me a way of dealing critically with the role the patriarchal distortion of religion played in homophobia.

The comparison to Henry James's similar trajectory is instructive. Like Santayana, James leaves America better to give expression to his secret self, but in so doing, he closely studies the effects on American men and women of both the Puritan ethics of freedom and equality they assume and its patriarchal sexism and homophobia, in effect, studying both the psychological and ethical struggle to resistance to patriarchy. Santayana also experienced American homophobia at Harvard, and I believe Santayana's leaving America must be understood as grounded in the same dynamic of Henry James's moving and living abroad. Like James, Santayana turns to writing a long novel, a best seller when published, *The Last Puritan,* to explain what he takes to be the repressive sexual psychology of American homophobia and its disastrous consequences—personal and political—for American men.

---

[402] See Carol Gilligan and David A. J. Richards, *The Deepening Darkness: Patriarchy, Resistance, and Democracy's Future* (New York: Cambridge University Press, 2009), pp. 121–158.

[403] See Erich Auerbach, *Mimesis: The Representation of Reality in Western Literature* (Princeton: Princeton University Press, 2013), pp. 41, 72, 92, 119, 153–4.

Santayana's mother, Josefina Borras, had been married to a Bostonian merchant husband, George Sturgis, who died; they had three children. Josefina's second husband was Santayana's father, Agustin, who had been in the Spanish foreign service and who lived in Spain with their only son, George (born in 1863) and children by Sturgis only for a few years. Josefina was devoted to the Sturgises and contemptuous of Spanish culture and was determined that all her children would live with her in Boston for education. Agustin lived with his young son, George, in Spain and then took him to live with his mother in Boston in 1872. Agustin continued to live in Spain in Avila. The young son would visit, and their relationship was close, including frequent letters. Agustin was an atheist and had a philosophical temperament, and the father and son could talk, as I did with my father. Throughout Santayana's forty years of living in the United States, he lived in the two worlds—the first one, speaking Spanish to his reticent, chilling but dutiful mother and the other, living, eventually, at Harvard College with continual reminders in the form of letters from his father, living out his retirement in Avila.[404]

Unlike the more withdrawn homosexuality of Henry James, Santayana clearly fell in love with several young men, wrote poetry to one of them (including a student who died)[405] as well as letters expressing his love.[406] In his travels to Britain, letters about his relationship to Lord Russell (Bertrand Russell's sexually wayward and multiply married brother) and Lionel Johnson suggest a gay sex life as well.[407] His biographer observes of Santayana's loyalty to the wicked earl. There may have been the memory of an intense physical affair.[408]

Aside from his father, there was no greater influence on Santayana's development than his teacher, William James, who appreciated and supported Santayana's work but put his praise in rather homophobic forms for its "perfection of rottenness" and "moribund Latinity."[409] Cory, Santayana's assistant late in his life, speculates that James found the young man a "sissy" and reports Bertrand Russell as having told him, "I'm afraid

---

[404]   John McCormick, *George Santayana,* p. 41.
[405]   Id., pp. 49–51.
[406]   Id., pp. 103–105.
[407]   Id., pp. 63–69, 118–122.
[408]   Id., p. 119.
[409]   Quote at id., p. 56.

that James was altogether too much for Santayana."[410] William would have had similar views of his gay brother, Henry (see chapter 3).

There was, however, a much more serious expression of Harvard's institutional homophobia when he was proposed to President Charles W. Eliot for an assistant professorship in the department in 1898; Eliot responded,

> I agree with you that Dr. Santayana's qualities give a useful variety to the Philosophical Department and that he is an original writer of proved capacity. I suppose the fact to be that I have doubts and fears about a man so abnormal as Dr. Santayana. The withdrawn, contemplative man who takes no part in the everyday work of the institution, or of the world, seems to me to be a person of very uncertain future value. He does not dig ditches or lay bricks or white schoolbooks; his product is not of the ordinary useful, though humble, kind. What will it be? It may be something of the highest utility, but on the other hand, it may be something futile, or even harmful, because unnatural and untimely.[411]

Santayana, seven years an instructor, was prepared to resign if he were not advanced. Without shouting about it, he knew his strength. Eliot's doubts were answered, and he wrote in response, "I am very glad that you can say of him that he is a strong and healthy man and a good, gay, fresh companion. That testimony strikes me as important."[412]

If the life and work of Henry James, including living abroad, is a lifesaving response to the abusive homophobia of his family, Santayana's resignation from Harvard and his living abroad is, I believe, what he came to regard as a lifesaving response to the abusive institutional homophobia of Harvard. William James, the only member of the department to whom Santayana could talk on terms of humane understanding and mutual respect, had died in 1910. His beloved father had earlier died in 1893, seventy-nine years old. As his son wrote, "Deaf, blind, and poor. He had

---

[410] Id.

[411] Quoted at id., p. 97.

[412] Id., text and quote at p. 97.

desired his own death and had attempted to hasten it."[413] Now his mother had died at eighty-six and left him an inheritance. There were no personal relationships of value left, and he wrote to his beloved half sister, now living in Spain:

> I am very sick of America and of professors and professoresses, and I am pining for a sunny, quiet, remote, friendly, intellectual, obscure existence, with large horizons and no empty noise in the foreground. What I have seen in California and Canada—apart from the geography of these regions—has left no impression on my mind, whatever. They are intellectually emptier than the Sahara, where I understand the Arabs have some idea of God or of fate when I am here in the midst of the dull round a sort of instinct of courtesy make me take it for granted, and I become almost unconscious of how I hate it all. Otherwise, I couldn't have stood if for *forty years*.[414]

A letter to a friend explaining his leaving America in 1912 describes his dissatisfaction "with the haste and want of solidity to which everything invites one there. I never felt so much a foreigner in New England as I did of late. In Avila, where my two sisters are now, I have almost a home, and I was very happy in Madrid last winter, living with an old (female) friend who is all piety, patriotism, and affection running over for everybody."[415] Santayana certainly does not find in America in general or Harvard in particular affection running over for everybody.

Santayana's *The Last Puritan*

Both Henry James and George Santayana turn to fiction to explore their psychological and ethical reasons for leaving America, both responding to American homophobia. For James, as we have seen (chapter 4), his fiction explored how American patriarchy had compromised deeper values of

---

[413] Id., quoted at p. 199.

[414] Quoted at id., p. 209.

[415] Id., text and quote, p. 216,

conscience. Santayana's novel, *The Last Puritan*,[416] has a quite different character. It is, for one thing, structured as if an autobiography (the subtitle is *A Memoir in the Form of a Novel*), a memoir of Santayana, now living in Italy, reflecting on two former students he taught at Harvard College, Oliver Alden and Mario Van de Weyer. Oliver, who is the novel's main character, comes from a family with a Puritan background on both sides. Mario, a cousin of Alden's, is the son of an American man and Italian opera singer, thus Italian American. Santayana, who had loved several of his Harvard students, is making sense of their initiation into American manhood, and he does so with a quite clinical investigation of how a certain kind of New England Puritan family leads to the homophobic repression in a gay man of any erotic gay feeling, covered over by denial and displacement. It is a world I recognize in the psyche of my childhood when I could not put a name to what I was feeling, and to that extent, the novel is revelatory of the psyche of a boy in such circumstances. But the world Santayana describes continues well beyond boyhood, and the denial and displacement continue as well. This was not thankfully my world or the world around me after my boyhood, but it may well be the world Santayana knew and what he observed in the young men he knew and loved, and it may be that bitter unadorned truth that he tells us so precisely in this important novel about gay consciousness or, if you will, gay unconsciousness, which comes closer to the novel's achievement.

Santayana places his novel in a period of transition in attitudes to homosexuality, marked, near the end of the novel, in a letter Oliver receives from Mario, now at an Oxford college living in rooms once inhabited by Oscar Wilde. Mario observes that a friend warned him "not to mention this circumstances because the name of Oscar Wilde was taboo in that circle" but goes on to deny any one cared about the sexual scandal because no one there "minds that nowadays. But they abhor Oscar Wilde's rhetoric—mid-Victorian, middle-class, melodramatic, and worm-eaten with morality."[417] So the unspeakable is now to some extent spoken about, albeit dismissively and unsympathetically. But Oliver, who is gay, is much

---

[416] See George Santayana, *The Last Puritan: A Memoir in the Form of a Novel* (critical edition), coed. William G. Holzberger and Herman J. Saatkamp Jr. with an Introduction by Irving Singer (Cambridge, Mass.: MIT Press, 1994; originally published 1935).

[417] Id., p. 520.

more rigidly controlled by his homophobia than is Mario who is not gay. Santayana wants us to understand empathetically that world, which in an earlier world where homophobia was hegemonic would have meant gay men, like Oliver, were sometimes quite cut off from their erotic feelings. We now know or there is good evidence for believing that Emerson[418] and Thoreau [419] may have been gay in this way but quite disassociated from much (Emerson) or any (Thoreau) sense of it. Santayana wants to show us that world and to show what, in his view, were its negative consequences; he does not entertain the possibility that in some cases, there may have been good or some balance of good over bad as well in the ways gay men come to terms with living in a homophobic culture.[420]

Santayana is also reflecting on himself as a gay and Latin man, living and brought up in New England, himself shaped by its moral world but also, as an outsider, freer from its demands, and thus telling us why he fled America, when he was able, to save himself from American homophobia. And here he understood the negative side all too well (as men turn on other men homophobically, as Harvard did on him), and the novel explores it in-depth.

The character at the center of the novel is Oliver Alden, and the novel traces his background through both his grandfather, and his grandfather's two children, Nathaniel and Peter, Oliver's father. The narrative starts in the traumatic murder of the grandfather "by a moneyless tenant in a sudden explosion of hatred and despair," responding to his being "a hard landlord and a miser, grown rich on uncertain and miserable payments wrung from the poor." In words directly taken from Hawthorne's *The Scarlet Letter*,

---

[418] See, for a persuasive argument along these lines, Caleb Crain, *American Sympathy: Men, Friendship and Literature in the New Nation* (New Haven: Yale University Press, 2001), pp. 148–237.

[419] See, on this point, Laura Dassow Walls, *Henry David Thoreau: A Life* (Chicago: University of Chicago Press, 2017), pp. 239–41.

[420] On the probable origins of the thought and practice of democracy and human rights in the Franciscans, see Brian Tierney, *The Idea of Natural Rights: Studies on Natural Rights, Natural Law, and Church Law 1150–1625* (Grand Rapids, Michigan: William B. Eerdmans, 19970); Larry Siedentop, *Inventing the Individual: The Origins of Western Liberalism* (London: Allen Lane, 2015). On recent rethinking of Christian thought, See Roger Haight, *Jesus: Symbol of God* (Maryknoll, NY: Orbis, 2000); Margaret A. Farley, *Just Love: A Framework fo Christian Sexual Ethics* (New York: Continuum, 2006:.

Nathaniel could "never be at ease in this conscience! A scar of horror, if not of guilt, lay consciously on his breast, like that scarlet letter."[421]

Carrying this sense of guilt in his psyche leads, counterphobically, to an extraordinary moral punctiliousness in Nathaniel's outward sense of respectability but an almost unbelievable lack of human feeling for anyone, including his unfortunate half brother, Peter Alden, of whom Nathaniel is the guardian. (It is a mark of the patriarchal character of the narrative that no woman appears as a mother until later in the narrative, and she, as we shall see, rather monstrously so.) Peter, in contrast to his brother, makes the great mistake of taking an interest in other human beings outside his brother's narrow understanding of the moral community (excluding all foreigners, etc.), including with "persons of inferior education and a lower station in life,"[422] and Peter, to save him from evil influences, is sent for moral reeducation to a camp in Wyoming. Nathaniel, who wants to be free of custody of his brother, transfers custody to his half sister, Caroline Van de Weyer, who sends him to Exeter then Harvard. At Harvard, as part of an initiation in a club that required stealing a Bible from a chapel, when seized by a night watchman, dropped the bible in the man, inadvertently killing him. Peter was shipped abroad and began his wanderings around the world. Having inherited his fortune at twenty-one, he traveled, becoming a doctor, and sought remedies for his ailments with Dr. Bumstead in Connecticut.

At the urging of Dr. Bumstead, his daughter Harriet, with no interest in men (her intense attachments were to women) and less in Peter, marries him, and he, as a gesture to respectability but with little feeling for her, agrees. Peter Alden, absorbed in sailing his yacht, spent little time at home; "he never interfered with the child's education."[423] The son, Oliver, had none of the vices of his father, but in the view of his mother, "he harked back to his remoter ancestors and took everything seriously."[424] "[T]he Aldens had genuinely come over in the *Mayflower,* and Oliver had the inexpressible privilege of being descended from those famous Pilgrims, Priscilla and John Alden, immortalized by Longfellow."[425] Duty was the

---

[421]   George Santayana, *The Last Puritan,* p. 23.
[422]   Id., p. 34.
[423]   Id., p. 74.
[424]   Id., p. 74.
[425]   Id., p. 75.

boy's mission. "Life was essentially something to be endured, something grim."[426]

There is a nice counterpointing in the novel between the German governess's quite sensitive observation of the boy and his needs, and the mother's rather clueless invocation of gender stereotypes and insistence she won't allow "any sensuality, healthy or not in *her* house."[427] Condemning getting a cushion for the boy to sit in, Harriet refuses, "It is effeminate."[428] Her view, of course, prevails, though based, as the governess sees, on incorrect assumptions. Throughout the novel, the governess complains in letters home that there is no discussion in the home about the truth or how to argue about it, and that she is instructed by Mrs. Alden: "I musn't teach Oliver to make gestures or show his feelings. Gentlemen are not monkeys."[429] Oliver's education in boyhood was one "[o]nly nonhuman subjects were fit for the human mind, leading to puritan disdain of human weakness and of human genius"[430] When he goes to the public high school, he is initiated into "that herd-instinct, that sense that you must swim with the stream and do what is expected of you, which now became dominant in him."[431] "[He] now began to do at school everything that the school spirit demanded, which first and foremost was to play football."[432] "All his lessons and sports seemed to be taken up as duties, executed unswervingly, as if to get rid of them as quickly and thoroughly as possible, but at least there was a silent moment of peace as each duty—each enemy—was dispatched in turn."[433] Even as a boy, "Life was essentially something to be endured, something grim,"[434] and "it was his duty to rule. He knew how to do it."[435] Later in his life at college, Oliver plays football brilliantly but regards it as problematic: "Football brings out the fighting instinct, and you do things you wouldn't do in cold blood."[436] When asked why he plays when he

---

[426] Id., p. 99.
[427] Id., p. 90. For other uses of "effeminate" in the novel, see id., pp. 73, 333, 382.
[428] Id., p. 100.
[429] Id., p. 112.
[430] Id., p. 117.
[431] Id., p. 129.
[432] Id., p. 129.
[433] Id., p. 132.
[434] Id., p. 99.
[435] Id., p. 103.
[436] Id., p. 380.

doesn't like it and doesn't think it does any good, he replies that he must play for his school: "They needed me. It would have seemed selfish and effeminate."[437] His preference would have been to study philosophy, as he does at Harvard, studying Plato with Professor Santayana.[438]

The only interruption in Oliver's relentless education into patriarchal duty is when he is invited by his father to join him on his yacht and where he meets the English captain, James Darnley, called Lord Jim, after the protagonist of the Conrad novel. Aboard the yacht, his father is a different man "surrounded by deference and smiling affection,"[439] and observing in one of the few allusions to maternal feeling in the novel, that for him, "[T]he sea carries us like a nurse in her arms."[440] Oliver is shocked by the physically playful relationship between Jim and his father: "This outsider was behaving more like a son and the old gentleman more like a father. It is more than Oliver had ever seen anyone behave before." And Oliver entertains a question about himself that he never had before: "Was Oliver himself cold, shriveled, heartless, and unacquainted with the feelings of a son?"[441] Oliver and Jim now swim naked together. In the only erotic moment in the novel, Oliver experiences feelings he had never had before: "What a chest and what arms! Being stripped, he resembled, if not a professional strong man, at least a middle prizefighter in tip-top condition, with a deep line between the middle of his chest and back, and every muscle showing under the tight skin."[442]

Santayana is quite clear that erotic feelings of this sort must, in psychoanalytic terms, be repressed: "All sensation in Oliver was, as it were, retarded. It hardly became conscious until it became moral."[443] But Jim not only provokes in Oliver new erotic feelings but elicits new thoughts as, for the time in his life, Oliver talks intimately with another man who will hide nothing, who self-censors nothing. The first revelation is why Jim and others were court martialed by the British navy: "Because a few snotties had been overheard calling a spade a spade. Immorality in the British Navy"

---

437 Id., p. 382.
438 Id., pp. 412, 419–20, 497, 541.
439 Id., p. 148.
440 Id., p. 143.
441 Id., p. 150.
442 Id., p. 154.
443 Id., p. 158.

(presumably, talking about gay sex among sailors) and how Jim's mother, with whom he was close, supported him). Oliver now has a thought he had never had before: "Lord Jim's mother stands up for her young cub against the world, which my mother—I never saw it so clearly before—always stands up for the world against her young cub."[444] And Jim goes on to further revelations about Oliver's father—that he had killed a man as part of a fraternity prank at Harvard College (leading to his traveling abroad for many years) and that his father had developed a drug habit (presumably, opium). Jim cared for him when he was under the influence of the drug. Jim questions both the morality that "there was nothing between white and black"[445] and that fails to take human frailty seriously, "In this world, you have to take people as you find them."[446] Oliver turns on Jim for such revelations: "It was a breach of trust."[447] Jim correctly interprets Oliver's shock and rejects his condemnation as "the moral tantrums of a boy of sixteen."[448] Oliver sees how Jim cares for his father and apologizes to him, doing what boys do in such situations, putting his hand out to shake the hand of the other. "But Jim, not knowing the ways of the country, neglected to shake and took Oliver's hand affectionately in both his own, held it for a moment, and said, 'That's all right. I didn't give a thought,' and then proceeded to pat Oliver on the back. And Oliver, though his expectation and his pride were cheated, did somehow feel comforted. Pride began to seem insufficient and unnecessary. There was something else more genuine, more honest. This was the first time anyone had caressed him, since Fraulein, the German governess, twelve years before had stopped stroking his bare legs."[449] That night, Oliver slept longer than before, and Santayana explicitly invokes the unconscious: "It was as if in his unconsciousness—for he didn't remember to have dreamt—a muted voice had kept whispering with him, 'Sleep on—no hurry, no school, no family breakfast, nobody waiting. Rest, rest, rest. You are free.'"[450]

---

[444] Id., p. 165.

[445] Id., p. 163.

[446] Id., p. 167.

[447] Id., p. 168.

[448] Id., p. 168.

[449] Id., p. 172.

[450] Id., p. 173.

Santayana, at this point in the novel, brilliantly captures the experience of a repressed gay man falling in love—an experience I know at firsthand. There is, of course, sexual attraction, but there is something else that goes much deeper into the human psyche, the psyche of a young man who has never spoken to anyone about his sexual desires and may indeed, as in Oliver, be so deeply repressed them that he does not acknowledge their existence. Strong sexual attraction is here wedded to an honest and free and equal voice in the beloved, Jim, based on experience, that confronts Oliver with the falseness of the gender binary and hierarchy in which he has been imprisoned. Jim and Oliver's father are in an easy relationship, which belies gender hierarchy, and Jim is caring of his father's frailties and yet a perfectly competent man. And Jim speaks to Oliver in a way no one has ever spoken to him, exposing his rigid moralism as "the moral tantrums of a boy of sixteen." Oliver is, for a time, dethroned from his heretofore accepted perch in the gender binary and hierarchy, falling in love with someone who has seen him for the person he is and speaks to him in an honest, intimate voice critical of the false patriarchal self he has assumed to be in the nature of things. "The power of love upsets the order of things."[451] That is perhaps why we say we *fall* in love and why love so often flourishes in resisting patriarchy.[452]

Unfortunately, these moments with his father and Jim on the yacht do not lead to any deepening of Oliver's relationship to his father or Jim or anyone else in the novel. His mother's patriarchal moral tyranny over Oliver expresses itself in homophobic rage that Oliver should sail with Jim on his father's yacht, and the son supinely complies.[453] Later, when his father is seriously ill and commits suicide, Oliver aligns himself with his mother, not his father (feeling guilt for his choice).[454] Oliver clearly has fallen in love with Jim[455] but sees there is no future with him. (Jim has been having an affair with a married woman, Mrs. Bowler, and has a child by her.)[456] Oliver, who cannot acknowledge what he feels about all this, has

---

[451] Genesis Rabbah LV8, the epigraph of Carol Gilligan's *The Birth of Pleasure.*

[452] See David A. J. Richards, *Why Love Leads to Justice: Love Across the Boundaries* (New York: Cambridge University Press, 2016).

[453] See George Santayana, *The Last Puritan,* pp. 208–13, 217, 219–20.

[454] Id., pp. 329–30.

[455] Id., pp. 210, 226, 231, 259, 351, 508.

[456] Id., p. 255.

a dream arising from having attended a performance of Verdi's *Rigoletto* (Santayana, like me, loved Verdi's operas;[457] and *Rigoletto* is, for me, Verdi's version of *King Lear,* an opera he meant to write but never did. My view is he didn't because he had already written *Rigoletto*). In the dream, Mrs. Bowler is Maddalena, and Jim is her brother, who is to kill the duke. Oliver is Gilda, who, in the opera, saves the duke by substituting herself for him when he is about to be killed. Jim's father, a vicar, has arranged for the murder of the duke, but the person killed is Oliver.[458] In Oliver's dream, his love brings a father's revenge on him, not on his seducer. Jim and Oliver later meet again on a ship, and Jim, now financially desperate, effectively offers himself sexually to Oliver, who refuses, saying, "I hate pleasure."[459] Jim sees that Oliver is both gay and lacks the courage to act on his erotic feelings.[460] Later, Jim is killed in World War I.

Mario Van De Weyer, Alden's Italian American cousin, is introduced late in the novel largely as Santayana's way of counterpointing Oliver's increasingly rigid need of moral maxims and psychological lovelessness[461] (his "petrified conscience").[462] Mario could not be more different: he is close to and has lived with his opera singer mother, who loves him. Their poverty has, however, been relieved by the wealth of Oliver and his relatives. Oliver comes as well to believe that he loves Mario, a man, of course, who loves him.[463] When he meets him again, however, after a separation of several years, he sees that Mario, though Oliver thinks of him homoerotically as the "hyacinthine creature," is very much a ladies man. Women fall in love with him easily in contrast to Oliver, whom they repel (at least, two women reject Oliver's marriage proposals but were attracted to Mario).

The narrative ends in World War II. To Oliver's shock, Mario decides to fight in France against the Germans, a requirement of manhood: "If you're a man, you must be ready to fight every other man and to make love to every pretty woman."[464] With his sanguinary views on war as the test of manhood, Oliver suggests that he might better enlist for the Kaiser, but Mario is allied

---

457 See, John McCormick, *George Santayana,* p. 157.
458 See George Santayana, *The Last Puritan,* pp. 241, 263–66.
459 Id., p. 357.
460 Id., pp. 359–61.
461 Id., pp. 306–9.
462 Id., p. 317,
463 Id., pp. 341–343, 383, 477–78.
464 Id., p. 501.

with "the politics of Charles Maurras,"[465]—a French Catholic nationalist and profascist, not French politicians, "Free Masons and Jews, more than half of them."[466] Mario's views repel Oliver: "You expect everything to be smashed, and you don't seem to mind. You laugh and slyly enjoy the prospect. And a rancid conservative like you can't wait for war to be declared but must rush forward and enlist in order to smash everything."[467]

However, when the United States declares war on Germany, Oliver regards it as his duty as an American to fight: "I am going to fight the Germans whom I like on the side of the French whom I don't like. It's my duty."[468] He is killed in a car accident, after the armistice, swerving to avoid a motorcycle coming at him. His will leaves money to Jim's son. Mario survives the war, marries into an old Italian family in Rome, and is a supporter of Mussolini's fascism.[469] It is he who urges Santayana, living in Europe, to write about the life of his now dead friend.

What Santayana Tells Us about American Homophobia

Santayana turns to the novel in *The Last Puritan* to give voice, as James earlier did, to the experience of living under American homophobia. James, as we have seen in chapter 4, reveals aspects of his secret self and often uses women as alter egos. Santayana is altogether more direct both in its main character (Oliver Alden is clearly a repressed homosexual) and in its almost clinical interest in the initiations into patriarchal manhood of such an unhappy and divided man. The novel is, I believe, very much a work of love in the sense that Santayana had, as a student and teacher at Harvard College, not only known but loved such men and had experienced at firsthand how American institutional homophobia, including the institutional homophobia of Harvard College, has destroyed such men as the persons they could have been.

Santayana had himself been a Harvard student and a gay man and later a Harvard philosophy professor of international renown, so he knew at firsthand that American homophobia destroyed both love and lives. It was,

465 Id., p. 502.
466 Id., p. 503.
467 Id., p. 503.
468 Id., p. 555.
469 Id., pp. 499–504.

at the last, his own experience of the institutional homophobia of Harvard College that led him to leave Harvard and America for Europe. And Oliver Alden is not only based on one or another of the students he loved but on himself. Oliver is very much psychologically divided, as Santayana was, between his mother (described in a letter to his sister as the absolutely dominating force in all our lives)[470] and his beloved father, an atheist and philosophical, as his son was, and with whom the son could talk. Santayana had not, however, lived with his father since he was a boy, and Santayana captures the distance between father and son in Oliver's sense of distance from and yet attraction to his father. Peter Alden, because of his travels abroad and his diverse experiences of other cultures and people and ways of life, is much more an outsider to American culture than his wife or his son and observes with a sense of sadness and helplessness and detachment, for which, of course, he is importantly responsible, how damaged Oliver's psyche is by his rigid initiation into American patriarchy, largely stage-managed by Peter's wife, Harriet, whom he clearly never loved, nor she him. Santayana was himself puzzled by his parents' marriage and tried to capture the impact of such a loveless marriage on a son in *The Last Puritan*, as Oliver realizes, in the crucial scene on his father's yacht when he falls in love with Jim, not only that his mother never loved him but "Lord Jim's mother stands up for her young cub against the world, which my mother—I never saw it so clearly before—always stands up for the world against her young cub."[471] Falling in love with Jim has made this thought possible for Oliver, but because his love for Jim goes nowhere or is not allowed (by the homophobic rage of Oliver's mother) to go further, Oliver always complies with his mother's theatrical program for his life, including serving in a war as a good American man must—whatever his doubts about the war and its conception of friends and enemies: "I am going to fight the Germans whom I like on the side of the French whom I don't like. It's my duty."[472]

What makes her program patriarchal is that it is controlled by his mother's quite rigid conception and enforcement of the gender binary and hierarchy (the marks of patriarchy). As Proust saw,[473] women under

---

[470] Quoted in John McCormick, *George Santayana*, p. 213.

[471] George Santayana, *The Last Puritan*, p. 165.

[472] Id., p. 555.

[473] See, on this point, Carol Gilligan, *The Birth of Pleasure: A New Map of Love* (New York: Vintage, 2003), pp. 81–86.

patriarchy often come to regard themselves as more inflexible in the enforcement of patriarchal demands because under patriarchy, they think of themselves as the instrument of the superior hierarchical authority of the patriarchs, men. Men, precisely because they have this patriarchal authority, may be much more flexible in releasing themselves and others from patriarchal demands precisely because they have that authority as patriarchs, and women do not. It is part of the psychological brilliance of *The Last Puritan* that Santayana so clearly sees, with really a clinical eye, the role women can and do play in their son's initiation into patriarchy. He clearly knew this experience at firsthand.

But Santayana also shows us, in the scenes on his father's yacht with his father and Jim, how a kind of love he had never known before can free even a young man of sixteen as controlled as Oliver was from the psychological strangle hold of patriarchy over both his mind and heart. Oliver has thoughts and recognitions he has never had before. Why Jim? His erotic beauty is very much part of it, but also the freedom and honesty of his voice, speaking from experience (not from abstract moral demands) about what he had seen of gay love in the British navy and the moral hypocrisy of the patriarchs of the British navy that condemned it, and even of the human frailties that led Oliver's father to depend on opium. And there is his care for Oliver's father, something he had not seen in his own mother—care for either him or his father. Jim is more maternal, not bound by the gender binary, thus more humane. Jim is wholly unphilosophical, but his sense of ethics is democratic, rooted in experience—an experience available to anyone, whatever their background or class. The iron moralistic Puritan condemnations of gay sex or drug use make no sense to Jim, and Oliver sees and is attracted to this alternative democratic way of life and of ethical life.

But Oliver's love for Jim, which he acknowledges throughout the novel and at its very end,[474] does not ripen into anything deeper, in part, because his mother's homophobic rage forbids her son from any further trips on his father's yacht. And Oliver complies. Santayana's interest is in showing us that there was a way out, a road not taken, and he shows as well how patriarchy reasserts its power over the human psyche.

The mechanism of such patriarchal control is, as Santayana shows us, the boys' group, and Oliver's sense of himself as an American man is one with the demands of his all-male team, with competitive athletics (football)

---

474   George Santayana, *The Last Puritan*, p. 508.

as the model. Though Oliver admits he does not like athletics or see much point in it, he regards the all-male team, or the male band of brothers, as the measure of what is demanded. His reasons for going to war are based on this conception that he can no more deny the demands of his athletic team than he can deny the demands of American manhood once war with Germany has been declared.

What Santayana Tells Us about the Difficulties of Resistance

If Santayana had a mother, like Oliver Alden's, who enforced patriarchal demands, he, unlike Oliver, came to resist such demands, as we see in the excerpts from *The Life of Reason* earlier discussed. The influence of his atheist, philosophical father—living in Spain—played a role in this, but so did Santayana's own interests in philosophy and doing philosophy as he did. Santayana's naturalism took human nature as he found it to be, including our erotic passions, and argued against the traditional role religion had played in repressing these passions. American Puritanism was one such religion, and he focuses on it in *The Last Puritan*.

Oliver Alden is, however, also interested in philosophy, indeed intensely interested (before his death, he thinks he may become a professional academic philosopher), studying with Santayana himself at Harvard[475] and writing a paper on Plato, criticizing Plato for connecting love too closely to desire.[476] Santayana comments that neither Plato nor Emerson (he is writing in a room in which Emerson, as a student, lived) shaped his view. "[I]t was his own spirit that inspired him."[477] Love, Oliver argues, must be for "the absolute idea of the beautiful"[478] and must be completely and unselfishly intellectual with no admixture of sensuality. Santayana had written an essay in 1911, the year after the death of William James, on what he called "the genteel tradition" in American philosophy in which he argued that American thinkers (only Walt Whitman excepted) are uncritically confined within and by American Calvinism—"an expression of the agonized conscience."[479] Santayana regards Oliver's philosophizing

---

[475] Id., p. 412.
[476] Id., pp. 421–422.
[477] Id., p. 419.
[478] Id., p. 420.
[479] George Santayana, *The Genteel Tradition* (Lincoln: University of Nebraska

as an example of this tradition because its disassociation of thought from sensual feeling essentially replicates the moral prison in which, through his initiation into American patriarchy, Oliver is confined. The consequence is for Santayana that, unlike Mario, for Oliver it is impossible to "enjoy life on so many levels and identify himself with people of so many descriptions. If you wish to do right, to make yourself and the world better,"[480] but his moralism so disassociates thought from feeling that Oliver, so committed to doing what is right and just, cannot really think or act morally or justly, thus cannot resist injustice. Oliver to his credit himself sees the problem near the end of the novel, "How should it be possible to do good when you haven't discerned the good or to abolish injustice when you're not sure what would be just or to diffuse happiness when you have never tasted it?"[481] So Oliver goes to war for his country not because he has reflected on its justice but because to do otherwise would be inconsistent with his conception of patriarchal American manhood just as, earlier, he played for his football team without any pleasure or sense of its doing any good.

This is, I believe, the heart of Santayana's indictment of American Puritanism and the American philosophy that he came to believe uncritically supported it. He shows us through his clinical study of the initiation of Oliver into American patriarchy the damage such initiation inflicts not only on Oliver's capacity for love but on his capacity to resist injustice. Oliver is thus very much in the tradition of what other men, American artists, have shown to be similarly damaged by patriarchy (e.g., Hawthorne's Dimmesdale and Chillingworth or Melville's Ahab and Captain Vere or Henry James's Hyacinth).

What Santayana Tells Us about Reactionary Patriarchy: Anti-Semitism in T. S. Eliot and Ezra Pound

Santayana had spent some forty-five years working on *The Last Puritan*, publishing it in 1935. It is, in my judgment, not so much a novel but an almost clinical analysis of what Santayana, both a philosopher and a shrewd psychologist, had come to regard as the destructive Puritanism of

---

Press, 1998, originally published, 1967), p. 41.

[480] George Santayana, *The Last Puritan*, p. 486.

[481] Id., p. 516.

American homophobia and how difficult it was and would be for American men, initiated into its terms, to resist it. But there is another, even more important dimension to Santayana's achievement in *The Last Puritan*, one I am quite sure he did not intend but is the most revelatory, namely, what he tells us about the road not taken by Oliver Alden but taken by his friend Mario. It is a mark of a great psychological thinker, like Freud, for example,[482] that even when he takes a wrong turn (disowning his early interest in the voices of women), he shows with remarkable honesty how and why he came to that wrong turn. When it comes to the psychology of homophobia, Santayana is, I believe, an astute psychological thinker, and his integrity is most in evidence when he deals with what he takes to be the Oliver's wrong turn and Mario's right turn. He is, I believe, quite wrong about both, yet he shows us with great honesty why he, Santayana, came to his own wrong turn in exploring the two aspects of himself—his American Oliver and his Italian American Mario.

Santayana wrote *The Last Puritan* largely in the period between World War I and World War II (Santayana dies in 1952 at the age of eighty-eight in Rome, Italy), and he is responding to interpreting what he took to be the catastrophe for Western culture of World War I, as two other American artists did, both Americans, T. S. Eliot and Ezra Pound. Santayana had taught Eliot at Harvard College (Eliot found his lectures "soporific")[483] and would meet and talk with Pound in Italy near the end of his life.[484] Santayana ends *The Last Puritan* with World War I, and one can see why this very long and quite difficult novel was, to Santayana's surprise, a 1936 best seller in America and Europe, only second in sales and popularity to *Gone with the Wind*.[485]

America's intervention in World War I, which had been decisive both in the Allied victory and the resulting Treaty of Versailles, had made this country of enormous interest to Europeans. And Santayana, who had lived in America for forty years and then returned to Europe, seemed to many the best possible analyst of this new American democracy and more attractive

---

[482] See, on this point, Carol Gilligan, *The Birth of Pleasure*, pp. 216–28.

[483] See John McCormick, *George Santayana*, p. 99.

[484] See, on this point, id., pp. 399–418.

[485] See *The Last Puritan* at https://en.wikipedia.org/wiki/The_Last_Puritan; John McCormick, *George Santayana*, pp. 337–339.

because he was, in fact, so critical of the governing philosophy and religion of America, Puritanism, for which many sophisticated Europeans had contempt.

And the novel would be appealing to Americans in 1936 precisely for the same reasons that *Gone with the Wind* was appealing. *Gone with the Wind* offers a view of the American South, which would downplay its slavery and racism, thus falsifying historical memory.[486] And *The Last Puritan* was critical of the New England abolitionist political morality that motivated the Civil War, its abolition of slavery, and its ongoing criticism of Southern and American racism, which remained virulent when *The Last Puritan* was published (Southern racist lynchings continued with no adequate state or federal remedy). *The Last Puritan* could be read by Americans as supporting their isolationism (which had led to what many now regarded as their wrong-headed intervention in European imperialist wars) and their racism. And the villain was American Puritanism, which Santayana had now revealed and debunked.

Santayana is one of the very best critics, certainly of his period and long thereafter, of American patriarchal homophobia, but the personal significance for him of American homophobia (at the hands perhaps of his own mother and certainly of Harvard University) led him not to see other more enlightened aspects of American political morality. As far as one can tell, Santayana, who learned so much from and admired William James, never joins James as a public intellectual critical not only of American racism (Southern lynchings) but of American racist imperialism, leading to the Spanish-American War of which James, like Mark Twain, was a sharp critic.[487] One might have thought that Santayana, himself Spanish, might have at least been engaged by the issue, but in his correspondence with his sister, he remains noncommittal, seeing wrong on both sides.[488] Santayana's blithe insouciance in matters of political morality became much worse, and inexcusably worse, when, living in Italy, he embraced the anti-Semitism of the period as the source of World War I and all European woes and supported

---

[486] See, on this point, David W. Blight, *Race and Reunion: The Civil War in American History* (Cambridge, Mass.: Belknap Press of Harvard University Press, 2001).

[487] See, on this point, Robert D. Richardson, *William James: In the Maelstrom of American Modernism* (Boston: Mariner, 2006), pp. 38–85, 441–42.

[488] See John McCormick, *George Santayana*, p. 131.

Mussolini's version of fascism.[489] Edmund Wilson, who visited Santayana in Rome shortly after the war, explained the appeal of fascism for Santayana in starkly psychologically patriarchal terms: "Owing to his [Santayana's] approval of displays of 'virility.' And that although unsympathetic to the Germans, he had admired the officers in uniform during his student days in Berlin."[490] Even after World War II, when the monstrous inhumanity of European fascism becomes clear, Santayana finally condemns the excesses of Mussolini and, of course, Hitler, but he does not reconsider his essentially aristocratic views of an authoritarian political morality that would protect the "vital liberty" of philosophers like Plato and himself.[491] And though he remained an atheist until the end, he repudiated any Protestant search for the humane ethical teaching of the historical Jesus for an endorsement of some form of Catholic irrationalist mythology.[492]

Santayana had made a wrong turn, and the psychological acuity and honesty of *The Last Puritan* shows us how he came to make it. The real focus of *The Last Puritan* is always Oliver Alden, whose tragedy is clearly close to Santayana's heart—connected to young men he loved and lost and to his own sense of humiliation by Harvard institutional homophobia that leads him to leave America and Harvard for Europe. Santayana makes quite clear, however, that there was a time—Oliver aboard his father's yacht when he swims nude with and talks intimately with Jim—when love might have released this sixteen-year-old boy from the homophobia that would destroy him. Santayana writes a remarkable letter to Morton Fullerton, eventually the bisexual lover of Edith Wharton and a friend from Harvard College, about his choices in love in which sex and "sentimental love" are distinguished as inconsistent. The letter suggests that Santayana, unlike Oliver, certainly knew and acted on his gay desires but never saw or experienced the two as marrying.[493] Oliver could have taken that turn (say if his father had protected him from his mother's ranting homophobia). If he had, why wouldn't that be

---

[489] See John McCormick, *George Santayana*, pp. 352–367.

[490] See id., p. 407.

[491] See id., pp. 483-496; on "Vital Liberty," see id., p. 486. For his concluding statement of political theory, George Santayana, *Dominations and Powers: Reflections on Liberty, Society and Government* (New York: Charles Scribner's Sons, 1951).

[492] See George Santayana, *The Idea of Christ in the Gospels* (New York: Charles Scribner's Sons, 1946).

[493] See id., p. 71.

a basis for resistance? That is a question Santayana does not entertain, but we can and should. In fact, he shows us the way.

The alternative, as Santayana shows us, is Mario to whom everyone is sexually attracted and who certainly, unlike Oliver, integrates his sense of morality with his feelings and appetites. But when Oliver argues with Mario about fighting in World War I, Mario's reasons for fighting with the French against the Germans align him quite explicitly with anti-Semitism and fascism. At the end of the novel, Mario has married into a Roman noble family allied with the pope and supports Mussolini. So Santayana quite clearly shows us Mario's turn to fascism, explicitly interpreted by Oliver as appealing to the patriarchal manhood of *The Iliad* as his model[494] and to which Oliver responds, "You talk as if we were savages rightly wound round and held down by civilization."[495] Oliver quite clearly sees that the psychological heart of fascism is the shamed patriarchal manhood and propensities to violence of *The Iliad,* and that such impulses, once unleashed, could destroy "civilization" as, of course, they nearly did. What is remarkable is that Santayana should want us to see this in 1935 before the monstrously aggressive violence of fascism had been fully unleashed.

One of the reasons *The Last Puritan* is to me so compelling to me is that, in showing us the alternative choices of Alden and Mario, he reveals an alternative I and other racialized immigrant groups have faced, namely, what parts of the American tradition we will adopt and which parts we will abandon, or alternatively, work to change. It is, I think, psychologically understandable why other Italian Americans, like Justice Antonin Scalia, have chosen within limits to take certain features of American patriarchy (in matters of sexuality and gender) as central and used them in their narrow interpretations of constitutional principles of privacy and gender equality. [496] It is a way, as Randolph Bourne saw in his essay, "Trans-National America,"[497] that immigrant groups, in seeking to be assimilated,

---

[494] Id., p. 501.

[495] Id., p. 502.

[496] For fuller critique of Scalia's originalism as rooted in patriarchal sectarian religion, see David A. J. Richards, *Fundamentalism in American Religion and Law: Obama's Challenge to Patriarchy's Threat to Democracy* (Cambridge: Cambridge University Press, 2010).

[497] Randolph Bourne, "Trans-National America," *The Radical Will: Selected Writings 1911–1918,* ed. Olaf Hansen (Berkeley: University of California Press, 1977; first published, 1916), pp. 248–264.

may ostensibly in becoming more American and thus more successful and upwardly mobile in appealing to American conventional values lose a sense of the humane values that most distinguish their countries of origins.[498] I understand that, though I think the choice is quite wrong in terms both of the enduring values of American constitutionalism and of Italian secular humanism.[499] But Santayana shows us the alternatives, and I certainly understand how and why some of my fellow Italian Americans have made a different choice than I have. There are, however, alternative paths. If we don't see this and make it part of our understanding, we will unconsciously and uncritically come to regard hegemonic American patriarchy as the exclusive road to American manhood, much to the cost of our happiness and our democratic constitutionalism, which is founded not on a common ethnicity or religion but on universal human rights.

What Santayana does not understand, let alone appreciate, is that the American political liberalism, which grew out of Puritanism as it secularized, could and would embrace the rights of gay people to love, and much else, including a progressive understanding of the human rights of people of color, despised religious minorities (like the Jews), women and the like.[500] It was very much my own experience, when I read Santayana's *The Life of Reason* as an undergraduate at Harvard College in 1962 to 1966, that the ethical voices of people of color in the civil rights movement and of young men in the anti-Vietnam War movement were grounded in a reasonable and principled understanding of American constitutional values and principles. Both of these movements moved me: the civil rights movement because it questioned American racism (including the racialization of Italian Americans) and the antiwar movement because it arose from the experience of men resisting the patriarchal authority of their fathers (more on this later). So even then, before the discourse of gay rights had developed, I questioned Santayana's more aristocratic liberalism and wondered if there was an alternative, more egalitarian liberalism, which would ground voices like mine and others, resisting injustice. I would search for it and, when found, give it voice.

As I read *The Last Puritan* today, Oliver's retort to Mario seems to me quite right, though Mario, the Italian American, is close to his

---

[498] See, on this point, id., pp. 253–55.

[499] See, on this point, David A. J. Richards, *Italian American*.

[500] See, for my argument, along these lines, David A. J. Richards, *Toleration and the Constitution*.

opera-singing mother as I was to my opera-singing father. But Oliver had had no real loving mother, as I had, and his father was not both loving and egalitarian in matters of gender, as was my father. Yet we were certainly Italian American, but my parents clearly resisted the demands of Italian Catholic patriarchal culture, and my father taught me that Verdi's voice was a voice that resisted the destructive impact of Italian patriarchy on the private and public life of Italian men and women, which led me to question American patriarchy long before American culture did.

What I have come to think is that Santayana, for whom the issue of American homophobia was paramount in his concerns, had himself been so damaged by the patriarchal demands of his mother that when he came to resist American homophobia (as he clearly did), he regarded the whole of American philosophy, based on Puritanism, as not only bankrupt but dangerously so an experience of moral nihilism like that James Gilligan has analyzed as the psychological source of "political religions" (see chapter 2). But Santayana does not see what Hawthorne so clearly saw in *The Scarlet Letter*, namely, that the central values of a free and equal conscience in Puritanism that had been the basis of liberal political revolutions against monarchs could also be the basis of liberal resistance to patriarchal views of sexuality and gender,[501] as it has been.[502]

The consequence of the psychological damage that American patriarchal homophobia had inflicted on Santayana was, as often happens in response to abusive demands by a patriarchal figure, that his personal and political ethics uncritically absorbed patriarchy as the model for all relationships, which he carried into his philosophy—an odd mixture of naturalism (Spinoza) and Platonism.[503] Santayana never takes seriously that a group like the Jews were themselves the long-standing victims of Christian anti-Semitism in the same way gays were the victims of Christian homophobia, and he is thus vulnerable psychologically to anti-Semitism in a way he was not to homophobia. Because he sees no nonpatriarchal alternative and regards American patriarchy as unacceptable, he turns to sympathy with one of the most extreme forms of political patriarchy, fascism. It is appalling

---

[501] See, on this point, Carol Gilligan, *The Birth of Pleasure*, pp. 133–37.
[502] See Carol Gilligan and David A. J. Richards, *The Deepening Darkness*.
[503] For one of the better statements of his mature views, see George Santayana, *Scepticism and Animal Faith: Introduction to a System of Philosophy* (New York: Dover, 1955; originally published, 1923).

that so fine and skeptical a philosophical and psychological mind, who never could or would accept the ultimate truth of fascism (unlike Ezra Pound),[504] would nonetheless lend his authority to such a monstrously inhumane ideology at war with everything he believed in about humanism.

Our study of Santayana illuminates as well a larger movement of American thought, as, in the wake of World War I,[505] Americans like T. S. Eliot and Ezra Pound follow psychologically Santayana's path to self-exile from America and repudiation of American liberal values tinged by implicit or explicit anti-Semitism[506] and, in Pound's case, quite virulent anti-Semitism and aggressive public support of Mussolini's fascism while Italy and Germany were at war with the United States, leading to his trial for treason after the war.[507] Both poets write of the experience of moral nihilism after World War I in two of their most powerful poems, Eliot's *The Wasteland* (1922) and Pound's *Hugh Selwyn Mauberley* (1920). *The Wasteland*, beginning with "The Burial of the Dead" reads like the fragmented memories and voices of a World War I trauma victim, the poem referring, at its end, to "These fragments I have shored against my

---

[504] See, on the relationship between Santayana and Pound, John McCormick, *George Santayana*, pp. 399–418.

[505] See, on the reaction to World War I, Paul Fussell, *The Great War and Modern Memory* (New York: Oxford Univeristy Press, 2000; originally published, 1975).

[506] On Eliot's anti-Semitism, Christopher Ricks, *T. S. Eliot and Prejudice* (Berkeley: University of California Press, 1988); Anthony Julius, *T. S. Eliot, Anti-Semitism and Literary Form* (Cambridge: Cambridge University Press, 1995). See also Peter Ackroyd, *T. S. Eliot: a Life* (New York: Simon and Schuster, 1984), pp. 201, 297, 303-4, 331.

[507] On Ezra Pound's life and work, see A. David Moody, *Ezra Pound: Poet: Volume I The Young Genius 1885–1920* (Oxford: Oxford University Press, 2007); *Ezra Pound: Poet Volume II The Epic Years 1921–1939* (Oxford: Oxford University Press, 2014); *Ezra Pound: Poet Volume III The Tragic Years 1939–1972* (Oxford: Oxford University Press, 2015). On his turn to fascism, see Moody, op. cit., Volume II, pp. 133–312; on his speeches supporting Italian fascism and his trial for treason and its consequences, see Moody, op. cit., Volume III, pp. 3–444. See, for illuminating discussion, Hugh Kenner, *The Pound Era* (Berkeley: University of California Press, 1971); Hugh Kenner, *The Poems of Ezra Pound* (Lincoln: University of Nebraska Press, 1985).

---

ruins."[508] And "Hugh Selwyn Mauberley" explicitly references World War I fighting experience:

> These fought, in any case, and some believing, pro
> Domo, in any case . . . Some quick to arm, some for
> adventure, some from fear of weakness, some from fear
> of censure, some for love of slaughter, in imagination,
> Learning later . . .
>
> Some in fear, learning love of slaughter; Died some "pro
> Patria, non dulce non et decor" . . .
>
> walked eye-deep in hell believing in old men's lies, then
> unbelieving came home, home to a lie, home to many
> Deceits, home to old lies and new infamy;
>
> Usury age-old and age-thick and liars in public places.
>
> Daring as never before, wastage as never before.
> Your blood and high blood,
> Fair cheeks, and fine bodies;
> fortitude as never before
>
> frankness as never before, disillusion as never told in
> the old days, hysterias, trench confessions, laughter out
> of dead bellies.
>
> THERE died a myriad,
> And of the best, among them,
> For an old bitch gone in the teeth,
> For a botched civilization,
> Charm, smiling at the good mouth,
> Quick eyes gone under earth's lid,
> For two gross of broken statues,
> For a few thousand battered books.[509]

---

[508] See T. S. Eliot, *Collected Poems 1909–1962* (Orlando: Harcourt, 1968), pp. 53–76, at p. 69.

[509] Ezra Pound, *Hugh Selwyn Mauberley* (London: The Ovid Press, 1920), pp. 4–6.

Both Eliot and Pound resolve their moral nihilism by adopting forms of patriarchal political religion in which anti-Semitism plays an important role, for Eliot, high Anglicanism and for Pound, Italian fascism. Eliot's anti-Semitism is more muted than Pound's,[510] and he regarded his version of Christianity as a way of finding a way to resist both fascism and communism.[511] But it is really quite appalling to read today *After Strange Gods*,[512] based on lectures he delivered in 1933 at the University of Virginia. The book contains "a general diatribe against contemporary American civilization—its society was 'worm-eaten by Liberalism', and some parts of the United States had been 'invaded by foreign races.' A population should ideally be 'homogeneous'—linked by ties of 'blood kinship' and not 'adulterated' by other races. Specifically, he deprecates 'the presence of free-thinking Jews.' They are 'undesirable' in large numbers."[513]

Eliot later disavowed the book and refused to allow it to be republished, but its argument illustrates how far he had ethically sunk into reactionary anti-Semitism. The lectures were given, of course, in 1933 in racist Virginia, and the contrast is drawn, of course, to my beloved New York City, the city where I fell in love with a Jewish man and that sustained and nurtured us, as it has so many others, otherwise excluded and marginalized, in an America no longer so homophobic and racist that gays and people of color had to flee. We could and did resist, and there was now resonance for our resisting voices. It is striking, psychologically, how Eliot's repudiation of the Protestant liberal unitarianism of his parents required a much more patriarchal form of Christianity closer to Roman Catholicism and a Christianity still in 1933 deeply anti-Semitic, which Eliot does not question but enforces at a time when political anti-Semitism

---

[510] See, on this point, Peter Ackroyd, *T. S. Eliot, a Life*, pp. 201, 297, 303–4, 331. But see Christopher Ricks, *T. S. Eliot and Prejudice* (London: Faber and Faber, 1988); Anthony Julius, *T. S. Eliot and anti-Semitism and Literary Form* (Cambridge: Cambridge University Press, 1995).

[511] See his unpublished 1935 lecture, "The Christian in the Modern World," published as "Outside the Catacombs," in *The Times Literary Supplement*, July 7, 2017, No. 5962, at pp. 16–18.

[512] T. S. Eliot, *After Strange Gods: A Primer of Modern Heresy* (London: Faber and Faber, 1934),

[513] See Peter Ackroyd, *T. S. Eliot: a Life*, p. 201 (quotes included).

was in Germany now ferociously in power. American liberal Protestantism is for Eliot not patriarchal enough, and somehow the Jews are at fault.[514]

Pound's experience of moral nihilism is resolved in a much more complex, creatively innovative, idiosyncratic, disturbing, and so it seems to me, pluralistically American way. Pound never gives up the role that the Founders of the American Republic—Thomas Jefferson and John Adams, in particular—play in his search for universal political truth, but he combines it with an extraordinary syncretic amalgamation of Chinese Confucianism (which he admired for its "totalitarian" sense of social responsibility)[515] in which, in his poetry in "The Cantos," the American Founders and Chinese characters, drawn from Confucius, play a prominent role as well as other languages.[516] At the heart of the heady brew, however, lies his virulent and aggressive political anti-Semitism—the Jews responsible, as he came to believe and argue, for the catastrophe of World War I and all other human woes.[517] Even Santayana, when he met and talked with Pound in Italy during and after World War II, found his fascist ranting incoherent, preferring, as he put it in a letter, "the normal and the beautiful, not abortion or eruptions like EP."[518]

Santayana ends *The Last Puritan* with World War I. Santayana leaves me with a question. Is there a connection between resistance to patriarchy's repression of love and resistance to its role in unjust war? This is a question, which Santayana cannot even ask, let alone answer, as the psychology of the initiation of men into American manhood, a subject he so brilliantly studies in *The Last Puritan*, ends tragically, essentially, reenacting the tragedy at the heart of patriarchy. We need, now more than ever, to ask new kinds of questions about the patriarchal framework itself. To attempt to pose and answer this question, we turn to the resistance to patriarchal racism and homophobia of yet another gay American who leaves America for Europe, James Baldwin.

---

[514]   See, for fuller discussion, Peter Ackroyd, T. S. Eliot: a Life.

[515]   See A. David Moody, op. cit., Volume II, p. 248.

[516]   See Ezra Pound, *The Cantos of Ezra Pound* (New York: New Directions, 1996).

[517]   See, for full discussion, A. David Moody, op. cit., Volume II.

[518]   See John McCormick, *George Santayana*, p. 400.

CHAPTER 6

James Baldwin on Gay Love and Resistance

Like both Henry James and George Santayana, James Baldwin, afflicted by American homophobia, leaves America for Europe, and he came, through the experience of gay love, to find the remarkable voice of his essays, novels, and plays—a voice which questioned both American racism and homophobia. I recall reading some of his remarkable essays when a young man but, probably more importantly, seeing him on American television—flamboyantly effeminate but always intelligently indignant at the enormities of American racism. Baldwin was showing me and others that there was a path through resisting voice that resists not only American racism but homophobia as well. People did not speak of it at the time, because while Baldwin had published at least one novel, *Giovanni's Room*, dealing with homosexuality, he did not explicitly embrace the case for gay rights until later in his life. But there was for me, now as a young man well into the 1960s, no doubt that the voice I heard on American television was a voice like no other man then speaking in public: it simply could not be coded in the ways then conventional for the speech of men or of women. It was not sober and understated but emotionally florid and yet emotionally intelligent. It was sensitive and authentically expressive and indignant. It appeals to the heart and to the mind. It had a musical cadence beyond words yet deeply expressive, like Verdi's voice struggling to resist patriarchy by breaking out of its shackles on male voice. Was Baldwin in American terms a man or a woman? Whatever he was, his voice, connected to an effeminacy that even gay men of the period detested, broke through and challenged a barrier on voice. Ethically, he showed us a new world, another country, as he put it in one of his most profound novels (shortly to be discussed). I heard his voice as a gay voice that resisted American racism and eventually resisted American homophobia. Something was now possible that I had not anticipated, and I and others could learn from it, indeed be inspired by it. If him, against such odds, why not I? The classic virtue of manhood, courage, took on a new and deeper meaning for me in my search for democratic manhood.

It was, after all, the 1960s, and Baldwin played a significant role in the civil rights movement led by Martin Luther King Jr. His example moved me, as it did many others of my generation, and I want to explore here—consistent with my over-all argument—how he came to resist and how he revealed to me and others that there was a link between the evils of American racism and homophobia, namely, American patriarchy. I have discussed elsewhere in some details his novels and plays and will limit myself here to only a few of them that illustrate his development.[519] I will, however, discuss the essays in some depth.

Baldwin was born to Berdis Jones in New York City's Harlem Hospital on August 2, 1924, an illegitimate child who never knew who his real father was.[520] Baldwin's stepfather, David Baldwin, was a preacher and laborer who came to the North from New Orleans in the early 1920s and married Berdis; they would have eight children together in addition to James, the eldest child of the family. Reverend David Baldwin became, for Baldwin, in the words of his brilliant biographer and close personal friend, David Leeming, "The archetypal black father, one generation removed from slavery, prevented by the ever-present shadow and the frequently present effects of racial discrimination from providing his family with what they needed most—their birthright, their identity as individuals rather than as members of a class or a race."[521] In the pulpit, following the tradition of the pentecostal black church, David Baldwin "called down the wrath of God on the sinners of the white Sodom and Gomorrah"; at home, "the father's prophecy took the form of an arbitrary and puritanical discipline and a depressing air of bitter frustration, which did nothing to

---

[519] See David A. J. Richards, *Why Love Leads to Justice*, pp. 150–181.

[520] David Leeming, *James Baldwin: A Biography* (New York: Knopf, 1994), p. 4.

[521] Id., p. 5.

alleviate the pain of poverty and oppression."[522] The stepfather humiliated his stepson, "making fun of his eyes and calling him the ugliest child he had ever seen."[523] And "t]here were times in Baldwin's adolescence when he nearly came to blows with his stepfather. They fought because he read books, because he liked movies, and because he had white friends. For Reverend Baldwin, all these interests were a threat to the salvation, which could only come from God."[524] His bitterness and hardness alienated even members of his church, and he was less sought after as a minister. In his late years, he became suspicious even of his family, accusing them of wanting to poison him. Eventually, Reverend Baldwin lost his job and went mad; in 1943, he was committed to a mental hospital, where he died of tuberculosis. James Baldwin came to see that "this man, who frightened him so much that 'I could never again be frightened of anything else,' was a victim of a morally bankrupt religion and a morally bankrupt society, and that he was a black parody of that bankruptcy."[525]

That Baldwin was able at least to stand his ground against a father he and all his siblings came to hate was due to countervailing influences on his early life. The greatest such influence was his mother, to whom he remained close throughout his life. If his stepfather saw the world in terms of racist stereotypes, "Berdis Baldwin constantly reminded her children that people must not be put on pedestals or scaffolds, that people have to loved for their faults as well as their virtues and their ugliness as well as their beauty."[526] There was also a white schoolteacher, Orilla Miller, and her sister, Henrietta, and later Evan Winfield, who "included him in their family not only sharing cultural activities (taking him to the theatre) but as a participant in their political discussions."[527] These friends could not, however, help him with his blackness. Two African American teachers at Frederick Douglass Junior High School, which Baldwin—then called Jimmy—entered in the fall of 1935, afforded models of how to fill the gap: Countee Cullen (already an important poet of the Harlem Renaissance) and Herman W. Porter. Cullen, in particular, "brought him

---

[522] Id., p. 5.
[523] Id., p. 6.
[524] Id., p. 7.
[525] Id., p. 8.
[526] Id., p. 9.
[527] Id., p. 16

into the school's literary club, which he had founded, and spent a great deal of time working with him on both poetry and fiction."[528] Baldwin graduated from junior high school in the summer of 1938—"a summer during which he was to be nearly overwhelmed by sexuality and, almost at the same moment, by religion," becoming a rather successful preacher for a few years, which enhanced his self-confidence. On Countee Cullen's advice, he had applied to and been accepted in 1938 into the well-known De Witt Clinton High School in Bronx, where he was exposed to excellent largely white teachers, some with PhD's; formed close friendships with other boys, all white and Jewish; and read and wrote. Baldwin shared with one of these friends, Emile Capouya, that he had recently learned of his illegitimacy, and bursting into tears, he had decided his stepfather's church could not be his and left the pulpit. Capouya suggested to Baldwin that he should meet the black painter, Beauford Delaney, who lived in Greenwich Village. "Jimmy was not yet fully aware of his own homosexuality or of the demands of his vocation, and Beauford, himself a homosexual, a minister's son and an artist was there, as a father in art, to help his younger version of himself though a crucial passage."[529] Delaney would remain a good friend to Baldwin both in New York City and later in Paris, where they had each moved.

At the end of his high school and preaching careers, Baldwin felt increasingly trapped as the eldest male child of a family with a jobless father in ill health, a working mother, and eight hungry brothers and sisters; but at the same time, he felt pulled away from them by the sense of himself as an artist and as a gay man. For a while, he joined Capouya working at a defense-related job in New Jersey, but his heart was not in his work, and when a waitress refused to serve him because of his race, he exploded. In rage, he threw a mug at her; it missed but shattered the window behind her. He got away, "[b]ut what worried him more is the fact that he had been ready to commit murder, the fact that his *real* life was in danger, not from anything other people might do but from the hatred he carried in his heart."[530] After the death of his stepfather in 1943, Baldwin moved back with his family in their Harlem apartment, but soon after decided he had

---

[528] Id., p. 22.
[529] Id., p. 33.
[530] Id., p. 40.

to move again, living first with Beauford in Greenwich Village and then with others.

He had some affairs with women, including a white Jewish women, but more numerous one-night relationships with men, now telling Capouya that he was homosexual. Prejudice interfered with his sex life, as his manner was effeminate, and he was often verbally abused "as a 'queer' by men who acted very differently when they were alone with him. Baldwin was well aware then of the agony that plagued the lives of these ostensibly 'straight' males who roamed the streets and men's rooms of the village, searching for 'faggots.' Not being attracted to men whom he considered to be pretentiously effeminate—men who pretended to be women" and thus "inevitably found himself in bed with the more ambiguous sort, and he suffered the abuse that derived from their shame."[531]

The great love of these village years was Eugene Worth, an African American man who was not gay and with whom Baldwin did not have sex and who, like Rufus in *Another Country,* committed suicide in 1946 by jumping off the George Washington Bridge. Vivaldo, an Italian American, straight man who is Baldwin's voice in *Another Country,* comes to regard with guilt his failure of physical intimacy with Rufus as a failure of love when such love was desperately needed; and Baldwin himself, though as a gay man, expressed a similar remorse over the death of Worth, who had once wondered to Baldwin whether he, Worth, was in love with him. Baldwin confesses in one of his late essays, "I was to hurt a great many people by being unable to imagine that anyone could possibly be in love with an ugly boy like me. However, when he was dead, I realized that I would have done anything whatever to have been able to hold him in this world."[532] Baldwin had been breaking the love laws for some time but had not yet been in love and acted on such love. It is only when Baldwin goes to France that he confesses: "I fell in love. Or, more accurately, I realized, and accepted for the first time that love was not merely a general human possibility not merely the disaster it had so often been for me. It was among *my* possibilities, for here it was, breathing and belching beside me, and it was the key to life."[533]

---

[531] Id., pp. 45–46.

[532] See James Baldwin, *The Price of the Ticket, Collected Essays,* ed. Toni Morrison (New York: The Library of America, 1998), pp. 830–842, p. 833.

[533] James Baldwin, *No Name in the Street,* op. cit., pp. 365–66.

Baldwin was haunted by the death of Worth both as an artist (Rufus in *Another Country*) and man, expressing his own fears about the loss of love or the inability to love and a rage—the uncontrollable rage that frightened him in his response to the New Jersey waitress—that he might turn on himself. "Suicide was a subject that obsessed him throughout his life. He lost several close friends by that route and attempted it himself at least four times."[534]

Through friends, Baldwin was now introduced to writers, including Richard Wright, who read some of his work and liked it. Baldwin wrote essays but wanted to work on novels; he "had gone about as far as he could without facing his demons head-on."[535] By 1948, a good friend advised him, "Get out—you'll die if you stay here."[536]

The move from his home country to a foreign country was profoundly transformative for Baldwin. Falling in love for the first time in his life and with a white European man in Europe released both the astonishing ethical voice of his pathbreaking investigation of the psychology of American racism in his influential essay, *Notes of a Native Son* (1955) and the artistic voice that revealed this psychology in his first three pathbreaking novels, *Go Tell It on the Mountain* (1952), *Giovanni's Room* (1956), and *Another Country* (1962). Both the essay and the novels—probably Baldwin's most enduring achievements—arose from his loving gay relationship to a white man:

> Lucien Happersberger was a Swiss who had left home in search of excitement and success in Paris. In Lucien, Jimmy found the love of his life. He was a street boy, motivated at first more by the drive to survive in a hostile environment than by any homosexual cravings, but he came to love Jimmy with genuine depth. Apparently, oblivious to what people thought of their relationship, he did not mind being called Jimmy's lover even though, during the greater part of their friendship over the next thirty-nine years, he technically was not.[537]

---

[534] David Leeming, op. cit., p. 12.

[535] Id., p. 53.

[536] Quoted at Id., p. 54.

[537] Id., pp. 74–5.

During their several years together, Jimmy and Lucien developed an emotional closeness that Baldwin had never experienced before,[538] an experience Baldwin himself called "the love of his life." The love affair did not last. "Lucien was easygoing and relaxed about the relationship. Jimmy was not. He wanted a mate, Lucien wanted a copain who would understand his need for women as well. During the years that they knew each other, Lucien was to marry three times and to produce two children. The first marriage would occur within two years of their initial meeting."[539] Baldwin would go on to have many other sexual relationships to white and, increasingly, young black men, always seeking what he had discovered in his love affair with Lucien in what he imagined and hoped would be a long-term creative relationship of equals. Baldwin never found any such long-term relationship, in part "because he was drawn not to other homosexuals but to men who were sometimes willing to act homosexually, importantly, in response to the need for money and shelter or to what can only be called his personal magnetism and persuasiveness."[540] The resentment of these men "sometimes led to beatings and, in later years, to his becoming the victim of outrageous acts of embezzlement and theft,"[541] and he sometimes despaired (thus the suicide attempts).

Nevertheless, he held onto the sense of its possibility and, of course, its value, something he could not conceive before Lucien. "Every lover he had after Lucien had to compete with the memory of him, the possibility of his return or his presence down the street, next door, or in the next room."[542] Something in his relationship to Lucien opened Baldwin's heart and mind not only to the possibility and value of gay love but to its reality, which was, he discovered, close at hand if he could but grasp and hold onto it. It was the sense of this reality, so close at hand, that led to Baldwin's astonishing investigation of what held him and others back, namely, the violence directed at any love that challenged the irrational boundaries imposed by patriarchy—in particular, anti-Semitism, racism, sexism, and homophobia. Strikingly, "the love of his life," Lucien, was with him as death approached. Songs of Bessie Smith were on the television. These were songs he had

---

[538] Id., p. 75.

[539] Id., pp. 75–76.

[540] Id., p. 76.

[541] Id., p. 76.

[542] Id., p. 76.

listened to on the Swiss mountain with Lucien as he wrote his first novel. Now Lucien was there, and Bessie Smith was singing again.[543] It was when he lived intimately with Lucien in an isolated Swiss village that he found the creative voice of his essay *Notes of a Native Son* and his astonishing first novel, *Go Tell It on the Mountain*,[544] and Baldwin would continue to draw on the what he had learned from the relationship even after it ended, in his remarkable next two novels, *Giovanni's Room* and *Another Country*.

Baldwin broke the love laws with a man and a man who was white and from a different culture but in a way that Baldwin had never experienced before because he had never fallen in love and been loved in this way. It was this experience of real relationship—free and improvisatory, "full of laughter, food, sex, and above all, drink"[545]—that released Baldwin from the hold of the internalized racial stereotypes that afflicted his violently racist stepfather. Through loving experience, Baldwin came to see in himself and Lucien the same range of human thoughts and feelings and free voice in relationship (thus free of both the gender binary and hierarchy) and the centrality for both of them of the human need for loving and being loved, the north star of Baldwin's life and work. The question this raised for Baldwin is how and why such love had previously been for him so unthinkable, indeed the object of fear and anger and violence by others and himself. The question became real for Baldwin through the experience of gay love, and in several of his novels, he answers the question in terms of what divides gay men from such love or what brings a straight man to such love with a gay man.

In *Giovanni's Room*, David, a white American, had in Paris come to acknowledge and explore his homosexuality in a love affair with an Italian, Giovanni. When he abruptly rejects Giovanni in a rather savagely unfeeling way, ostensibly to marry a white woman, Giovanni confronts David with his coldness and terror and his resulting self-deceived failure of relationship, which would poison his life. "Giovanni has no one to talk to and no one to be with, and where he has found a lover who is neither man nor woman, nothing that I can know or touch."[546] What David cannot and

---

[543] Id., p. 385.

[544] See James Baldwin, *Go Tell It on the Mountain, Early Novels and Stories*, ed. Toni Morrison (New York: The Library of America, 1998), pp. 1–215.

[545] David Leeming, *James Baldwin*, p. 75.

[546] See James Baldwin, *Giovanni's Room, Early Novels and Stories*, ed. Toni

---

will not see is what Giovanni had seen revealed in him in their passionate love, that he is "neither man nor woman." Similarly, in *Another Country*, when Vivaldo, a straight man, unburdens his heart to and eventually makes love to a gay man, Eric, he sees that Eric lives in the truth of human love and relationship. "It was a quality to which great numbers of people would respond without knowing to what it is that they are responding. There is great force in the face and great gentleness. But as most women are not gentle, nor most men strong, it is a face that suggested, resonantly, in the depths, the truth about our natures."[547] The truth about our natures is that the gender binary and hierarchy—the heart of patriarchy—are false and destructively false because they cut us off from loving relationships based on freedom and equality.

Baldwin saw this destructive force as quite general, cutting off straight women and men, as well from real relationship, as when, in *Another Country*, Vivaldo and his married woman friend, Cass, approach having a relationship in which Vivaldo can speak of his deepest worries. Then Vivaldo draws back, "feeling his hope and his hope of safety threatened by invincible, unnamed forces within himself."[548] Baldwin now could see from experience that his stepfather's demonization of whites was as false as his idealization of blacks, resting on the violence and lies by which patriarchy enforces the gender binary and hierarchy, violence and lies that Baldwin had himself endured, as an effeminate and "strange" boy at the hands of his stepfather and so many others. Everything we know about trauma and the violence Baldwin endured at the hands of his stepfather and others was traumatic, and it clarifies how Baldwin, a child, would have identified with his aggressor, absorbing his gender stereotypes into his own psyche, clarifying why he would, before Lucien, have acted on his homosexual feelings in self-punishing ways.

Perhaps Baldwin never entirely freed his personal life from the burdens of such trauma, but his love affair with Lucien showed him there was a way out and he was to spend the rest of his life showing others what he had discovered though, tragically, he never fully realized his hope for enduring

---

Morrison (New York: The Library of America, 1998), pp. 221–360, pp. 334–5.

[547] James Baldwin, *Another Country* (New York: Vintage International, 1990; originally published, 1960), p. 330.

[548] Id., p. 237.

---

love with another man. It is a mark of the continuing power of patriarchy that it sometimes remains intractably at work in our intimate lives, long after we have resisted it elsewhere. Nonetheless, effectively freed, for the first time in his life and from the gender binary and hierarchy that enforces patriarchy by repressing resisting voice, Baldwin found the voice to write his first great essay and most brilliant novel—a novel in which he shows what he had learned through the experience of love about how patriarchy destroys love, as it had destroyed his stepfather. Lucien was at this time his lover and companion.

What Baldwin had discovered that would make the subject of his essays, novels, and plays was both an astonishing insight into the personal and political psychology of patriarchy, and it was a corresponding insight into how culture, in particular, American culture, had both constructed its sense of identity in terms of this repressive psychology and yet made possible and imperative a resisting voice that might and would and should challenge its injustice. Baldwin was himself to exemplify such liberal voice for Americans, white and black, gay and straight, of his remarkable generation of both transformative political change and reaction, in which he came to play an increasingly important role as a public figure in America's vibrant civil society.

Baldwin explains how he came to a sense of the American dimension of the problem in "Stranger in the Village,"[549] the last essay in *Notes of a Native Son*.[550] He reflects on his experience of living with Lucien in an isolated Swiss village, where no blacks had ever been seen. Baldwin was struck by the response to his strangeness of the Swiss: "All the physical characteristics of the Negro, which had caused me, in America, a very different and almost forgotten pain were nothing less than miraculous— or infernal—in the eyes of the village people. In all this, in which it must be conceded, there was the charm of genuine wonder and in which there was certainly no element of intentional unkindness. There was yet no suggestion that I was human: I was simply a living wonder."[551] The very different response to him of the Swiss prompted reflection on the distinctive history of America in which blacks were coercively brought

---

[549] See James Baldwin, "Stranger in the House," *Collected Essays,* ed. Toni Morrison (New York: The Library of America, 1998), pp. 117–129.

[550] See James Baldwin, *Notes of a Native Son,* id., pp. 5–116.

[551] Id., p. 119.

to America as slaves stripped of their history, and yet in contrast to the relationship of European imperialists to the blacks and other ethnicities they ruled over in distant colonies, American blacks were intimately part of American culture, including, paradoxically, its ideals of democracy and human rights. It was this very intimacy and the contradiction of slavery and racism to their democratic ideals that led Americans to "the idea of white supremacy"—an idea central to "the heritage of the West"—but "Americans made themselves notorious by the shrillness and the brutality with which they have insisted on this idea." Americans did not invent the idea, but "it has escaped the world's notice that these very excesses of which Americans have been guilty imply a certain, unprecedented uneasiness over the idea's life and power, if not, indeed the idea's validity." What it called for was to deny the "human reality" of black people, with whom they lived so closely—their "human weight and complexity and the strain of denying the overwhelmingly undeniable forced Americans into rationalizations so fantastic that they approach the pathological."[552] It was only when Baldwin came to Europe (fleeing a country he thought he despised) and fell in love with a white European that he realized how American he was and how much his own psyche, as an American black, was framed by its distinctive history, both its democratic ideals and its savage racism. What Baldwin came to realize on his Swiss mountaintop with Lucien is that, in light of this history, American blacks "could turn his peculiar status in the Western world to his own advantage, and it may be to the great advantage of the world. It remains for him to fashion out of his experience that which will give him sustenance and a voice."[553]

What such voice could show us, Baldwin now writing in his own resisting voice as a black American, is that because of both their democratic ideals and their racism, "Americans are as unlike any other white people in the world as it is possible to be." For example, "the American vision of the world—which allows so little reality, generally speaking, for any of the darker forces in human life and which tends until today to paint moral issues in glaring black and white—owes a great deal to the battle waged by Americans to maintain between themselves and black men a human separation, which could not be bridged. It is only now beginning to be borne in on us that this vision of the world is dangerously inaccurate and

---

[552] Id., pp. 126–7.
[553] Id., p. 128.

perfectly useless. For it protects our moral high-mindedness at the terrible expense of weakening our grasp of reality."[554]

"Stranger in the Village" leads to the question, How had such a dangerously unreal and unjust separation become part of the fabric of American life? Once Baldwin realized how deeply American he, a black and gay American, was, he saw that exploring racism within the American black community, something he knew at firsthand from his stepfather, was a way of understanding the personal and political psychology of American racism generally. If blacks, so clearly the victims of American racism, could themselves reactively embrace a form of it that would reveal the power of the psychology that sustains racism, something American blacks and whites, as Americans, tragically shared. Falling in love with a European white man in Europe—showing him that he could love and be loved— released Baldwin from the fear and anger he had experienced in his sexual life in America, an uncontrollable rage that he had come to fear in himself (the incident with the New Jersey waitress). It is often a feature of thus falling in love that each of the lovers, in falling in love with and coming into real relationship with the individual they come to love, come to know and understand the web of relationships stretching from early childhood forward that made the beloved the person he or she is, including the traumas and losses, the love and hate, the hopes and fears, which are always part of the complex fabric of a human life. Baldwin experienced such a love for and with Lucien; thus, through the experience of being loved for the complex person he was, he could see himself and give honest voice to the web of persons and relationships that shaped his psyche, including the rage and anger he absorbed from his violently racist stepfather.

Baldwin thus writes, while living with Lucien, his intimately autobiographical first novel, *Go Tell It on the Mountain*,[555] about a young black man, John Grimes, modeled on Baldwin and his early relationships, at the time Baldwin first found his voice as a magnetic religious preacher, a vocation that he soon abandoned but a vocation that prefigures the compelling and truthful ethical voice of his novels and essays. (At times, Baldwin seems like the thundering and piercing Jonathan Edwards of his time.) John is portrayed as in love with an older black straight boy, Elisha,

---

[554]   Id., pp. 128–9.

[555]   See James Baldwin, *Go Tell It on the Mountain, Early Novels and Stories*, ed. Toni Morrison (New York: The Library of America, 1998), pp. 1–215.

his teacher, and though their relationship is not sexual at all, it is John's love for Elisha that brings him to a sense of his own voice as a preacher (just as, later on, it would be Baldwin's sexual love for Lucien that would lead to his voice as an essayist and artist). What the novel is essentially about is John's struggle for voice and for love, coming to understand his struggle in light of the impact on him of the three main influences on his early life—his mother, his violent stepfather, and his stepfather's sister, all of whom moved from the South to Harlem and were important persons in his early life. The question explored in *Go Tell It on the Mountain* is why his preacher stepfather not only did not love as his mother did but was indeed consumed and ultimately destroyed by hatred.

What makes the novel so riveting is that Baldwin focusses on the damage to love in intimate life as the key to understanding how blacks and whites, living, unlike Europeans, so closely together, could accept a racism that requires their separation. The damage Baldwin identifies is the moral injury inflicted on the human psyche by the patriarchal love laws, an injury that he analyzes as the source of his stepfather's violently self-destructive racism, which arises, reactively, as a response to the racism of Southern whites.

The racism of Southern whites rested on the racialized pedestal that ascribed to all white women an idealized purity and unjustly ascribed to all blacks a degraded, indeed rapacious sexuality, and thus rationalized extraordinary forms of violence (lynchings) directed at any suggestion or suspicion of sex between black men and white women, much of which was, in fact, consensual. Sex between white men and black women, often exploitative, was, in contrast, conventional, though officially condemned because it was supported by the stereotype of degraded black sexuality. What kept American whites and blacks in the American South, who were otherwise so intimately connected, apart was the internalization of the patriarchal love laws, which held Southern white women, in particular, on a tight leash of patriarchal control of their sexual desires and love lives. Antimiscegenation laws were thus very much at the American heart of darkness, expressing itself in a wanton violence and irrationalist dehumanization. As Baldwin put the point, what American racism called for was to deny the "human reality" of black people, with whom they lived so closely. Their "human weight and complexity and the strain of denying the overwhelmingly undeniable forced Americans into rationalizations so fantastic that they approach the pathological."[556] It was precisely because intimate affections and love, including sexual love, were so humanly natural among people so intimately connected, as blacks and whites in the American South clearly were, that the moral injury inflicted by the violently irrational repression of such love made thinkable what should have been unthinkable, the massive cultural dehumanization of people of color.

What Baldwin comes to see in his stepfather is that, brought up in the racist South as he was, his own racism against whites mirrored the basis of the racism of whites, since both accepted the unjust terms patriarchy imposed on intimate life. Patriarchy draws its power and appeal from the way it rationalizes the abridgement of basic human rights of whole classes of persons by dehumanizing them through enforcing stereotypes that, in a vicious circularity, arise from the repression of the resisting voice of those who might and would challenge such stereotypes. It is these stereotypes that idealize those who conform to patriarchal demands on a pedestal and denigrate those who do not conform. The only difference between white and black racism is whom they idealize or denigrate. Both seek to control sex and love to the ends of patriarchy, as they understand it. For blacks like Baldwin's stepfather, since the racialized pedestal unjustly ascribed to all blacks a degraded sexuality, resistance to such unjust images in the black churches led to insistence on a form of idealization of good black women's sexuality that rested on repression of sexual voice, and a corresponding devaluation of any women who had a free sexual voice and lived accordingly. There was to be no friendship or love across the boundaries patriarchy required.

What Baldwin shows us in his first novel is the effects of the patriarchal pedestal (good asexual vs. bad sexual women) on the psychology and ethics of black men and women of the South. Baldwin is mainly concerned with the impact of this form of the pedestal on men like his stepfather, who was first urged on Gabriel (based on Baldwin's stepfather) by Gabriel's devout mother and, after a history of sexual dalliance, adopted by him at her death when he becomes a minister. In the novel, Gabriel's devotion to her ideals takes the form of marrying Deborah, a woman scorned by other black men as tainted because she had been raped by white men. In dreams he has before deciding to marry her, Gabriel first dreams of having armored himself in

---

[556] Id., pp. 126–7.

chastity, about to be stoned, and then battling (he wakes with a nocturnal emission) and then dreams of being on a cold mountaintop and asked by a voice to go higher, finally coming to the sun and to peace.[557] As his dream shows, he married Deborah not from love but from a sense of better meeting his religious ideals, which disfavor any sexual feeling for the woman he marries; in fact, she is childless. Gabriel is then attracted to and has an affair with a young woman, Esther, who gets pregnant by him. He refuses to consider her proposal—to leave his wife and run off with her—because he regards her as a fallen women.[558] Esther is repelled by his dishonesty, his fear, and his shame, which in turn shames her: "[b]efore my *God* —to make me cheap, like you done, done . . . I guess it takes a holy man to make a girl a real whore."[559] Gabriel steals money from Deborah to help Esther leave for Chicago; she dies in childbirth, leaving a son, Royal, whom Gabriel never acknowledges his own and is killed as a young man. After the boy's death and before her own, Deborah confronts Gabriel with the truth, questioning his judgment about not going with the women he evidently sexually loved but regarded as a "harlot" ("Esther weren't no harlot,"[560] Deborah opines). "He has," Deborah says, "done the wrong thing both ethically and before God."[561] Both Esther and Deborah identify Gabriel's sense of the pedestal as the root of what cuts him off from any real relationship to them or to any person or God. The heart of Gabriel's problem is that his enforcement of the patriarchal love laws rests on an irrationalist propensity to violence at any challenge to his patriarchal authority, including his violence against and thus moral injury to his own capacity for love, and his violence against others, including his gender-bending stepson.

There can be little doubt that Baldwin, whom his stepfather found ugly, effeminate, and "strange," came to see his own plight, as a black gay man, as at one with the pedestal's denigration of black sexual women. In his first play, *The Amen Corner* (1968), Baldwin studied the same issue from the perspective of a black woman minister, Sister Margaret, who, like his stepfather, reacts to the racism she endured by placing herself on

---

557 See James Baldwin, *Go Tell It on the Mountain*, op. cit., pp. 105–107.
558 Id., p. 126.
559 Id., p. 128.
560 Id., p. 143.
561 Id., pp. 142–144.

an idealized pedestal, breaking any real loving relationship to her husband and son. As Baldwin put the point of the play, "Her sense of reality is dictated by the society's assumption, which also becomes her own, of her inferiority. Her need for human affirmation, and also vengeance, expresses itself in her merciless piety, and her love, which is real but is also at the mercy of her genuine and absolutely justifiable terror, turns her into a tyrannical matriarch."[562] Baldwin had come through the experience of love to see his own internalized fear and anger as arising from his own internalization of his stepfather's violence against any form of sexual love that defied patriarchal controls, a violence that black women under patriarchy could and did enact as well. In contrast, John's love for Elisha leads to his resonant voice as a minister, which clearly anticipates the voice Baldwin would find through his love for Lucien. Baldwin would not and did not make his stepfather's disastrous mistake.

Baldwin elsewhere describes the boundaries that the racialized pedestal, when absorbed into the minds and lives of blacks, imposes on any possibility of real relationships among them, a traumatic break in relationship "like one of those floods that devastate counties, tearing everything down, tearing children from their parents and lovers from each other, and making everything an unrecognizable waste."[563] The consequence is damning:

> You very soon, without knowing it, give up all hope of communion. Black people, mainly, look down or look up but do not look at each other, not at you, and white people, mainly, look away. And the universe is simply a sounding drum; there is no way, no way whatever, so it seemed then and has sometimes seemed since, to get through a life, to love your wife and children or your friends or your mother and father or to be loved.[564]

---

[562] James Baldwin, *The Amen Corner* (New York: Vintage International, 1996), at p. xvi.

[563] James Baldwin, "The Fire Next Time," *Collected Essays,* ed. Toni Morrison (New York: The Library of America, 1998), pp. 291–347, at p. 304.

[564] Id., p. 304.

The pedestal kills real sensual relationships of mutual voice, thus kills relationships:

> To be sensual, I think, is to respect and rejoice in the force of life, of life itself, and to be *present* in all that one does, from the effort of loving to the breaking of bread. The person who distrusts himself has no touchstone for reality—for this touchstone can be only oneself. Such a person interposes between himself and reality nothing less than a labyrinth of attitudes.[565]

The pedestal is one component of this "labyrinth of attitudes," a stereotypical assumption that cuts one off not only from the voice of others but from one's own personal emotional voice. It thus stultifies emotional intelligence, without which love is narcissism. Baldwin had seen this in his father and other preachers and had come, for this reason, to be skeptical about the Christianity of the black churches in particular and of established religion in general. He would be skeptical to the end of his life, though his own voice, as an essayist and artist, was an ethically transformative voice that he first found as a black minister.

The importance of his homosexuality to Baldwin's life and work, only dealt with peripherally in *Go Tell It on the Mountain,* is stage central in his second novel, *Giovanni's Room,* dedicated to Lucien. *Giovanni's Room* contrasts with his other five novels in both style and content. Whereas all the other novels deal with complex webs of interpersonal relationships, *Giovanni's Room* has the starkness of Greek tragedy and has no black characters. It is about the relatively short sexual relationship of a white American, David, living in Paris and an Italian bartender, Giovanni. There are two other gay characters, Jacques and Guillaume, Giovanni's boss whom he murders and Hella, an American woman whom David will ask to marry him at the end of the novel. The narrative voice of the novel is David, the white American who had had a gay relationship with another boy when young and then abruptly ended it and thought of himself and acted thereafter as straight. Giovanni, in his village in Italy, had had a child with a woman. The child and woman died in childbirth, and he comes to Paris to escape. Quite handsome, he becomes a bartender in a gay bar,

---

[565] Id., pp. 311–12.

where he meets and falls in love with David. Both David and Giovanni are white, quite good-looking and neither effeminate, so Baldwin is editing out of the narrative issues that were, in fact, central to his own struggles as a black gay man. Their passionate sexual affair lasts a few months in Giovanni's one-room apartment, which becomes for them both a kind of new world of thought and feeling but one confined, claustrophobically, to Giovanni's room. Abruptly, David abandons Giovanni, who is distraught in losing the person he thought was the love of his life. He loses his job when Guillaume sexually exploits and then falsely accuses him of theft and murders him, and at the end of the novel, he is punished by the guillotine. Hella, when she discovers the nature of David's relationship to Giovanni, rejects him, and David clearly will settle into a life quite like the ostensibly straight men Baldwin knew in New York City who haunted gay bars to pick up gay men like Baldwin, with whom they have sex and for whom they have contempt.

Baldwin's voice in the novel is the novel's victim, Giovanni (since Italians were racialized in both France the America). Baldwin sometimes uses Italian ethnics to capture his experience as a black men, as he does in *Giovanni's Room* and would again do with Vivaldo in his next novel, *Another Country*, and with Jerry and his Sicilian friends in his fourth novel, *Tell Me How Long the Train's Been Gone* (1968).[566] Giovanni's voice is, as one would expect, wonderfully intelligent, funny, loving, and compelling (like Baldwin's), and his indictment of David in the gripping scene of David's rejection of him has the force of an ethical sermon on the problematic and crippling homophobia of American manhood in a man like David, who cannot love the one man who loved him and whom he loved, settling instead for a life of self-deception and furtive homosexual liaisons. David would remain haunted to his death by a sense of moral guilt and responsibility for Giovanni's death, killing the man he loved, as the violence of homophobia requires.

Baldwin's motives in writing *Go Tell It on the Mountain* arose from his experience of and desire to understand and make sense of his stepfather's violence and its intrapsychic impact on him, as a gay man. It was because his stepfather's violence against Baldwin was so clearly directed at his stepson's effeminacy and strangeness that Baldwin saw so early the roots

---

[566] See, for example, James Baldwin, *Tell Me How Long the Train's Been Gone* (New York: Dell, 1968), at pp. 118–19.

of such violence in patriarchy, albeit a black reactive interpretation of patriarchy, which he saw had poisoned not only the intimate lives of white men and women but blacks as well. It is this insight, arising from his close observation of his stepfather and of himself and others, that led him in *Giovanni's Room* to offer one of the first and most piercing indictments of American homophobia, which cold cruelty rests, as it did with David, on an irrational panic at any threat to a self-conception of American manhood that men like David could not question, though its costs to them and others were, for Baldwin, catastrophic. Baldwin strips race from the novel because he wants to identify the American pathology as rooted in a powerful conception of American manhood and womanhood, which extended to both whites and blacks, both of whom Baldwin came to see, through his love for a European white man in Europe, as deeply American.

Baldwin's most ambitious attempt to bring together his insights into American racism, sexism, and homophobia is his third novel, *Another Country*. In one of his most remarkable later essays, "No Name in the Street" (1972), Baldwin wrote of these insights in terms of an American disassociation that could not connect the evils of public life to those of private life:

> I have always been struck, in America, by an emotional poverty so bottomless and a terror of human life, of human touch, so deep, that virtually no American appears able to achieve any viable, organic connection between his public stance and private life. This is what makes them so baffling, so moving, so exasperating, and so untrustworthy.[567]

Another Country examines the moral injury inflicted on American private life by the patriarchal love laws, in particular, the interlinked evils of American racism, sexism, and homophobia. What Baldwin wanted to expose for discussion was the connection between public stance and private life, and *Another Country* thus examines a broad range of cases in which conforming to or breaking the love laws is the center of discussion, sometimes leading to disaster, sometimes liberation through love, resisting

---

[567] James Baldwin, *No Name in the Street, Collected Essays,* ed. Toni Morrison (New York: The Library of America, 1998), pp. 353–475, at p. 385.

patriarchy. These include a black straight man's (Rufus's) disastrously violent sexual affair with a white Southern woman. Vivaldo, a white writer and the closest friend of Rufus who fails to give Rufus the support he needs when his depression will lead to committing suicide, leading Vivaldo wondering if he should have made love to Rufus, and Eric, a gay American actor who had had an unhappy love affair with Rufus and would soon find love in France with a younger man, Yves, and on his return to America, has a sexual affair with Vivaldo, which helps Vivaldo resolve his guilt about Rufus and better understand the problems in his sexual affair with Rufus's black singer sister, Ida. Eric also has an adulterous affair with Cass, the unhappily married white wife, with two children, of a successful American novelist, Richard, leading to the end of the marriage, and the possibility for Cass of a life in which she might realize more fully both her need for real relationships and a vocation that might fulfill her.

The heart of the novel is Vivaldo's interracial love for Rufus's black sister, Ida. Baldwin later wrote of "My heroine, Ida, who in effect dictated a great deal of the book to me."[568] While it is clear that Ida loves Vivaldo and Vivaldo loves her, though the relationship is fraught with misunderstanding. Ida, an ambitious and talented singer, has an affair with a rather repelling agent to advance her career, as Vivaldo has an affair with Eric. Nonetheless, Ida's internal life only emerges into the open late in the novel, as she and Vivaldo acknowledge to each other what they have each done, making love to others, and what they have been struggling within their relationship (namely, the specter of Rufus, whom they both loved and failed). What is striking about the Ida-Vivaldo relationship is that they are lovers and also ambitious artists and that they come to a sense of the value of their love, as now free and equal, through honest voice, finally opening up to one another about the legitimacy of their ambitions and their common love of Rufus.

Baldwin shows us in *Another Country* what he had come to understand about being American when he found love in Europe with a European man, namely, that breaking the love laws could release an ethical voice that resisted the injustices of patriarchy. For this to be possible, we need to find in our intimate relationships "another country"—a love based in freedom and equality on the basis of which a good and just life would be possible.

---

[568] James Baldwin, *Notes of a Native Son, Collected Essays,* ed. Toni Morrison (New York: The Library of America, 1998), pp. 707–713, at p. 708.

Breaking the love laws may, if patriarchal domination of women by men remains unquestioned, be disastrous (Rufus and his Southern mistress). But failure to break the love laws (Vivaldo not having a love affair with Rufus) may also be disastrous, if it reflects a homophobic panic leading to a disastrous failure of love. And breaking the love laws may be the key to new relationships if, like the adultery of Cass and Eric or the love of Eric and Yves or the love of Eric and Vivaldo or the love of Eric and Cass or, finally, the love of Vivaldo and Ida, it frees people from the patriarchal disassociation, which has blighted their lives and makes possible a life lived in the truth and value of free and equal love—another country.

Baldwin may have tried to do too much in *Another Country*, but its ambition is to show us quite concretely what our lives might be like if we took seriously what he had come to believe was the heart of the greatest evils in American cultural and political life—its racism, sexism, and homophobia. Its narrative is undoubtedly sometimes forced, more working out the abstract logic of Baldwin's insight into the importance of breaking the love laws than plausibly showing us how lives embody these insights. A gay man may certainly love and help straight friends, as Eric does transforming the lives of Vivaldo and Cass, but in the context of the novel, his erotic availability and goodness, as a kind of gay savior, strain credulity, exemplifying the kind of idealization of sexuality of which Baldwin was usually so skeptical. Nonetheless, the novel has moments of shattering tragic force (the suicide of Rufus) and of transcendent erotic power (as Baldwin relives his love affair, now ended, with Lucien, narrating the only relationship in the novel that seems deeply loving, the love of Eric and Yves in France, a love that Eric believes will end as Yves matures).

Baldwin continued to write novels: *Tell Me How Long the Trains Been Gone* (1968), *If Beale Street Could Talk* (1973), and *Just Above My Head* (1979). These novels draw upon Baldwin's experience as now a public celebrity and an influential activist in the civil rights movement; it was a telegram from Baldwin, over the violence in Birmingham calling for action by the federal government, to then attorney-general Robert Kennedy that led to an angry meeting with Baldwin and other black leaders in New York City, a meeting that may have prompted a speech by President Kennedy that he would propose pathbreaking civil rights rights legislation.[569] Baldwin also now increasingly depended on the love of his family and their children,

---

[569] See David Leeming, *James Baldwin*, pp. 222.

including their active involvement in helping manage his demanding life of writing and public appearances (he was particularly close with his brother, David, who was a manager of his affairs). Baldwin had, of course, been the eldest child in a large family, and thus had been a caretaker of his younger brothers and sisters, and the sensitivity of his treatment of young children in his works arose from this experience (e.g., *Go Tell It on the Mountain* and his short children's novel, *Little Man, Little Man,* written from the point of view of black boys in Harlem).[570] Baldwin never forgot the traumatized boy in the sometimes violent and unhappy man. While he fled America to find his voice in Europe and continued largely to live in Europe, he had deeply missed his family and no doubt experienced guilt for abandoning them, and his now frequent visits to America allowed him to reconnect and deepen relationships, which were to prove among the most supportive in his later life. Baldwin continued to have love affairs with younger men, and after the murders of Medgar Evers, Martin Luther King Jr., and Malcolm X, all of whom he knew personally and admired, he was drawn to young black militant men and was involved with and supported, as did his close friend, the actor, Marlon Brando, the Black Panthers, and others.[571] These experiences, including a sense for him of the emotional hollowing of his celebrity, are drawn upon in his three later novels.

Baldwin had increasingly returned to the United States both to observe and participate in the civil rights movement—the most important challenge to American racism in our history. His essays, for example, are often a personal narrative of both what he observed and experienced during his increasingly frequent returns, riveting, indignant, and incisive. And many of my generation of liberal whites, who often despaired, as Baldwin did, in response to the murder a number of both white and black leaders of resistance, some of whom (like Medgar Evers and King practiced nonviolent resistance), found in Baldwin's essays and in his increasingly frequent appearances on American television, the honest, uncompromising ethical voice we then desperately needed to hear to keep alive our own resisting voices and hopes during a dark, increasingly reactionary time— the presidencies of Richard Nixon and Ronald Reagan.

---

[570] See James Baldwin, *Little Man Little Man: a Story of Childhood,* written by James Baldwin and illustrated by Yoran Cazac (New York: The Dial Press, 1976).

[571] See Id., pp. 290–95.

Baldwin had been born and brought up in Harlem but had experienced the effects of Southern racism in the psyches of his stepfather, mother, and aunt, all of whom have moved from the South to Harlem. Now for the first time in his life, Baldwin went South as a celebrity and told us truths we have never heard before about the character of racism in the South, which arose, as he showed us, from the terror racist Southerners brought to the enforcement of the love laws, including—as Baldwin, a gay black man, insists on showing in harrowing personal terms—its homophobia. His words from *No Name in the Street* (1972) bear repeating:

> I have written elsewhere about those early days in the South, but from a distance more or less impersonal. I have never, for example, written about my unbelieving shock when I realized that I was being groped by one of the most powerful men in one of the states I visited. He got himself sweating drunk in order to arrive at this despairing titillation. With his wet eyes staring up at my face and his wet hands groping for my cock, we were both, abruptly, in history's ass-pocket. It was very frightening, not the gesture itself but the abjectness of it, and the assumption of a swift and grim complicity: as my identity was defined by his power, so was my humanity to be placed at the service of his fantasies. This man, with a phone call, could prevent or provoke a lynching. Therefore, one had to be friendly, but the price for this was your cock.
>
> This will sound an exaggerated statement to Americans, who will suppose it to refer, merely, to sexual (or sectional) abnormality. This supposition misses the point, which is double-edged. The slave knows, however, his master may be deluded in this point, that he is called slave because his manhood has been or can be or will be taken from him. In the case of American slavery, the black's right to his women, as well as to his children, was simply taken from him, and whatever bastards the white man begat on the bodies of black women took their condition from the condition of their mother: blacks were not the only stallions of the slave-breeding farms! And one of the many results of this loveless, money-making

conspiracy was that, in giving the master every conceivable sexual and commercial license, it also emasculated them of any human responsibility—to their women, to their children, or to themselves. The results of this blasphemy resound in this country, on every private and public level, until this hour. When the man grabbed my cock, I didn't think of him as a faggot, which, indeed, if having a wife and children, house, cars, and a respectable and powerful standing in the community, mean anything, he wasn't. I watched his eyes, thinking, with great sorrow, *The unexamined life is not worth living.*[572]

What is poignant about this observation is that it centers not only on the moral injury the love laws inflict on blacks but on whites. Baldwin's second and most important play, *Blues for Mister Charlie* (1964), further explores this observation. The play arose from the racist murder of Emmett Till and the resulting trial and acquittal, dramatizing the very different ways the black and white communities interpret the evidence given to the court. The play takes seriously the burdens nonviolence imposed on a black community subject to racist violence, but its main attention is on the burden Southern racism imposed on the two white men, Lyle Britten (the store owner who murders a black boy for disrespectfully speaking to his wife) and Parnell James (a wealthy liberal newspaper editor). Parnell is a close friend both of the black family of the boy who was killed, and of Lyle, and is caught between the opposing parties at the trial. Both Parnell and Lyle have slept with black women in the town, but Lyle, seeking respectability, married a white, well-educated librarian, Jo, whereas Parnell has continued to sleep with blacks, expressing both his desire and ambivalence: "Out with it, Parnell, the nigger lover! Black boys and girls! I've wanted my hands full of them, wanted to drown them, laughing and dancing and making love, making love—wow!—and be transformed, formed, liberated of this gray-white envelope."[573] Both Lyle and Parnell broke the love laws, sleeping with black women, but Lyle did so in the clandestine way white man of the

---

[572] James Baldwin, *No Name in the Street, Collected Essays*, ed. Toni Morrison (New York: The Library of America, 1998), pp. 353–475, at pp. 390–91.

[573] See James Baldwin, *Blues for Mister Charlie* (New York: Vintage International, 1992), at p. 106.

South did, acting on the racialized pedestal that idealized white women as asexual and degraded black women as sexual. Thus, Lyle marries a good white woman to preserve his respectability, and indeed, the motive for the murder of the black boy is a perceived insult to his white wife. Parnell is in a very different place, himself regarding his breaking of the love laws as the explanation for his ethical feeling for blacks and his objection to Southern racism. Of all the people who testify at the trial, only Parnell speaks truthfully, and he later challenges Lyle for making his wife, Jo, lie at the trial that the black boy sexually assaulted her, when in fact he only spoke disrespectfully. The pathos of the play—blues for Mr. Charlie—is the pathos of Parnell, now regarded as a renegade to the white race and, at the end of play, allowed by blacks to "walk in the same direction."[574] Parnell exemplifies Baldwin's lifelong view that American racism inflicted devastating moral injury on whites, in particular, on their intimate sexual lives.

When Baldwin met Martin Luther King Jr., he commented, "Reverend King is not like any preacher I have ever met before. For one thing, to state it baldly, I liked him."[575] He was thinking, of course, of his stepfather and the other such ministers he had known. King was clearly a counterexample to Baldwin's negative view of black preachers, "[w]hat he says to Negroes, he will say to whites, and what he says to whites, he will say to Negroes. He is the first Negro leader in my experience, or the first in many generations, of whom this can be said."[576] But Baldwin, for all his admiration of and active support for King and his movement, did take critical note of a problem in black leadership, including King: "[o]ne of the greatest vices of the white bourgeoisie on which they have modeled themselves is its reluctance to think, its distrust of the independent mind."[577] Even King had uncritically absorbed a conventionality, which mirrored white conventionality, acquiescing, for example, in pressure brought "to force the resignation of his (King's) extremely able organizer and lieutenant, Bayard

---

[574] Id., p. 121.
[575] James Baldwin, "The Dangerous Road Before Martin Luther King," in James Baldwin, *Collected Essays,* ed. Toni Morrison (New York: The Library of America, 1998), pp. 638–658, at p. 638.
[576] Id., p. 639.
[577] Id., p. 655.

Rustin."[578] The resignation had been forced by Rustin's homosexuality. For Baldwin (a gay man), yielding to such pressures reflects the hypocritical public face of sexual conventionality, compromising the central aim of the civil rights leadership, recognition of the human rights of all on equal terms, which "necessarily carries with it the idea of sexual freedom: the freedom to meet, sleep with, and marry whom one chooses."[579] Baldwin is making reference to the racist obsession with miscegenation; the response of such conventionality is: "I am afraid we must postpone it [the right to sexual freedom] for the moment, to consider just why so many people appear to be convinced that Negroes would then immediately meet, sleep with, and marry white women; who, remarkably enough, are only protected from such undesirable alliances by the majesty and vigilance of the law."[580] The issue of sexual freedom is not, Baldwin argues, peripheral to the civil rights movement, but central, as the Supreme Court itself recognized in 1967 when it struck down anti-miscegenation laws in *Loving v. Virginia*.[581]

Baldwin found in Martin Luther King Jr. a preacher in many respects quite different from his stepfather but sensed in some areas the same kind of dishonest sexual voice, required by patriarchal conventionality that he found in his stepfather. The problem, of course, arose from the ways in which the black churches, in resisting the racialized pedestal, adopted a form of the pedestal to accentuate their own sexual virtue and, correlatively, condemning any blacks who deviated from it (for example, Bayard Rustin). The problem was, if anything, aggravated when some black churches under King's leadership became active in the civil rights movement. In order to be credible critics of dominant racist opinion (with its racialized pedestal), protesters had to be, if anything, hyper-respectable in the terms of Southern white respectability, including the pedestal.[582]

---

[578]   Id., p. 656. The purging of Rustin from the Southern Christian Leadership Conference, where King had wanted Rustin appointed as coordinator and publicist, was King's response to a grotesque threat by Adam Clayton Powell that, otherwise, he would publicly state that King and Rustin had had a homosexual affair; see Taylor Branch, *Parting the Waters*, pp. 328–9.

[579]   James Baldwin, "The Dangerous Road Before Martin Luther King," *Collected Essays*, ed. Toni Morrison (New York: The Library of America, 1998), pp. 638–658, at p. 653.

[580]   Id., pp. 653-4.

[581]   See Loving v. Virginia, 388 US 1 (1967).

[582]   See, on this point, Marisa Chappell, Jenny Hutchinson, and Brian Ward,

King had been prepared for this role by the ways in which, as a black man, he had accommodated himself to its public requirements of respectable manhood once he decided that his vocation was that of his father and maternal grandfather, a Baptist minister.

There was, of course, a problem of black manhood under racism correlative to the problem of black womanhood, the consequences of which Orlando Patterson has argued are still very much with us.[583] The racialized pedestal defines the problem, a pedestal that allowed white Southern men to indulge their sexuality on black women while rigidly controlling the sexuality of white women; the sexual desire of white women for anyone, let alone for black men, was such a threat to this ideology (rationalizing lynching) because it threatened the idealized pedestal itself (a point Ida Wells-Barnett had powerfully made).[584] Black men were correlatively trapped in a kind of sexual cage. Any sexual interest in white woman called for lynching and their ability to protect their own black women was compromised by the terms of white racism, which rationalized its sexual exploitation of black women on the basis of dehumanizing stereotypes of black sexuality as of animals, not of humans. The more promiscuous the sexuality of blacks, the more they accommodated themselves to the racist stereotype. Black men like King had as strong sexual interests as white men, but their manhood as Baptist preachers required that they keep their sexual interests undercover, so to speak, conforming in their public roles to idealized roles of husband and father and hold their wives under comparable idealizing controls, all to make the appropriate public statement in rebuttal of the racialized pedestal. It was as much a role at which black men like King played as it was for Tolstoy when he decided that, as a man, he must play to the hilt the roles of husband and father.[585] James Baldwin, a gay man and an outsider to this conception of manhood,

---

"Dress Modestly, Neatly . . . as if You Were Going to Church: Respectability, Class, and Gender in the Montgomery Bus Boycott and the Early Civil Rights Movement," in Peter J. Ling and Sharon Monteith, *Gender in the Civil Rights Movement* (New York: Garland Publishing, 1999), at pp. 69–100.

[583] See Orlando Patterson, *The Rituals of Blood: Consequences of Slavery in Two American Centuries* (Washington, DC: Civitas, 1998).

[584] See, for her brilliant analysis, David A. J. Richards, *Women, Gays, and the Constitution*, pp. 182–190.

[585] For fuller exploration of this point, see David A. J. Richards, *Disarming Manhood*, pp. 43–91.

shows us the price in real relationships black men and women paid when they took this line, and he apparently sensed with the sensitivity and psychological insight of the great artist he was that King had paid and was paying such a price.[586]

Bayard Rustin paid such a price, not so much as a black man but as a gay man, as both white (Muste) and black (King) leaders, who received indispensable advice and support from Rustin, broke with him, in the case of King, on no real ground whatsoever other than baseless accusations by Adam Clayton Powell Jr. And Eldridge Cleaver turned on Baldwin for his homosexuality and for his supposed rejection of his blackness.[587]

Such hurtful expressions of homophobia arise from a larger problem in the black male leadership of the civil rights movement, namely, patriarchy. The problem is further illustrated by their sexist failure to acknowledge the absolutely crucial role black women played in starting, leading, and executing the nonviolent forms of civil disobedience central to the successes of the civil rights movement. It was pivotally important, in this connection, that the Montgomery bus boycott not only began in the 1955 refusal of a woman, Rosa Parks,[588] to obey the laws governing segregation on buses, but that its initial groundswell of support came spontaneously from women and that women were disproportionately involved in the boycott itself.[589] This ethical leadership of women had become so conspicuous that when black male leaders of Montgomery first met to discuss tactics and some urged

---

[586] For fuller exploration of this point, see David A. J. Richards, *Disarming Manhood*, pp. 172–80.

[587] David Leeming, *James Baldwin*, p. 292.

[588] See Taylor Branch, *Parting the Waters: Martin Luther King and the Civil Rights Movement 1954–63* (London: Papermac, 1988), pp. 128–34, 139, 655.; see also Taylor Branch, *Pillar of Fire: America in the King Years 1963–65* (New York: Simon & Schuster, 1998).

[589] See, on these points, Mary Fair Burks, "Trailblazers: Women in the Montgomery Bus Boycott," *Women in the Civil Rights Movement*, eds. Vicki L. Crawford, Jacqueline Anne Rouse, and Barbara Woods (Bloomington: Indiana University Press, 1993), pp. 71–84; Belinda Robnett, *How Long? How Long?: African-American Women in the Struggle for Civil Rights* (New York: Oxford University Press, 1997), pp. 53–70; Lynne Olson, *Freedom's Daughters: The Unsung Heroines of the Civil Rights Movement from 1830 to 1970* (New York: Scribner, 2001), pp. 87–131; Taylor Branch, *Parting the Waters*, p. 149.

keeping their names secret, E. D. Nixon, a railroad porter and admirer of A. Philip Randolph, exploded in rage at their timorousness in comparison to the courage of women:

> Let me tell you gentlemen one thing. You ministers have lived off their wash-women for the last hundred years and ain't never doing anything for them. We've worn aprons all our lives. It's time to take the aprons off. If we're gonna be men, now's the time to be men.[590]

Nixon's trenchant, salty observations question a black manhood that was apparently less ready, willing, and able effectively to resist injustice than womanhood. Constance Baker Mottley, an NAACP lawyer during this period, notes in this connection that, as regards nonviolence:

> [King] sometimes had problems with young men who believed that violence was the answer, but [w]hen he preached nonviolence to the largely elderly females in those Birmingham churches at night, King was preaching to the converted. They were always there, night after night. Strong black women had always set the tone in Southern black communities.[591]

We are only now, in the light of the feminist project to recover women's roles in history, coming to some understanding of the role women played not only in mass demonstrations throughout the South but important leadership roles.[592] These women included, among many others, Ella

---

[590] Taylor Branch, *Parting the Waters*, p. 136.

[591] Constance Baker Mottley, *Equal Justice Under Law* (New York: Farrar, Straus and Giroux, 1998), p. 157.

[592] See, for important studies, Peter J. Ling and Sharon Monteith, *Gender in the Civil Rights Movement;* Lynne Olson, *Freedom's Daughters;* Belinda Robnett, *How Long? How Long?;* Vicki Crawford, Jacqueline Anne Rouse, and Barbara Woods, *Women in the Civil Rights;* Bettye Collier-Thomas and V. P. Franklin, eds., *Sisters in the Struggle: African American Women in the Civil Rights-Black Power Movement* (New York: New York University Press, 2001); Paula Giddings, *When and Where I Enter..The Impact of Black Woman on Race and Sex in America* (New York: William Morrow and Company, 1984).

Baker,[593] Septima Clark,[594] Diane Nash,[595] and Fannie Lou Hamer.[596] King was enough of a patriarchal man to maintain the Baptist tradition that top leadership was rightly kept in the hands of men; some of these women, notably Ella Baker, resisted him on this and other points. But these and other women were drawn into such active participation, including leadership roles (for example, the role of Diane Nash in proposing the Birmingham campaign) by something that moved them, as women, in King's prophetic ethical voice and in his actions. The patriarchal problem was not just King's, of course; it was endemic in the civil rights movement. One of the important motives to feminism was the ethical empowerment of some women by participation in the civil rights movement that led them to question its sexism and sexism generally, both as an aspect of racism and as an independent evil.[597]

The problem illustrated by both the homophobia and sexism of the civil rights movement is patriarchy, a problem, as we have seen, also very much at work in white leaders of human rights movements (Muste). It was a particular problem in the civil rights movements because of the leadership role played by the black churches and their uncritically patriarchal conceptions of religious authority, and no one was more critical of this fact than, as we have seen, James Baldwin, whose stepfather was a preacher in one of the black Christian churches.

Baldwin did not regard the problem as unique to black Christianity. Baldwin knew and admired Malcolm X as well, as a leader of black resistance to racism and was horrified by his murder. In writing his screenplay on the life of Malcolm *One Day When I Was Lost* (1972), a revised form of which was made into a movie on Malcolm directed by Spike Lee after Baldwin's

---

[593] See Taylor Branch, *Parting the Waters,* at pp. 231–3, 258, 264, 273–6, 292–3, 317, 392, 466–7, 487, 518; Taylor Branch, *Pillar of Fire,* pp. 192–3, 439, 457.

[594] See Taylor Branch, *Parting the Waters.*, pp. 263–4, 290, 381–2, 573, 576–7, 899; Taylor Branch, *Pillar of Fire,* pp. 124, 191.

[595] See Taylor Branch, *Parting the Waters,* pp. 279–80, 295, 392, 424, 428–9, 437, 439m 449, 455, 466–7, 487, 559m 588, 712, 754, 892–3; Taylor Branch, *Pillar of Fire,* pp. 54–5, 68, 139–41, 165, 285, 524, 553, 559, 579, 587, 599.

[596] See Taylor Branch, *Parting the Waters,* pp. 636, 819; Taylor Branch, *Pillar of Fire,* pp. 57, 71, 74, 109, 179, 219, 240, 329, 458–9, 461, 465, 474, 481, 547–8.

[597] See, on this development, *Sara Evans, Personal Politics: The Roots of Women's Liberation in the Civil Rights Movement and the New Left* (New York: Vintage Books, 1980).

death,[598] Baldwin naturally sees in Malcolm's turn to the racism of the Black Muslim faith as akin to the racism of his stepfather's Christianity; but it is when Malcolm rejects the racism of this version of Islam for the more traditional Islam that embraces all races and ethnicities that Baldwin perceives his true moral stature as a black leader. If the racism of whites motivated the murder of Martin Luther King Jr., Baldwin sees the patriarchal racism of the black Muslim faith, now challenged by Malcolm, as what leads to his murder.

The great importance of both Bayard Rustin and James Baldwin to the civil rights movement is that because they broke the love laws as gay black men loving white men, they had, as black men repudiating the gender binary and hierarchy in their love lives, come to see something other black men could not or would not see until much later, namely, the uncritical role patriarchy continued to play in their conceptions of authority. In this, they compromised their own ethical authority, rooted in a struggle for human rights, by not recognizing the crucially important role women and gay men played in that struggle at every level.

Baldwin lived until 1987 and thus saw the emergence from the civil rights movement of second-wave feminism and gay rights. There had always been a feminist edge to Baldwin's art and essays because, as we have seen, it was through releasing himself from the gender binary and hierarchy in his love for Lucien that breaking the love laws gave rise to the remarkable resisting voice of all his work. This feminist edge appears in his earliest essays on homosexuality and is starkly clear in his later essays.

His early essay, "The Male Prison" (1954), discusses Andre Gide's homosexuality.[599] What rivets Baldwin's attention is the way Gide dealt with his homosexuality in his remarkable *Madeleine*,[600] in which he discusses his sexless marriage to his cousin, Madeleine. Baldwin does not discuss his own homosexuality in the essay, but he expresses dismay at the shocking way Gide, confessedly a gay man, dealt with this marriage,

---

[598] See, for discussion, David Leeman, *James Baldwin*, pp. 284–302.

[599] See James Baldwin, "The Male Prison," *Collected Essays*, ed. Toni Morrison (New York: The Library of America, 1998), pp. 231–235 (first published, 1954).

[600] See Andre Gide, *Madeleine*, trans. Justin O'Brien (Chicago: Elephant Paperbacks, 1952).

namely, his arid idealization of her as "an utterly disincarnate love,"[601] "the least carnal perturbation to whom would have been an insult."[602] Gide had himself been shocked when his fellow gay artist, Marcel Proust, told him that in creating gay characters in his great novel, he had always attributed the good features of gay men he had observed to his female characters and their abject, bad features to the gay men he portrayed in his novel.[603] For Gide, this was dishonest to Proust's own experience as a gay man and thus unconscionable in terms of his demanding Protestant conscience.[604] Gide thought of himself, as a gay man and artist, as always honest to his experience. What he tells us about his marriage to his cousin is unflattering to both him and her, but honest. In his one explicit apologetic work about homosexuality, *Corydon*,[605] the only form of homosexuality he defends is the one he preferred, namely, pederastic sexual relations to quite young boys. What understandably shocks Baldwin is the narrowness of Gide's experience, in particular, the role that idealization played in what he called love for his cousin. Baldwin had come to see the idealized pedestal as what marks the lack of any real loving relationship between persons as individuals. It is not the lack of sex in Gide's marriage to his cousin that shocks Baldwin, but that the relationship is so idealized that he is never in a real relationship to her, or she to him, and Baldwin would clearly see this as a failure of love in all relationships, heterosexual and homosexual, the consequence of what he calls "the male prison," which is patriarchal masculinity.

Another early essay, "Preservation of Innocence" (1949),[606] questions the conventional condemnation of homosexuality as unnatural and offers

---

[601] See Id., p. 16.

[602] Id., p. 17.

[603] See, on this point, Didier Eribon, *Insult and the Making of the Gay Self,* trans. Michael Lucey (Durhajm: Duke University Press, 2004), at p. 86.

[604] For a plausible defense of Proust as breaking through the unspeakability of homosexuality and thus preparing the way for its honest discussion and ethical evaluation, see Didier Eribon, *Insult and the Making of the Gay Self,* pp. 23–140.

[605] See Andre Gide, *Corydon,* trans. Richard Howard (New York: Farrar, Straus Giroux, 1983; original French edition, 1983).

[606] See James Baldwin, "Preservation of Innocence," *Collected Essays,* pp. 594–600 (first published, 1949).

an explanation for the "hysteria" leading to the "present untouchability" of male homosexuals:

> Let me suggests that his present debasement and our obsession with him corresponds to the debasement of the relationship between the sexes, and that his ambiguous and terrible position in our society reflects the ambiguities and terrors, which time has deposited on that relationship as the sea piles seaweed and wreckage along that shore.[607]

The problem, as Baldwin sees it, is the falseness to experience of the gender binary itself that men and women correspond to its terms:

> It is observable that the more we imagine we have discovered, the less we know and that, moreover, the necessity to discover and the effort and self-consciousness involved in this necessity make this relationship more and more complex. Men and women seem to function as imperfect and sometimes unwilling mirrors for one another, a falsification or distortion of the nature of the one is immediately reflected in the nature of the other. A division between them can only betray a division within the soul of each. Matters are not helped if we thereupon decide that men must recapture their status as men and that women must embrace their function as women; not only does the rigidity of attitude put to death any possible communion, but having once listed the bald physical facts, no one is prepared to go further and decide of our multiple human attributes, which are masculine and which are feminine. The recognition of this complexity is the signal of maturity; it marks the death of the child and the birth of the man.[608]

---

[607] See Id., p. 595.
[608] See Id., pp. 596–7.

"Freaks and the American Ideal of Manhood" (1985)[609] and "The Price of the Ticket" (1985),[610] published late in this life, deal with his own personal experience as a gay man, the first with the kind of abuse he endured as a black gay man, the second with the importance in his life as a gay artist of his relationships to various artists, and in particular, Beauford Delaney.

In the most striking of these essays, "Freaks and the American Ideal of Manhood," Baldwin frankly discusses his early life as a young gay black man in New York City, in which there was much gay sex but no love: in a world in which "humiliation is the central danger of one's life. Since one cannot risk love without risking humiliation, love becomes impossible."[611] Baldwin's experience was one of continual violence directed at his being gay:

> The condition that is now called gay was then called queer. The operative word was *faggot*, and later pussy, but these epithets really have nothing to do with the question of sexual preference: You were told simply that you had no balls.
>
> I certainly had no desire to harm anyone, nor did I understand how anyone could look at me and suppose my physically capable of *causing* any harm. But boys and men chased me, saying I was a danger to their sisters. I was thrown out of cafeterias and rooming houses because I was *bad* for the neighborhood.
>
> The cops watched all this with a smile, never making the faintest motion to protect me or to disperse my attackers; in fact, I was even more afraid of the cops than I was of the populace."[612]

---

[609] See James Baldwin, "Freaks and the American Ideal of Manhood," *Collected Essays*, pp. 814–29 (first published, 1985).

[610] See James Baldwin, "The Price of the Ticket," *Collected Essays*, pp. 830–42 (first published, 1985).

[611] See James Baldwin, "Freaks and the American Ideal of Manhood," *Collected Essays*, pp. 814–29 (first published, 1985), p. 817.

[612] Id., p. 819.

Such violence, including being beaten by mobs of boys and men, were elicited by Baldwin's sense of his effeminacy:

> It wasn't only that I didn't wish to seem or sound like a woman, for it was this detail that most harshly first struck my eye and ear. I am sure that I was afraid that I already seemed and sounded too much like a woman. In my childhood, at least until my adolescence, my playmates had called me a sissy. It seemed to me that many of the people I met were making fun of women, and I didn't see why. I certainly needed all the friends I could get, male or female, and women had nothing to do with whatever may trouble might prove to be.[613]

It is this kind of experience that led Baldwin, though deeply unhappy, not to be "even remotely tempted by the possibilities of psychiatry or psychoanalysis" because "anyone who thought seriously that I had any desire to be adjusted to this society had to be ill—too ill, certainly, as time was to prove, to be trusted."[614] His problem was a matter of American culture,

> the American ideal of masculinity. This ideal has created cowboys and Indians, good buys and bad guys, punks and studs, tough guys and softies, butch and faggot, black and white. It is an ideal so paralytically infantile that it is virtually forbidden—as an unpatriotic act—that the American boy evolves into the complexity of manhood.[615]

He now saw developments within feminism as the key to taking seriously and resisting the pernicious role gender continued to play in our culture: "The present androgynous *craze* strikes me as an attempt to be honest concerning one's nature."[616] He concludes,

---

[613] Id., p. 823.

[614] Id., p. 816.

[615] Id., p. 815.

[616] Id., p. 827.

But we are all androgynous, not only because we are all born of a woman impregnated by the seed of a man but because each of us, helplessly and forever, contains the other—male in female, female in male, white in black and black in white. We are a part of one another. Many of my countrymen appear to have found this fact exceedingly inconvenient and even unfair, and so, and very often, do I. But none of us can do anything about it.[617]

We are, Baldwin argues, androgynous, by which he means that the gender binary and hierarchy do not correspond to human experience—men have characteristics ascribed to women and women those ascribed to men so that the gender binary is false and falsifying and does not correspond to what we experience in real relationships between equal persons with free voices. It was the experience of such a relationship with Lucien—the first loving gay relationship in his life—that led him to see the cultural role that America's rigid enforcement of the gender binary and hierarchy had played not only in crippling his own capacity to love but the lovelessness that he came to see motivated racism, sexism, and homophobia as well. Long before American feminists like Carol Gilligan gave a name to this phenomenon, Baldwin found his vocation and voice in exploring the role the love laws played in sustaining both black and white racism, as well as sexism and homophobia, as I believe my argument has now shown. It is an astonishing achievement of both psychological and ethical insight, confirming yet again the power of art to deepen our understanding of our common humanity in ways that other disciplines are not yet able to do.

Near the end of his life, Baldwin was working on his last play, *The Welcome Table,* that he did not live to finish,[618] in which the main characters were women, and its main character Edith, living in the South of France, is modeled on the black singer-dancer Josephine Baker. Baldwin was coming to believe that the best way to express his own complexities was through the prism of a woman artist and the way her love and her art challenged conventional barriers, in the same way that Tennessee Williams, another gay American artist, would find in Blanche DuBois in *Streetcar Named Desire* the fullest expression of his life as a gay man seeking a voice and

---

[617] Id., pp. 828–9.

[618] For discussion, see David Leeming, *James Baldwin,* pp.. 372–78.

resonance for his struggles for love and vocation and the tragic forces in American masculinity that not only refused to see such love for what it was but destroyed and maimed it. Baldwin was, of course, acutely sensitive, as a gay man, to how patriarchy killed loving relationships between men, and he knew, from the experience of his loving relationship to Lucien, that it was that experience that gave rise to his voice resisting patriarchy. Like D. H. Lawrence in *Women in Love,* Baldwin believed that we will not have taken seriously the deepest injustices that afflict us until we resist patriarchy in our intimate lives and thus make possible not only love between women and men but between men and men.

What a late essay like "Freaks and the American Ideal of Manhood" shows us, in terms starker and more personal than Baldwin had ever used before, is the violence he endured, which he saw from the beginning to be rooted in his gender-bending gay lifestyle or, even before he had a sex life, in his gender-bending "strangeness." It is his great achievement to give voice to the roots of this violence in a conception of American manhood and womanhood that, in demanding compliance with the love laws that held people in their racist or sexist or homophobic place, destroyed the possibility of love and real relationship, indeed gave rise to violence to any love that challenged the rigid gender binary and hierarchy. What makes Baldwin's achievement so remarkable is that he saw the central issue, patriarchy, in such complex and nuanced ways, interconnecting evils (racism, sexism, and homophobia) not usually seen whole but in compartments. Is it perhaps because, as a black man who was gay and loved white men and black and gender-bending, he saw and experienced all these evils as one and found nonetheless a love that resisted all of them, giving him both life and voice to tell his terrible and terrifying story with such emotional force and yet intellectual precision? If there is any example of how challenging the gender binary and hierarchy makes life and love and ethical voice possible, it is James Baldwin.

No one had dealt with these issues in the way Baldwin did, and his work and life remain resonant as much now as ever. For my part, Baldwin deeply moves me, as I share his experience of falling in love with another man of a different ethnic and religious background (he, Jewish from Eastern Europe; me, Catholic and Italian American). It was, as I told Donald at the time, like waking up from a kind of sleepwalking. I had lived for so long with muted expectations about human relationships since my relationships had been based, until the few years before we were introduced by a mutual friend, on a secret self that I could not disclose to those I most loved and who loved me (my parents and my sister). My love and my sense of vocation as a law professor were married. My voice for gay rights arose from our love, and both of us were empowered by each other to protect what we had discovered from a world still hostile and homophobic but also to resist that world and its attendant evils not only of homophobia but anti-Semitism, racism, and sexism. All my work should be understood against this background. Love changed everything for both of us.

CHAPTER 7

Resistance and Creativity in the Work of James Joyce, Mark Twain, William Faulkner, and James Gilligan

Not only gay men have resisted patriarchy, and such men through resistance have shown that patriarchy harms not only women but men as well, a topic to which I turn in the next two chapters. I focus here on two artists, James Joyce and Mark Twain (with reference as well to the tragic vision of William Faulkner), and the American psychiatrist and student of male violence, Dr. James Gilligan. All these men are skeptical of the conceptions of heroism of patriarchal manhood and offer compelling visions and arguments for an alternative conception, what I call democratic manhood. Their reasons for resisting patriarchal manhood center on the damage patriarchy inflicts on men, the topic of this book.

James Joyce on His Struggle to Resistance

In his remarkable autobiographical novel, *A Portrait of the Artist as a Young Man*,[619] James Joyce, under the name Stephen Daedalus, brilliantly explores his life in Ireland from his memories as a baby to boy to young man, ending with his decision that he must (like Henry James, George

---

[619]   James Joyce, *A Portrait of the Artist as a Young Man* (New York: Penguin, 1992; first published, 1916).

Santayana, and James Baldwin) leave Ireland for "some mode of art as freely as I can and as wholly as I can, using for my defence the only arms I allow myself to use—silence, exile, and cunning."[620] The issue is not for Joyce about homosexuality, but as much for the gay men I have discussed. Joyce's secret self is his sexuality and his growing sense of a need to resist the highly patriarchal Catholic constraints on sexuality he had once taken so seriously.

It is also about his relationship to his parents—his improvident and often drunken father and his loving and pious mother, as well as his many siblings. Joyce was attracted to his father's wayward ways. (He thinks of him almost as a brother,[621] but it is quite clearly his mother who nurtured his early literary interests.) Resistance for Joyce takes the form not only of leaving Ireland but leaving the church, which calls for him to argue with his mother and refuse to do what she regards as his religious duty, which means breaking her heart. In fact, Joyce omits certain facts from his narrative. His father had, in a drunken state, beat his wife while recovering from one of her pregnancies,[622] and in fact, Joyce's mother was to die shortly after he first left Ireland[623]—a fact not discussed in the novel, but which must have made the separation from her all the more painful for him. Moreover, though Joyce in the novel mentions his romantic attraction to a young woman and his sex with a prostitute, he does not advert to the pivotal reason for his leaving Ireland, falling in love with an Irishwoman, Nora Barnacle, whom he was to marry and would share his life to its end. Nora is the model for Molly Bloom in *Ulysses*.

Reading *A Portrait of the Artist as a Young Man* shocked me, revealing things I thought only I had experienced myself as once a young Catholic man in its astonishing treatment of the psyche of a boy exposed to Catholic teaching on sexuality. No book, in my judgment, better captures the experience of a young Catholic man, deeply religious and well educated. In Joyce's case, he went to quite demanding Jesuit schools, struggling with his own growing sexual desires and actions (going to a prostitute), but he was also taking into his psyche the grotesque images of hell, including

---

[620] Id., p. 269.

[621] See id., p. 98.

[622] See Richard Ellmann, *James Joyce rev. ed.* (Oxford: Oxford University Press, 1983), p. 41.

[623] See id., pp. 129–30, 136.

Bosch-like retributive figures that the Jesuits vividly describe as the condign retribution for even having such desires.[624] Joyce's writing at this point, which goes on and on like a terrifying incantation, a relentless horror movie (the images are that vivid), without end, is extraordinary, capturing something like my own personal experience of forbidden sexual desires in my Catholic home. Like Joyce, I was as a boy very religious, and the question of a vocation came up, as it does in Joyce's narrative (he rejects the idea). Southern Italian Catholicism with its roots in Pagan culture and art (ancient Rome and Greece) is not, however, as terrifying as Irish Catholicism being taught by Jesuits to model one's manhood on "the life of Saint Francis Xavier—a great soldier of God."[625] My father insisted that I go to public schools, and our priests were not Jesuits, but rather gentle Capuchin monks whose piety appealed to my parents as religiously genuine and humane, important values for them. Their model was more Francis of Assisi than Francis Xavier. The idea of our Capuchins as soldiers of any sort was preposterous. But still, Joyce very much captures just how terrifying and damaging such teaching is in the life of a boy and young man, and imparted by patriarchal priests, God on earth. I still have memories of my endless weekly confessions as a boy, always confessing my sexual sins (masturbation) almost obsessionally. My family knew nothing of this; it was my secret world, just as Joyce's sexuality was his secret world.

Joyce also writes of something else: abusive punishment by a Father Dolan for an offense for which Joyce is not culpable,[626] an experience I never had. His sense of innocence and indignation leads him to complain to the rector,[627] which prefigures his later resistance, the heart of the novel. But Joyce is intellectually drenched in Catholic teaching, Thomism. As his closest friend in the novel, Cranly, a kind of intimate confessor, observes of Joyce after Joyce tells him he has lost his religious faith: "Your mind is supersaturated with the religion in which you disbelieve."[628]

Other young friends of Joyce share his disbelief, but their religious emancipation takes the form of either a commitment to Irish nationalism (against the British oppressors) or to some conception of utilitarian

---

[624] See James Joyce, *A Portrait of the Artist as a Young Man*, pp. 109–58.
[625] See id., p. 115.
[626] See id., pp. 53, 75–76.
[627] See id., pp. 58–61.
[628] Id., p. 261,

universal brotherhood and pacifism.[629] But Joyce's resistance take the form of rejecting both Irish nationalism and more universalistic ideals, as well as rejecting religious belief which is, for him, essentially sexually repressive and inhuman.[630] What haunts him is the vision of himself as an artist,[631] and it is finding his voice as an artist that leads him to leave Ireland though his work would continue to be placed in Ireland. He would write in English, but create a new language in English that was his own, not bound to either Ireland nor to England.[632] Above all, Joyce does not share their sense of manhood, he is skeptical of it, in particular, the Jesuit idea of becoming a "soldier of God" or the secular idea of becoming a soldier for Ireland, a skepticism connected to Joyce's lifelong hatred of violence.[633]

The heart of *A Portrait of the Artist as a Young Man*—as the remarkable resistance narrative it is—shows the roots of resistance. Joyce quite clearly shows how and why he lost confidence in all the traditional sources of authority around him, including not only his father, his mother, his church, his nation, and his friends. In consequence, the novel ends with a kind of lonely heroism that has nothing to do with patriarchal manhood, which Joyce came to see was empty and oppressive in all its dimensions, whether religious (Catholicism) or secular (nationalism). *A Portrait of the Artist as a Young Man* ends with a long and moving conversation between Joyce and his intimate, Cranly, in which Cranly argues that, even if Joyce is right about religion, should not the suffering and care of his mother (having nine children and an improvident and abusive husband) lead him, as an act of love, to do as she wishes?[634] Joyce earlier writes of "his mother's sobs and reproaches,"[635] and his response to Cranly that he has not known love does not ring true. As Cranly quite clearly sees and Joyce, guilt ridden, will not acknowledge that his mother loved him and he her. And we know that, in fact, his resistance turned on the sexual love of his wife, Nora, who shared his exile and nurtured and sustained him, and he meets her the year after

---

[629] See, for example, id., p. 213.

[630] On rejecting Irish nationalism, see id.,

[631] See id., pp. 183–184.

[632] See, on this point, id., pp. 205, 220.

[633] See Richard Ellman, *James Joyce*, pp. 68, 70.

[634] See James Joyce, *A Portrait of the Artist as a Young Man*, pp. 259–267.

[635] Id., pp. 243–44.

his mother's death, and his love of Nora and of his mother were seamless, as the love of men for women often is.[636]

Why can't Joyce deal honestly with the importance of love in his resistance in his autobiography? He certainly had no such problem in his art. His great novel, *Ulysses,* certainly debunks the patriarchal manhood and womanhood of the Homeric poem on which it is based, as both its protagonist, Bloom, and his sexually adulterous wife, Molly, explore an alternative conception in which a gentle and humane man, Bloom, and his sexual wife are a world apart from the Ulysses and Penelope of Homer. Joyce here shows us a living and vital alternative, an antipatriarchal conception of both men and women, and sexual desire and love are unashamedly at its center.[637]

It was through his powerful sexual relationship to Nora that Joyce became the artist he wanted to be, as through her love (like Baldwin's love for Lucien) he finally overcame the shame over sexuality that his abusive Catholic Jesuit teachers had inculcated in him, including not only his own feelings of shame over his sexuality but the shame men under patriarchy are supposed to feel at the adulterous sexuality of their wives. To that extent, *Ulysses* should, I believe, be understood as one of the great modernist ethical protests against the shame culture of patriarchy, which Joyce had experienced at firsthand. At the end of *A Portrait of the Artist as a Young Man,* Joyce goes to encounter the reality of experience and to forge in the smithy of my soul the uncreated conscience of my race.[638] His achievement was to have created the new conscience I call democratic manhood.

Mark Twain on Comic Democratic Manhood and William Faulkner on the Tragedy of Patriarchal Manhood

In his important essay "Come Back to the Raft Ag'in, Huck Honey!," first published in 1948, the great American literary critic Leslie Fiedler argued that some of the most important masterpieces of American fiction,

---

[636] See Richard Ellman, *James Joyce,* pp. 292–5.

[637] For fuller discussion, see Carol Gilligan and David A. J. Richards, *The Deepening Darkness: Patriarchy, Resistance, and Democracy's Future* (Cambridge: Cambridge University Press, 2009), at pp. 203–209.

[638] James Joyce, *A Portrait,* pp. 275–76.

Mark Twain's *Adventures of Huckleberry Finn* notably among them, are resistance narratives to American racism and homophobia because they celebrate, all of them, the mutual love of a *white man* and a *colored*.[639] And Fiedler's great book, *Love and Death in the American Novel*,[640] ends with a brilliant interpretation of *Huckleberry Finn* as perhaps the greatest American novel because it carries its critique of American manhood further and deeper than any other American novelist.[641]

I agree with Fiedler's subtle and profound analysis of this masterpiece, its depths hidden by its unpretentious vernacular style, hilarity, sense of irony, and subject matter (a tale of boyhood written by the boy). Nothing else Twain wrote (and his output was prodigious and usually quite popular) is quite like it, and we know he is drawing on his own boyhood experience in Hannibal, Missouri, with other rambunctious American boys, including, apparently, a man of color he knew, the model for Jim in the novel,[642] and another boy whose father was a drunk, the model for Huckleberry Finn and his wayward, drunken father.[643] His art was pathbreaking in the development of American letters: "Mark Twain's baton began to mute the Anglican symphony and strike up the rhythms of American jazz."[644] And no human voices save his own mother's caught his imagination quite like those of the Negro slaves.[645] (Twain was born and raised in the antebellum period and the novel is set in that period; slavery was all about him, and his family had owned one slave, whom they sold.)

Huckleberry Finn is written in Finn's astonishing voice, very much the voice of someone outside of American patriarchy. How was Twain capable of finding and writing in such a voice? Twain was apparently close to both his father and mother and siblings (the death of one of his beloved brothers was one of his most traumatic early experiences). Twain's father, Marshall Clemens, was a judge, "an educated, eloquent, ambitious man, claimant to British peerage, apostle of the Southern honor code, a visionary

---

[639] See Leslie Fiedler, "Come Back to the Raft Ag'in, Huck Honey," in *A New Fiedler Reader* (Amherst, NY: Prometheus, 1999), pp. 3–12, at p. 7.

[640] Leslie Fiedler, *Love and Death in the American Novel* (New York: Criterion Books, 1960).

[641] See id., pp. 553–591.

[642] See Ron Powers, *Mark Twain: A Life* (New York: Free Press, 2005), p. 12.

[643] See id., pp. 34–35.

[644] Id., p. 8.

[645] Id.

of the America to come." As justice of the peace, "[h]e held the power of life and death over other men. This version of Marshall Clemens reigned as a titan in Sammy's consciousness."[646] And the affection of son and his mother, Jane Clemens, "deepened in his early years, as did her influence on his character. She reinforced Sammy's enchantment with language. Mark Twain marveled at the 'unstudied and unconscious pathos' of her native speech. When stirred to indignation, 'she was the most eloquent person I have heard speak.'"[647] However, Twain's father encountered disastrous business dealing, and he died of pneumonia at the age of forty-nine; his son was eleven and immediately went to work, as his mother urged, as an apprentice to support the family, which continued in other jobs long after, as Twain worked at a range of jobs, including being a captain on a Mississippi River boat, and traveling widely both in America and abroad. His travels abroad continued when he became a best-selling writer, including traveling abroad with his beloved wife and children (all girls).

Twain did not leave America in the way Henry James, George Santayana, and James Baldwin did, but he developed his remarkable eye and voice from the kind of internal exile he endured as he early on had to work for his family while continuing in his travels both in America and elsewhere throughout the rest of his life. Twain's travels played the role as the stimulus to the independence of his voice that the travel abroad of James, Santayana, and Baldwin played in empowering their creative and resisting ethical voices. My sense is that his sense of the resilience of young boys against the odds, very much at the heart of *Huckleberry Finn*, was at heart of his own life and finding of his artistic voice, which in *Finn*, a relatively late novel, is a work of American genius about the damage American patriarchy inflicts on men and boys and how they come to resist it. In this, Twain's artistic journey is closer to that of Charles Dickens, whose artistic voice arises from his own sense of trauma when, as we have seen, as a young man, he is apprenticed by his father in a job and young boy detests (chapter 3).

Huckleberry Finn is, I believe, a study of human nature, which, in the novel, is always contrasted to something Huck Finn rebels against, namely, the attempts of the Widow Douglas, among others, to "sivilize"

---

[646] Id., p. 40.
[647] Id., p. 40.

him.[648] There is no mother in the novel, but there is a violent, drunken, racist father,[649] who at one point kidnaps and threatens to kill his son.[650] (the father dies by the end of the novel.) Finn escapes. Finn is effectively an orphan, cared for by guardians like the Widow Douglas and her sister spinster, Miss Watson (the sisters live together), rather devout Christians and always needling Finn to improve his ways. "Sivilization" is proslavery and racist, and when the slave, Jim, runs away from his owner, Miss Watson, because she is planning to sell him to a more severe owner and tells Huck, who is also running away, that he is a fugitive slave, Huck worries and confides, "People would call me a low down abolitionist [sic] and despise me for keeping mum,"[651] but replies, "I ain't agoing to tell."[652] The narrative of the novel is about the escape and wanderings, often together but not always, of Finn and Jim on a raft on the Mississippi River. Jim is married with children and escapes with the intention to rejoin his family.

Their adventures include one, when they are separated, in which Finn encounters an aristocratic Kentucky family, the Grangerfords, who take him in, and Finn befriends their son, Buck. The Grangerfords have been in in a long blood feud with another family, the Shepherdsons, but the families go to the same Christian church where Christian love is preached to all. Nonetheless, when a boy and girl from the two families fall in love and marry, the families explode into homicidal violence, including the death of all male Grangerfords, including Buck. Finn, uncomprehending of all this violence, watches his friend being killed. Finn cannot understand and is untouched by the psychology of shame of the patriarchal love laws.

Jim and Finn rejoin in the raft, but two confident men, claiming to the long-lost son of an English duke (the duke of Bridgewater) and the other the Lost Dauphin, the son of Louis XVI of France, join them and proceed to use them in various fraudulent schemes, including stealing the money left by a deceased man to his family. In order to save the family, Finn reveals their scheme and then discovers that the two men have now

---

648 Mark Twain, *Adventures of Huckleberry Finn*, in *Mississippi Writings* (New York: The Library of America, 1982; originally published, 1884), pp. 625–912, p. 625.

649 See id., pp. 650–651.

650 See id., pp. 652–653.

651 Id., p. 666.

652 Id., p. 666.

sold Jim to a family, Silas and Sally Phelps, who plan to return him to his owner for the reward.

Tom Sawyer is the nephew of the Phelps family, who have never met Tom. Finn pretends he is Tom in order to secure Jim's freedom, which he is about to secure rather easily.

When Tom (now pretending to be Finn) himself arrives, he confabulates a bizarre complex scheme to secure Jim's freedom, which leads to Tom being injured in the leg. He is cared for by Jim, who nonetheless is returned to the Phelps family. Tom's aunt Polly arrives and reveals the true identity of Tom and Finn and that Jim's owner has died and given him freedom in her will. Tom knew about Jim's freedom but nonetheless confabulated the complex to free Jim. He had, unlike Finn, no interest as such in freeing Jim. Jim can return to his family. Finn learns that his father is dead and that he has money and is free. Confronted with Sally Phelps's desire to adopt and "sivilize" him, Finn flees out west.

The central contrast in the novel is between proslavery and racist "sivilization" and the love that emerges between Jim, the fugitive slave, and Finn, the orphan. Both are quite alone, and as they flee from their persecutors on the raft, they experience on the raft real affection for each other. Jim tenderly calls Huck "honey."[653] Jim talks to Huck on the raft of his plan that "when he gets enough, he will buy his wife, which is owned on a farm close to where Miss Watson lives and they will both work to buy the two children. If their master won't sell them, they'll get an ab'litionist to go and steal them."[654]

Early on, Huck experiences a crisis of conscience over not giving a fugitive slave up but muses: "Then I thought a minute and say to myself to hold on, s'pose you'd done right and give Jim up, would you feel better than what you do now? No, says I, I'd feel bad—I'd feel just the same way I do not. Well, then, says I, what's the use of you learning to do right when it's troublesome to do right and ain't no trouble to do wrong?"[655]

Later in the narrative, the crisis of conscience leads Huck to write a letter to Jim's owner about where Jim is, and he writes the following:

---

[653] See Mark Twain, *The Adventures of Huckleberry Finn*, op. cit., pp. 672, 675, 707, 715, 735, 738, 867.

[654] Id., p. 711.

[655] Id., p. 714.

I felt good and all washed clean of sin for the first time I had ever felt so in my life, and I knowed I could pray now. But I didn't do it straight off, but laid the paper down and set there thinking—thinking how good it was all this happened so, and how near I come to being lost and going to hell. And went on thinking. And got to thinking over our trip down the river; and I see Jim before me; all the time, in the day, and in the night-time, sometimes moonlight, sometimes storms, and we a floating along, talking, and singing, and laughing. But somehow I couldn't seem to strike no places to harden me against him, but only the other kind. I'd see him standing my watch on top of his'n, 'stead of calling me, so I could go on sleeping; and see him how glad he was when I come back out of the fog; and when I come to him again in the swamp, up there where the feud was; and such-like times, and would always call me honey, and pet me, and do everything he could think of for me, and how good he always was; and at last I struck the time I saved him by telling the men we have small-pox aboard, and he was so grateful and said I was the best friend old Jim ever had in the world and the *only* one he'd got now; and then I happened to look around, and see that paper.

It was a close place. I took it up, and held it in my hand. I was a trembling, because I'd got to decide, forever, betwixt two things, and I knowed it. I studied a minute, sort of holding my breath, and then says to myself.

"All right, then, I'll *go* to hell"—and then tore it up.[656]

What Huck remembers is something he has never felt for and received from anyone else in his life: intimate affection and love with another man, indeed a man of color, his secret self. On the raft, Huck and Jim are lovers in a state of nature, before "sivilization" separated them into master and slave, white and black. The experience of love between them is more real for Huck Finn that any of the authorities, religious and secular, that condemn such love, and it is love that frees Finn's voice, "All right, then I'll

656 Id., pp. 834–835.

go to hell." It is that truth that Lesie Fiedler saw: it is love between men, and such love arises in the human psyche it empowers a voice stronger than "sivilization", whether patriarchal religion or law. Finn is outside patriarchy in a way his erstwhile and ingeniously intelligent friend, Tom Sayer, is not and who thus cannot respond to Jim, despite his goodness to him when he is injured, in a human way.

Twain marks Huck Finn's resistance to the demands of patriarchal manhood in two striking ways: first, in the Grangerford episode, that he is dismayed by the fratricidal blood feud, elicted by a couple breaking the love laws, leading to the killing before his eyes of his friend, Buck, and second, his love for Jim that itself breaks the love laws because he is resisting the gender binary and hierarchy of patriarchy. Huck Finn embodies a new kind of American manhood, democratic manhood, one that is skeptical of patriarchal violence and of the object of such violence, any transgression of the patriarchal love laws. Twain in this novel is carrying the critique of patriarchal manhood of Hawthorne and Melville even further and deeper, revealing the role that both racism and homophobia play in such manhood, and how only a new kind of love not only between men and women but between men and men can release them from patriarchal demands with new ethical possibilities for American democracy.

It is no accident that Twain became a prominent American critic of the role patriarchal religion played in American culture and politics, and the role the shaming of patriarchal manhood played in America's turn to imperialistic wars in the late nineteenth century, for example, the Spanish-American War. There was in American experience the possibility of new forms of egalitarian relationships between persons and thus forge a democratic manhood.

The Adventures of Huckleberry Finn is as ethically serious and profound a book by an American man about American manhood as has ever been written, but it is also a comic masterpiece of hilarious adventures and misadventures, including Huck dressed as a woman and other feigned identities and much lying (Huck is shocked at one point when he speaks the truth) that is written in his vernacular voice. Comedy sometimes is rooted, I think, in an underlying sense of dysfunction and loss or at least coming close to such loss and then, thankfully, veering away, so we can see a way out from such loss, more bearable because so real about human frailty and so apparently harmlessly funny. *Huckleberry Finn* is one of the most successful examples of this genre, and it resonates so deeply in the

American psyche because Twain is showing us our ethical heart of darkness (our racism), how the love laws enforce it, and how there is in our humanity or the humanity of those less burdened by patriarchy a way out, what I call love across the boundaries, something Twain marks as close to nature. (Jim and Huck on the raft, "Swimming and tender as lovers are, he would always call me honey and pet me.") Twain writes *Hucklebery Finn* during a period in American history he himself named "the Gilded Age"[657]—one of the most racist and sexist periods in American history as Americans tried to forget the radical ethical abolitionism (condemning both racism and sexism) that motivated the Civil War, in effect, reflecting a psychology of loss of memory and voice, the marks of trauma, and the Civil War was traumatic both for the North and South.[658] Its brilliance is that Twain, great artist that he is and a Southerner, finds a voice during this period to tell us the terrible truth about our most profound national evil and how we sustain it through irrationalist violence and how a boy and a fugitive slave show us that the way out is, in fact, in our human natures, as natural as love itself. And Americans laughed, which made it all comically bearable.

There is another much more unbearably tragic way to tell us the same truths only in a quite different narrative by another very great American artist and Southerner, who shows us a Southern family over several generations enacting the tragedy. I mean, William Faulkner and perhaps his greatest and most densely complex novel, *Absalom, Absalom!* published in 1936. The narrative is largely told by a Southerner, Quentin Compson, to his roommate and close friend, Shreve, at Harvard College and is based on Quentin's own memories as well as the memories of his father and grandfather and deals with the period before, during, and after the Civil War. It is a patriarchal family tragedy, very much in the spirit of *The Oresteia*, and the tragedy arises from the patriarchal ambitions of a newcomer to Mississippi, Thomas Sutpen, coming from a poor, nonslave holding family in West Virginia but insulted by a black servant of a white family for his poverty and setting out to make his fortune in the deep, slave-holding South. Sutpen first successfully seeks his fortune in Haiti, where he is awarded by a wealthy planter by wedding the planter's daughter

---

[657] See, on this point, Ron Bowers, *Mark Twain: A Life*, 328, 351, 400, 417, 604.

[658] See, for fuller discussion, David W. Blight, *Race and Reunion: The Civil War in American Memory* (Cambridge, Mass.: Belknap Press of Harvard University Press, 2001).

and having a son by her, Charles Bon. When he finds his wife is part black, Sutpen abandons his wife and child, leaving them, in recompense, his fortune. Sutpen comes to Mississippi to make his fortune through a plantation and marries the daughter of a local merchant and has two children, Henry and Judith. At the University of Mississippi, Henry and Charles become friends, and when Henry brings him home, Charles and Judith are attracted to each other and plan to marry, as the Civil War begins in which both Charles and Henry fight for the South. Sutpen forbids the marriage of Charles and Judith. Henry believes his objection is because they are half siblings and refuses to regard this as a bar to his friend's marriage to his sister. It is a different matter, however, when the father explains that the reason for his prohibition is not incest, but racist. Charles, despite Henry's objection, persists in his desire to marry Judith, and Charles kills him. The rest of the narrative continues the story of those left after the killing, including Henry, who returns to his home at the end, a broken man, and is burned to death in a fire. Nothing good happens to anyone, including the father, Thomas, who is killed by the father of a girl, whom Thomas rejected when she gave birth to a girl, not a boy.

No one in the narrative questions the destructive power of patriarchy in the life of Sutpen or his son, Henry, or in the life of the South, except Shreve in the conversation at Harvard with his friend, Quentin Compson, that is most of the novel. Shreve is an outsider to Southern patriarchal culture and tells his friend at the end of the novel that the South will flourish precisely because the products of miscegenation, now so despised, "will conquer the Western hemisphere." And Shreve concludes, after listening to these horrors, that Quentin hates the South. In response, Quentin, at the novel's end, repeats at least six times, "I don't hate it."[659]

The relationship between the half brothers, Henry and Charles, is expressly psychologically mirrored in the novel by the relationship between Quentin and Shreve.[660] And Faulkner, an extremely precise psychological artist, writes of their relationship: "not at all as two young men might look at each other but almost as a youth and a very young girl might out of virginity itself—a sort of hushed and naked searching, each look burdened

---

[659] William Faulkner, *Absalom, Absalom!*, *Novels 1936–1940*, ed. Joseph Blotner, Noel Polk (New York: The Library of America, 1990; originally published, 1936), pp. 5–311, at p. 311.

[660] See id., p. 275, "Charles-Shreve and Quentin-Henry."

with youth's immemorial obsession not with time's dragging weight which the old live with but with its fluidity: the bright hells of all the lost moments of fifteen and sixteen."[661] This is an intimate relationship, perhaps even homoerotic in its suggestion of gender fluidity. We know Quentin commits suicide. Faulkner is, I believe, drawing a parallel between the violence of patriarchy directed at interracial love between a man and woman (murder) and its homophobic violence against same-sex love (suicide)—the only love that allows Quentin to find and speak in his own voice, Quentin's secret self. So Shreve is right: Quentin is seething with rage, but rather than resisting the patriarchy that legitimates that rage, he tragically turns the rage on himself. The enactment to patriarchy has no end but feeds on itself.

So these two great Southern American artists—the one comic, the other tragic—tell us the same story of patriarchy and its links to racism and homophobia. Twain finds his voice outside patriarchy; Faulkner is very much within it and insisting we see its remorseful and tragic consequences as it is passed mindlessly from father to son.[662]

James Gilligan on Patriarchal Violence and Homophobia and Love as Therapy

Both James Gilligan and his work were first introduced to me when I began teaching with his wife, Carol Gilligan, at a seminar, currently called Resisting Injustice, at New York University School of Law. Carol and I have now taught the seminar for well over ten years when she moved from Harvard University to becoming university professor at New York University. Our collaboration has been richly rewarding for us both, leading to a coauthored book, *The Deepening Darkness: Resistance, Patriarchy, and the Future of Democracy*, published in 2009, and another such book, *Darkness Now Visible: The Trump Presidency, Patriarchy's Resurgence, and a Call to Resistance*, published in 2018. I started teaching a seminar with Jim several years ago, Retribution in Criminal Law Theory and Practice, and thus have gotten to know him and his work quite well. I have already

---

[661] See id., p. 247.

[662] For a brilliant treatment of Faulkner's rather tormented psychology and life, including disastrous alcoholism, see Philip Weinstein, *Becoming Faulkner: The Art and Life of William Faulkner* (Oxford: Oxford University Press, 2010).

discussed and used some of Jim's work in chapter 2 and will explore more of it in chapters that follow.

My interest here is to place James Gilligan's life and work in the context of the other men (Joyce, Twain, and Faulkner) who, like him, were empowered to find a voice in themselves that, because it resisted patriarchal demands on men, showed us the range of evils that harm men that arise from their initiation as men into patriarchy. James Gilligan is one of these men—a man with a strong artistic temperament and artistic interests whose work as a psychiatrist is continuous with that temperament and those interests (not least his love of Dostoevsky and fascination with Nietzsche on the psychology of guilt and shame and William James on religion). The central topic of his life's work has been violence in men, its sources and how responsibly to understand and deal with it.

His book, *Violence*,[663] is a pathbreaking investigation of the psychological roots of violence in men arising from the shaming of manhood and is based on his own work as a psychiatrist of such violent men. The book is a study of what he learned, during the period 1977–1992, when he led a team of colleagues from Harvard teaching hospitals in providing mental health and violent prevention services to the Massachusetts prison system, after two United States district courts, reacting to an epidemic of suicides, homicides, and other violence throughout the prison system, ordered the state to bring the level of psychiatric services in the prisons up to community standards. As medical director of the Massachusetts prison mental hospital for the "criminally insane" at Bridgewater, Massachusetts, and clinical director of the Prison Mental Health Service, he supervised the training and clinical practice of psychiatrists, psychologists, and social workers in the understanding and treatment of violent offenders.

Gilligan explains how he came to be the kind of American man interested in such questions in the remarkably personal prologue to *Violence*. It is a family history that begins with what he heard as a boy in Nebraska about his physician grandfather's role in investigating the tragic violence in the family of an Irish immigrant and a half-breed Indian squaw in which the father's violence against the mother's favorite son led to the death of the son (the exact nature of the son's death is not clear). The story resonates with Gilligan as he then recounts his own experience of violence in his own

---

663   James Gilligan, *Violence: Reflections on a National Epidemic* (New York: Vintage, 1997).

family, inflicted by his physician father on his elder and younger brothers and, at least once, on his mother. Gilligan, like the son of the squaw, was his mother's favorite and was not himself the victim of his father's violence, though he was clearly traumatized by the violence all about him and the fact that his father was regarded as a respectable pillar of the community.

The violence inflicted on his elder brother is particularly shocking: "On one occasion, when I could not have been older than five or six, my father struck my older brother—who was then five years older than I—so hard that he was hurled across a good-sized living room. I remember being terrified that my father might accidentally kill my brother. It was a violent scene. I remember the tears, my mother trying to restrain my father, my father's rage, my brother's fear, and the injuries that became the unspeakable secrets we were never to utter."[664] It turns out that this brother, John, was gay, and his early death was for Jim a matter of deep and continuing grief.

The prologue is Jim's explanation for how, as a psychiatrist, he became absorbed in violent men. Jim had known and loved such a man as his father and had come to regard the problem of violence as a problem not only for criminals but for the entire culture of American patriarchal manhood. What makes his work with violent criminals, whom most Americans marginalize as not one of us, so remarkable is that Jim refuses to objectify even the most violent of criminals because his own experience has been that this violence is in all American men, including men like his father, because it arises from the harms American patriarchy inflicts on men.

His work shows that patriarchy—the gender binary and hierarchy— was the basis of the vulnerability to shame and violence he found in the psychology of the aggressively violent men he studied in American prisons. Any threat or insult to their sense of patriarchal manhood was experienced as humiliation, eliciting uncontrollable violence. But there was another discovery even more important: the vulnerability to violence of these men rested on often appalling developmental injuries to their sense of self as men, and that the injuries masked their underlying sense of shame that they were as incompetent—both in their personal and employment lives—as many of them were. Among these injuries were not only abuse by parents and others but a lack of any of the social and educational advantages that might have made them more competent to advance in the highly

---

[664] James Gilligan, *Violence*, p. 13.

competitive society around them. Their vulnerability to uncontrollable violence was the only way they could express their sense of value as men, and there was an inverse psychological relationship between their violence and their voice or, rather, lack of voice. As their voices were supported and strengthened, their vulnerability to violence plummeted.[665]

Further psychological research on the psychology of violent people, directed at both others (homicide) and themselves (suicide), has revealed that the apparently instinctive aggressive violence elicited by humiliation arises from developmental injuries that disable people from reflecting on or thinking about why they are thus prompted to violence. The lack of affect regulation is thus tied to a lack of "mentalization," to themselves forms of incompetence that are the object of shame.[666] Therapy for such lack encourages precisely a voice that mentalizes that there is such a gap and understanding and dealing with its psychological destructiveness, the experience of which is what leads one into therapy.

The inverse psychological relationship between patriarchal violence and voice was both confirmed and strengthened in a reform experiment in San Francisco jails.[667] Here, through forms of individual and group therapy and theater work, the prisoners came to sensitize themselves to their own propensities to violence and its roots in trauma and abuse and became critics of the patriarchal gender roles they had once assumed to be in the nature of things. When they listened to people who had suffered loss arising from killing people they loved (some of them had killed), some of them experienced an emotion, guilt, that they had used the mask of shame not to acknowledge or feel in themselves. They wept.

What this work shows is both that highly patriarchal shame cultures continue to exist in the United States, and America's high rates of violence should be understood as the consequence of our allowing or encouraging such shame cultures to exist. The propensity to violence of these men, including murders, was connected to insults to their sense of patriarchal

---

[665] See, on all these points, James Gilligan, *Violence*.

[666] See, for an excellent study along these lines, Peter Fonagy, Gyorgy Gergely, Elliot L. Jurist, Mary Target, *Affect Regulation, Mentalization, and the Development of the Self* (New York: Other Press, 2004). See also Rosine Jozef Perelberg, ed., *Psychoanalytic Understanding of Violence and Suicide* (London: Routledge, 1999).

[667] See, for discussion of this experiment, Sunny Schwartz and David Boodell, *Dreams from the Monster Factory* (New York: Scribner, 2009).

manhood, as was revealed by the men themselves in therapy as they found a voice to discuss both their violent acts and the connections of such violence often to family histories of abuse and neglect. What is revelatory about this work is that American prisons, despite their historical origins as institutions intended to bring criminals to a sense of guilt and remorse, not only do not bring prisoners to a sense of guilt but are institutions that shame them as men eliciting and exacerbating their propensities to violence. Indeed, the conditions in American prisons themselves inflict violence and humiliation both by guards and fellow prisoners. Perhaps, the most telling point in his analysis is the role homophobia played in sexual relations among men in our prisons, which prisons encouraged as a way in which prisoners could hierarchically and violently control one another, as patriarchy requires. Prisons are, for Gilligan, thus a case study in the culture of American homophobia, as any possibility of love, let alone sexual love, between men (as equals) is culturally framed as an insult to a manhood that structures all such relationships, including those to women, in terms of a rigid gender binary and hierarchy deviation from which requires violence and sometimes homicidal violence.[668] American prisons are, in effect, war zones in which the prisoners, often divided by gang groups based on ethnicity and race, war on one another; and the authorities sometimes encourage and even stage-manage such violence, as patriarchal men do (as in wars).[669]

What enabled Gilligan to see the violent men he studied as persons was that he had freed himself, as a man and a psychiatrist, from the extraordinary repressive burdens American patriarchy imposes on male voice. To know Jim Gilligan is to know that his own way of dealing with the traumatic losses he suffered in his early life (including not only his father's violence but his beloved mother's early death and the death of good friends in a car accident that he survived) was through both education and personal love, the latter culminating in his marriage to Carol and his relationships to his own children (three sons and their wives, his

[668] See, on this point, James Gilligan, *Violence*, pp. 76, 81, 83–84, 156–57, 164, 171, 189.

[669] See, on gladiatorial matches in American prisons managed by corrections officers, James Gilligan, *Violence in California Prisons: A Proposal for Research into Patterns and Cures* (Sacramento: Diane Publishing Co. 2000, edited with an introduction by California State senator Tom Hayden).

daughters-in-law) and grandchildren, but a love itself framed on terms that, quite remarkably in my opinion, resist patriarchy. Through freeing his own voice from patriarchy, he was also able to form caring relationships of a man to another man in his work with violent prisoners, in particular, men lower in the gender hierarchy, that patriarchy forbids and indeed finds unnatural and unthinkable. That is why his psychological analysis of homophobia in American prisons, clearly not unconnected to his love for his gay brother, reveals a larger psychological truth about how patriarchy damages men— holding them into the rigid, competitive, and aggressive patterns required by the gender binary and hierarchy. Therapy, as Gilligan, has practiced it with prisoners is itself a work of love across the boundaries, caring for them and helping them come to see how they might release themselves from the patriarchal cycle of violence that has destroyed them.

No aspect of Jim Gilligan's study of violence in American prisons more riveted and compelled me than his investigation of the centrality of homophobia in American prisons, so thick, as he once put it to me, that you had to cut through it to see what keeps American prisons in place. It is, he argues, not just incidental to an all-male environment, for it is not psychologically central to other all-male environments, many of which foster brotherhood and team effort. But Gilligan sees homophobia—the fear and hatred of all forms of intimacy on equal terms between men—as what keeps prisons going, as American prisons effectively encourage a homophobic violence between men, maintaining the gender binary and hierarchy, as the only way to keep order. (In fact, it is the only way to keep order under patriarchy.) Men, thus already victimized by patriarchy in the wider society, become the instruments of maintaining patriarchy in American prisons. The larger lesson to be drawn from this, I believe, is that the psychology of American patriarchy, largely enforced by men against men, harms all men by holding them in antidemocratic relationships to other men, relationships unjustly based on and perpetuating hierarchy and inequality, incendiary violence and hatred instead of friendship and brotherhood. Friendship and love of man for man is driven underground, men's secret self.

It was these discoveries that led Gilligan to understand as well the violence of his own father and the American men like his father, dangerously prone to uncontrollable violence in their personal and public lives, because their sense of themselves as men had been so damaged by their initiation into patriarchy. Gilligan's father was, in fact, a respected member of his community, a hardworking physician. Thus, Gilligan analyzes the American problem of violence as by no means limited to violent criminals, but extending it as well to men like his father whose propensities to violence were masked by a patriarchal culture some of whose leaders are, precisely because they are leaders, allowed much broader scope in indulging violence in their personal and even their political lives because, in a patriarchal order, they are the patriarchs or they and others think of themselves in such terms. It is this insight that has led Gilligan plausibly to extend his views of male violence to political fascism and contemporary terrorism as forms of "political religion" (see chapter 2).

What his work reveals, I believe, is that America is not the exclusively guilt culture it is sometimes supposed to be, but it also retains uncritically and indeed supports a questionable shame culture on issues of gender and sexuality that contradict our deeper democratic values of equal voice and indeed that we cannot deal with the American epidemic of violence until we address the deeper questions of humiliating forms of economic inequality that are, in his view, responsible for such violence (perpetuating our unjust shame culture, harming men).[670] Education and love made resistance to the cycle of patriarchal violence he had experienced in his father possible for Jim, and he has thus seen, because of this, that the American mindless obsession with retribution in criminal justice has only perpetuated the same self-destructive cycle of violence for American men generally, which injures us all (see chapter 7). As he has learned in his life, he calls for a social democratic justice guaranteeing the equal opportunities for all to education and love.[671]

Resistance for Gilligan arose from his ethical voice as an American man, himself victimized by this largely invisible shame culture and the harms it inflicted on his own family (his brothers and mother), exposing these harms in American prisons and beyond. What is at the heart of his life and work is that patriarchy harms men as well as women.

---

[670] See James Gilligan, *Why Some Politicians Are More Dangerous Than Others* (Cambridge, UK: Polity, 2011).

[671] See id.

American Criminal Justice as Our Heart of Darkness

On the basis of Jim Gilligan's insights, it is time for Americans of conscience to ask themselves ethical questions about criminals and our unjust treatment of them in a prison system that is the scandal of the civilized world. Why have we allowed this to happen? The key to our national problem is, I believe, the degree to which the ways in which patriarchy harms men have not been part of our public debate.

There has undoubtedly been some progress, as the gay movement raised such fundamental questions of constitutional privacy about the long-standing criminalization of gay/lesbian sex that our constitutional law has now accepted their arguments[672] and indeed extended the right to protect the right of gays and lesbians to marry.[673] That movement was empowered by the voices of gay men and lesbians, including my own, that broke the homophobic silencing of voice central to patriarchy, claiming a right to love that resonated broadly with Americans as a basic human right that all Americans enjoy and should enjoy on equal terms.

That right has not, however, been extended on fair terms to the draconian American drug laws, which enforcement has been highly racialized. The issue of racism in American criminal law has now, however, led to greater resistance than ever, a resistance that joins a broad coalition of Americans, men as well as women. Such resistance may be more effective now than it has ever been, largely because people of color have now not only resisted through Black Lives Matter, but leading black scholars, including Michelle Alexander, have now given pith and focus to the issue through the remarkable documentary, _13th_.[674] We would note, as particularly stark and disgraceful example, what the Nixon adviser John Ehrlichman acknowledged as the basis for Nixon's War on Crime: "We knew we couldn't make it illegal to be either against the war or black, but by getting the public to associate the hippies with marijuana and blacks

---

[672] See Lawrence v. Texas, 539 US 558 (2003), criminalization of gay/lesbian sex unconstitutionally violated the constitutional right to privacy.

[673] Obergefell v. Hodges, 135 S.Ct. 2584 (2015), the right of constitutional privacy extends to the right to marry of gays and lesbians.

[674] _13th_, directed by Ava DuVernay (2016).

with heroin, and then criminalizing both heavily, we could disrupt these communities."[675]

It is something of a tragedy for the cause of racial justice in the United States that, during the long period of the largely Republican war on drugs, both otherwise liberal whites and blacks were complicitous with mass incarceration, as James Forman Jr.'s recent book cogently argues. Forman, a black scholar now at Yale Law School and the son of a leading civil rights advocate, shows how black leaders were drawn into complicity and makes his case on the basis of black people he represented as a public defender in the District of Columbia. The power of the narrative is precisely that he insists that we see the issue from their point of view and the harms black politicians inflicted on them.[676] From my perspective, the assumptions behind such complicity, including "warrior policing,"[677] bespeak the power of patriarchy in black culture (divide and conquer), dividing politicians and the police from other blacks, whom they refuse to take seriously or treat humanely. We are, thankfully, now in part inspired by the election of Barack Obama (who was critical of mass incarceration) in a new period of black resistance, and it is time for all of us to join this resistance against a Trump administration that mindlessly repeats our worst, most ethically egregious mistakes.

Such resistance, in my view, must take seriously several issues largely ignored in the United States since Nixon. First, there is the injustice on liberal grounds of respect for human rights of America's retributive drug laws.[678] Second, we should fundamentally question American retributivism as the rationale for continuing America's highly racialized death penalty[679]

---

[675] May 13, 2009, interview of John Erhlichman by G. Kerlikowske, heard in the documentary movie, *13th*, directed by Ava DuVernay (2016).

[676] See James Forman Jr., *Locking Up Our Own: Crime and Punishment in Black America* (New York: Farrar, Straus and Giroux, 2017).

[677] Id., p. 170.

[678] See, on this point, David A. J. Richards, *Sex Drugs, Death, and the Law: An Essay on Human Rights and Overcriminalization* (Totowa, NJ: Rowman and Littlefield, 1982), pp., 157–212; Douglas N. Huask, *Drugs and Rights* (Cambridge, UK: Cambridge University Press, 1992); Douglas Husak, *Legalize this! The Case for Decriminalizing Drugs* (London: Verso, 2002); Douglas Husak, *Overcriminalization: The Limits of the Criminal Law* (Oxford: Oxford University Press, 2008).

[679] For critiques of the death penalty, see David Garland, *Peculiar Institution:*

as well as for the appalling state of our prison system, which has long outlived any of the justifications once offered in its support.[680] I agree with Michel Foucault that the prison system, as classically developed in America and Europe during the Enlightenment, not only no longer serves any legitimate purpose (it certainly does not reform its dominant founding purpose) but largely maintains a docile and often racialized underclass, attenuating the effects of revolt [such treatment] may arouse.[681] There are

---

America's Death Penalty in an Age of Abolition (Cambridge, Mass.: The Belknap Press of Harvard University Press, 2010); James Q. Whitman, *Harsh Justice: Criminal Punishment and the Widening Divide between America and Europe* (Oxford: Oxford University Press, 2003); Robert A. Ferguson, *Inferno: An Anatomy of American Punishment* (Cambridge, Mass.: Harvard University Press, 2014); Carol S. Steiker and Jordan M. Steiker, *Courting Death: The Supreme Court and Capital Punishment* (Cambridge, Mass.: Belknap Press of Harvard University Press, 2016). For a defense, see Matthew H. Kramer, *The Ethics of Capital Punishment: A Philosophical Investigation of Evil and Its Consequences* (Cambridge, UK: Cambridge University Press, 2011).

[680] For critiques of the American prison system, including its underlying assumptions and suggestions for alternatives, see Philip Zimbardo, *The Lucifer Effect* (New York: Random House, 2007); Craig Haney and Philip Zimbardo, "The Past and Future of US Prison Policy Twenty-Five Years after the Stanford Prison Experiment," *American Psychologist*, July 1998, Vol. 53, No. 7, pp. 709–727; Norval Morris, *The Future of Imprisonment* (Chicago: University of Chicago Press, 1974); Richard L. Lippke, *Rethinking Imprisonment* (Oxford: Oxford University Press, 2007); Andrew von Hirsch, *Doing Justice: The Choice of Punishments* (New York: Hill and Wang, 1976); Andrew von Hirsch, *Censure and Sanctions* (Oxford: Oxford University Press, 2003); Andrew von Hirsch, *Past or Future Crimes: Deservedness and Dangerousness in the Sentencing of Criminals* (Manchester: Manchester University Press, 1986); Franklin E. Zimring and Gordon J. Hawkins, *Deterrence* (Chicago: University of Chicago Press, 1973); Alfred Blumstein, et al., *Deterrence and Incapacitation: Estimating the Effects of Criminal Sanctions on Crime Rates* (Washington, DC: National Academy of Sciences, 1978); Jeremy Travis, et al., *The Growth of Incarceration in the United States: Exploring Causes and Consequences* (Washington, DC: The National Academies Press, 2014); Paul H. Robinson and John M. Darley, "Does Criminal Law Deter? A Behavioural Science Investigation," *Oxford Journal of Legal Studies*, Vol. 24, No. 2 (2004), pp. 173–205.

[681] Michel Foucault, *Discipline and Punish: The Birth of the Prison System*, trans. Alan Sheridan (New York: Vintage Books, 1977), p. 303. For further

thankfully alternatives, some of which would take seriously violence as the central purpose for prisons and use our best psychiatric and therapeutic understanding about how violence may be prevented, including alternatives to prisons that better deal with preventing violence.[682] America—a nation famously creative and innovative—needs to turn its creativity to thinking about and developing such humane alternatives.

Why is our criminal justice system so problematic? It rests, in my judgment, on the American heart of darkness—so dark that our democracy has, until quite recently, been unable to face what it has done and mindlessly continues to do. The experience of other democratic advanced democracies, with whom we reasonably compete ourselves, offers reasons for doubt that democracy itself requires such institutions. These countries have lower crimes rates that we do and have abolished the death penalty and held unconstitutional forms of solitary confinement still used and defended in American prisons; they also have lower sentences that we do, and some of them have developed different approaches to prisons and even undertaken alternatives to prison, including constitutionally required democratic review of prison conditions. Yet, I repeat, all these countries have lower rates of violent criminality than we do.[683]

What is most profoundly revelatory about Gilligan's work—something no one else has brought to democratic public discussion before him—is an analysis of the role patriarchy, based on a shame culture (see chapter 2), plays in the psychology of violence, which is largely male on male violence. His insights arose from his close study of violent men as a prison psychiatrist over several decades. The propensity to violence of these men, including murders, was connected to insults to their sense of patriarchal manhood, as was revealed by the men themselves in therapy as they found

---

discussion of Foucault, see David A. J. Richards, *Why Love Leads to Justice: Love Across the Boundaries* (Cambridge: Cambridge University Press, 2016), pp. 225–229.

[682] See James Gilligan and Bandy Lee, "Beyond the Prison Paradigm: From Provoking Violence to Preventing It by Creating 'Anti-Prisons' (Residential Colleges and Therapeutic Communities," *Ann. NY Acad. Sci.* 1036: 300–324 (2004).

[683] See, on all these points, James Q. Whitman, *Harsh Justice: Criminal Punishment and the Widening Divide between America and Europe* (Oxford: Oxford University Press, 2003). See also James Gilligan, *Preventing Violence* (New York: Thames & Hudson, 2001).

a voice to discuss both their violent acts and the connections of such violence often to family histories of abuse and neglect. What is revelatory about this work is that American prisons, despite their historical origins as institutions intended to bring criminals to a sense of guilt and remorse, not only do not bring prisoners to a sense of guilt but are institutions that shame them as men eliciting and exacerbating their propensities to violence. Indeed, the conditions in American prisons themselves inflict violence and humiliation both by guards and fellow prisoners. Perhaps, the most telling point in his analysis is the role homophobia played in sexual relations among men in our prisons, which prisons encouraged as a way in which prisoners could hierarchically and violently control one another, as patriarchy requires. Prisons are, for Gilligan, thus a case study in the culture of American homophobia, as any possibility of love, let alone sexual love, between men (as equals) is culturally framed as an insult to a manhood that structures all such relationships, including those to women, in terms of a rigid gender binary and hierarchy deviation from which requires violence and sometimes homicidal violence.[684] American prisons are, in effect, war zones in which the prisoners, often divided by gang groups based on ethnicity and race, war on one another; and the authorities sometimes encourage and even stage-manage such violence, as patriarchal men do (as in wars).[685]

What enabled Gilligan to see what he came to see is that he came to see the violent men he studied as persons, having freed himself, as a man and a psychiatrist, from the extraordinary repressive burdens American patriarchy imposes on male voice. Through freeing his own voice from patriarchy, he was able to form relationships of a man to another man, in particular, a man lower in the gender hierarchy, that patriarchy forbids and indeed finds unnatural and unthinkable. That is why his psychological analysis of homophobia in American prisons reveals a larger psychological truth about how patriarchy damages men—holding them into the rigid,

---

[684] See, on this point, James Gilligan, *Violence,* pp. 76, 81, 83–84, 156–57, 164, 171, 189.

[685] See, on gladiatorial matches in American prisons managed by corrections officers, James Gilligan, *Violence in California Prisons: A Proposal for Research into Patterns and Cures* (Sacramento: Diane Publishing Co. 2000, edited with an introduction by California State senator Tom Hayden).

competitive, and aggressive patterns required by the gender binary and hierarchy.

But what his approach reveals as well is how and why American criminal justice expresses the American heart of darkness. The American prison system—through the racialized mass incarceration earlier discussed—is largely occupied by the men on the lowest rung of American patriarchy, men President Trump calls losers. Michel Foucault is, I believe, quite right that the prison system today no longer has any legitimate public purpose, and what drives it is something we refuse to see because it is so painful to see, let along admit, namely, it supports and rationalizes the injustice we inflict on some of the most unjustly disadvantaged people in American culture, in effect, so dehumanizing them that they lose their capacity to resist the injustices they have suffered. What Foucault does not see but seems to me clear, in light of Gilligan's revelations, is the role patriarchy plays in rationalizing this ethical monstrosity in liberal modernity, in particular, in the United States. It is a system largely created by men and is about men; and men, because of the force of patriarchy in their own lives, psychologically frame such institutions in patriarchal terms, which elicits the levels of violence, rationalized as just retribution, that distinguish American criminal justice from other democracies in the world. In effect, criminality by the disadvantaged breaks from their role in the gender hierarchy, and thus shame the manhood of more advantaged men, eliciting illimitable violence that cannot be reasonably justified. What distinguishes America is, I believe, that patriarchy is and has remained stronger here than elsewhere, which may be connected to the continuing power here of patriarchal religion, including our Puritan traditions.[686]

---

[686] On the symmetry of religious and secular punishments, see Samuel Y. Edgerton Jr., *Pictures and Punishment: Art and Criminal Prosecution during the Florentin Renaissance* (Ithaca: Cornell University Press, 1985), pp. 30–32. Perhaps in this connection Nietzsche's most powerful critique of religion comes when he quotes at length the grisly punishments endorsed both by Aquinas and Tertullian, as both Aquinas and Tertullian take such pleasure, even delight, in the tortures of the damned, exemplifying the psychology of ressentiment of Christian ascetics. See Friedrich Nietzsche, *On the Genealogy of Morals*, trans. Douglas Smith (Oxford: Oxford University Press, 1996), pp. 33–34. Consider, in this context, what may underlie Nietzsche's criticism of Kant's acceptance of the lex talionis ("Even with Old Kant: The Categorical Imperative gives off a whiff of cruelty," id., pp. 46–47), namely, that Kant,

Its highly retributive models of divine punishment, whatever their merits on religious grounds, are an illegitimate model for punishment in a secular culture committed to the values of the First Amendment, including both the protection of free exercise and the prohibition of established churches. In contrast, other constitutional democracies sharply constrain the degree to which retributive arguments justly impose constraints of justice on punishment along the lines of HLA arguments for limiting punishment by principles of fairness and personal culpability (condemning scapegoating) and proportionality principles that align the metric of sanctions with underlying moral judgments of relative wrongness (none of which requires punishment or any punishments in particular, as Kant's lex talionis mistakenly supposes).[687]

Gilligan's argument illustrates the importance of our approach that extends feminist analysis to men as well as women. The problem, as I see it, is that psychologically patriarchy bears most heavily on men and boys, whose initiation into patriarchy occurs much earlier than that of girls and women. The consequence is that any institution run largely be men for men is likely to raise the most profound ethical questions about the justice of our institutions.

---

a secular philosopher, uncritically endorses, here and elsewhere, normative views that derive from sectarian religion's grisly conceptions of hell, not from a secular ethics. Nietzsche may be quite right about this. For Kant's theory of punishment, see Immanuel Kant, "On the Right to Punishment and to Grant Clemency," pp. 472–477, Immanuel Kant, *Practical Philosophy*, trans. ed. Mary J. Gregor (Cambridge: Cambridge University Press, 1999).

[687] See H. L. A. Hart, *Punishment and Responsibility: Essays in the Philosophy of Law Second Edition* (Oxford: Oxford University Press, 2008); see also R. A. Duff, *Punishment, Communication, and Community* (Oxford: Oxford University Press, 2001).

CHAPTER 8

Philip Roth on Traumatic American Manhood and Paths to Resistance

There is a contemporary author, only recently deceased (2018), whose work deals quite precisely with the role trauma has played in American manhood and womanhood in both personal and public life (including our propensity to fight unjust wars, to be discussed in a later chapter), namely, Philip Roth. Roth's novels are especially resonant for me because his artistic voice expressed liberal resistance to two unjust burdens that American culture imposed on his sense of self, namely, his sense of himself as an outsider to a Christian American culture of anti-Semitism (Roth was Jewish) and an outsider as well to the sexual repression he experienced in the sexual Puritanism both of American culture and the Jewish culture in which he was born and brought up (including sexual relationships to non-Jewish women, breaking the love laws, and never having children).[688] Both these burdens resonate with my own experience during the historical period from which Roth's novels arise, namely, my sense of self as a racialized Italian American and as a gay man outside the repressive Catholic culture in which I was born and brought up. The analogies are, I believe, exact and show yet again how much straight and gay men share, their secret selves, when they come to a sense of the injustice of American patriarchal

---

[688] See, for illuminating discussion of Roth's life and works, Claudia Roth Pierpont, *Roth Unbound: A Writer and His Books* (New York: Farrar, Straus & Giroux, 2013).

gender roles and resist. What makes Roth's novels of special interest to the argument of this book is the focus of five of his later novels on the role trauma plays in inflicting moral injury on both men and women, and the role of voice in resistance.[689]

Early Work: *Goodbye, Columbus* and *Portnoy's Complaint*

Roth was brought up during World War II. His biographer, Claudia Roth Pierpont (based in part on interviews with Roth), observes,

> He was hugely impressed by the manliness of the guys who'd been in the war, particularly since he felt himself to be, he says, "A good little Jewish boy, a sissy"—a kid more brains than brawn. (He is quick to add, however, that he did not appear this way to others.) The romance of manliness that runs through Roth's work may have its beginnings in the experiences of a wartime child.[690]

What counted as being "a good Jewish boy" is very much the subject of Roth's early short story, *Goodbye, Columbus*,[691] which I read in my first year at Harvard College. It is written in the voice of Neil Klugman, a young man, like Roth, brought and up and raised in Newark (Newark is the locus of Roth's artistic imagination in the same way as London was for Dickens and Dublin for Joyce). Neil meets Brenda Patimkin, whose father, a successful Jewish businessman, had moved the family from Newark to Short Hills, a notably much wealthier and higher status community in New Jersey. Brenda, who goes to Radcliffe, is strongly attracted to Neil and he to her, and she introduces him into her family, including her parents, her older brother Ron (who is on the verge of marrying Harriet), and her younger sister, Julie, served by a black maid, Carlotta. Neil and Brenda are strongly attracted to one another and have a sexual affair; at Neil's insistence (for

---

[689] See, for illuminating discussion, Aimee Pozorski, *Roth and Trauma: The Problem of History in the Later Works (1995–2010)*, (New York: Bloomsbury, 2011).

[690] Claudia Roth Pierpoint, *Roth Unbound*, p. 17.

[691] Philip Roth, *Goodbye, Columbus, Novels & Stories 1959–1962*, ed. Ross Miller (New York: The Library of America, 2005), pp. 7–108.

---

his pleasure), Brenda gets a diaphragm. When Brenda's mother discovers the diaphragm (left in Brenda's drawer at home), she writes her daughter, now back at Radcliffe, about her outrage at such premarital sex with a boy who, thus repaid "the hospitality we were nice enough to show to him, a perfect stranger."[692] Brenda weeps at disappointing her parents' expectations for her as a good girl, and Neil is furious that Brenda so negligently left the diaphragm where her mother might discover it. The couple, who once thought themselves in love and Neil thought of marrying her, break up. The issue of possible marriage had come up at Ron's wedding party when an uncle, seeing the romance of Brenda and Neil, comments that a marriage woud very much be in Neil's interest; and Ron seems to expect and approve of such a relationship. Ron had now after college been drafted into his father's business, and Neil sees how he listens constantly to a record, *Goodbye, Columbus,* that celebrates Neil's happiest years on the Ohio State football team. Ron, a good boy, is counterpointed in the story to Neil, a bad boy. Ron's romantic mythologization of himself as a football hero anticipates the same theme of Roth's later novel, *American Pastoral,* to be shortly discussed.

Roth's early novel, *Portnoy's Complaint,* brought him fame and best-selling royalties; Roth was now a celebrity and a rich man[693] but also the object of condemnation by, among others, Jews, who found his revelations of Portnoy's sexual life as confirming, rather than contesting, anti-Semitic stereotypes of Jewish sexuality.[694] Alexander Portnoy, in whose voice the novel is written, is decidedly not a Jewish good boy at least if we understand such goodness as settling into a monogamous marriage with children to a Jewish girl. His sexual passions are for a succession of non-Jewish girls (shiksas). The more non-Jewish, apparently the better, culminating in the Monkey, Mary Jane Reed (evidently a former prostitute and relatively uneducated), with whom he has a sexual three way with an Italian prostitute in Rome. The narrative is in the form of an interminable psychoanalytic session with Dr. Spielvogel, confessing his struggles as a boy with a controlling mother over body functions, in particular, his frequent masturbations. It is a confessional narrative of male vulnerability

---

[692] Philip Roth, *Goodbye, Columbus,* p. 103.

[693] Claudia Roth Pierpont, *Roth Unbound,* pp. 62–63.

[694] See, for discussion of this point, Pierpont, *Roth Unbound,* pp. 62–68.

not only to women but to sexual appetites and put in terms of shamed manhood:

> Is this what has come down to me from the pogroms and the persecution? From the mockery and abuse bestowed by the *goyim* over these two thousand lovely years? Oh my secrets, my shame, my palpitations, my flushes, my sweats! The way I respond to the simple vicissitudes of human life! Doctor, I can't stand any more being frightened like this over nothing! Bless me with manhood! Make me brave! Make me strong! Make me *whole*! Enough being a nice Jewish boy, publicly pleasing my parents while privately pulling my putz! Enough![695]

When Portnoy pleas with Spielvogel, "Make me *whole!*" he reveals a psyche in contradiction with itself, publicly pleasing his parents, but privately living sexual secrets, beginning in the sexual freedom experienced first in masturbation and then in sexual affairs with shiksas. Portnoy's public life is that of a distinguished New York lawyer: valedictorian of his high school, editor of the *Columbia Law Review*, and an antidiscrimination official in the New York City mayoralty of the liberal Republican, John Lindsay. But he experiences his private sexual life as shamefully secret, and yet the novel is hilariously sexually uninhibited, quite pornographic really in its expression of Portnoy's sexual imagination and adventures, all framed by his critical humor about Christianity, including its founder—"the Pansy of Palestine."[696]

The key to the novel's remarkable popularity and its continuing appeal is the hilarious voice it unashamedly gives to the shameful secrets of a manhood living in what boys and men experience sometimes as an unjust Puritanical prison, as I did as a gay men during the period Roth wrote and as he did as a straight man. It is striking that, in exposing in this way the vulnerabilities of sexual desire that men sometimes experience as a shameful loss of control (feeling desire when we don't want it, and not feeling it when we do), Roth is writing very much along the same lines

---

[695] Philip Roth, *Portnoy's Complaint, Novels 1967–1972*, ed. Ross Miller (New York: The Library of America, 2005), pp. 279–468, at p. 302–303.

[696] Philip Roth, *Portnoy's Complaint*, p. 394.

as Augustine of Hippo's *Confessions* and *City of God*. Augustine and Roth are writing confessions from the same experience and the sense in both that a beloved mother intrusively attempts to control its expression.[697] For Augustine, the mother is his Christian mother, Monika, opposing his pagan father; for Portnoy, it is a Jewish mother, and Roth writes powerfully of how a young boy at age four ("I hardly know what sex I am")[698] is enveloped by "a mother's vitality"[699] and love, and how a father, though patriarchally domineering in other areas, did not extend his control here: "What a mix-up of the sexes in our house!"[700] The contrast, of course, is that Augustine aligns himself with his mother's strictures on sexuality (abandoning sexuality altogether), and Roth sets himself on a path of resistance, as his later novels show, not only to Augustinian anti-Semitic Christianity but to Jewish constraints on sexual life.

Alternative Models of Manhood: *Ghost Story* and *Counterlife*

Roth's resisting voice culminates in five later novels—*Sabbath's Theater* (1995), *American Pastoral* (1997), *I Married a Communist* (1998), *The Human Stain* (2000), and *The Plot Against America* (2004) that I want to discuss at some length. However, among his other works before these novels, two novels mark his own imaginative path to resistance.

The first of these, *The Ghost Writer* (1979), explores Roth's own path of resistance to his father's domineering voice that appears in so many of his novels. Roth, writing in the voice of his alter ego, Nathan Zuckerman, writes of Zuckerman's relationship to two other Jewish writers, modeled on Bernard Malamud and Saul Bellow, both of whom were models for Roth's art and recognized and supported him. The novel registers three competing male voices, a disapproving father, an artist, E. I. Lonoff, modeled on Malamud, whom Zuckerman visits, and an artist modeled on Bellow. Zuckerman is an overnight guest at E. I. Lonoff's New England

---

697 For fuller discussion of Augustine along these lines, see Carol Gilligan and David A. J. Richards, *The Deepening Darkness: Patriarchy, Resistance, and Democracy's Future* (Cambridge: Cambridge University Press, 2009), pp. 102–118.

698 Philip Roth, *Portnoy's Complaint*, p. 307.

699 Id., p. 307.

700 Id., p. 306.

farmhouse, where he meets both Lonoff's wife and a student, Amy Bellette, a young woman of indeterminate foreign background who was a former student of Lonoff and who may have been his mistress. Zuckerman, with an active imagination searching for artistic models, imagines Bellette is Anne Frank, an iconic figure in the understanding of the Nazi persecution and murder of European Jews and an aspiring writer and a woman writer at that, whose diaries are now universally read and admired. As Zuckerman imagines Anne Frank, she and her family are among the most secular of European Jews, which explains why Christians are so moved by her diaries. For Zuckerman, as for Roth, the persecution and murder of Anne shows how little anti-Semitism has to do with whether Jews are good boys and girls by Christian standards. Anti-Semitism is altogether more irrational and unjust, and Jews have no reason to comply with such standards. Indeed, they have good reason to resist them, a claim central to Roth's resisting voice in his novels.[701]

The second novel, *The Counterlife* (1986), was inspired by Roth's life in London with the actress Claire Bloom, who was Jewish, as he broke free from the isolated life of a E. I. Lonoff that he had once imagined for himself and theatrically imagined and explored lives that break free of once accepted constraints.[702] Roth, who had a serious heart condition, also framed this novel, as he would with his later novels, around death and the anti-Semitism he experienced both in Israel and London. The novel imagines two lives: Zuckerman's brother and Zuckerman himself, in one version of which the brother dies, and the other Zuckerman dies. Zuckerman's brother (based on Roth's elder brother, Sandy) leads a more conventional Jewish family life than his brother, a dentist with a wife and children, but having adulterous affairs with a Swiss woman in Basel and with his dental assistant at home (both of which he disclosed to his brother). He is altogether a Jewish good boy but, like Portnoy, with sexual secrets, and he resents his brother's greater freedom and artistic success. (Sandy, Roth's brother, had wanted to be a painter but ended up an advertising man; in fact, the relationship of the brothers was loving.) Zuckerman travels to Israel and encounters and resists the two forms of Jewish fanaticism he encounters there: the first, the anti-Semitism of

---

[701] For illuminating discussion of Roth's use of Anne Frank in this novel, see Claudia Roth Pierpont, *Roth Unbound*, pp. 108–11, 114–22.

[702] See Pierpont, *Roth Unbound*, pp. 141–157.

Jewish settlers with their contempt for American Jews who refuse to live in Israel, and the second, a psychopathic Jewish terrorist. It is here in Israel that Zuckerman, arguing with a settler and speaking clearly in Roth's voice, realizes how American he is and how much he values American constitutionalism:

> I went on, the fact of it was that I could not think of any historical society that had achieved the level of tolerance institutionalized in America that had placed pluralism smack at the center of its publicly advertised dream of itself. I could only hope that Yacov Elchanan's solution to the problem of Jewish survival and independence turned out to be no less successful than the unpolitical, unideological "family Zionism" enacted by my immigrant grandparents in coming, at the turn of the century, to America, a country that did not have at its center the ideal of exclusion.[703]

Zuckerman, who in this version dies, leaves a manuscript about his brother's life and adulteries, about his trip to Israel, and his life in Britain with an Englishwoman, Maria, with whom he had fallen in love. The brother, after Zuckerman's funeral, breaks into his apartment and destroys those parts of the manuscript that deal with his life. Maria does not, however, destroy the manuscript dealing with Zuckerman's life with her and her family, including an anti-Semitic mother and sister, though she believes Zuckerman has misrepresented her mother and sister. Zuckerman writes in the manuscript about his experience in Britain both with the Christian anti-Semitism of Maria's mother and sister and in a restaurant when a British women conspicuously speaks of the "smell" of the Jewish Roth dining with a Christian woman. Maria is not herself anti-Semitic and loves Zuckerman, but she realizes that their relationship cannot endure in the context of her family connections and British genteel Christian anti-Semitism. London and life with Bloom would pale for Roth, and his return to the United States would lead to the five deeply American novels that are his most enduring artistic achievement.

---

[703] Philip Roth, *Counterlife, Novels & Other Narratives 1986–1991*, ed. Ross Miller (New York: The Library of America, 2008), pp. 1–304, at p. 50.

Bad Boys: *Sabbath's Theater*

All these novels—*Sabbath's Theater, American Pastoral, I Married a Communist, The Human Stain,* and *The Plot Against America*—feature characters who have experienced either directly or indirectly war trauma (*Sabbath's Theater, The Human Stain,* and *The Plot Against America*) or the trauma of terrorism (*American Pastoral*) or the trauma of child abuse (*I Married a Communist*), and several combine several such kinds of trauma. All of them, however, explore deeper levels of trauma that dominant American stereotypes of manhood and womanhood inflict on men as well as women, what I earlier called moral injury, damaging moral character, both by bullying men and women into accepting stereotypes of manhood and womanhood that betray life and love lived from conviction, and silencing or crippling resisting voice. All Roth's works are haunted, as I have already observed, by the form these stereotypes take in the developmental experience of Jewish boys and men, starting in the idea of good versus bad Jewish boys that Roth hilariously explores, as we have seen, in *Portnoy's Complaint.* The depth of the problem for Roth is that these stereotypes of American manhood are themselves not only anti-Semitic but racist as well, and that the Americanization of immigrant Jews (like other immigrants like my own Italian Americans) can require them to disown their own experience of unjust persecution, crippling both their reflective values of justice and thus their capacity to resist the deepest injustices in American constitutional and political history, for example, the founding of the United States Constitution in slavery, the traumatic Civil War over slavery and racism, and our failures to address the racism that continued to flourish after the Civil War and continues to do so. Both slavery and racism are themselves in their nature traumatic, dehumanizing groups of people on irrational grounds, and thus exposing them to unjust treatment, including atrocities like slavery and lynching. European anti-Semitism has had a similar character, culminating in the genocidal murder of six million Jews. Roth's work in these five novels asks whether the Americanization of American Jews itself continues to inflict on Jews and other immigrants such trauma and thus disables them from seeing it or crippling their resistance to it. And the novels explore as well the connections of such traumas and their consequences to perpetuating sexism and homophobia in the name of gender stereotypes that remain uncritically patriarchal.

The first two of these novels—*Sabbath's Theater* and *American Pastoral*—expose the depth of this problem of being a good or bad boy from opposing comic and tragic perspectives. Mickey (Morris) Sabbath is a latter-day Alexander Portnoy, but unlike Portnoy, he is not torn between being a good boy in public and a sexually bad boy in private. He is as sexually obsessed, as hilariously as Portnoy, but has not opted for being as well in public life a respectable and accomplished lawyer and citizen, as Portnoy did. Mickey is an artist, not, however, a mainstream artist but a kind of bad boy artist, using puppetry to express his sexual desires and imagination as the key to his works (including an early and unsuccessful interpretation of *Macbeth* in New York City). His erotic art gets him in trouble with the then moralistic police and judges of New York (Catholic, of course), and he is arrested and tried when he performs one of his erotic puppet shows at Columbia University and a Barnard woman student is drawn to and fascinated by his show, at which time Mickey is arrested and tried. Mickey, in consequence, becomes a folk hero to New York liberals and ends up teaching his art at a college up state with his second wife on the faculty as well.

Mickey manages to turn every opportunity into disaster. His first wife, Nikki, performed in his early plays, but disappears mysteriously (Mickey imagines he killed her); and his second wife, Roseanna, abandoned by her mother and abused by her father, is an alcoholic ending in a half-way house, hating Mickey as much as he hates her. His great sexual love is a Croatian married immigrant, Drenka Balich, who has sex with many men outside her marriage, but regards Mickey as her great love, saying "My American boyfriend."[704] She dies, however, plunging Mickey into grief, expressed by masturbating on her grave (as another former lover of Drenka did as well). And Mickey loses his college job when his erotically explicit phone conversation with a student is made public, leading to a sexual harassment charge that is the ground for his discharge.

The novel is haunted by death, written after the death of a former lover of Roth.[705] Mickey, after all his emotional and professional losses, thinks about suicide. (The last section of the novel is "To Be or Not To Be.") A New York couple, the Cowans, remembering his theatrical work in New

---

[704] Philip Roth, *Sabbath's Theater*, *Novels 1993-1995*, ed. Ross Miller (New York: The Library of America, 2010), pp. 373-787, at p. 754.

[705] See Claudia Roth Pierpont, *Roth Unbound*, p. 189.

York and his trial, take him in, but he manages to alienate them both by his sexual advances to the wife (a periodontist) and sexual interest in their young daughter; they throw him out. At the end of the novel, Mickey dresses himself in the American flag given to Mickey's family after his beloved brother, Morty (an accomplished athlete), was killed fighting Japan in World War II. The death of his brother traumatized Mickey's mother (who fell into a lasting depression), and Mickey himself is still furious at all Japanese people (including the Japanese woman at his college who leads the sexual harassment charge against him). At the novel's end, Mickey masturbates on the grave of his beloved Drenka, and he is arrested and then released by her policeman son. Mickey decides he will not commit suicide. The last lines of the novel are: "And he couldn't do it. He could not fucking die. How could he leave? Everything he hated was here."[706]

Sabbath's Theater is artistically one of Roth's most remarkable works, taking us into the damaged psyche of an artist, whose sexual desire and imagination motivate his public artistic voice in a way Portnoy never could or did. Like Roth, Mickey is resisting the sexual constraints that imprison men. When he tries to seduce Mrs. Cowan, Mickey says, "God, I'm fond of adultery. Aren't you? A world without adultery is unthinkable. The brutal inhumanity of those against it."[707] The voice here is certainly Roth's, who had, for example, an adulterous affair while married to Claire Bloom.[708] (They eventually divorce.) But Mickey's resistance, unlike Roth's, is crippled, and Roth traces his destructiveness to the traumatic death of his good boy American brother and his resulting bottomless rage at those who have humiliated and abandoned him or, in Drenka's case, left him alone, including rage at the idea of patriotic American manhood that led his brother to his death. Mickey, of course, not only harms the two women he married but anyone who would befriend him. And he harms himself, turning his rage suicidally on himself. The power of trauma extends, Roth shows us, not only in silencing resisting voice but crippling it.

Sabbath's Theater reads, despite its preoccupation with death, as a comic novel, and it is important to ask why humor in this novel as well as *Portnoy's Complaint* and others allowed Roth to go so far in giving expression to the sexual desires and imagination of men, including artists. There is a long

---

706   Philip Roth, *Sabbath's Theater*, p. 787.
707   Philip Roth, *Sabbath's Theater*, p. 679.
708   See Claudia Roth Pierpont, *Roth Unbound*, p. 143.

tradition, exemplified by Erasmus's *In Praise of Folly* and Shakespeare's use of the fool in both comedies like *As You Like It* and *Twelfth Night* and tragedies as profound and harrowing as *King Lear*.[709] In these and other cases, putting sometimes the most cutting criticisms of current religious and political arrangements in the voice of a humorous fool allows a person to say things that could not and would not otherwise be said, let alone listened to. Erasmus, for example, was illegitimate and gay, and was able to expose criticisms of the religion and politics of Catholic Europe that might, as a serious argument, have led to a charge of heresy, a charge that was made against Luther.[710] Folly, the speaker in *In Praise of Folly*, is, however, not only funny but a woman, and Erasmus is able to say things that would not otherwise be said or heard. Roth was not illegitimate or gay, but he was Jewish and was to explore domains of sexual desire and experience condemned and silenced not only by Christians but Jews, some of whom condemned him precisely for telling family secrets (namely, that Jewish boys and men, being human, were as sexual as everyone else), secrets best kept from the goyim (Irving Howe),[711] drenched, as they were, in anti-Semitic stereotypes of Jewish sexuality. Jewish humor has always drawn its vital critical edge from the way it made possible a critical voice to be spoken and heard that was otherwise silenced. Roth in *Sabbath Theater* develops this tradition into profound art, giving expression to domains of sexual desire and experience not otherwise acknowledged and how unjust repression has rendered resistance so difficult and sometimes psychologically crippling, if not impossible.

Good Boys: *American Pastoral*

Roth's next novel, *American Pastoral*, is the tragic companion to *Sabbath's Theater*. *Sabbath's Theater* explores a bad boy resisting artist and is comic; *American Pastoral* is about the ultimate Jewish good boy, the Swede

---

[709] See Erasmus, *Praise of Folly*, trans. Betty Radice (London: Penguin, 1993). On Erasmus and the relationship to Shakespeare and Rabelais, see Walter Kaiser, *Praisers of Folly* (Cambridge: Harvard University Press, 1963)

[710] For a brilliant and illuminating recent discussion of both Erasmus and Luther, see Michael Massing, *Fatal Discort: Erasmus, Luther, and the Fight for the Western Mind* (New York: Harper, 2018).

[711] See Claudia Roth Pierpont, *Roth Unbound*, pp. 132–34.

Lvov, and is unbearably tragic, as the daughter he loved, Merry, becomes a terrorist against the Vietnam War, killing some four people. The novel is framed, as is the next novel, *I Married a Communist,* in the voice of Roth's alter ego, Nathan Zuckerman. In both novels, Zuckerman explores his own relationship as a boy to other boys or men he admired. In *American Pastoral,* Zuckerman, now an older man and established artist, has been asked to lunch with another Jewish boy he enormously admired, Swede Lvov, as if some serious matter was to be discussed. Swede conspicuously did not look Jewish, but Scandinavian (thus the name Swede). He was admired at their high school for his athletic prowess. No one seemed more American, less Jewish, and he was admired by Zuckerman and other boys for this reason. At lunch, Swede mentions only the three sons he has had with his second wife and surprises Zuckerman by not discussing more serious issues that he had expected him to discuss. Later, Zuckerman attends the reunion at this high school, where he meets Swede's brother, Jerry Lvov, a physician who tells him not only that Swede had died but that he had endured the trauma that his sixteen-year-old daughter, Merry, had become a terrorist, exploding a bomb at a local store, which had killed an admired doctor. The remaining novel is Zuckerman's discovery of the story of Swede, his first wife, Dawn Dwyer; their daughter, Merry; and their wider family, including not only Jerry but their demanding father (Merry's grandfather), Lou Lvov.

In contrast to his brother, the physician Jerry, Swede had never questioned his father's demanding authority, and indeed, unlike his brother, he had followed his father into the glove business in Newark. He fell in love with and married Dawn, a Catholic Irish girl who had been a New Jersey beauty queen, and a competitor in the Ms. America pageant. (She lost.) Lou Lvov opposed the marriage (Dawn was not Jewish), but Swede insisted, the one time he resisted his father's authority. Both Swede and Dawn were regarded as models and exemplars of American manhood and womanhood, and so regarded themselves and were regarded as an ideal American couple, he handsome, she beautiful. And Swede thought of himself as Johnny Appleseed, modeling his posture and walk and sense of self in terms of an American mythology he uncritically adopted as his private mythology and never questioned.[712] Dawn undertakes a business of raising cows, and Merry, their daughter, sometimes works with her.

---

[712] See, for illuminating commentaries on this point, Claudia Roth Pierpont,

Swede and Dawn, like Roth, were brought up in the period after World War II, when America was triumphant and entered into an unexpected position of economic and political dominance on the world stage as well as extraordinary economic prosperity (thus American pastoral). Swede prospered running his father's glove business, and the family moves to suburbs where most of their neighbors are not Jewish or Italian or Irish, but American Wasps. Swede and Dawn are living out the American dream, but their sense of American virtue is confronted by the Vietnam War and Nixon's refusal to end the war in timely fashion. Swede himself opposes the war, but in discussions in the family, he acts as an intermediary, leaving his father, Lou, to exercise his aggressive dominance in discussion, including his hatred of all Republicans and the enormity of Vietnam. Lou is modeled on Roth's aggressively dominant father; like Roth's father, Lou had only a high school education but had strong opinions that he expressed forcefully. We hear in Lou the kind of bullying in conversation that Roth had endured as a son to such a father—"opinionated, dominating, exasperating, and profoundly humane."[713]

Whereas, however, Roth had resisted his father, finding his artistic voice in education at Bucknell and later the University of Chicago. Swede lacks such education and such a voice, something his brother, Jerry, ascribes to his supine compliance with his father's authority. His father opposed the Vietnam War and so did his son, but in family discussions, it is his father's aggressive repudiation of the Vietnam War and Nixon that Merry hears and comes to accept, becoming more extreme in her denunciation of the Vietnam War than her grandfather and certainly than her father. Strikingly, Merry has a stutter, an impediment to expressive speech. Swede refuses to accept the opinion of a therapist that the family dynamics may have something to do with her stutter. He is an American hero, and nothing in the family life of such a hero can be responsible for Merry's problem in speaking. Merry, influenced by antiwar activists she meets in visits to New York City and lacking speech and furious at an America she identifies with her parents, turns, like Jim Gilligan's humiliated men, to terroristic violence, exploding bomb at a post office, killing a doctor. Merry disappears into the antiwar underground.

Roth Unbound, pp. 214-15.; Aimee Pozorski, *Roth and Trauma*, pp. 44–49.
[713] Claudia Roth Pierpont, *Roth Unbound*, p. 224.

Both Swede and Dawn are traumatized by what their daughter has done and never are able to understand what happened. Swede deals with Dawn's depression by supporting her having an expensive face-lift in Switzerland, restoring her beauty. The marriage deteriorates; Dawn insists they move from the house Swede loves to a house built by a WASP architect with whom Dawn has an affair. Swede also has an affair with Merry's therapist. We learn nothing of Swede's divorce and remarriage and children, but his life centers on finding his daughter. He learns something about her from a young woman, Rita Cohen, a deranged antiwar activist who claims to know Merry. (It is not clear she does.) She demands money and sex from Swede; he gives money and is repelled by her sexual demands. Five years later, Rita tells Swede that his daughter now works in an animal shelter in Newark, and Swede reconnects with her, discovering that, after killing three other men by bombs, she has become a nonviolent Jain. Swede consults with his brother, who tells him he must go to the police. Swede refuses to listen; Merry must have been brainwashed by others to commit such acts and cannot be treated as a responsible moral agent. He continues to see his daughter until she dies and never tells his wife he is seeing her, living with an unbearable secret he only shares with his brother. Such secrets kill love, and the marriage is over. Swede will move on to another marriage and other children (three sons), continuing to live the American dream as he understands that dream. But he is tragically alone.

There is something Swede cannot and will not see, something connected to his conception of being an American, which has so colonized his psyche that he lacks the convictions of his father's sense of injustice, resisting both American anti-Semitism and racism, thus resisting the racist imperialism of the Vietnam War. His identification with a mythological Americanism has inflicted moral injury, itself traumatic, damaging moral character arising from uncritically accepting a conception of American manhood that bullies men and women into accepting stereotypes of manhood and womanhood that betray life and love lived from conviction and silencing resisting voice. Swede's trauma may have been transmitted to his daughter. Her stuttering is a lack of voice, a lack of voice which infuriates her both in her mother and father. What infuriates her is that her father and mother see and live America stereotypically, and her hatred of America becomes her hatred of her parents. But like them, she sees America stereotypically only not good (like them) but murderously evil. Swede's tragedy is that his own trauma, which is invisible to him (as patriarchy often is for men), has been reenacted by his daughter, inflicting yet further trauma. This is American tragedy, and patriarchy's force is at the heart of it.

Boys' Choices of Models of Manhood: Violence or Nonviolence?

I Married a Communist

I Married a Communist is written, like *American Pastoral*, in the voice of Nathan Zuckerman, but here, Zuckerman begins not with admiration of a fellow high school student, Swede, but with the impact on him as a boy and man of one of his high school teachers he most admired, Murray Ringold, and his younger brother, Ira Ringold. The novel unfolds as a discussion between Nathan and Murray, as Murray discloses the truth of his brother's history as a Communist committed to violent revolution along Stalinist lines. It was his brother's Communism that led, during the McCathy period, to Murray losing his teaching position, though he is eventually reinstated. Murray was never a Communist and teaches Nathan the value of critical thinking, modeled on the similar influence on Roth of his male high school teacher, Bob Lowenstein. Though Lowenstein did not, in fact, teach English, "His presence had been a kind of legitimization: the first real sign, Roth says, that I could attach brains to manliness."[714] Roth is chronicling here, as he earlier had in *The Ghost Writer*, his own search for alternative models of manhood to his demanding father. Both the models before him call for resisting injustice: the one through violence, the other through nonviolent voice.

Zuckerman had, as a boy, been captivated by Ira Ringold's ethical force in resisting the injustices of American political and cultural life after World War II, in particular, American racism. The Communist Party had appealed to Ira because it was the only political party that took seriously this injustice. The Democratic Party was ethically flawed by its dependence on Southern racist politicians and the Republican Party by its dependence on the racism of American business. Only the Communist Party took seriously the injustice of American racism and its support of imperialism, and Ira joined it very much under the influence of the proletarian working

---

[714] Claudia Roth Pierpont, *Roth Unbound*, p. 231.

class Communist Johnny O'Day, whom Ira first met when he served in Iran; for Ira, O'Day was a model of American manhood.

Zuckerman learns from Murray that Ira was "the product of a brutalizing family—the only Jewish family in Newark's all-Italian First Ward" and had "left high school to dig ditches and to work in the zinc mines of Northern New Jersey then joined the army right after Pearl Harbor."[715] Roth models Ira on the men returning from World War II he had admired as a boy, in particular, an ex-GI, Irving Cohen, who had married Roth's cousin and who was "beaten up in the army because of his outspoken views—as Ira is beaten up and called 'a nigger-loving Jew bastard' for protesting army segregation."[716] Zuckerman learns that Ira had murdered someone at sixteen and, though he had denied it to Zuckerman's father, was by conviction a fanatical Stalinist Communist and had become a celebrity radio star, Iron Rinn. Ira's undoing was his disastrous marriage to the beautiful actress Eve Frame with a daughter from a previous marriage whom Ira despised. "[C]ulturally pretentious and a secretly Jewish anti-Semite, she is giddily submissive to any show of strength. When the marriage fails, she is persuaded by crusading right-wing snobs to write a lurid expose titled *I Married a Communist*"[717] that leads to both Ira and Murry losing their jobs.

Boys' Secrets and Women's Resistance: A Contemporary Hester Prynne?

The Human Stain

The Human Stain is again written in the voice of Nathan Zuckerman but now an older man and published author living alone in the Berkshires, where he develops a close friendship with Coleman Silk, a retired professor of classics who is a neighbor. Zuckerman has now had prostate surgery and is impotent and no longer sexually active with women,[718] and his

---

[715] Claudia Roth Pierpont, *Roth Unbound*, p. 231.

[716] Id., p. 232.

[717] Id., p. 235.

[718] See Philip Roth, *The Human Stain*, *The American Trilogy 1997–2000*, ed. Ross Miller (New York: The Library of America, 2011), pp. 705–1038, at p. 929.

attachment to Coleman is more homoerotically intimate than any such male-male relationship in Roth. The intimacy incudes Zuckerman at one point dancing with Silk to "Bewitched, Bothered, and Bewildered" sung by Frank Sinatra:

> There was nothing overtly carnal in it, but because Coleman was wearing only his denim shorts and my hand rested on his warm back as if it were the back of a dog or a horse, it wasn't entirely a mocking act. There was a semiserious sincerity in his guiding me about on the stone floor, not to mention a thoughtless delight in just being alive, accidentally and clownishly and for no reason alive—the kind of delight you take as a child when you first learn to play a turn with a comb and toilet paper.[719]

At three points, Roth cites Aschenbach's surprised discovery of his homosexual desire in *Death in Venice* as relevant to understanding what Zuckerman is now feeling.[720] It is certainly not Aschenbach's carnal passion but an intimate feeling for another man that was new to Zuckerman and to Roth's art.

Zuckerman is drawn to Coleman because he sees in the experience of this highly intelligent and learned man and writer the same struggle for manhood that preoccupied his own life, as we can see in the novels of Roth we have discussed so far. The struggle for both Zuckerman and Coleman was with and against a powerful conception of American manhood and the degree to which one would accept or resist that conception of manhood and the consequences of such a choice both for private and public life. As Zuckerman asks himself of Coleman after his death, "Was he merely being another American and, in the great frontier tradition, accepted the democratic invitation to throw your origins overboard if to do so contributes to the pursuit of happiness? Or was it more than that? Or was it less?"[721]

---

[719] Philip Roth, *The Human Stain*, p. 728.
[720] For references see Philip Roth, *The Human Stain*, pp. 752, 763, 863.
[721] Philip Roth, *The Human Stain*, pp. 1013–14.

Zuckerman asks this question only after Coleman's death when he has finally learned what "was Coleman's way of becoming a man."[722] Coleman had been born to a light-skinned black middle-class family, a highly intelligent and ambitious boy, with a devoted mother and Shakespeare-loving father and a sister, Ernestine, and a brother, Walt. Coleman was not only a gifted student but a gifted golden gloves fighter and wanted to pursue the latter as a way of going on scholarship to a better university; his father, however, insisted that he go to Howard. After returning from fighting in World War II, Coleman enrolled at NYU, where he received stellar grades, and realized that he could pass as white. After being rejected by a white girl when he took her to his home and she realized he was black, Coleman met a Jewish girl, Iris, whom he married (they had four children), and told her he is Jewish. It was after his marriage to Iris that Coleman told his mother (his father had died) that he had told Iris his parents were dead, and they were Jewish, not black. His mother was anguished. "He was murdering her,"[723] and she told him, "You think like a prisoner. You do, Coleman Brutus. You're white as snow, and you think like slave."[724] Coleman always "did love secrets"—a way "to force himself to ignore his feelings, whether of fear, uncertainty, even friendship, to have the feelings but have them separately from himself."[725]

Coleman became a classics professor, and in inventing his version of American manhood, he took as his model, *The Iliad*. He had broken his mother's heart and thus shown that he could kill love "on behalf of his heroic conception of his life":

> Anybody who has the audacity to do that doesn't just want to be white. He wants to be able to do that. It had to do with more than just being blissfully free. It's like the savagery in *The Iliad*, Coleman's favorite book about the ravening spirit of man. Each murder there has its own quality, each a more brutal slaughter than the last.[726]

---

[722] Philip Roth, *The Human Stain*, pp. 1007–8.

[723] Philip Roth, *The Human Stain*, p. 833.

[724] Philip Roth, *The Human Stain*, p. 834.

[725] Philip Roth, *The Human Stain*, p. 797.

[726] Philip Roth, *The Human Stain*, pp. 1014–15.

However, Coleman brilliantly succeeded in altering his personal lot, only to be ensnared by the history he hadn't quite counted on.[727] That history, which he thought he could ignore, caught up with him when, in response to two black woman students not attending his class, he asked, "Does anyone know these people? Do they exist, or are they spooks?"[728] The term was regarded by the students as racist, and they lodge a complaint. Coleman responded that the charge was "preposterous"[729] and rejected it without any sensitivity to issues of race (a blindness arising from his closely held secret self and the model of aggressively armored manhood, based on *The Iliad*, he had defensively adopted, burying his secret in denial). But he had not taken seriously that, in his former role as faculty head raising standards as required by a college president who had now department, he had made enemies who would take the accusation seriously. His wife, Iris, a liberal woman of the left, was shocked by the accusation and unexpectedly died, and one of his children, a daughter, condemned his action. Coleman believed the accusation killed her, and he retired from the faculty. It was at this point that he met Zuckerman. In fact, the novel was not inspired by the scandal of Anatole Broyard, the writer who had passed as white (in fact, Broyard's parents had themselves passed as white, quite unlike Coleman in the novel),[730] but by the experience of Roth's close friend, Melvin Tumin, the Jewish Princeton sociologist who had used the word *spooks* in his class and was charged by the university with racism.[731]

Zuckerman was drawn to Coleman because of what he took to be his moral individualism, as a Jew, long before his death and the disclosure of his secret self. But Coleman had confided in Zuckerman as well about his sexual affair with a woman janitor at the college, Faunia Farley. Zuckerman had received an anonymous letter condemning the affair as exploitative of an uneducated, working class woman, which introduces into the novel its other great theme, arising from Roth's indignation about the moralistic response to President Clinton's relationship to Monica Lewinsky, namely, disproportionately condemnatory American sexual Puritanism. In making

---

[727] Philip Roth, *The Human Stain*, p. 1015.

[728] Id., p. 710.

[729] Id.

[730] See Bliss Broyard, *One Drop: My Father's Hidden Life—a Story of Race and Family Secrets* (New York: Back Bay Books, 2007).

[731] Claudia Roth Pierpont, *Roth Unbound*, p. 253.

his case, Roth-Zuckerman references Hawthorne, who had pointed to "the calculated frenzy with what Hawthorne (who in the 1860s lived not many miles from my door) identified in the incipient country of long ago as 'the persecuting spirit'; all of them eager to enact the astringent rituals of purification that would excise the erection from the executive branch."[732]

In fact, *The Human Stain* is the novel of Roth's closest to the themes of Hawthorne's *The Scarlet Letter,* even containing a character, Faunia Farley, as much a fallen woman in her world as Hester Prynne was in hers, and the only character who speaks in an ethical voice that condemns the models of sexuality that oppress both women and men.[733] Unlike Hester, however, both her children have died, and she does not survive but is killed with her lover, Coleman, by her ex-husband, Lester Farley, a damaged Vietnam War veteran whose memories of the atrocities in Vietnam vividly display how destructively posttraumatic stress disorder colonizes the imaginations and lives of its victims. Both Faunia and her ex-husband Farley are both traumatically damaged people, and the novel explores here the traumatic abuse that patriarchy inflicts both on women and men and its tragic consequences for both. Faunia came from a rich and privileged background. She was sexually abused by her stepfather from the age five and ran away at the age fourteen, marrying a dairy farmer, the ex-Vietnam vet, Lester Harley. When the farm loses money, Lester beats her, and she leaves him with their two children and has affairs with different men, ending with Coleman. The two children die in a fire, and Faunia keeps their ashes under her bed; she tries to commit suicide at least twice. Lester blames her for the children's death and is homicidally furious at her affair with Coleman. He has himself been profoundly damaged by the traumas of fighting the Vietnam War (he had two tours), and the novel brilliantly takes you into his paranoia and delusional rage and the violence that leads him to kill Coleman and Faunia.

Faunia has been unjustly traumatized by both her stepfather and ex-husband, very much in the position of a fallen woman in her world that Hester occupies in her world. Her condition is, of course, much more desperate than Hester's and she lacks Hester's prophetic feminist imagination. But in a remarkable scene in which she talks to and about a

---

[732] Philip Roth, *The Human Stain,* p. 706.

[733] For illuminating discussion of this point, including references to Hawthorne in other novels, see Aimee Pozorski, *Roth and Trauma,* pp. 80–86, 109–11.

crow (reminding one of the crow in Dickens's *Barnaby Rudge*), this woman, whom others assume is illiterate, gives piercing ethical voice to the injustice of the codes of purity that oppress women and men:

> "That's what comes of being hand-raised," said Faunia. "That's what comes of hanging around all his life with people like us. The human stain," and without revulsion or contempt or condemnation. Not even with sadness. *That's how it is*—in her own dry way, that is all Faunia was telling the girl feeding the snake: we leave a stain, we leave a trail, we leave our imprint. Impurity, cruelty, abuse, error, excrement, semen—there's no other way to be here. Nothing to do with disobedience. Nothing to do with grave or salvation or redemption. It's in everyone. Indwelling. Inherent. Defining. The stain that is there before its mark. Without the sign it is there. The stain so intrinsic it doesn't require a mark. The stain that *precedes* disobedience, that *encompasses* disobedience and perplexes all explanation and understanding. It's why all the cleansing is a joke. A barbaric joke at that. The fantasy of purity is appalling. It's insane. What is the quest to purity, if not *more* impurity? All she was saying about the stain was that it's inescapable. That, naturally, would be Faunia's take on it: the inevitably stained creatures we are. Reconciled to the horrible, elemental imperfection. She's like the Greeks, like Coleman's Greeks. Like their gods. They're petty. They quarrel. They fight. They hate. They murder. They fuck. All their Zeus every wants to do is to fuck—goddesses, mortals, heifers, she-bears—and not merely in his own form but, even more excitingly, as himself made manifest as beast. To hugely mount a woman as a bull To enter her bizarrely as a flailing white swan. There is never enough flesh for the king of gods or enough perversity. All the craziness desire brings. The dissoluteness. The depravity. The crudest pleasures. And the fury from the all-seeing wife. Not the Hebrew God, infinitely alone, infinitely obscure, monomaniacally the only god there is, was, and always will be, with nothing better to do than

worry about the Jews. And not the perfectly desexualized Christian man-god and his uncontaminated mother and all the guilt and shame that an exquisite unearthliness inspires. Instead the Greek Zeus, entangled in adventure, vividly expressive, capricious, sensual, exuberantly wedded to his own rich experience, anything but alone and anything but hidden. Instead the *divine* stain. A great reality-reflecting religion for Faunia Farley if, through Coleman, she'd known anything about it. As the hubristic fantasy has it, made in the image of God, all right, but not ours—*theirs*. God debauched. God corrupted. A god of life if ever there was one. God in the image of *man*.[734]

The crow, like Faunia, is an outsider, having been brought up by humans and no longer one with her species. It is because Faunia, like Hester, is now outside the framework of conventional patriarchal codes of manhood and womanhood that she can see their injustice so clearly, trying to keep people in patriarchal prisons of religion, race, gender, or sexuality that are falsely defined as purity and, in fact, are not based on real experience.

I think of Carol Gilligan's reading[735] of the biblical text of Eve in the Garden of Eden as Eve created because man needed a "partner,"[736] and Eve breaks the patriarchal taboo on knowledge based on experience. (Seeing "that the fruit of the tree was good to eat and ate it"[737] and giving the apple to her husband to eat, "the eyes of both of them were open.")[738] Like Carol, Roth's Faunia Farley sees the freeing of sexuality as linked to resistance; erotic desire is the stain: "The stain that *precedes* disobedience, that *encompasses* disobedience and perplexes all explanation and understanding." Roth has often been condemned as a misogynist and responded that he loved women, and they have been and are crucial figures in his life and development.[739] Patriarchy deforms both men and women, which the *The*

---

[734]   Philip Roth, *The Human Stain,* pp. 928–29.

[735]   Personal conversation, and ongoing unpublished works.

[736]   Genesis 2:19, *The New English Bible* (Cambridge: Cambridge University Press, 1972), p. 2.

[737]   Genesis 3:6, id., p. 3.

[738]   Gensis 3:7, id., p. 3.

[739]   See, on this point, Claudia Roth Pierpont, *Roth Unbound,* pp. 236–7.

Human Stain clearly shows and explores. But the deformed men (Coleman Silk and Lester Farley) are in comparison to a deformed woman like Faunia Farley, blind, cruel, and quite alone, while Faunia looks at human experience clearly and calls for a more tolerant and loving approach: "God in the image of *man*." She is, I believe, Roth's Hester Prynne.

The Plot Against America as Prophetic Novel

The Plot Against America is the only one of the five novels written in the voice of Philip Roth, and it is the voice of Roth as a young boy at ages seven to nine. It is artistically the least impressive of the five novels, lacking not only the surrealistic imagination, wild humor, and psychological depth of the earlier novels but written flatly to simulate a historical narrative. It is written ostensibly as a historical novel imagining an America in which Franklyn Roosevelt loses the election of 1940 to Charles Lindbergh, who had had strong sympathies with Hitler's fascism and whose speech, "Who are the war agitators?" on September 11, 1941, to the America First Committee's rally in Des Moines, pointing to Jews as one of the three groups agitating for America to enter World War II, is reprinted at the end of the novel.[740] What it tells us about the depth of American anti-Semitism before World War II would be of continuing historical interest even if its fictionalized version of history were of little historical interest. It was written during the administration of George Bush and reflects understandable worries of many Americans during that period that there were fascist elements in the politics that brought him to power, including both the unjust war in Iraq to which he mindlessly led the American people and his war on the rights both of women and gays and lesbians. After the election of Donald Trump, its analysis may now be regarded as prophetic, on which I want to comment later.

The interest of the book, from the perspective of my argument here, is what is artistically best in the novel, namely, the fear-ridden world of Philip Roth as a young boy and as an American Jew, fears shared with his parents, extended family, and friends, and how they responded to those fears. We follow the young Roth as a boy, long before his resistance to

---

[740] See Philip Roth, *The Plot Against America*, *Novels 2001–2007*, ed. Ross Miller (New York: The Library of America, 2013), pp. 97–458, at pp. 452–58.

his father at age sixteen, still intimately close with his loving mother and under the spell of his demanding and opinionated father and close to his older brother, Sandy, and under the influence as well of other boys, some of whom tempt him to be what he regards as a bad boy, though he is, at this point, certainly a good boy. His confusion and temptations, including running away from home, are made wonderfully and humorously real.

The great interest of the novel, from my point of view, is its investigation of the impact of the traumatic election of Lindbergh on American Jews, some of whom, including Philip's aunt, are complicitous with the government's policies directed against Jews, and others resist, some by joining the war on behalf of the British in Europe, others (Roth's father and mother) resisting here. The choice between violent and nonviolent resistance (the central issue in *I Married a Communist*) is central yet again, only here posed by a democratically triumphant political anti-Semitism, which threatens real harms to American Jews.

The choice is posed in the novel by the reaction of Roth's parents (Bess and Herman) to three young men who respond differently to the injustice Jews now face: the son, Sandy, Roth's older brother; Alvin, the nephew the Roths took in after his loss of both his father and mother; and Seldon Wishnow, a boy of Roth's age whose father commits suicide, leaving the boy and his distraught mother, both of whom Roth parents support.

After Lindbergh's election, Rabbi Lionel Bengelsdorf, who marries Roth's aunt, joins the Lindbergh administration, supporting its Just Folks program under which Jewish boys will live with WASP families in other parts of the country to advance their Americanization. Sandy is not only attracted to the program but joins it, living with a farming family in Kentucky. When Roth's aunt tries to persuade Sandy to join a White House dinner in which Lindbergh greets a Nazi official, Roth's father put his foot down, demanding his son not to go. Eventually, Sandy loses all interest in politics as he develops an interest in girls.

Alvin was the nephew and ward of Herman Roth after the deaths of his beloved brother and the brother's wife and lived with the Roths, sharing a room with the young Philip, who, in the absence of his brother in Kentucky, became close to him. Rather than working in business with a man he hated, Alvin goes off to Canada to fight in Europe for Britain and returns a broken man, having lost his leg. His traumatic war experience and injury change him for the worse, and he infuriates Herman Roth, Philip's father, by working for a disreputable dealmaker in an illegal game-machine business that used thugs. Alvin and Herman had had violent disagreements in the past (for example, over Alvin's going to fight the Nazis rather than going to college), but at a dinner for Alvin and his fiancée (the daughter of the dealmaker), Herman's expressed contempt for what Alvin has done with his life escalated into something that had never happened before, namely, physical violence between the nephew and the uncle who had devoted himself to him, inflicting injuries on both. By this time, anti-Semitic mobs had killed Jews elsewhere in the country, including the Jewish journalist, Walter Winchell, who announced his candidacy to run against Lindbergh in the next election. Herman had refused to get a gun to protect himself and his family, not listening to an Italian American neighbor, Mr. Cucuzza, who had a gun and offered it to Herman. Herman had insisted on nonviolent democratic change through voting but now exploded into physical violence with his own nephew, illustrating the dynamic of traumatically inflicted moral injury, as the violence of anti-Semitic mobs is acted out by Jews against Jews. Philip Roth comments,

Prior to that night, it would have been as impossible for me to envision him [his father] beating somebody up—let alone battering bloody his beloved older brother's fatherless son—as to imagine him atop my mother, especially as there was no taboo stronger among Jews with our impoverished European origins and our tenaciously held American ambitions than the pervasive, unwritten prohibition against settling disputes by force. In that era, the common Jewish propensity was by and large nonviolent as well as nonalcoholic, a virtue whose shortcoming was the failure to educate the bulk of the young of my generation in the combative aggression that was the first law of other ethnic educations. [Consequently, in my high school] fewer fistfights broke out than in any of the neighborhood schools in industrial Newark, where the ethical obligations of a child were differently defined and schoolmates demonstrated their belligerence by means not readily available to us.[741]

Herman now takes the gun and thinks the family should have moved to Canada, as a neighbor had done. By way of explanation, Roth reminds us that Alvin had been traumatized by fighting the Germans, and the consequence was that now "he wants to fight. He's like the very fathers he wanted to be rid of. That's the tyranny of the problem, trying to be faithful

---

[741] Philip Roth, *The Plot Against America*, pp. 368–9.

to what he's trying to be rid of."[742] And Roth's father, Herman, was now father to Alvin and himself was burdened by the trauma of anti-Semitism inflicted on Jews by America First.

The Wishnow family lived downstairs from the Roths, and Sheldon was their only son. The father, dying of cancer, committed suicide, leaving a distraught wife and son. The Roths took care of them, but Philip took an intense dislike to Sheldon, who was too intelligent (class valedictorian), absorbed in chess, and threw "a ball like a girl."[743] He sought after Philip's friendship in a way that repelled him. Philip's response was to suggest to his aunt that the Wishnows, as part of the Lindbergh program for resettling Jewish families elsewhere and thus Americanizing them, be transferred; the Wishnows, mother and son, are sent to live in Kentucky. The family is unaware of what Philip did, and he is guilt-ridden when in fact a KKK mob in Kentucky kills the mother, and Sheldon is left alone and terrified. It is at this point that both Roth's mother and father intervene, the mother calling the Kentucky family who had taken in Sandy earlier to take in Sheldon (which they do), and Herman and Sandy drive all the way to Kentucky to retrieve Sheldon. Sheldon comes to live with the Roths, "the person in the twin bed next to mine shattered by the malicious indignities of Lindbergh's America."[744]

One of the striking features of *The Plot Against America* is that we get a view of Roth's parents much closer to the truth (in contrast, say, to the imagined parents of *Pornoy's Complaint*), including notably his mother Bess's loving and tender concern for the confusions of her young son, and his father's passionately held convictions about "the idea of fair play,"[745] as central to what it is to being an American. By this test, "He [Lindbergh] dares to call us *others?* He's the *other*. The one who looks most American— and he's the one who is least American!"[746] The novel also captures, as other novels so, the father's domineering qualities. In Roth's autobiographical *Patrimony*, written after his mother's death about his caretaking of his beloved father now in decline, Roth records his shock that his mother, shortly before her death, tells her son she is considering divorce. What had

---

[742] Philip Roth, *The Plot Against America*, p. 372.

[743] Philip Roth, *The Plot Against America*, p. 227.

[744] Philip Roth, *The Plot Against America*, p. 430.

[745] Philip Roth, *The Plot Against America*, p. 332.

[746] Philip Roth, *The Plot Against America*, p. 333.

been endurable when her husband was absent at work become unendurable for her when he had retired. As she puts it to her son,

> "He doesn't listen to what I say," she said. "He interrupts all the time to talk about something else. When we're out, that's the worst. Then he won't let me speak at all. If I start to, he just shuts me up in front of everyone, as though I don't exist."[747]

It was the domineering of his father that Roth came to resist through his art, but it is a resistance he learned from his father, as he tells us in *The Plot Against America*. When it came to Lindbergh's resurgent America First politics, "My father chooses resistance."[748] So too did his son.

The Plot Against America reads today in the age of Trump's America First politics as prophetic. The very term, *America First*, central to Lindbergh's politics has now become the guiding light of Trump's politics. Herman Roth's words come now powerfully to mind: "The one who looks most American—and he's the one who is least American!"[749] No one has written more sensitively or acutely than Roth about how Americanization can tear the moral heart out of more recent immigrants to the United States, including, of course, Jews, the Irish, Italians, as well as more recent immigrants. Roth saw this in Jews, as I have in Italian Americans.[750]

Martha Nussbam has trenchantly commented from this perspective on Roth's early short story, "Eli, the Fanatic" (1959), depicting the travails of Eli, an American Jewish lawyer who has so assimilated WASP values that he represents a community of such values who wants legally to reject the just claims of Orthodox Jews in their community and what havoc this wrecks on him when he comes to resist.[751] Stereotypes of American patriarchal

---

[747] Philip Roth, *Patrimony: A True Story, Novels and Other Narratives 1986–1991*, ed. Ross Miller (New York: The Library of America, 2008), pp. 581–732, at p. 602

[748] Philip Roth, *The Plot Against America*, p. 428.

[749] Philip Roth, *The Plot Against America*, p. 333.

[750] See David A. J. Richards, *Italian American: The Racializing of an Ethnic Identity* (New York: New York University Press, 1999).

[751] See Martha C. Nussbaum, "Jewish Men, Jewish Lawyers: Roth's 'Eli, the Fanatic,' and the Question of Jewish Masculinity in American Law," in Saul Levmore and Martha C. Nussbaum, *American Guy: Masculinity in American*

manhood and womanhood are very much central to this process, and Roth's novels show us how this is done and how disastrous it is both for minorities and for American ethical and political culture.

I am struck by the resonances in my own experience both as an Italian American (with an opera-singer, civil engineer father) and a gay man (with my secret self) with what Roth tells us about his own struggles with and against American manhood. Roth was very much a straight man, yet he captures with great force how American stereotypes of manhood (reflecting a long history of American racism, extreme religious intolerance [anti-Semitism], sexism, and homophobia) bully boys and men into compliance with the demands of these stereotypes, including boys and men themselves afflicted by the injustices these stereotypes mindlessly inflict, including, as he shows us, American Jews and, I would add, Italians as well as gays and others. He also shows us, consistent with Carol Gilligan's work on moral injury, how the initiation into manhood, enforcing these stereotypes, traumatically requires young boys to conceal or repress love and convictions inconsistent with their demands, silencing the voice of resistance. The great interest of *The Plot Against America* is that it so beautifully shows a young Philip Roth at ages seven to nine struggling between models of being a good or bad boy, only later at age sixteen resisting his own father as he enters into an education that leads to his finding his voice as an artist. It was at that age that I also began, as earlier chapters show, to read the novels of Dickens and Henry James and to see that a space for resistance was possible though I would not embrace it until many years later. And like Roth, it was my father, whom I loved, who lit my way in the darkness and whose great humanity and capacity for caring love were my northern star in my own path to love. My father was not, like Roth's father, domineering. Quite the contrary, he was always a man to whom one could talk honestly about our political and other differences (he was a Republican and I was not), and I first found my resisting voice in these conversations with him and the example of his remarkably egalitarian marriage to my mother, herself highly intelligent, loving, and an independent force. Men, like Roth's father and my own, often live much more complex, gender-bending lives and love that we think, living under the radar of patriarchy, and their sons study their complexities, as Roth and I clearly did, and find possibilities for resistance through voice that enrich their lives and the lives of others.

Law and Literature (Oxford: Oxford University Press, 2014), pp. 165–201.

I suppose what compels me about Roth is that, though a straight man, he should have found his brilliantly revelatory artistic voice through releasing his sexual imagination in ways that shocked conventional patriarchal pieties and that yet resonated with so many men as well as women. Humor, Jewish humor, was very much part of it, as if, like Erasmus, he was less heretical (though he was certainly a heretic) because he made us laugh despite ourselves, as Christians laugh as a Jew mocks "the Pansy of Palestine." Roth's artistic voice arose, I have come to think, from freeing his sexual voice not only from the hypocrisies of American Puritanical manhood (which he and many knew to be false) but from the censorship of Jewish fear of the goyim. He clearly broke the love laws in his sexual relationships to non-Jewish women (shiksas), and he had no children with this two wives (the first died in an accident, the second, Claire Bloom, who was Jewish, he divorced) nor with the many other women with whom he had affairs, some adulterous.[752] Sabbath's views on the good of adultery may have been close to Roth's, and resonate today with the many women and men who have come to regard adultery, as Esther Perel tells us,[753] as sometimes a moral good, indeed a personal and ethical liberation. Roth's work was always shaped by the political world around him, which was America during and after World War II and was my world as well. It was a world of extraordinary wealth and power for Americans, the world of *American Pastoral*, but it was also the world of resistance movements—the civil rights and antiwar movements and the sexual revolution, leading to second-wave feminism and gay/lesbian/transgender rights and also the reactionary politics to these movements of the Republican Party, in the presidencies of Richard Nixon, Ronald Reagan, the Bushes (father and son), and now Donald Trump.

Roth's artistic voice, empowered by his freeing of his sexual imagination, was rooted, I have come to think, in what empowered second-wave feminism as well as gay/lesbian/transgender rights, namely, freeing sexual voice from the blinders and repressions patriarchy had imposed on men and women, gay and straight and thus freeing ethical voice to see

---

[752] For fuller discussion of Roth's sexual life and its connections to his art, see Claudia Roth Pierpont, *Roth Unbound*.

[753] Esther Perel, *Mating in Captivity: Unlocking Erotic Intelligence* (New York: Harper, 2007); *The State of Affairs: Rethinking Infidelity* (New York: HarperCollins, 2017).

and acknowledge the evils of American racism, anti-Semitism, sexism, and homophobia that the trauma of American patriarchy had rendered invisible to many American men, as the Trump election shows. And we should remember that he suffered condemnation for it from some Jews, some quite learned, which must have deeply pained and distressed him, and may clarify why—like Henry James, Joyce, and Baldwin—he lived abroad (in Prague and in London) for some years, an exile from his beloved New York City, to which he eventually came home to write the astonishing five novels I have discussed.[754] Roth was, from the perspective of Carol Gilligan and myself, a cutting-edge feminist,[755] showing what few other male writers of his generation showed us, how patriarchy harms not only women but men, and yet because of the power of the initiation of boys into patriarchy, men cannot see what harms them though it has deeply shaped their lives, sometimes destroying them and those they love (Swede Lvov). Feminism, as Carol and I understand it,[756] is the most important liberatory movement of the age because it alone addresses the unjust harms patriarchy inflicts on both men and women, entrenching the ethical and constitutional evils of racism, anti-Semitism, sexism, and homophobia. It is the marginalization of feminism in American discourse that has, I believe, led to the nescience and irratinalism expressed in the Trump election. Nothing could be more important or more needed. But we must first see the dimensions of the problem before we can grapple with our ethical and constitutional responsibilities.

The philosopher Theodor Adorno came to believe that it was not argument that could reveal the deepest injustices that persist, but the subversive voice of cutting-edge artists like Samuel Becket, whom he particularly admired.[757] His argument, as I understand it, is that both our intellectual and emotional natures were interpersonally mimetic, and art, being mimetic, could more deeply reveal and express our repressed and ethical warped natures, revealing the injustices that we could not see or acknowledge because forms of injustice had so damaged us, repressively

---

[754] This point was suggested to me by Phillip Blumberg.

[755] See Carol Gilligan and David A. J. Richards, *Darkness Now Visible.*

[756] See Id.

[757] See Theodor W. Adorno, *Aesthetic Theory,* trans. Robert Hullot-Kentor (Minneapolis: University of Minnesota Press, 1997).

alienating thought from emotion, destroying resisting voice.[758] Adorno is an enormously obscure thinker,[759] and his artistic preferences are sometimes simply preposterous (he hated all American jazz, for example).[760] But when it comes to the role patriarchy plays in sustaining some of the most profound injustices that afflict us, I have come to think that certain art can play a crucial role in making visible what patriarchy requires us to keep invisible, and thus I have come to see in these terms the good sense in Adorno's argument. And the problem particularly centers, I believe, on men, who played the decisive role in electing Donald Trump. Philip Roth's art is, in my judgment, an example of the kind of art we need, showing how much patriarchal stereotypes of manhood destroy men not only personally but men as citizens who ostensibly value democracy. It is why he and other artists have played the central role in my argument that they have.

The Plot Against America is a prophetic novel in the same sense that the earlier discussed *The Scarlet Letter* and *Moby-Dick* were prophetic novels. All these novels reveal evils in forms of democracy, whether the Puritan democracy of *Scarlet Letter* or antebellum American Jacksonian democracy in *Moby-Dick* or the appeal of America First democracy in *The Plot Against America*, and all these novels resist the ways in which democracy was now self-destructively in contradiction with itself. Trump may be closer to Ahab and certainly to Lindbergh than we like to think.

The Plot Against America is set in the election of 1940, when pacifist isolationism was powerful in American politics (represented by Lindbergh)

---

[758] See Id., On mimesis in artistic representation, see Erich Auerbach, *Mimesis: The Representation of Reality in Western Literature,* trans. Willard R. Trask (Princeton: Princeton University Press, 2003; first published, 1953).

[759] See, for example, Theodo W. Adorno, *Negative Dialectics,* trans. E. B. Ashton (New York: Continuum, 2007; first published, 1966); Theodor Adorno, *Minima Moralia: Reflections from a Damaged Life,* trans. E. F. N. Jephcott (London: Verso, 2005; first published, 1951). For illuminating commentary on Adorno and the Frankfurt School, see Martin Jay, *Adorno* (Cambridge: Harvard University Press, 1984); Martin Jay, *The Dialectical Imagination: A History of the Frankfurt School and the Institute of Social Research, 1923–1950* (Berkeley: University of California Press, 1996; first published, 1973); Martin Jay, *Reason After Its Eclipse: On Late Critical Theory* (Madison: University of Wisconsin Press, 2016).

[760] See, for example, Theodor W. Adorno, *Essays on Music* (Berkeley: University of California Press, 2002), pp. 470–500.

---

and Franklin Roosevelt recognized the threat of fascist aggression to both European and Americans but knew Americans were not yet ready for war (that would require attack on Pearl Harbor on December 7, 1941), but tried to prepare America for what he knew would come (getting Congress to pass the Lend Lease Act in March 1941 to aid Great Britain). By this time, American Jews knew about the increasingly virulent anti-Semitism in Germany and were accordingly fearful of the force anti-Semitism had in American politics and culture, reflected in Lindbergh's earlier mentioned speech, "Who are the War Agitators?" on September 11, 1941 to the America First Committee's rally in Des Moines, pointing to Jews as one of the three groups agitating for America to enter World War II.[761] Roth shows how Lindbergh might have been elected in 1940 precisely because the sense of being American in 1940 was so framed by our history of racism and anti-Semitism. America First was the cosmetic slogan of his campaign because it trumpeted as American a deeply WASP Americanism, which marginalized not only people of color but recent immigrants, Jews and Catholics (the Irish and Italians). The novel's plot, written in the voice of Roth as a Jewish boy at this time, thus begins, "Fear presides over these memories, a perpetual fear."[762] It is thus a novel about Jewish fear and explores the range of Jewish responses to a fear that is now quite realistic, ranging from complicity to violent resistance to nonviolent resistance to leaving America (for Canada). Members of the Roth family, including relatives and friends, move through all these stages. Even Roth's father abandons nonviolence and regrets not leaving America.

The novel shows how politically powerful America First can be, as a cosmetic label to cover the invisible forces of patriarchy that Lindbergh mobilizes. Carol Gilligan and I argue in *Darkness Now Visible*[763] that Trump's populist politics had the appeal it had because he mobilized forces of patriarchy in American culture and politics, using America First as a cosmetic label, as Lindbergh did in Roth's novel, to cover the reactionary forces to which he appealed not only racism and anti-Semitism, as in *The Plot Against America*, but sexism and homophobia as well. Trump's version of America First had the appeal it did because it trumpeted a politics based

---

[761] See Philip Roth, *The Plot Against America*, *Novels 2001–2007*, ed. Ross Miller (New York: The Library of America, 2013), pp. 97–458, at pp. 452–58.

[762] Philip Roth, *The Plot Against America*, p. 97.

[763] See Carol Gilligan and David A. J. Richards, *Darkness Now Visible*.

on a rigid gender binary (masculine vs. feminine) and hierarchy (men over women), the DNA of patriarchy, denigrating the woman candidate he opposed in those terms as well as the people of color, religions, women, gays and lesbians and transgendered, and others who supported her. Carol and I argue that such politics had the appeal it did because many men and women were still deeply initiated into patriarchy, and this traumatically inflicted on men in particular moral injury that made them vulnerable to Trump's politics of fear and anger at those unsettling the patriarchal order of things, thus shaming these men, eliciting fear and anger. What surprised so many of us in the election of Donald Trump arises from what we failed to take seriously, the personal and political psychology of trauma that patriarchal institutions inflicted on so many Americans. Patriarchy was invisible to so many because trauma (depriving us of both speech and memory) was not recognized or taken seriously, thus acted out its repressive demands in irrationalist fear and anger akin to fascist politics. Such fear and anger has, under Trump's presidency, been most starkly visited on immigrants, quite precisely repeating the same pattern of irrationalist fear without any evidentiary basis visited during the period of Roth's novel (World War II) on Japanese Americans. Michiko Kakutani, whose Japanese American family had been unjustly subject to internment, recently pointed to the strength of the analogy:

> Under President Donald Trump, the news is filled with pictures and stories of families and children being held in detention centers. History is repeating itself. This time without even the pretext of war and with added heartbreaking cruelty. Under Mr. Trump's "zero tolerance" border enforcement policy, nearly 3,000 children were separated from their parents, and while the administration later halted these separations, it neglected to keep proper records and is now struggling to find and reunite families.
>
> Once again, national safety is invoked to justify the roundup of whole groups of people. Once again, racist stereotypes are being used by politicians to ramp up fear and hatred. And once again, lies are being used to justify

actions that violate the most fundamental Americans ideals of freedom, equality, and tolerance.[764]

Philip Roth, in *The Plot Against America* that was conceived and written during the presidency of George Bush, explores such vulnerability in an earlier historical period; and it is a vulnerability very much arising from a conception of American manhood and womanhood based on the feminization as unmanly of outsiders to WASP America. Roth was clearly concerned that he saw this vulnerability as well in American politics during the Bush presidency. What might easily have happened in 1940 was happening then as America, after 9/11 now visibly at threat, was vulnerable to a politics of fear and anger that could be mobilized to fight a disastrous unjust war and war as well on the rights of women and sexual minorities. We are vulnerable to such politics because the trauma of manhood leads to an identification with American manhood that, like Swede Lvov, tragically blinds us. Roth shows us in these novels, culminating in his prophetic novel, the blindness that led men and women to be vulnerable to Trump's fear and anger. His art thus performs the invaluable role that Adorno argued was the crucial contribution of art to giving voice to the most intractable injustices and calling for resistance.

---

[764] Michiko Kakutani, "When History Repeats," *The New York Times*, Sunday, July 15, 2018, SR 1, 4–5, at pp. 1 and 4.

CHAPTER 9

Masculinity and Resistance in the Movies of John Ford and Clint Eastwood

My argument has so far explored the role that a secret self has played in a number of artists, largely male novelists, who have given voice to their secret selves, aspects of themselves as men that patriarchy requires them not to acknowledge but to which their art gives voice, and thus resists patriarchy. And we have seen as well the role that finding such a resisting voice played in forms of political analysis and action advancing justice (Ruth Benedict, James Baldwin, and James Gilligan).

American movies have also played an important role in defining and exploring masculinity, and no movies more so than Westerns, many of which I saw with my family as a boy and young man. I want here to examine, in light of my argument, the work of two great American artists, John Ford and Clint Eastwood, whose work came, I believe, to question American patriarchal masculinity in a genre often taken to promulgate, not question, such masculinity. Ford is of particular interest to my argument as his secret self (homosexuality) was, so I argue, the voice of resisting patriarchy that we find in his art.

John Ford

John Ford is today prominently known for his Westerns. Among the best known are *Stagecoach* (1939) that introduced John Wayne to American audiences, *My Darling Clementine* (1946), *Fort Apache* (1948), *She Wore a Yellow Ribbon* (1949), *Rio Grande* (1950), and his masterpiece, *The Searchers* (1956). All these movies feature conflicts between Amerindian tribes and Americans, three of them deal with the US Cavalry in particular. *Sergeant Rutledge* (1960) also deals with a black cavalry officer, falsely accused of rape. *The Man Who Shot Liberty Valance* (1962) deals with a lawless Western town, terrorized by Liberty Valance, and the conflicting approaches of an idealistic young lawyer and a more realistic and experienced rancher in dealing with Valance, who is eventually killed. Military service in the Civil War is the subject of *The Horse Soldiers* (1959), and here, the conflicting approaches are between the colonel successfully leading a cavalry campaign against the confederacy and a physician committed to his profession. Differences in approach among military officers in dealing with a defeated Indian tribe, the Cheyenne, is the subject of *Cheyenne Autumn* (1964).

The relationships among men, usually in highly disciplined and hierarchically ordered military service, are Ford's dominant theme in all these movies, with comic relief supplied by drunk, usually Irish soldiers. Ford, born in Maine, was preoccupied by his Irish immigrant background, thinking of himself as a rebel.[765] Only one of his movies, *The Quiet Man* (1952), is set in a rather idealized Ireland: an American ex-fighter, retired after remorse over the death of his opponent in a fight, moves to Ireland and woos and marries a spirited Irish girl. But another movie, *How Green Was My Valley* (1941), set in Wales, beautifully and sensitively narrates the tragic story of a Welsh coal family, told from the point of view of the youngest son, a boy; the older sons, facing a lack of opportunity in the declining coal industry, emigrate to America; the beloved father dies in a coal accident; the beautiful sister marries for wealth, not pursuing the man she loves, and is deeply unhappy; the boy and his beloved mother are left.

There is a similar sensitivity of treatment in dealing with the struggles of young men in *Young Man Lincoln* (1939), losing the woman he loves, and the remarkable *The Grapes of Wrath* (1940). The latter shows a family

---

[765] See, for a magisterial biography on Ford's life and works, Joseph McBride, *Searching for John Ford* (Jackson: University Press of Mississippi, 2011).

now struggling against the depression, leaving the dust bowl for California, all seen through the eyes of the son. The central relationship here is the heartrending relationship of son to his mother, who, at the end, urges her son to leave to find a better life though his leaving breaks both their hearts. All these four movies, not Westerns in any sense, expose what is, I believe, the beating heart of Ford's remarkable art: the sense in men's lives of traumatic loss that they carry with them stoically—whether the remorseful, expatriate fighter; the Welsh boy, who has lost his brothers and sister and father; the young Lincoln, who has lost the woman he loved; or the broken hearted young man and his mother in the dust bowl.

Patriarchy requires that men must rigidly observe the gender binary and hierarchy, not acknowledging the thoughts and feelings and sensitivities that might be regarded as feminine. But as we have seen, the heart of Ford's art found and explored precisely this voice, which is a voice of resistance, and I believe Ford's art is best understood and valued when seen in this way. Ford was, however, deeply conflicted about the sources of his art, indeed apparently concealed a secret self that was not only sensitive and tender but also apparently a closeted homosexual,[766] and not always very closeted.

Maureen O'Hara, who was in several Ford movies, writes in her 2004 memoir, 'Tis Herself:

> I walked into his office without knocking and could hardly believe my eyes. Ford had his arms around another man and was kissing him. I was shocked and speechless. I quickly dropped the sketches on the floor then knelt down to pick them up. I fumbled around slowly and kept my head down. I took my time so they could part and compose themselves. They were on opposite sides of the room in a flash. The gentleman Ford was with was one of the most famous leading men in the picture business (probably Tyrone Power).[767] He addressed a few pleasantries to me, which were forced and awkward then

---

[766] See, on this point, Nancy Schoenberger, *Wayne and Ford: The Films, the Friendship, and the Forging of an American Hero* (New York: Doubleday, 2017), pp. 55, 135–43.

[767] See, for this claim, Id., p. 139.

quickly left. Not a word was said, and I played it out as I
hadn't seen a thing.[768]

"Later," she writes, "that actor approached me and asked, 'Why didn't
you tell me John Ford was a homosexual?' I answered, 'How could I tell
you something I knew nothing about.'"[769]

Nancy Schoenberg, in her book, *Wayne and Ford*, continues O'Hara's
narrative as follows:

O'Hara later speculates that Ford struggles with
homosexual feelings, and it gave her insight into the
problems in his marriage—the separate bedrooms, his
insulting her, the periodic drinking, and the lack of
outward affection they showed to each other. I now believe
there was a conflict within Ford and that it caused him
great pain and turmoil.[770]

Another way that conflict expressed itself was in Ford's propensity to
uncontrollable rage, including punching Maureen O'Hara in the jaw[771] and
also punching a lead actor in *Fort Apache*, Henry Fonda, in the jaw. "The
two never spoke again."[772]

O'Hara's account has, unsurprisingly, been contested by Ford's friend
and admirer, Peter Bogdanovich, on the basis of Ford's supposed affair with
Kate Hepburn.[773] But O'Hara plausibly argues of Ford:

His fantasies and crushes on women like me, Kate
Hepburn, Anna Less, and Murph Doyle—all of whom he
professed love for at one time or another—were just balm
for his wound. He hopes each of us would save him from
these conflicted feelings but was later forced to accept
that none of us could. I believe this ultimately led to my

---

[768] Quoted at Id., pp. 139–40.
[769] Quoted at id., p. 140.
[770] Id., p. 140.
[771] Id., p. 140.
[772] Id., p. 77.
[773] Id., p. 141.

punishment and his downward spiral into an increased reliance on alcohol.[774]

O'Hara's account of conflict in Ford rings true and the conflict is also in his art where I believe he found a way to give voice to the side of men that patriarchy ignored, denigrated, and silenced not only in the non-Western movies already discussed but in the Westerns themselves as well as in the movies dealing with men's experience of war in World War II—*They Were Expendable* (1945) and *The Wings of Eagles* (1957). Ford came to know that experience intimately as he served in the military during World War II with the four other American movie directors who joined him in making remarkable documentaries during the war of the war and the American men who fought the war and the ravages of the war (Frank Capra, John Huston, George Stevens, and William Wyler), including, in the case of George Stevens, of the Holocaust.[775] Ford served as captain in the United States Navy and was both at the Battle of Midway filming *The Battle of Midway* (1942), where he was injured, and at D-Day, where he was so sickened by the carnage that he went on a drunken bender.[776] His service included making innumerable movies (1940–1945) about the war and the American soldiers who fought it both in the Pacific and in Europe.[777]

The Westerns made after World War II, many of which closely study men in military service, work from this experience, and are for this reason so remarkable for what they tell us about American manhood in a military service supposedly rigidly defined by the gender binary and hierarchy that mark patriarchy. Ford shows us it is hardly as rigid as we might think. The movies show us the some leaders are stupid and racist in dealing with the rather noble enemy, the Apache, and other officers try to resist (*Fort Apache*); and other leaders think outside the patriarchal box and seek and realize peace with the Indians in unconventional ways (*She Wore a Yellow Ribbon*); and quite good military leadership under patriarchy may be and is in tension not only with marriage but in relationships to children, here,

---

[774] Quoted at Id., pp. 140–41.
[775] See, for a magisterial study, Mark Harris, *Five Came Back: A Story of Hollywood and the Second World War* (New York: Penguin, 2014).
[776] See, on this Mark Harris, *Five Came Back*, pp. 310–19.
[777] See, for a list of the movies, Joseph McBride, *Searching for John Ford*, pp. 800–801.

a son who admires and wants to serve with his father. However, the movie ends with the officer, rather than killing Apaches as he was ordered, saving American children from the Apaches in Mexico, who have kidnapped them (*Rio Grande*). Even ostensibly patriarchal men (military leaders) do and can resist patriarchal injustices.

It was not only Ford's life that was, as Maureen O'Hara trenchantly observed, in conflict with patriarchy but, more importantly, his voice as an artist, which he pursued relentlessly throughout his life, making innumerable movies, both silent and talkies. It was precisely because Ford masked so much of himself that he always refused any suggestion that he was an artist, rather than a tough, demanding, rather alcoholic man, living largely in a small world of other men devoted to him whom he ruled imperiously and sailing with them on his yacht. Any threat to that world and his control of it was for him shaming and incendiary, leading, as we have seen, to his shocking violence against several of his distinguished actors.[778] We can see this world of men, his world, in his movie based on the Eugene O'Neill sea plays, *The Long Voyage Home* (1940). It is a world of men on a ship closely bound emotionally to one another alienated from the world of women and children. The movie is very much a tale of male friendship and love, as Ford shows these men drunkenly and joyfully dancing with one another. It is not a world of men that we are usually allowed to see, yet Ford, the artist, insists that we see it.

Ford's divided self—the secret self of his art and the public self of a tough guy—is given powerful expression in the two antagonist men in a late movie, *The Man Who Killed Liberty Valance*. The movie is set in a lawless town, terrorized by Liberty Valance and in his gang; the marshall is ineffective. The two men are Tom Doniphon, who believes violence is needed to combat the gang, and Ransom Stoddard, an idealistic young lawyer who has just arrived in town to practice law. Ransom has been brutally beaten by Valance and is nursed back to health by townspeople, including a young woman, Haillie. Doniphon has long been in love with Haillie and has built a house in which they will live as a married couple; Ransom falls in love with Haillie as well. His gentleness and vulnerability attract her, and she falls in love with him; Doniphon, furious and traumatized, burns the house down. The story is told some years after these events; Ransom is

---

[778] See, in general, Joseph McBride, *Searching for John Ford;* Nancy Schoenberger, *Wayne and Ford.*

now a US senator married to Haillie, and they return to attend the funeral of Doniphon. Ransom, as man of conscience, tells newspapermen what happened between him and Doniphon. Doniphon insisted to Ransom that he had to learn to use a gun to fight Liberty Valance and trains him in the use of a gun. To the surprise of everyone, when Valance comes to kill Ransom, Ransom's gun fire apparently kills Valance, and he is acclaimed, and people want to elect him to political office, beginning what was to be a long political career. It is Doniphon who nominates Ransom for political office. When Ransom hesitates because he believes a killer like himself should not be elected, Doniphon discloses it was he, not Ransom, who in fact killed Valance, firing at the same time Ransom fired. Now Senate Ransom, guilt ridden, confesses the truth to the newspapermen. One of them responds, "This is the West, sir. When the legend becomes fact, print the legend." They do not print the truth. A false picture of heroic manhood takes the place of the more complex picture of a broken-hearted man, Doniphon, who nonetheless saved the man Haillie loved and whom he has come to like. Ford in this late work clearly shows the difference between idealized patriarchal manhood and the more complex reality, and how it is the latter, not the former, that we mythologize politically. Few movies more powerfully contest this mythology.

Male friendship and love is the subject, ironically, of Ford's two remarkable movies about military service in World War II, a service he knew intimately. *They Were Expendable* deals with the friendship of two officers, one in charge and the other working for him, running a PT boat squadron during and after the fall of the Philippines to the Japanese. Naval superiors refuse to acknowledge the usefulness of the squadron in battle, until the squadron decisively proves itself in sinking a Japanese destroyer. The squadron continues to prove its worth until Japanese force whittles it down. The two officers are air lifted back in order to train other squadrons, but the remaining officers and men are left to face the onslaught of the Japanese (the expendable). The movie is an honest treatment not of victory but of the bitter taste of defeat during one of the darkest periods for America in World War II. It is one of the best war movies ever made because it speaks from experience, an experience Ford knew at firsthand.

The Wings of Eagles is even more directly from Ford's experience and the most gender-bending of his movies. It is about a remarkable man Ford knew well, Frank "Spig" Wead, and the history of naval aviation from its inception until World War II. Wead, played by John Wayne, is depicted as a daredevil and rather flamboyant airman, challenging conventional naval protocol, but completely devoted to his work as an airman and the men with whom he works, most notably, his mechanic, Jughead Carson. His wife, Min, played in the movie by Maureen O'Hara, loses patience with their way of life, and they separate. (Their two daughters hardly know their father; a young son earlier died.) Wead has an accident while at home, falling down the stairs, breaking his neck. His recovery results from the devoted care not of his wife, but of Jughead Carson:

> Carson (Dan Dailey) assigned as Wead's nurse, masks his concern with a smoke screen of wisecracks and even a song-and-dance routine. Carson's seeming callousness (and Ford's) is actually a way of facing the unbearable. Making a joke out of Wead's infirmity gradually banishes his self-pitying despondency and restores his fighting spirit. Carson seems totally devoted to Wead, almost as if an unspoken homosexual attachment, and becomes more of a "wife" than Min ever manages to be. Wead's sexual impotence turns him into the perpetual observer, fantasizer, and romanticizer of history, a personally dysfunctional but artistically creative role in life much like that played by Ford himself.[779]

Finally, Wead becomes a screenwriter, who in fact works for Ford, who appears in the movie, played by Ward Bond. The movie is autobiographical not only because Ford is a character in it but because, as his grandson believed,

> the film is a disguised autobiography of his grandfather. Both Ford and Wead had restless, wandering natures that made them gravitate to lives of action, but because of physical infirmities, they had to be content with largely vicarious adventures. Both turned to moviemaking as a substitute for military careers. Both found ways of serving in World War II but as observers rather than combatants. And more significantly, both men were unable to balance

---

[779] Joseph McBride, *Searching for John Ford*, p. 582.

their careers with satisfying home lives. They neglected their families for the sake of their careers and also perhaps because feelings of sexual inadequacy made them prefer masculine companionship.[780]

Ford's voice as an artist was not, unlike Wead's, substitutive for a life of mindless military adventure, precisely because the voice in all the movies I have discussed so critically observes the traumas and burdens of men living under patriarchy and thus resists them. Ford's secret self was not only his sexuality but a sense of himself as an ethnic outsider, Irish and rebellious, and the cultural ethnicity (Catholic homophobia) as an outsider reinforced the secret self of his sexuality. Both these aspects of his secret self spoke to my own experience, as gay and Italian American. What held Ford together was creating a small world of men devoted to him in which he could despotically rule, but paradoxically, it was this way of life that made possible the artistic voice in his movies that increasingly questioned American racism (his interest in the wars against Amerindians is a place holder enabling him to explore prejudice against the Irish) and to show as well how much the gender binary falsified the experience of the men he knew, including men who fought in our wars, who, under all their well-advertised machismo, could be so caring, tender, and compassionate. The culmination of this art is *The Searchers*. Only Ford could create

> the most complex and fascinating character in Ford's entire body of work, Ethan Edwards (John Wayne). A former Confederate soldier, mercenary for Emperor Maximilian in Mexico and freewheeling outlaw, Ethan enigmatically returns to his brother's family three years after the end of the Civil War. Ethan is secretly in love with his brother's wife, Martha, as we told nonverbally by their gestures and by the couple's theme music, "Lorena," from a haunting Civil War ballad by Reverend H. D. L. Webster about an unconsummated adulterous romance ("We loved each other then, Lorena, / More than we ever dared to tell . . ."). Shortly after Ethan's return, Martha is raped and murdered, and her husband and son killed by

---

[780] Id., p. 580.

a band of Comanches led by Chief Scar. Scar carries off the two survivors of the massacre, nine-year-old, Debbie Edwards, and her womanly sister, Lucy, who herself is soon raped and killed. Ethan spends five years searching for Debbie with his young partner, Martin Pauley, an adopted member of the Edwards family who... is part Indian.[781]

Ethan is a racist, contemptuous of Martin Pauley and clearly traumatized by seeing the raped body of the woman he loved. When they finally track down Ethan's niece, Debbie Edwards, they learn she has become one of Scar's wives, and she tells them she now regards herself as a Comanche and does not want to go back. Ethan says he would rather kill her than allow her to live with a Comanche (she has broken the love laws), and tries to kill her, but Martin blocks his way. Ethan is injured by a Comanche arrow as they escape. Martin nurses him back to health and tells Ethan that he wishes him dead and could kill him. "That'll be the day," Ethan replies, and they return home. When they learn they can attack the Comanche camp, they do so, with Ethan killing Scar. Debbie now tells Martin she is willing to go back but flees when Ethan finds her and pursues her on horseback. Martin pursues frantically worried that Ethan will kill her, as he has promised to do. But Ethan sweeps her up into his saddle, saying "Let's go home," one of the most moving moments in cinema. In the last iconic scene, Martin joins the woman he loves, and Debbie to a family that loves her; but Ethan is alone outside, as the door closes on him.

Ford captures in Ethan Edwards his own sense of loneliness as an outsider and how the traumatic losses men suffer express themselves in violence often against outsiders and yet how men through love resist and do resist (Ethan's love for Debbie's mother). Ford's portraits of mothers in *How Green Was My Valley* and *The Grapes of Wrath* suggest the love that sustained him and may have been the basis of his art, as it was in the life of James Baldwin. Like James Baldwin, he may never have found the lover he sought and needed, but like Baldwin as well, he found in the voice of his art a way of speaking from his secret self about the injustices patriarchy inflicts on men and how men can and do resist. Ford centered his life in

---

[781] Joseph McBride, *Searching for John Ford*, p. 553.

this voice and in the resonance it had for American men as well as women. To this extent, like the other artists I have studied, he communalized the traumas of American manhood, and we learned how much we shared itself a kind of love. It is striking that it was any threat to his control of the voice of his art that expressed itself in physical assaults of his actors, a passion for control that suggests moral injury to the capacity to love and trust. After all, we fall in love; we do not will it. There is loss here, indeed moral injury, in Ford's passion for control—a control replacing the vulnerabilities of love. But Ford, like Baldwin, came to regard his artistic voice as the only experience of truth and love he had ever known, and any threat to that was an attack on the only thing that gave meaning to his life. This explains as well his relentless productivity, as if he could not live if he was not giving voice to this art, giving voice to his secret self.

Clint Eastwood's Journey to Resistance

The philosopher Drucilla Cornell has recently powerfully argued that the movies of Clint Eastwood reflect a critique of American masculinity analogous to that I have found in the movies of John Ford.[782] She is, I believe, quite right, and I draw on her account here, in particular, those parts of it that my account clarifies.

Richard Schickel, a close friend of Eastwoods, has written an illuminating biography of Eastwood,[783] who is still alive and working in 2018. (The biography was published in 1997.) Schickel tells us,

> What feeds Clint's temper is a profound sense of the world's unreliability. He was a child of hard times. Born in the first year of the depression, his first memories are of dislocation, as for several years he and his family moved from place to place annually trying to stabilize their economic lot. His parents were good people, he loved them, he vaguely understood the pressures they were under, but he hated the loneliness their travels imposed on

---

[782] See Drucilla Cornell, *Clint Eastwood and Issues of American Masculinity* (New York: Fordham University Press, 2009).

[783] Richard Schickel, *Clint Eastwood: a Biography* (New York: Vintage, 1997).

him—always the new kid on the block and in the school, wondering how he got there. When he recalls these years, the angry note in his voice is unmistakable.[784]

Anger is a recurrent feature of Eastwood's personality, indeed "outrage. For the institutions he encountered in those years (late adolescence and early manhood)—educational, economic, and governmental—were unresponsive, insensitive, and clumsy in their impositions."[785] Eastwood never claimed" trauma or even unbearable hardship for these experiences,"[786] but he drew from these two features of his work: distrust of institutions and "the celebration of characters variously subversive, antisocial, and rebellious. In a phrase, place the rage for order in the service of a different kind of order."[787]

The differences from Ford are striking. Eastwood began his career as a very handsome and increasingly accomplished actor, and he loved women having affairs, several marriages, and a number of children, two sons and five daughters, that he cared for and some of whom worked for and with him.[788] Eastwood has little interest in the relationships among men in military institutions, a central preoccupation of Ford's art. Like Ford, however, Eastwood works as a director with a small group, and he is very much in charge. Unlike Ford, he gives his actors a lot of leeway and is in life easygoing and reticent. But there is the anger, the source of his art and, I believe, the growing resistance to patriarchal manhood that his movies increasingly reflect.

As James Gilligan has shown, anger in men often arises from a shaming of their sense of patriarchal manhood, expressing itself in violence. Eastwood appeared as an actor as Dirty Harry Callahan in five commercially successful movie—*Dirty Harry* (1971), *Force Magnum* (1973), *The Enforcer* (1976), *Sudden Impact* (1983), and *The Dead Pool* (1988), and directs as well as acts in *Sudden Impact*. Callahan, a San Francisco detective, is a maverick, and his anger is as much directed against the violent criminals he relentless pursues, as it is against the laws and

---

[784] Id., p. 15.
[785] Id.
[786] Id.
[787] Id., p. 16.
[788] See, in general, Richard Schickel, *Clint Eastwood*.

practices (including constitutional rights) that constrain such police work, a war by a loner against the system as much as against the criminals.

In these early movies, Callahan's retributive anger is very much along the lines Jim Gilligan describes as not resisting patriarchal manhood but enacting it. Such manhood is shamed by any insult to its sense of its status in the gender binary and hierarchy, and Callahan's anger is very much elicited by his view of himself as a God-like dispenser of retributive justice (at the top of the gender hierarchy) personally insulted by the wrongdoing of those below him (and criminals are always below), and thus lashing out with violence against them always regarded as deserved. Even in *Sudden Impact*, which he directed, though the avenger is a woman vigilante who was brutally raped, as was her sister (permanently damaged physically and psychologically), Callahan, who is pursuing her for killing all the men who raped her and her sister, lets her off, as God's just avenger.

The impulse to anger in these movies and others later is retribution, but there is a remarkable shift between the endorsement of retribution in these movies (Callahan acting as judge, jury, and executioner of retributive justice) and the much more skeptical exploration of this theme in later movies, reflecting, I believe, Eastwood's sense of men's secret self and growing resistance to the patriarchal manhood he once embraced.

There is already a more complex, nuanced investigation of police officers like Callahan in two movies, *Tightrope* (1984) in which Eastwood acts and directs and *In the Line of Fire* (1993 in which Eastwood acted but did not direct. Both movies are discussed by Drucilla Cornell together, exploring what she calls "dancing with the double, reaching out from the darkness within."[789] In *Tightrope*, a divorced police officer, Block, who lives with his two young daughters, is pursuing a killer of prostitutes. The officer himself uses the service of prostitutes, and the killer observes him having sex with one of them whom he then kills. "Block and the killer are locked in a dance, each pursuing the other in turn, sharing a darkness, which [s]ome of us have under control, while some act it out. The rest of us try to walk a tightrope between the two."[790] *In the Line of Fire* features remarkable performances by Clint Eastwood and John Malkovich, who have a doubling relationship. Eastwood plays a secret service agent disgraced when he failed to save President Kennedy from assassination;

---

[789] Drucilla Cornell, *Clint Eastwood and Issues of American Masculinity*, p. 40.
[790] Id., p. 42.

Malkovich an ex-CIA agent assassin compelled to kill a friend. Both have been traumatized. The Malkovich character in revenge now intends to assassinate the president, and Eastwood is to defend him. Both are quite lonely and broken (the effects of trauma), and there are intimate conversations by phone between them in which they both see how much they share, albeit now opposing one another. The Eastwood character, however, forms a loving sexual relationships with a woman secret service agent, who supports him in finding the strength to defeat the assassin. There is a comparable relationship in *Tightrope* to a woman rape counsellor and activist to similar effect.

These movies introduce three new themes in Eastwood's work, which he explores in his later movies: trauma, its connections to violence and retribution, and the reparative place of love.

Eastwood's movies increasingly focus on the experience of trauma in male experience. In *A Perfect World* (1993), an escaped criminal, played by Kevin Costner, takes a young boy as a hostage from his family who are Jehovah's Witnesses, where he has not been permitted to play as boys usually are, including not celebrating Halloween. The criminal is pursued by a police officer, played by Eastwood, who realizes that he made a mistake when the criminal was a boy in insisting on a harsh sentence for car theft, an experience that traumatized the boy leading to a life of criminality; the boy has also been abused by his father. The escaped criminal befriends the boy, who experiences the pleasures of play he had never previously known. The criminal is unjustly killed, and the Eastwood's character is aggrieved by his death, for which he feels responsible.

The most brilliant and probing of Eastwood's investigation of the traumatic experience of boys and its tragic consequences is one of his darkest and most disturbing movies, *Mystic River* (2003). Three young Irish American boys, good friends, are shown playing hockey in the streets of Boston. One of them is taken away by two men, who kidnap and sexually abuse him for four days, until he escapes. The scene shifts to the three boys as adults, no longer close friends: the abused boy is now rather broken man with a child and married to a woman who understands nothing of his experience; another is an ex-criminal, also married, whose daughter is killed; and the third is a police officer who pursues the killer. The broken man happened to see his former friend's daughter the night of the murder at a bar, and later, when he saw an older pedophile abusing a boy in a car, he beat him up, bloodying his hands. His wife comes to believe, wrongly, that he killed the girl and so informs his ex-con friend, who kills retributively his wholly innocent former friend. Few works of art more powerfully explore the effects of trauma on boys and how it may lead to a self-righteously retributive violence, which is profoundly unjust, here rooted in precisely the self-righteous conviction of a man like Dirty Harry Callahan.

The Unforgiven (1993) offers yet another harrowing portrait of the destructive force of retributivism, here rooted in the anger of women. A prostitute in a Western town has been beaten and disfigured by several cowboys whom she sexually insulted, and the sheriff orders compensation in terms of horses given to the prostitutes. The prostitutes regard this as inadequate punishment and try to hire gunmen who will enforce harsher retribution, killing the cowboys. The sheriff will not permit any vigilantism and brutally beats one such gunman who comes to town to be hired by the prostitutes. An aging gunman and outlaw, Manny, played by Eastwood, has now become a farmer and been reformed by his Christian wife, now deceased. The farm is no longer profitable, and to support his two small children, Manny, with the help of a friend and fellow outlaw and gunman, Logan, takes on the job the brothel offers. The sheriff brutally beats to death Logan, who is a man of color. Manny kills the sheriff and the men who disfigured the prostitute and disappears, probably moving to San Francisco with his children, and becomes wealthy with the money the prostitutes have given him.

The traumas men experience in war, whether on the just or unjust sides, are depicted in *American Sniper* (2014) as well as in *Flags of Our Fathers* (2006) and *Letters from Iwo Jima* (2006). *American Sniper* explores the traumatic war experiences, based on his memoir, of the legendary sniper Chris Kyle, who massed a record number of kills on the battlefield during his ten-year experiences on the battlefield of the Iraq War during his career as a Navy SEAL. At the end of the movie, having returned to the United States and his wife and son and daughter, Kyle is murdered by a fellow soldier and trauma victim he tried to help. Few movies more powerfully explore the devastating effects of war on soldiers, and in light of the sense today of that war's injustice, they indict such wars. The other two movies deal with the experience of American soldiers fighting on Iwo Jima in the Pacific during World War II; the latter with the experience of Japanese soldiers fighting at the same time and place. Enemies, as men, share the common experience of trauma in war.

The reparative power of love is the subject of two recent movies, *Million Dollar Baby* (2004) and *Gran Torino* (2008). In both, a man is alienated from his own children and yet becomes a loving father to outsiders to his world. In *Million Dollar Baby*, Eastwood plays a man, who runs a gym and has successfully trained fighters in the past and who is alienated from his own family—in the first, from his daughter to whom he writes letters, which she sends back unanswered. We are never told the nature of the rupture. In *Gran Torino*, a man, who fought in Vietnam and shows evidence of trauma, had endured the loss of his beloved wife and is quite disaffected from his two sons and rejects any attempts they make to repair the breach. These curmudgeonly men develop, however, deep attachments to nonfamily members.

In *Million Dollar Baby*, the attachment is of a conventionally sexist man from a very masculine world (fighting) to a gender-bending young woman who eventually persuades him to train her and becomes a champion. The girl is herself alienated from her family of origin, who has only a mercenary interest in her unconventional success. She is seriously injured in her last fight, and there is no promise of any recovery. She asks her trainer to kill her using drugs. He does so and disappears. A friend, who works with him at the gym, writes a letter to his disaffected daughter about his friend's remarkable love for this young woman.

In *Gran Torino*, the unlikely attachment is of a conventionally racist Vietnam veteran to a young man, an Hmong immigrant from Vietnam, and his sister. The young man is bullied by a Hmong gang, and the veteran takes an interest training him in a more conventionally American masculine strength to resist the Hmong gang. The Hmong gang, in revenge, brutally rapes the sister. He sacrifices his life to save them and leaves the young boy his prized possession, a Gran Torino automobile.

In both these movies, Eastwood is exploring love across the boundaries of gender and ethnicity, showing its power in enabling men to resist injustice. The nature and power of such love between a man and woman is the subject of *The Bridges of Madison Country* (1995). The movie begins with the two children, a man and woman, reading their now-deceased mother's journals and discovering, to their shock, her adulterous four-day affair with a photographer. The photographer, played by Eastwood, had come to the town to photograph the bridges and met the married woman with two children, played by Meryl Streep. The wife is from Southern Italy, where her husband met her during World War II and married her.

The husband and children are away for several days, and the photographer and wife have a passionate sexual affair, the deepest such experience in either of their lives. As earlier observed, adultery breaks the love laws, and the experience sometimes opens both the woman and man to a new sense of life's creative possibilities. The woman here is tempted to leave her marriage and is on the verge of doing so, but the photographer, who loves her, sees that she cannot do so because of the harm to her children and her husband. The loss for him is devastating, shown in a brilliant cinematic moment as she sees him in a downpour, weeping as the sky weeps. The photographer, inspired by their love, brings out a book of his photographs, a step he had never taken before. At the end, the two now-adult children are moved by what they discover about their mother and her love for her children. Inspired by her example, the son decides to revive his marriage, and the daughter to leave her unhappy marriage.

We earlier saw that John Ford found his creativity in giving voice to his secret self (his sexuality and ethnicity), and very likely, like James Baldwin, he never found the personal love he sought. The treatment both of women and children in Eastwood's work suggests his relationships to the women he loved and the children he cared for made possible for him not only a rich personal life but to clarify his own development from the retributive simplicities of Dirty Harry Callahan to the complexities of his later works with their striking skepticism about the retributivism he had once trumpeted. Eastwood came through such relationships to give voice to a secret self of sensitivity and emotional intelligence that the traumatic initiation of boys into patriarchy bullies into silence, requiring men to deny what they love. Eastwood, a man who always loved music (he wrote the music for *Mystic River*), did not like Moss deny his love, which is, I believe, the key to his remarkable art that communalizes a journey he shows us men can and should take, much to their own good and the good of others, including resisting the injustices that patriarchy enforces to divide us from our common humanity.

CHAPTER 10

How Patriarchy Harms
Men: Unjust Wars

For me and college-age young men of my generation, the experience of two resistance movements—the civil rights movement (see chapter 7) and the anti-Vietnam War movement—raised for us new challenges to the conceptions of manhood that were once conventionally American. The Vietnam War was the more personally challenging of the two because as college students, we were then ourselves subject to the draft. I was then at Harvard College (1962–1966) and would then do graduate work at Oxford University (1966–1968) and study law at Harvard Law School (1968–1971). Both the constitutionality and the morality of the Vietnam War were for us real, not abstract, questions, and I like others came to regard the war as wrong both in its ends and means. Because I was granted deferments during the relevant period, I did not confront the question of what I would do if drafted, but I certainly was one of those young men of my generation who came to resist the war morally and politically.

It was difficult for me and other similarly minded young men because our views on service in the war collided with the views of our fathers, some of whom at least had served in other less questionable wars, most notably, World War II. And the central issue was, for them and us, American manhood. One of the few times in my life that my father and I deeply disagreed was over Vietnam, and it was painful for me to resist him on such an issue because as should now be clear, he had been not only an unusually loving father but, to my way of thinking, a deeply ethical and humane man.

But we did disagree, and my resistance turned on my skepticism about the authorities who had gotten us into the war as well as my skepticism about men, like my father, who aligned themselves with those authorities. Many American young men of my generation experienced the same wrenching intergenerational conflict (see, for example, James Carroll's moving memoir dealing with his war resistance and conflicts with his father, discussed below). So it is fair to say that for us, as American men in the making, resistance to patriarchal authority was very much part of our sense of what we should do as men, and it was that resistance that was also supported by our support for the civil rights movement, in particular, after Martin Luther King Jr., opposed the war, and our resistance would later develop in our support for second-wave feminism and gay rights. We were, as men, very much in transition from what I call patriarchal manhood to democratic manhood. But we were now part of an antiwar resistance movement drawing significant support from the soldiers fighting in Vietnam, and in time, we democratically changed American policy. It was unforgettable, life-changing experience but, as I note later, one often forgotten today. We need now, more than ever, to understand the importance of such antiwar resistance and connect it to resistance to patriarchy, for nothing has more harmed men that their complicity with wars unjust both in their ends and means.

The earlier discussion of *The Oresteia* (chapter 2) showed what I called patriarchy hiding democracy could lead to the contradictions in the argument of the play justifying, on the one hand, the Athenian democracy as a solution to the internal cycle of violence among Athenian citizens but, on the other, rationalizing the unjust imperialistic wars that the democracy fought, ending, disastrously in its defeat. Athenian politics, in particular its decision to break the truce with Sparta and initiate the Peloponnesian War, illustrates the problem as Thucydides in his classic history drily observes, "What made war inevitable was the growth of Athenian power and the fear that this caused in Sparta."[791] In cultures still highly patriarchal and thus dominated by the shaming of manhood eliciting violence, the mere fact of inequality is an insult to male honor, eliciting aggressive violence lacking reasonable justification. Imperialistic wars—often between competing imperialisms (for example, World War I)—historically have this character, and it may be a good reason to worry about Donald Trump, as I later argue,

---

[791] Thucydides, *History of the Peloponnesian War,* p. 49.

that he is such a patriarchal man (in particular, in a period when China increasingly seems to be our equal).[792]

Killing even in war is always psychologically fraught for the men who have fought in wars in human history in which, as we now know, many men refuse to kill.[793] The military training required better to enable soldiers to kill, as in Vietnam, may itself be quite costly in human terms, including post-traumatic stress disorder.[794] There is, however, another side to the psychology of men fighting in wars. They sometimes form extraordinarily close bonds, based on equality and reciprocity, to one another; as Sebastian Junger recently put the point, "What the army sociologists, with their clipboards and their questions and their endless meta-analyses, slowly came to understand was that courage *was* love."[795]

It is the psychological force of patriarchy that, even in democracies, has historically enlisted men in service of unjust wars, often rationalized by supposed insults to patriarchal manhood, insults sometimes made by women, who mindlessly condemn men as unmanly when they resist such wars, as some British women did in World War I. Patriarchal men and women, deprived of any free and equal democratic voice, lack the competence to resist both unjust wars and their enlistment in service of such wars. Many wars in human history are unjust both in their ends and means, and patriarchy—whether hiding in democracy or rationalizing autocratic regimes—crucially explains how men and women, clearly

---

[792] See, on this point, Graham Allison, *Destined for War* (New York: Houghton Mifflin Harcourt, 2017).

[793] See, on this point, Lt. Col. Dave Grossman, *On Killing: The Psychological Cost of Learning to Kill in War and Society* rev. ed. (New York: Back Bay Books, 2009; first published, 1995).

[794] See, on this point, id., pp. 251–299. See also John Shay, *Achilles in Vietnam: Combat Trauma and the Undoing of Character* (New York: Scribner, 1994). For a psychoanalytic study of military indoctrination, see Chaim F. Shatan, "Bogus Manhood, Bogus Honor: Surrender and Transfiguration in the United States Martin Corps," (1977) *Psychoanalytic Review*, 64(4): 585–610.

[795] See Sebastian Junger, *War* (New York: Twelve, 2010), p. 239; see also Sebastian Junger, *Tribe: On Homecoming and Belonging* (New York: Twelve, 2016); Chris Hedges, *War Is a Force that Gives Us Meaning* (New York: Public Affairs, 2014; first published, 2002).

---

harmed by their deaths and injuries in such wars, nonetheless are the instruments of such injustice.[796]

American experience illustrates why Americans in the age of Trump might and should worry about this, for we have historically not been exempt from what Thucydides observed of the Athenian democracy's propensity for fighting unjust wars, as Carol and I argued about the Spanish-American War, World War I, the Vietnam War, and the war in Iraq.

The context of the first two wars must be understood in terms of the reactionary American politics of the post-Civil War period. America in the late nineteenth and early twentieth centuries was at a vulnerable transitional moment away from the anti-racism of the Reconstruction Amendments to an increasingly racist culture (importantly supported both by American politicians and by the Supreme Court of the United States in *Plessy v. Ferguson*)[797] attracted for this reason to European models of racist imperialism to its own version of imperialism.[798] The North and South, which had fought a civil war ultimately over slavery and the cultural racism that rationalized it, buried its enduring ethical meaning as white men in the North and South found common ground in racist imperialist ventures abroad.[799] The rather extreme and populist racism of this period explains how Americans could be and were drawn into unjust imperialist wars; and America First nationalism—in which gender played a central role—was at the heart of its politics.

The role of irrationalist appeals to gender, provoking Americans into an imperialistic war, is shockingly visible in the Spanish-American and Philippine-American Wars in which Theodore Roosevelt's conflicted psychology of manhood, as an American leader and provocateur, played

---

[796] See, for an illuminating general study of war and democracy, John Ferejohn and Frances McCall Rosenbluth, *Forged Through Fire: War, Peace, and the Democratic Bargain* (New York: Liveright, 2017).

[797] 163 US 537 (1896)

[798] See, on this point, Stephen Kinzer, *The True Flag: Theodore Roosevelt, Mark Twain, and the Birth of American Empire* (New York: Henry Holt and Company, 2017); Kristin L. Hoganson, *Fighting for American Manhood: How Gender Politics Provoked the Spanish-American and Philippine-American Wars* (New Haven: Yale University Press, 1998).

[799] See, on this point, David W. Blight, *Race and Reunion: The Civil War in American History_*(Cambridge, Mass.: Belknap Press of Harvard University Press, 2001).

so pivotal a role, as many scholars have cogently observed.[800] Roosevelt had had to struggle to conform to then dominant conceptions of manhood; when he first appeared as a legislator in the New York Assembly, both his clothes and manner and voice "led the newcomer [to] quickly become known as 'Oscar Wilde,' after the famous fop who, coincidentally, had arrived in America earlier the same day."[801] After the traumatic deaths of both his beloved mother and wife at roughly the same time, he recovered his always fragile sense of manly self by a physically demanding period of hunting and riding in the American West,[802] about which he would later publish a multivolume study, *The Winning of the West*. [803] Roosevelt had no patience and indeed turned on any man with "a certain feminine reticence," and accordingly, "he would write of Henry Adams and 'that other little emasculated mass of inanity', Henry James, that they were 'charming men, but exceedingly undesirable companions for any man not of strong nature.'"[804] Roosevelt belligerently supported the Spanish-American War in rhetorical terms that William James, who had taught Roosevelt at Harvard, observed, "Not a word of the cause, one foe is a good as another, for aught he tells us. He swamps everything together in one flood of bellicose emotion." Of his former student, "he is still mentally in the *Sturm und Drang* period of early adolescence."[805] (Like Trump, I wonder?) Roosevelt was a passionate anglophile, which explains his modeling of American manhood along imperialist lines and explains as well his later passionate advocacy of our entering into World War I on Britain's side,

---

[800] See, for example, Gail Bederman, *Manliness and Civilization* (Chicago: University of Chicago Press, 1995), pp. 170–215; Kristin L. Hoganson, *Fighting for American Manhood: How Gender Politics Provoked the Spanish-American and Philippine-American Wars* (New Haven: Yale University Press, 1998); Stephen Kinzer, *The True Flag: Theodore Roosevelt, Mark Twain, and the Birth of American Empire* (New York: Henry Holt, 2017); Kim Townsend, *Manhood at Harvard: William James and Others* (New York: W. W. Norton, 1996), pp. 256–86; Edward J. Renehan Jr., *The Lion's Pride: Theodore Roosevelt and His Family in Peace and War* (New York: Oxford University Press, 1998).

[801] Edmund Morris, *The Rise of Theodore Roosevelt* (New York: Random House, 1979), p. 144.

[802] Id., pp. 229–34, pp. 264–276.

[803] See id., pp. 474–48, 484.

[804] Quoted at id., p. 425 (footnotes omitted).

[805] Cited in Kim Townsend, *Manhood at Harvard*, p. 244.

285

urging his sons to serve (one was killed),[806] yet another example of the tragic role American patriarchal manhood played in rationalizing service in unjust wars.

Even, however, during this period, there was notable resistance to America's propensity to initiate unjust wars, as the example both of William James and Mark Twain clearly shows.[807] Both men had lived for long periods in Europe (James as a boy,[808] Twain as an established author)[809] and were accordingly skeptical of Theodore Roosevelt's America First nationalism. In contrast, Roosevelt, like other Americans of his period (including Woodrow Wilson)[810] publicly inveighed about recent immigrants from abroad because of their "hyphenated Americanism;"[811] the threat was "a flabby cosmopolitanism that led in turn to flabby patriotism."[812] Wilson was also a virulent racist, which informs his version of America First nationalism.[813] Patriarchy both uses and enforces unjust stereotypes (here immigrants), clearly here connected to rationalizing imperialist wars. No one of this period better identified" the stupidity and injustice" of such thinking than William James feeding an ethical "blindness with which we all are afflicted in regard to the feelings of creatures and people different from ourselves."[814] And no one better debunked the specific anti-immigrant stereotypes than a feminist woman of this period, Jane Addams, who worked closely at Hull House with immigrants, finding among them "an unquenchable desire that charity and simple justice shall regulate men's

---

[806]   See, for fuller discussion, Edward J Renehan Jr., *The Lion's Pride.*

[807]   On Twain's resistance, see Stephen Kinzer, *The True Flag.*

[808]   See, on this point, Robert D. Richardson, *William James: In the Maelstrom of American Modernism* (Boston: Houghton Mifflin, 2006), pp. 11–24.

[809]   See, on this point, Ron Bowers, *Mark Twain: A Life* (New York: Free Press, 2005), pp. 414–31, 580–98.

[810]   See, on this point, Michael Kazin, *War Against War*, p. 114.

[811]   Edward J. Renehan Jr., *The Lion's Pride*, p. 115.

[812]   Id.

[813]   See, on this point, PBS American Experience, *The Great War*, aired on April 12, 2017.

[814]   See William James, "On a Certain Blindness in Human Beings," *Writings 1878–1899* (New York: The Library of America, 1992), pp. 841–60, at p. 841.

relations."[815] Addams went on to connect what she had experienced with anti-militarism, putting a limit to revenge.[816]

It was never clear that World War I—a war among competing European imperialisms—was just either in its ends or means, and our entry into that war was probably unjustified, as perhaps most Americans in that period reasonably believed. It was an instance, to be repeated, as we see later in Vietnam, of the "best and brightest" (Woodrow Wilson and, for a time, John Dewey and Walter Lippman) leading us into disaster because they would not listen to, indeed repressed, democratic resisting voices.[817] Once the United States declared war, the Wilson administration—sensing the illegitimacy of its decision to enter the war—turned with repressive violence on any opponents of the war, perhaps the most egregious violation of free speech in American history, as our constitutional law has now come to regard it.[818] The consequence was such outrage at Wilson's policies that Americans after the war refused to endorse the League of Nations and a resurgent America First nationalism made us an isolationist power.[819] Wilson's mismanagement of the terms of peace—imposing extraordinary demands for reparations on a defeated Germany—so insulted Germans that the "shame of Versailles" motored as John Maynard Keynes warned it might in his remarkable psychological exploration of the role a rigidly Puritanical patriarchal religion played in his tragic mismanagement of the peace treaty,[820] the rise of aggressive fascism in Italy and Germany, as well as in Spain and Japan. America's isolationism disastrously made

---

[815]   Jane Addams, *Newer Ideals of Peace* (Urbana: University of Illinois Press, 2007; originally published, 1906), p. 10.

[816]   Id., p. 17. See, for useful background, Jean Bethke Elshtain, *Jane Addams and the Dream of American Democracy* (New York: Basic Books, 2002).

[817]   See, on these points, Jeremy McCarter, *Young Radicals: In the War for American Ideals* (New York: Random House, 2017), pp. 159–190.

[818]   See, on this point, David A. J. Richards, *Free Speech and the Politics of Identity* (Oxford: Oxford University Press, 1999).

[819]   See, on all these points, Michael Kazin, *War Against War: The American Fight for Peace 1914–1918* (New York: Simon & Schuster, 2017).

[820]   John Maynard Keynes, *The Economic Consequences of the Peace* (available at ReadaClassic.com 2010, originally published 1919). On Keynes's analysis of Wilson's psychology, see David A. J. Richards, *The Rise of Gay Rights and the Fall of the British Empire: Liberal Resistance and the Bloomsbury Group* (New York: Cambridge University Press, 2013), pp. 120–122.

politically impossible any reasonable attempt, of the sort Churchill urged on the British parliament,[821] to stop such aggressive nationalism before it was too late. It was too late, leading to the catastrophe of World War II.

The most stark and instructive recent example in recent American history of the psychological roots of unjust wars in patriarchy is the role of what David Halberstam called "the best and the brightest" in initiating and executing the unjust Vietnam War.[822] It is an appalling narrative of how some of the best educated, most liberal-minded American men, first in the Kennedy and then the Johnson administrations, led us into and escalated this war on the basis of false assumptions both of its background and of the character of the enemy never critically examined until the dimensions of their miscalculations and their lies to the American people became disastrously evident, and even then the appropriate response under the Nixon administration was unjustly delayed, costing many more innocent American and Asian lives.

Men, so obsessed by their own sense of themselves as successful American men, could not question what they took to be their successful lives and were thus acutely sensitive, as patriarchal men always are, to the shaming of their manhood inflicted by any sense of defeat. This psychology is most starkly displayed by President Lyndon Johnson himself, who refused to believe that Ho Chi Minh, the leader of a small, technologically backward, largely agrarian nation, could defeat America's extraordinary industrial and technological superiority ("Raggedly-ass little fourth-rate country," Lyndon Johnson called it during the great debates),[823] and indeed put the issue of America's response to alleged attacks by the Vietnamese at Tonkin Bay to reporters in sexist and homophobic terms, "I didn't just screw Ho Chi Minh, I cut his pecker off."[824] Halberstam concludes,

> *Machismo* was no small part of it. He has always been haunted by the idea that he would be judged as being insufficiently manly for the job that he very much wanted

---

[821] See, on this point, David A. J. Richards, *Disarming Manhood,* pp. 196–7, 199, 208–9.

[822] See David Halberstam, *The Best and the Brightest* (New York: A Fawcett Book, 1992, originally published, 1969).

[823] Ibid., p. 512.

[824] Id., p. 414. See, for other examples of Johnson's sexist and sometimes homophobic emoting, id., pp. 298, 373, 425, 499–500, 522.

to be seen as a mean; it was a conscious thing. He was very much aware of *machismo* in himself and those around him, and at a moment like this [escalating military force in Vietnam] he wanted the respect of men who were tough, real men, and they would turn out to be the hawks. He had always unconsciously divided the people around him between men and boys. Men were activists, doers, who conquered business empires, who acted instead of talked, who made it in the world of other men and had the respect of other men. Boys were the talkers and the writers and the intellectuals sat around thinking and criticizing and doubting instead of doing.[825]

At the end,

> Doubt itself, he thought, was an almost feminine quality. Doubts were for women. On another issue, when Lady Bird raised her doubts, Johnson had said of course, she was doubtful. It was like a woman to be uncertain. Thus, as Vietnam came to the edge of decision, the sides were unfair, given Johnson's makeup. The doubters were not the people he respected; the men who were activists were hawks, and he took sustenance and reassurance that the real men were for going ahead.[826]

It was always Johnson's sense that, after Kennedy's assassination, the best and brightest supported him, and he was as much hostage to their worship of American manly success as they were to his.[827] "[Johnson] was a relentless man who pushed himself and all others with the same severity and demanded, above all other qualities, total loyalty, not loyalty in the traditional sense, not positive loyalty, but total loyalty, not just to office or party or concept, but loyalty first and foremost to Lyndon Johnson."[828] Since Johnson was older than they and thus closer to the

---

[825] Id., p. 531.

[826] Id., p. 532.

[827] See, on this point, id., pp. 305–306.

[828] Ibid., p. 433.

political impact of McCarthy's irrationalist conspiracy about the loss of China, he was more vulnerable than they to the confusion of China and Vietnam, but their support after Kennedy's death strengthened, if anything, Johnson's confusion with its consequences not only in Vietnam but for his poverty programs and the future of the Democratic Party as a liberal and progressive party, which could win elections. Men (a boys group, in effect, with Johnson at its apex, demanding total loyalty) stood together over Vietnam, disastrously so for them and us. At the end, the damage to ethical intelligence was all too evident: few acknowledged mistake: "there was no sense of remorse, nor even on why they failed to estimate correctly. The faults, it seemed, were not theirs. The fault was with this country, which was not worthy of them."[829] The analogy to Hitler, at the end turning on the German people, is inescapable. How, psychologically, could this happen, and in admired liberal leadership of the United States of America, rightly still honored, as by me among others, for its domestic achievements dealing with long-standing injustices of race and poverty? Is it just, as Johnson's biographer Robert A. Caro observes, "Ruthlessness, secretiveness, deceit—significant elements in every previous stage of Lyndon Johnson's life here destroyed him." Caro goes on to comment, "Not always, however, sometimes these other elements—the anger at injustice, the sympathy, empathy, identification with the underdog that added up to compassion—had been expressed, by this master of the political gesture, in gestures, deeply meaningful."[830]

In the American experience of unjust wars, what makes the Vietnam War remarkable is not the resistance (which had occurred earlier), but that the resistance, like British objectors to World War I, originated among the soldiers, fighting the war and was, for the first time in American history, widespread, resonant, and effective—the American people were persuaded the war must be brought to an end without victory. Unlike World War I, the American law of free speech had evolved so now antiwar speech was now fully protected constitutionally.[831] Such resistance was also importantly connected to the civil rights movement whose leader, Martin

---

[829] Id., p. 656.

[830] Robert A. Caro, *The Years of Lyndon Johnson: The Passage of Power* (New York: Vintage Books, 2012), p. 536.

[831] See, on this point, David A. J. Richards, *Free Speech and the Politics of Identity.*

Luther King Jr., had now come out in opposition to the war.[832] What was the connection?

What seems crucial is that the Vietnam War was imperialist and, like other imperialisms, racist. But the achievement of the civil rights movement was both to reveal American racism for what it was (based on violence and lies) and to do so through nonviolence, *satyagraha*. What made nonviolence such an effective and resonant strategy was that nonviolent ethical voice was conspicuously met by violence and lies, thus exposing the irrationalism of racism, resting on the violent repression of resisting voice. The voice of the civil rights movement was thus a human voice resisting injustice, releasing the men and women of the movement from the ways American patriarchy had repressed their voices and, as other Americans came to see, their voices as well. Resistance to patriarchy thus empowered democratic voice.[833]

It was American voices, thus ethically empowered, that made psychologically possible resistance by the soldiers serving in Vietnam to the war, giving voice to their experience of the war, as they came to see that the aims and means of the war were themselves racist and that democratic voice could and should resist such an evil, both abroad and at home. Even the American men, like Tim O'Brien, who struggled with their consciences whether to serve in Vietnam and served, came to see and write about the moral injury they had thus suffered, acknowledging for the first time in their lives the unjust power patriarchy had over American men: "My conscience told me to run, but some irrational and powerful force was resisting, like a weight pushing me toward the war"[834]—a power rooted in the shaming of manhood and, as O'Brien came to see, cowardice.[835] O'Brien thus sees in himself the conflict between his vulnerability to the shaming of his manhood and the ethics of guilt arising from a conscience concerned with harms to others, shame-covering over guilt. This is the realization Tolstoy, a man who had fought in Russian wars and who also came to, leading him, however, to resistance (in his case, pacifism).[836]

---

[832]   See, on this point, David A. J. Richards, *Disarming Manhood*, p. 226,

[833]   See, on all these points, David A. J. Richards, *Disarming Manhood*.

[834]   Tim O'Brien, *The Things They Carried* (Boston: Mariner, 2009; originally published, 1990), p. 49.

[835]   See Id., pp. 54–58.

[836]   See, for fuller discussion, David A. J. Richards, *Disarming Manhood*, pp.

Resistance to the Vietnam War was empowered by the resistance of young men to the patriarchal authority of their fathers, who neither understood nor supported their sons. The human dimensions of such resistance is the subject of James Carroll's moving memoir of his own resistance to Vietnam and to his father, an Air Force lieutenant general who chose Vietnamese targets for American bombs.[837] The issues ran together for Carroll for two reasons, the first of which was that his father was an Air Force lieutenant general connected to Vietnam and the second was that Carroll had begun adulthood by fulfilling his father's abandoned intention of joining the Roman Catholic priesthood, and Francis Cardinal Spellman, a militant anti-Communist, was a close friend of Carroll's parents.[838] When Carroll comes, as a matter of conscience, to resist the Vietnam War, his resistance to his father was not only over Vietnam but over Carroll deciding he had to leave the priesthood as well. What connects the two issues for Carroll is his own questioning of the patriarchal turn in Roman Catholicism, writing later an important book about how Christianity had been patriarchally distorted when it became the established church of the Roman Empire, including its role in supporting anti-Semitism.[839]

Have Americans learned anything from the Vietnam War? Later events suggest we have not. Part of the problem is that contemporary Americans know so little about that war and thus fail to appreciate its significance as a resistance movement in which men, centrally, resisted patriarchy. In the seminar, Resisting Injustice, that I coteach with Carol Gilligan, we have the students watch the documentary, *Sir, No Sir,*[840] and they are shocked that, as well educated as they are, they did not know what the movie documents about the resistance of American soldiers, serving in Vietnam, to the war. We have, they argued, been told a false story about our history, a loss of memory and voice covered over by lies and distortions, and many of them see an analogy to race: false stories about the Civil War and slavery and the virulent racism, which followed the Civil War. With

---

43–91.

[837] See James Carroll, *An American Requiem: God, My Father, and the War that Came Between Us* (Boston: Houghton Mifflin, 1996).

[838] See, on this point, Id., pp. 70–73.

[839] See James Carroll, *Constantine's Sword: The Church and the Jews: A History* (Boston: Houghton Mifflin, 2001).

[840] See *Sir, No Sir* (2005).

respect to Vietnam, attempts to tell the truth are sometimes rationalized as symptoms of pathology, "the Vietnam syndrome." Karl Marlantes, who served as a marine in Vietnam and received the Navy Cross, reviewing an important book dealing with the lies told by our politicians about the war at the expense of the lives of our soldiers, trenchantly responds to this rationalization:

> If by Vietnam syndrome we mean the belief that the US should never again engage in (a) military interventions in foreign civil wars without clear objectives and a clear existing strategy, (b) "nation building" in countries about whose history and culture we are ignorant, and (c) sacrificing our children when our lives, ways of life, or "government of, by, and for the people" are not directly threatened, then we should never get over Vietnam syndrome. It's not an illness; it's a vaccination.[841]

Such loss of memory and voice are the marks of trauma, often connected to patriarchal demands. Unfortunately, the trauma for Americans of 9/11 exposed patriarchal America's vulnerability to the shaming of manhood as a response to that attack and elicited from our leadership, not wisdom. It was yet another catastrophically unjust American war, forgetting everything we should have learned from Vietnam, thus the loss of memory and voice. Resistance was for this reason less effective than it should have been when political leaders used patriarchal demands to secure and sustain themselves in power, leading, as we argued in our book, to President George Bush's taking us into an unjust war in Iraq, which has had catastrophic consequences, including mindlessly unleashing terrorism in Iraq, Syria, Afghanistan, and elsewhere. Why was resistance to that war so ineffective? Why did even Hillary Clinton support it (when Barack Obama did not)? Carol Gilligan and my indictment of patriarchy in our earlier—linking policies of unjust war to the attack on the rights of women and gays and lesbians—identifies why patriarchy is and remains such a

---

[841] Karl Marlantes, "The Bloody Pivot: Twenty-four days of nonstop urban battle that turned the tables in Vietnam," *The Wall Street Journal* Saturday/Sunday, June 3–4, 2017, C5,C6, at C6, reviewing Mark Bowden, *Hue 1968* (New York: Atlantic Monthly Press, 2017).

threat to democracy not only in the United States under the leadership of President Trump but to the many other democracies, which appear also to be leaning as well to forms of populist nationalism often based on patriarchal values hostile to values of universal human rights.

It is for this reason that I believe that the analysis of patriarchy as a threat to democracy is so important to democrats everywhere, so we do not have to learn yet again of how the patriarchal imperialisms that exploded in the violence of World War I and the forms of fascist patriarchy that almost destroyed civilization in World War II (both modeled on the Roman Empire) unleashed the most catastrophic forms of savagery in human history. I make this case in this book by a form of argument, as Virginia Woolf urged, that unites men and women in a common struggle to understand and resist the ways in which patriarchy unjustly divides them from one another and thus resist the injustices that patriarchy has supported and perpetuated throughout human history. My guideline for democracy's future calls for democratic free and equal voice—democratic both in its voice and in its aims—that understands that the failure within democracies to see the problem of patriarchy shows the psychological hold on our psyches of patriarchy, and the consequences, as history shows, are catastrophic.

The election of Trump, in which patriarchal male rage played so prominent a role, should thus especially worry us not only in domestic but in foreign policy. There is also reason to worry about a personality defect he shares with Lyndon Johnson, but that is, in Trump's case even worse, namely, the demand, like Johnson's, for total loyalty but, unlike Johnson, the central role his family apparently is playing in his administration. Both the demand for total loyalty and the centrality of family do not bode well for constitutional government, a fact Trump—for whom a family business has been the paramount model from his father to him to his children—apparently cannot understand or take seriously. In effect, as with Johnson, there is again a boys' club, totally loyal, with Trump at the apex. The historical example on which Carol Gilligan and I focus in *The Deepening Darkness*—how Augustus ended the Roman Republic and its consequences—may be especially prophetic today. The Roman Republic was well on its way to the imperialism of the Roman Empire when Augustus took power, but his founding of the autocracy of the Roman Empire now removed any constraints on the imperial military power of Rome. As Tacitus acidly put the point, "There was nothing left of the fine old Roman character. Political equality was a thing of the past: all eyes was for imperial commands. [A]t Rome, consults, senate, knights, precipitately became servile."[842] The consequence was to unleash violence unjust both in its ends and means, and yet rationalized as the pax Romana: "Tacitus has a Caledonian war leader tell his men that the Romans 'create a desolation and call it peace.'"[843]

---

[842] Cited in Carol Gilligan and David A. J. Richards, *The Deepening Darkness,* at p. 50.

[843] Adrian Goldsworthy, *Pax Romana: War, Peace and Conquest in the Roman World* (New Haven: Yale University Press, 2016), p. 2.

CHAPTER 11

Why Men Must Join Women in Resistance

Democracy at Threat

Trump could not have had the political appeal he had if American men understood the ways in which patriarchy harms not only women, but them as men. So American men are at a point in our history in which it is time to take seriously what our greatest artists, joined by anthropologists, philosophers, and psychiatrists, have been telling us as men since Hawthorne and Melville and others wrote. Failure to do so may be perilous not only to ourselves but to the value we place on constitutional democracy.[844] As I conclude the argument of this book, I want to underscore several features of Trump's politics that seem to me to threaten our democracy and conclude on why we must, as men, embrace a feminism, based on resisting the gender binary and hierarchy, through which we can join with women in freeing democracy from patriarchy and preserve, protect, and defend our constitutional democracy.

Men are quite capable as moral persons of coming to see the moral injuries patriarchy has inflicted on them and join with other men and women in sharing their experiences, communalizing the moral injury patriarchy has inflicted on them and, on that basis, resisting and forming

---

[844] See, on this point, Timothy Snyder, *On Tyranny: Twenty Lessons From the Twentieth Century* (New York: The Duggans Books, 2017).

296

a more perfect democratic union.[845] Trump's election and its consequences call for such resistance from us all, men as well as women. I have too much respect for American men for the courage they have shown when democracy has been at threat to think they cannot meet this challenge, as they move responsibly from patriarchal to democratic manhood. We need now, amidst the irrational fears and angers unleashed by Trump's politics,[846] a courage founded on democratic manhood.

Connections between the Attack on Immigrants and Unjust Wars

There is American history closer at hand that seems highly relevant in justifying worries about both Trump's domestic and foreign policies, namely, his war on immigrants and an aggressive foreign policy. As we saw, there was such a connection between the war on recent immigrants of both Theodore Roosevelt and Woodrow Wilson and the unjust wars into which they led the American people. Their worry was evidently not that immigrants would be less industrious or more crime-prone than other Americans (both of which may have been false then as they are clearly false now).[847] Rather, their worry evidently was that what they called "hyphenated Americans" would be likely to take more cosmopolitan attitudes to other nations and thus be more likely to resist mindless America First aggressive nationalism. Trump's war on immigrants (whether illegal immigration from Mexico or legal immigration by a religious group, Muslims) was the very center of his America First campaign, and we know Stephen Bannon's conservative fanaticism arose from his conviction that Islam was an aggressive threat to America, and that it was Bannon who engineered the anti-Muslim travel ban of which the American judiciary was understandably so skeptical on constitutional grounds of First Amendment guarantees protecting free exercise and forbidding established

---

[845] On the importance of communalizing in repairing moral injury, see David A. J. Richards, *Why Love Leads to Justice*, pp. 209–33.

[846] See, on the role of these emotions in Trump's populist politics, Martha C. Nussbaum, *The Monarchy of Fear: A Philosopher Looks at Our Political Crisis* (New York: Simon & Schuster, 2018).

[847] See, on this point, Bret Stephens, "Only Mass Deportation Can Save Us," *The New York Times*, Saturday, June 17, 2017, A23 (op-ed).

churches. Trump's attack on immigrants is thus constitutionally much more questionable that earlier anti-immigration policies, but it is also much more dangerous in terms of our foreign policy goals. Its mindless intolerance (stereotyping all Muslims as terrorists) confirms the irrational fears Islamic terrorists foment of the West as crusaders once again unjustly attacking Islam, as they had during the Crusades. It is the kind of insult that shames the highly patriarchal manhood of the terrorists and others, and thus elicits violence and even war.

We need to take instruction in these circumstances from the American ethical leaders who, in the earlier historical period, worried about America's propensity to initiate unjust wars, to wit, William James and Jane Addams. James notably protested both American imperialism[848] and the virulent racism of American lynchings.[849] In his important 1910 essay, "The Moral Equivalent of War,"[850] James was particularly concerned with the kind of mindless militarism he condemned in the policies of Theodore Roosevelt but, after considering pacifist (Tolstoy) and feminist alternatives, concludes that the war-party is assuredly right in affirming and reaffirming that the martial virtues, although originally gained by the race through war, are absolute and permanent human goods.[851] He proposes a moral equivalent of war, namely, mandatory public service for young people, as a way of redirecting and civilizing these "virtues." James certainly sees the role that the gender binary plays in framing these issues but, working within the binary as a fixed feature of male human nature, looks forward, through such alternatives, "to a future when acts of war shall be formally outlawed as between civilized people."[852]

In contrast, the ethical and psychological brilliance of Jane Addams's framing of the same issue (American aggressive militarism) is the way she investigates the question through her close study of recent immigrants she knew from her work at Hull House, precisely the immigrants that Theodore Roosevelt and Woodrow Wilson would condemn as "hyphenated

---

[848] See, on this point, Robert D. Richardson, *William James: In the Maelstrom of American Modernism* (Boston: Houghton Mifflin, 2006), pp. 380–85.

[849] See, on this point, Id., pp. 441–42.

[850] William James, "The Moral Equivalent of War," *Writings 1902–1910* (New York: The Library of America, 1987), pp. 1281–1293.

[851] Id., p. 1290.

[852] Id., p. 1289.

Americans." What Addams saw in her experience of these immigrants was not a threat but an ethical impulse of care and concern arising from "the opportunity and necessity for breaking through the tribal bond."[853] In a period when immigrants were demonized as "the scum of Europe,"[854] Addams closely observed and appreciated the humane capacities she saw in the immigrants she knew at firsthand—the "old German potter . . . his life . . . illumined with the artist's prerogative of direct creation," the humane rationality of Southern Italians "congregate[d] in cities where their inherited and elaborate knowledge of agricultural processes is unutilized,"[855] the courage of Russian immigrant victims of religious and political persecution with their experience of the "bittersweet martyrdom,"[856] and "the most recently immigrated Jews" with their "refreshing insistence upon the reality of the inner life."[857] Addams entered into the world of these people, coming to understand their struggles in a new environment and how little their struggles and gifts were taken seriously or appreciated. Addams also saw in American immigrants "the power of association that comes from daily contact with those who are unlike each other in all save the universal characteristics of man, suggestions of a new peace and holiness. It would seem as if our final help and healing were about to issue forth from broken human nature itself, out of the pathetic striving of ordinary men, who make up the common substance of life, from those who have been driven by economic pressure or governmental oppression out of a score of nations."[858] Addams argues that what she has discovered from work with and listening to immigrants is an alternative to William James's search for a moral equivalent to war: "the substitution of nurture for warfare, analogous to that worldwide effort to put a limit to revenge,"[859] the psychological root of a militarism Addams finds also in the American criminal justice system, including prisons.[860] Unlike James, Addams challenges the gender binary itself and frames her argument in terms of an ethics of care along the lines we advocate that challenges the binary.

---

[853] Jane Addams, *Newer Ideals of Peace,* p. 10.

[854] Id., p. 16.

[855] Id., p. 38.

[856] Id., p. 40.

[857] Id., p. 40.

[858] Id., p. 11.

[859] Id., p. 17.

[860] See, on this point, id., pp. 33–35.

Like the insights of James Gilligan into American criminal justice, Addams's insights arise from her close and intimate study of persons (in Gilligan's case, criminals; in Addams, immigrants) marginalized and even held in contempt, based on crude stereotypes. Like Gilligan, Addams listens to the voices of such groups, appealing to experience. What she finds are forms of rationality between diverse people that break down the stereotypes that politicians use to divide them from one another and other Americans and indeed lead to a sense of common ethical values that they share with all of us, "an unquenchable desire that charity and simple justice shall regulate men's relations."[861] It is one of the great ethical strengths of the American immigrant experience that its diversity can and sometimes does lead to respect for the common values such people share or come to share on terms of freedom and equality. It is this experience that explains the role universal values of human rights have played and increasingly have come to play as the foundations of American constitutionalism, values we share with other constitutional democracies.

The fact that the central feature of Trump's America First nationalism was the Muslim ban, followed close by his draconian views on illegal immigrants, clearly shows the stark inconsistency between his now visible patriarchy and the values of constitutional democracy, universal human rights. As with other American leaders in the past, who used the attack on immigrants as a way of advancing policies of aggressive war, Trump's attacks on immigrants may be linked to a readiness for aggressive unjust wars, as it has been so linked in the past.

American Transnationalism

It was during the period that Jane Addams was developing an alternative interpretation of William James's search for a moral equivalent of war that the American pragmatist, Randolph Bourne, a student at Columbia of John Dewey and Franz Boas, wrote in a similar spirit and on the same basis of America not as a melting pot into the English-American but developing not a nationality but a trans-nationality.[862] Just as Addams had closely

---

[861] Id., p. 10.

[862] Randolph Bourne, "Trans-National America," *The Radical Will: Selected Writings 1911–1918*, ed. Olaf Hansen (Berkeley: University of California

observed the diverse immigrants at Hull House, Bourne closely studied the diverse immigrant groups in the progressive schools at Gary Indiana, which welcomed children from thirty nationalities. He observed, "They merge, but they do not fuse."[863] What is emerging is something quite new: "In a world that had dreamed of internationalism, we find that we have all unawares been building up the first international nation, the continent where for the first time in history has been achieved the miracles of hope, the peaceful living side by side, with character substantially preserved of the most heterogeneous people under the sun."[864]

Bourne came to disagree with his revered teacher, John Dewey, and once good friend, Walter Lippman, about their support of America entering into World War I (both later recanted their views), in part because he perceived that Woodrow Wilson's attacks on hyphenated Americans, as those who opposed the war, was a way disastrously of quashing dissent to an unjust war.[865] What emerged from one of the periods of the most egregious violations of free speech by the federal government in American history was the development of the robust and muscular protection of free speech in the United States the we now enjoy, including the constitutional protection of speech resisting governmental policies while we are at war (thus the robust resistance to the Vietnam War, which changed minds and policies).[866] Bourne clearly sees in his essay that the attacks on hyphenated Americans by, among others, Woodrow Wilson and Theodore Roosevelt, were a way of repressing wholly just antiwar views in favor of the militaristic views of more established American ethnic groups, noting that many such groups are in the part of the nation with much fewer recent immigrants, that is, the American South,[867] with their patriarchal codes of honor, preserving in America "mediaeval codes of dueling" that have led in Europe to World War I and "the spirit that inflames it and turns all its energy into mutual destruction."[868] Why, Bourne, himself an English-American, asked "have [we] not heard copiously and scornfully

---

Press, 1977; first published, 1916), pp. 248–264, at p. 262.
[863] See Randolph Bourne, "Trans-National America," at p. 255.
[864] See id., p. 258.
[865] See, for full discussion, Jeremy McCarter, *Young Radicals.*
[866] See, on this point, David A. J. Richards, *Free Speech and the Politics of Identity.*
[867] See, on this point, Randolph Bourne, "Trans-National America," p. 253.
[868] Id., p. 259.

of hyphenated English Americans?"[869] More recent immigrant ethnic groups, Bourne insists, have "a right to a voice in the construction of the American ideal."[870] "They must be heard."[871] This shows, I believe, the close connection between what Bourne so valued in the American democratic experiment, our pluralism, and our constitutional traditions that are now grounded in respect for universal human rights, including free speech that we share with other constitutional democracies but are here more muscular in part because we have learned how robust protections of speech assure to all Americans, including recent immigrants, that all Americans are in a common enterprise. It is not what we are now that concerns us but what this plastic next generation may become in the light of a new cosmopolitan ideal.[872] From Bourne's perspective, it is precisely less assimilated immigrant groups that may, given American protections of free speech, have the most to contribute to reasonable democratic debate in service of democracy and universal human rights.

It has certainly been my own experience, both as a gay man and an Italian American, that American constitutional traditions of free speech empowered an ethical voice in me (a voice that sometimes surprised me) that resisted the ways in which American patriarchy would otherwise have disabled me from understanding and living in the truth and value of gay love and in the richly humane and artistic traditions of my nation of origin, not least the expressive, emotionally truthful voice of Italian opera, which the Italians, of course, invented on the model of Greek tragedy in the Florentine Camerata.[873] It was the voice—intelligent and musically expressive—of my father, the civil engineer and opera singer, my first model for democratic manhood. I recall the sense of shock I felt when I first stood before a law school class, teaching Criminal Law and Constitutional Law, and found a voice in me that could give full expression to my heart and mind in a way I had never before in my life. It still shocks me, having lived so much of my life believing that love and my secret self could not be one. (I was thirty when I met my partner.) Only in America, I now realize,

---

[869] Id., p. 251.

[870] Id., p. 263.

[871] Id., p. 264.

[872] Id., p. 250.

[873] See, on this point, "Florence," in Stanley Sadie, ed., *The New Grove Dictionary of Opera Volume 2* (London: Macmillan, 1992), at pp. 232–240.

could I have found voice in that way. Just as I had now found love, I had now found my vocation, and they were one search and one consummation. I came as an Italian American and gay man to the same realization Philip Roth apparently came to as an American Jew in *Counterlife*, arguing with a Zionist in Israel: "I went on, the fact of it was that I could not think of any historical society that had achieved the level of tolerance institutionalized in America that had placed pluralism smack at the center of its publicly advertised dream of itself."[874] That is what Bourne saw when he opposed the America First nationalism of Woodrow Wilson, joined by the best and brightest. American values and universal human rights are now the same thing, and any threat to them, as by the Trump presidency's war on truth (which is, as Hannah Arendt made clear, the political psychology of political fascism's war on liberal values) is a threat to American democracy itself. What many Americans, including Italian Americans like myself, should learn from the history of warring on hyphenated Americans (as my family certainly were) is to refuse the kind of racialized Americanization Trump offers, setting us now against other contemporary immigrants who do not share our ethnicity or our religion. And we should take seriously the features of Trump's presidency that undermine democracy itself, not least his appalling war on a free press. It is a threat we must resist.

Does Trump Threaten American Democracy?

In his recent book, *On Tyranny: Twenty Lessons from the Twentieth Century*, the Yale historian Timothy Snyder reviews the twentieth century history of the collapse of democracy in Italy in the 1920s and in Germany in the 1930s, in the Soviet Union after the 1917 revolution and in Russia in the 1990s (Putin's subversion of democracy) and in Eastern European countries after World War II and raises the question whether Trump's politics in the United States suggests reasons for believing we may be on the verge of a similar collapse in the United States and what Americans should do to resist such a threatened collapse.[875] Snyder emphasizes the

---

[874]   Philip Roth, *Counterlife*, in Philip Roth, *Novels & Other Narratives 1986–1991*, ed. Ross Miller (New York: The Library of America, 2008), pp. 1–304, at p. 50.

[875]   Timothy Snyder, *On Tyranny: Twenty Lessons from the Twentieth Century* (New York: Tim Duggan Books, 2017). For studies to similar effect, see

following features of the undermining of democracies in all these nations: the tendency to obey authoritarian leaders in advance of their mandates; the failure to defend institutions; one-party states; citizen failures to take responsibility for resisting evils like anti-Semitism, racism, and sexism; the important role of paramilitaries in enforcing fascist violence; intemperate language; the loss of a sense of truth in politics; the dependence on populist slogans rather than attention to the print media, including reading books, that prompt reasonable investigation; the undermining of the distinction between public and private life reflected in absorption in the leader's personality; the failure to learn from peers in other countries; not listening for dangerous words enforcing irrational prejudices; not staying calm when the unthinkable happens; not patriotically resisting to defend enduring political values of human rights; and not developing the civic courage to resist. There are reasons, he argues, for believing that Trump's politics exemplifies a number of them, and that a reasonable concern for history requires concern that his politics may be undermining our constitutional democracy.

The argument of *Darkness Now Visible*, which emphasized analogies between Trump's politics and political fascism, is certainly consistent with Snyder's argument, indeed explains its accuracy and force. Trump's politics and its success (the Republican Party now in power in two branches of the national government and perhaps, in time, the third) reflect a number of the historical analogies Snyder adduces, not least, his shallow bromides, the roles that lies and distortions have played in his polities, his attack on the independent print media, his blatant appeal to misogyny, the supine Republican compliance with and indeed support of his policies, the forms of paramilitary violence by his supporters—encouraged by Trump—against their opponents,[876] his uncritical passion for antidemocratic authoritarians like Putin, who have subverted Russian democracy and have apparently tried to subvert ours,[877] and many others. There is, however, one notable

---

Carol Gilligan and David A. J. Richards, *Darkness Now Visible: Patriarchy's Resurgence and Feminist Resistance* (Cambridge: Cambridge University Press, 2018); Timothy Snyder, *The Road to Unfreedom: Russia, Europe, America* (New York: Tim Duggan Books, 2018); Yascha Mounk, *The People vs. Democracy: Why Our Freedom Is in Danger and How to Save It* (Cambridge, Mass.: Harvard University Press, 2018).

[876] See, on this point, Timothy Snyder, *On Tyranny*, pp. 43–46.
[877] See, on this point, id., pp. 27–31.

difference between today and the examples cited by Snyder: the resistance movements that have arisen in this country and that Carol and I have supported. There is also the explanatory and normative focus of my argument in what I believe is central to Trump's politics and to resistance to this politics: American patriarchy and voices resisting patriarchy.[878]

Snyder correctly indicts Americans as citizens for their lack of critical interest in our history, accepting an America First ideology in which "[e]very reference to the past seems to involve an attack by some external enemy upon the purity of the nation."[879] This is not, as Snyder correctly observes, the American constitutional tradition: "As the Founding Fathers debated our Constitution, they took instruction from the history they knew. Concerned that the democratic republic they envisioned would collapse, they contemplated the descent of ancient democracies and republics into oligarchy and empire."[880] When will we be worthy of them? It is time to take seriously, as they would have, of the compelling evidence *now* before us that we now know what the real threat to democracy now is, as it has always been, namely, patriarchy, and to take up arms to resist. Only an alliance between men and women—united in a sense of the harms patriarchy inflicts on both men and women—is adequate to this challenge, as I now argue.

Alternative Models of Manhood: Trump and Obama

Against the backdrop of the once hegemonic cultural patriarchy in America, traditional masculinity is today more fragile and contested than it has ever been. Gender binaries have become more obviously porous, challenged by queer and transgender Americans. Not only women's but also men's lives have become less constrained by gender, no longer dichotomous but a fluid spectrum.[881] Trump's racism and misogyny mobilized a reactionary politics that relied on bullying, lies, and violence to reverse these developments. Without in any way seeking to mask his

---

[878] Snyder mentions Trump's sexism, but it is not central to his argument. See id., p. 75.

[879] See id., p. 121.

[880] Id., p. 9.

[881] We are grateful to Lucy Kissel for suggesting this way of putting our argument.

intention, Trump set out to repudiate everything that Obama had stood for and represented: his race, his feminism, his embrace of the Constitution in its deepest intention, and above all, his manhood. In contrast, as Carol Gilligan and I show in *Darkness Now Visible,* Trump trumpeted his brand of patriarchal manhood and showed contempt for Obama's very different manhood in the blatantly false birther claims about Obama he relentlessly pressed until late in his campaign.[882] It is illuminating to contrast his background with Obama's, illustrating the alternative models of manhood they put on offer.

The most striking difference in the background of Trump and Obama is their very different relationships to their fathers. Obama, as we shall see, barely knew his father, and it is the love of his mother and her parents that nurtured and sustained him and gave direction to his demanding education and his idealism. None of the well-researched books on Trump's life show any remotely comparable family constellation and certainly not demanding education and idealism.[883] Trump's family was highly patriarchal even by the standards of the period. The patriarch was his "gruff and demanding" father, Fred Trump, a hard-driving and successful real estate developer in Queens, keenly committed to training his sons for a life of fierce competition. "Be a killer," he told them over and over; he insisted that they work, delivering papers, but he also indulged them in the way that a man with hard-won riches did. When it rained or snowed, he let the boys deliver their newspapers via chauffeured limousine. "You are a king," said Fred to Donald.[884] His mother, who had immigrated from Scotland, was "as tough, stubborn, and ambitious as her husband,"[885] sometimes working for him in the business, and she was, unlike her husband, "charming and unafraid to be the center of attention at a party—a bit of a performer."[886] In this one respect, the son is more like the mother than the father.

---

[882] See Michael D'Antonio, *The Truth About Trump* (New York: Thomas Dunne Books, 2016), pp. 284–96.

[883] See Michael D'Antonio, *The Truth About Trump* (New York: Thomas Dunne Books, 2016); David Cay Johnston, *The Making of Donald Trump* (Brooklyn: Melville House, 2016); Michael Kranish and Marc Fisher, *Trump Revealed: The Definitive Biography of the 45th President* (New Yorik: Scribner, 2016).

[884] See Michael D'Antonio, *The Truth About Trump* (New York: Thomas Dunne Books, 2016), p. 39.

[885] Id., p. 36.

[886] Id., p. 38.

Donald, at once spoiled and patriarchally controlled, bridled at his father's demands. Unable to control him, he was sent to New York Military Academy, where he found a war veteran teacher, Theodore Dobias, who "became his real role model," with Dobias helping him "to adapt and thrive in an environment where macho concepts of strength and masculinity prevailed."[887] Another cadet, "Harry Falber, would recall that the systematic bullying among the students was far more troubling than the discipline meted out by the staff. Though not quite *Lord of the Flies*, the culture at the school was 'full of aggression,' said Falber, and a mob mentality sometimes prevailed."[888] In *Darkness Now Visible*, Carol Gilligan and I set out several papers from our male students that give a vivid sense of such initiations, and I quote from them here. One of them depicted his initiation into his college fraternity, which he describes as "a night of torture" at the end of which they were "literally covered in blood." The student is clear as to what this brotherhood was about. They were "indoctrinated by nothing but pain-inducing patriarchal norms."

> Our initiation, the last day of pledge-ship, consisted of a night of torture. We were first stripped down to our underwear and forced into a small bath of ice, where we sat for an hour. We were then herded into a room full of sand, spread evenly over a brick tile floor. In that room, we were told that "on the count of three" we must all drop to our knees at the same time so that only one loud thump could be heard in the room. We were told to remove our legs from under us so that our knees hit the ground, buckling without any support. After hitting the ground, we were forced to spin in a circle so that the topis of our bare feet would drag across on the floor. My friends who were ridiculed the most for being unfit as a pledge brother were harassed the most during this event, as older brothers would jump in and grind their feet among the brick and sand while they spun. The older brothers were yelling things like "faggot" and "pussy," as time and time again, we fell to the floor. The master of the fraternity

---

[887] Id., p. 44.
[888] Id., pp. 44–45.

would yell, "As one! You're not dropping as one!" This, of course, was a ploy. Regardless of how well we dropped, we were destined to drop thirty times.

By the end of this nightmare, each one of us was covered in blood, and perfect rings of blood surrounded each one of us where our feet had been spinning.

Finally, all of us lined up outside on the driveway, sitting Indian style in six rows. At 3:00 a.m. in the morning, it was twenty degrees outside. We were individually doused with water to ensure our discomfort. There was nothing to keep us warm but a fire at the front of the first row. Different older brothers would get up and make speeches, usually involving a story about a time they had an unusual and objectifying sexual experience. Our backs twisted and ached only to be momentarily relieved as the head master yelled, "Switch!" in which case, the front row quickly scurried to the back of the formation to allow the fire to warm the next closest row. As we sat there, objects were thrown at our heads like ice or empty beer cans. Finally, as the sun rose, the nightmare was over. We were all officially "brothers" in a fraternity, indoctrinated by nothing but pain-inducing patriarchal norms.

Another student who had attended an Ivy League university told a similar story. He had joined a fraternity in which the brothers also had bonded over a manhood proven by objectifying women and the dehumanizing of gays. In the initiation, the first prize was the "yellow jersey" (YJ) that was awarded to the young man who had achieved the most stunning sexist adventures with women— "[t]he brother with the craziest story of how he hooked up with a woman, what he did to her, or even how he disrespected her in a way that would make us laugh the most." The YJ—yellow jersey—was worn on campus by the winner of this contest.[889]

Dobias would later observe that Trump's father was "really tough on the kid. He was very German. He was very tough," but Dobias also

---

[889] See Carol Gilligan and David A. J. Richards, *Darkness Now Visible*, pp. 24–26.

"taught that winning wasn't everything. It was the only thing."[890] "A good but not stellar student, he [Trump] became one of Dobias's favorites and absorbed the sense of superiority that was preached at NYMA with the consistency of a drumbeat. Rigidly hierarchical and hypermasculine, the academy required physical sacrifice, and the cadets were denied a world of experiences and relationships enjoyed by friends back home—no moms and dads, no brothers and sisters. In school plays, female roles were played by boys in drag."[891]

Trump's initiation into a version of American patriarchy is, even by the standards of that period, one of unusual traumatic loss not only separation from his family and siblings but a military school experience full of "systematic bullying among the students," leading to Trump's identifying with the aggressor whose violence he had experienced, leading to uncritical acceptance of its "[r]igidly hierarchical and hypermasculine" ideals as the way of life and indeed key to his business and political success. There was nothing in his experience that would challenge leading a way of life that he never thought of as a choice. It was the key to his father's success and to the military distinction of Theodore Dobias, thus the celebration of unbridled business and the role of military advisers in his presidency. His elder brother by eight years, Freddy Jr., whom Trump loved and admired, fared much less well, abandoning the business that his father had intended him to lead, pursuing a professional and personal life independent from his father as an aviator and then divorced from his wife and two children, rejoining the business and sinking into alcoholic abuse and early death at forty-three.[892] By many reports,[893] Freddy was gay and homophobia, both his own and that of his family and culture may have played a role in his decline and death. Freddy, unlike Donald, had never fought his father[894] but, not having developed the armor of competitive masculinity that Trump had imbibed at military school, was wounded by his father's overbearing ways when the father brought him into the business. For Donald, "Trump men were supposed to be tough, even when dealing with each other,

[890] Id., p. 43.

[891] Id., p. 45.

[892] Id., pp. 59–65, 154–55.

[893] Michael Wolff, *Fire and Furty: Inside the Trump White House* p. 72 (London: Little, Brown, 2018).

[894] Michael D'Antonio, *The Truth About Trump*, p. 59.

but when his father lashed out at Freddy, he was so hurt he seemed to physically shrink. It was hard to watch."[895] Trump, now having accepted a version of his father's and Dobias's conception of patriarchal masculinity, "couldn't help but torment Freddy when they were together. 'What's the difference,' asked Donald contemptuously, 'between what you do and driving a bus?'"[896] Trump "would count his brother's death as a formative and even defining episode in his life,"[897] but whatever grief he felt did not lead him to question the conception of manhood he had by now fully embraced. Trump "blamed his brother for letting others take advantage of him. He was, in other words, a sucker. 'Freddy just wasn't a killer,' said Donald. He didn't defend himself, which was 'a fatal mistake.' Fred's death had taught Donald to keep his guard up one hundred percent."[898]

With his brother's departure to a career in aviation, Donald took over his role in his father's business, learning and elaborating his ruthless ways. When he marries, "[h]is parents' marriage was his model. 'For a man to be successful, he needs support at home, just like my father had from my mother, not someone who's always griping and bitching.'"[899] So success or the image of success plays an important role in his choice of wives, but only the first of them, Ivana, is closely involved in his business affairs (like Trump's mother), and all of them are from abroad, less likely to be influenced by the new conceptions of personal life of second-wave feminism, "someone," in Trump's misogynist view of feminism, "who's always griping and bitching." And there is an element both in Trump's marriages and personal and business life that his father would not have understood or endorsed, something he may have learned in the raucous men's world of the military academy and its sometimes brutal and traumatizing initiations into patriarchal manhood, namely, the ancient patriarchal idea that really successful men are judged by their uninhibited sexual success at attracting, getting, and sometimes exploiting desirable women—the more the better. This was Trump's robustly publicized (by him) "playboy image"[900] cultivated by him in his choice of wives, "stereotyping feminine,

---

[895] Id., p. 59.
[896] Id., p. 65.
[897] Id., p. 154.
[898] Id., p. 135.
[899] Michael Kranish and Marc Fisher, *Trump Revealed*, p. 79.
[900] Id., p. 153.

long-legged, ample chested, with big hair." "Ivana, Marla, and years later, a Slovenian model, Melania Knauss, were all New York City outsiders with distinctive accents, two from Eastern Europe and one from a small town in Georgia. None had been born to privilege. As Trump grew older, the age gap grew bigger. Publicly, the women grew quieter too."[901] And there were also his affairs, some involving sexual harassment.[902]

In the early 1980s, Trump's interests shifted; Barbara Rees, who had worked for him for years, observed of this shift: "I think that was the beginning of the end of him being a serious businessman. And he moved into being a cartoon."[903] He had been a successful businessman, more so than his father, as Trump moved the family business from Queens to Manhattan, culminating in the symbol of his Manhattan success, Trump Towers. But Trump now became invested in celebrity in the unique media environment of New York City, and Trump was both a symptom and catalyst of what Christ Hedges has called the American "empire of illusion."[904] For Trump, any celebrity story was good celebrity, and he wrote in one of his books, "I play to people's fantasies. I call it truthful hyperbole. It's an innocent form of exaggeration—and a very effective form of promotion."[905] A number of psychiatrists and mental health experts have commented on Trump's grandiose narcissism, including not only his lack of truthfulness and intellectual curiosity but how any shaming of his alleged achievements elicits savage fighting back and violence.[906] Trump's seemingly privileged childhood was, in fact, a traumatic initiation into patriarchal manhood, dominated by a father showing little loving interest in his son as an individual but dictating that the son comply with the father's image of what a man must be--tough, hypermasculine, a killer. Grandiose narcissism, as a psychological disorder, arises from such parental abuse and neglect, which is reasonably clear in Trump's development—a child traumatically separated from intimate relationships and thus unloved

---

[901]   Id., p. 153.

[902]   Id., pp. 162-64.

[903]   Id., p. 101.

[904]   See Chris Hedges, *The Empire of Illusion: The End of Literacy and the Triumph of Spectacle* (New York: Nation Books, 2009).

[905]   Michael Kranish and Mark Fisher, op. cit., p. 105.

[906]   See Bandy Lee, *The Dangerous Case of Donald Trump: 27 Psychiatrists and Mental Health Experts Assess a President* (New York: A Thomas Dunne Book, 2017).

as an individual, a trauma that expresses itself in identification with an image, a false self and vulnerable to anger at any challenge to this image.[907] This external self thrives in living in public responsive to approbation and admiration of this image, acutely sensitive to shame and anger, much less responsive to the inner voice of guilt and remorse for ethical lapses. Trump very much lived in this way, and celebrity was an important part of what sustained and energized him, including the image of a successful business tycoon in the *Apprentice* series of national television.[908] Trump himself has celebrated his own narcissism and corresponding lack of personal relationships when he wrote of his wives as good people, "But I'm married to my business. It's been a marriage of love," going on to trumpet the virtues of his narcissism. "Narcissism can be a useful quality if you're trying to start a business. A narcissist does not hear the naysayers. At the Trump Organization, I listen to people, but my vision is my vision." His advice is, "Don't overthink things. (The day I realized it can be smart to be shallow was, for me, a deep experience.) And think of yourself as a one-man army. You must plan and execute your plan alone."[909] Thinking of oneself "as a one-man army" is the world of the men of Homer's *Iliad*, what I earlier called a shame culture, and Trump lives in and has thrived in the patriarchal shame culture still very much alive in American culture and politics, as the 2016 election made quite clear.

If Trump has a psychological disorder (as he certainly does), he is well aware of it and quite clearly regards it not as a deficit but as a strength in the way narcissism sometimes plays a role in the life and works of other public figures, sometimes for good and sometimes for ill—artists, national leaders like Hitler and Stalin, politicians, celebrities, and others. If Carol Gilligan and I are right in *Darkness Now Visible*, his political success in the 2016 election turned on the authenticity of his narcissistically displayed patriarchal misogyny and the remarkable fact that American men and women were still so patriarchal that his narcissistic rage elicited a

---

[907] See, on the psychological roots of narcissism, Heinz Kohut, *The Analysis of the Self: A Systematic Approach to the Psychoanalytic Treatment of Narcissistic Personality Disorders* (Chicago: University of Chicago Press, 1971); Heinz Kohut, *The Restoration of the Self* (New York: International Universities Press, 1977). See also Andrew P. Morrison, ed., *Essential Papers on Narcissism* (New York: New York University Press, 1986).

[908] See Michael Kranish and Marc Fisher, *Trump Revealed*, pp. 210–20.

[909] Id., p. 168.

comparable irrational rage in them. What reason could such an intelligent man have for questioning his own narcissism when it has been so successful, however damaging to our democracy, as Carol and I also argue? Resistance to the policies of such a man, as we also argue, must come from others.

The contrast of Obama's manhood to Trump's could not be more starkly dramatic. Obama's presidency was the culmination not only of the bridge from Selma—the Civil Rights movement and Martin Luther King—but of all the resistance movements of the 1960s and '70s. Although these movements differed in their focus—civil rights, the Vietnam War, women's liberation, gay rights—they all dismantled the culture of patriarchy, its politics and its psychology. The new progressive manhood of Obama was aligned with Martin Luther King's conviction that in the end, the force of truth and the power of justice will prevail. It was also arguably inspired by the role resistance to patriarchy played in Obama's development, as the son of a mother who had resisted white racist patriarchy.[910] We can see the consequences of such resistance not only in the more democratic manhood of men such as Obama but the resonance such manhood had for the Americans who elected him by majorities much larger than those of Donald Trump. In fact, despite his assertions to the contrary, Trump, like George W. Bush in the election of 2000, received fewer votes than his opponent. We can see in the more fluid gender arrangements that are now a reality for more people a potential for a truly feminist resistance in that Americans including American men may now be more open to ending patriarchy than ever before in American history.

Obama barely knew his Kenyan father, though he had a lively imagination about him. When he did actually meet him on his father's short visit to Honolulu, he soon "began to count the days until my father would leave."[911] Obama developed his liberal and humane values in relationship with his mother and her parents, Toot and Gramps, and to the second man his mother married, the Indonesian Lolo, with whom they lived in Indonesia for several years. Obama's mother was not only passionately committed to the resistance movements of the '60s, a passion she imparted to her son, but she had broken the patriarchal love laws by

---

[910] See David A. J. Richards, *Resisting Injustice and the Feminist Ethics of Care,* pp. 118–141.

[911] Barack Obama, *Dreams from My Father: A Story of Race and Inheritance* (New York: The Three Rivers Press, 2004), p. 68.

marrying a black man. In patriarchal terms, she had committed the highest crime and misdemeanor for women, breaking the love laws by falling in love with and marrying a man of color—not once but twice.

In his remarkably revealing autobiography, written before he entered politics, Obama writes movingly of how, observing Barack's disappointment in his father, his mother explains to him the pressures his father, a Kenyan man, was under. He had abandoned the marriage in part because his Kenyan family "didn't want Obama blood sullied by a white woman"[912] and in part because his ambition drove him to accept an offer to attend Harvard that did not cover the expenses of bringing his wife and baby. What strikes Obama after all these years is the kind of love his mother had for his father: "the love of someone who knows your life in the round, a love that will survive disappointment."[913]

Obama clearly came to see and understand his mother as a whole human being with sexual interests, including fantasies that had been forbidden to a white middle-class girl from Kansas, the promise of another life, warm, sensual, exotic, different."[914] The autobiography also tells us that his mother and her parents were devoted to his education, wanting him to go to the best private school in Honolulu, Punahou. And it was Obama's mother who, when he was a boy, woke him early each morning to teach him English lessons for three hours before he went to school. When he bridled at this regime, her response was, "This is no picnic for me either, buster."[915]

There are, however, two features of his mother and father that Obama understates in his autobiography. First, in David Remnick's recent study of Obama's life, Obama's mother, Ann Dunham, emerges as a serious, demanding, and committed intellectual—"an indefatigable researcher"[916] and an anthropologist doing fieldwork in Indonesia on the lives and futures of the craftsmen of central Java for her doctoral dissertation during her son's last three years at Punahou and completing her dissertation in 1992.[917] During this period, Dunham remained in close contact with her son who

---

[912] Barack Obama, *Dreams from My Father: A Story of Race and Inheritance* (New York: The Three Rivers Press, 2004), at p. 126.

[913] Obama, *Dreams from My Father*, p. 127.

[914] Barack Obama, *Dreams from My Father: A Story of Race and Inheritance* (New York: The Three Rivers Press, 2004), p. 124.

[915] Barack Obama, id., at p. 48.

[916] David Remnick, *The Bridge*, p. 86.

[917] See David Remnick, *The Bridge*, pp. 83–90.

---

was living with her parents; her thesis supervisor, the granddaughter of John Dewey, Alice Dewey, observed, "She *adored* that child, and they were in constant touch. And he adored her."[918] Her dissertation, *Peasant Blacksmithing in Indonesia: Surviving and Thriving Against All Odds,* was over a thousand pages in manuscript and in-depth study of "the history, beliefs, and skill of nearly every inhabitant of the village—its intricate and evolving social, religious, and class structures and its cultural formation through centuries of foreign and indigenous influence."[919] While continuing work on her dissertation, Dunham worked for the Ford Foundation in the nineteen-eighties; she was "concerned about women's rights and their livelihoods."[920]

Second, Obama's autobiography ends with a long visit to Kenya in which he tries to find out more about his father, now deceased. Obama does confirm the qualities his mother had observed in his father: his generosity[921] and his universalistic ethical values.[922] He also learns about his patriarchal grandfather called "the Terror,"[923] who had rejected Christianity for Islam because its teachings on nonviolence "was foolish sentiment, something to comfort women,"[924] and had demanded that his son leave his white wife, Obama's mother.[925] Obama learns that his father's obedience to his father reflects the wider and deeper patriarchal culture of Kenya, in which arranged marriages, polygamy, and wife beating and child beating are endemic.[926] He also learns that his father's rather American

---

[918] Quotation of Alice Dewey, cited in David Remnick, *The Bridge,* p. 84.

[919] David Remnick, *The Bridge,* p. 86. Her dissertation has now been published. See S. Ann Dunham, *Surviving against the Odds: Village Industry in Indonesia,* ed. Aice G. Dewey and Nancy I Cooper (Durhan, NC: Duke University Press, 2009). For a recent illuminating biography of Obama's mother, see Janny Scott, *A Singular Woman: The Untold Story of Barack Obama's Mother* (New York: Riverhead Books, 2011).

[920] Quoted from Mary Zurbuchen, who worked with Dunham at the Ford Foundation, cited in David Renick, *The Bridge,* p. 88.

[921] Barack Obama, *Dreams from My Father,* p. 336–7.

[922] Barack Obama, *Dreams from My Father,* p. 348.

[923] Barack Obama, *Dreams from My Father,* p. 369.

[924] Barack Obama, *Dreams from My Father,* p. 407.

[925] Barack Obama, *Dreams from My Father,* p. 422.

[926] See, on these points, Barack Obama, *Dreams from My Father,* pp. 386, 390, 402–7, 434,

idealism conflicted with an increasingly corrupt Kenyan politics, leading to professional failure, unhappy marriages, and alcohol abuse (culminating in the auto accident in which he died). What Obama understates is what he had been spared by not living with this man who had beaten one of his wives and children in Kenya.[927] What he learned in Kenya and earlier from his aunt Auma in the United States was "utterly at odds with [his] long-held myth of his father's grandeur, a myth propagated by his loving and well-meaning mother."[928] The effect on him was liberating:

> Now as I sat in the glow on a single light bulb, rocking slightly on a hard-backed chair, that image [of his father] had suddenly vanished. Replaced by . . . what? A bitter drunk? An abusive husband? A defeated, lonely bureaucrat? To think that all my life, I had been wrestling with nothing more than a ghost! For a moment, I felt giddy; if Auma hadn't been in the room, I would have probably laughed out loud. The king is overthrown, I thought. The emerald curtain is pulled aside. The rabble of my head is free to run riot; I can do what I damn well please. For what man, if not my own father, has the power to tell me otherwise? Whatever I do, it seems, I won't do much worse than he did.[929]

Why, in his autobiography, would Obama understate both his mother's intellectual distinction and the extent of his father's and even Lolo's violence?[930] Obama's autobiography is written very much as a struggle to find himself as a man of color whose black father was never much of a reality in his life. Calling his book *Dreams from My Father,* he frames his narrative in the patriarchal terms dominant in such narratives in our culture (men drawing their sense of ethical identity from their fathers). The truth of the matter is much more radical: it was his mother's care, joined by that of his grandparents and Lolo, who had nurtured his own ethical voice.

---

[927] See David Remnick, *The Bridge,* pp. 63, 246–7.

[928] David Remnick, *The Bridge,* p. 246.

[929] Barack Obama, *Dreams from My Father,* pp. 220–1.

[930] For evidence of Lolo's physical abuse of Obama's mother, see David Maraniss, *Barack Obama: The Story* (New York: Simon & Schuster, 2012), p. 243.

His ethical identity was forged in a remarkably honest and unidealized relationship to a mother whom he came to see both as a sexually loving woman (challenging the patriarchal love laws) and as an accomplished intellectual and feminist activist. The narrative of his autobiography really explodes the framework within which it is written, which is to say that it comes to see patriarchy as a lie: "The king is overthrown, I thought . . . I can do what I damn well please. For what man, if not my own father, has the power to tell me otherwise?"

Obama thus experienced at firsthand both his mother's resistance to the patriarchal love laws, and his father's lack of resistance, opening his heart and mind to what makes such resistance so liberatory yet so difficult and the lack of resistance sometimes so tragic. What such resistance makes psychologically possible is breaking through the ethnic and other stereotypes that divide us and keep us from loving another as an individual. It was in loving relationship to such a resisting woman (who loved his father as an individual) that Obama came to accord authority to her liberal and humane values, including the moral authority of women's voices and experiences. Obama dealt with the experience of loss—the loss of his father, the feeling of separation as a man of color from his white mother and grandparents—not through identification with patriarchal stereotypes of manhood but by staying in relationship to the real, individual people whom he loved and who loved him. Both his mother and Toot were strong, adventurous women, loving men while holding to their own ambitions and sense of themselves. (Toot earned more money than her husband.) Obama stayed in loving relationship to unidealized real women (including a mother, who did not sacrifice her sexual or her intellectual life) and an unidealized real man, Gramps, who showed his grandson a white man who resisted his grandmother's racist fears[931] and introduced him to a black poet who helped Obama think about and through these issues.[932]

Indeed, his mother, an anthropologist, may have imparted to her son an interpretive ability not to confuse culture and nature, and thus to be sensitive to the ways in which the power of patriarchy rests on this confusion. Through his mother and grandmother one suspects, Obama came to his own vibrant relationship with a strong woman, Michelle Obama, and subsequently with their two daughters. In *Dreams from My*

---

[931] See Barack Obama, *Dreams from My Father*, pp. 87–8.
[932] Barack Obama, *Dreams from My Father*, pp. 89–91.

Father, he identifies a "strong, true love" with an equal as what saves men from the "male cruelties" that destroyed his father.[933] In doing so, he shows us a manhood that is democratic, not patriarchal.

It is striking that, while describing his youth as "living out a caricature of black male adolescence, itself a caricature of swaggering American manhood,"[934] it is relationships to women who either challenge his quest for racial identity (Joyce by her search to be an individual[935]) or prod him (Regina) to greater honesty (using the name Barack, which is closer to his real roots, his Kenyan father)[936] or tongue lash him into a sense of larger ethical responsibility that transcends race.[937] While both Joyce and Regina are evidently fictionalized, the underlying experience they reflect is clearly not that of a patriarchal man who is not in this way moved by the authority of women's resisting ethical voices.[938] Its roots in Obama's life are clear. Obama writes that even when young and talking to black friends at "*white folks* this or *black folks* that, 'I would suddenly remember my mother's smile, and the words that I spoke would seem awkward and false.'"[939] One senses as well that when in New York, Obama faces the option of conventional upward mobility that so many others in his place took or would take. His choice to do community work in Chicago was very much in line with the ethical voice nourished by his remarkable mother.

It is this universalistic ethical sensitivity,[940] rooted in his mother's ethics of care, that can explain how and why it was that, for Obama,

[933] Barack Obama, *Dreams from My Father: A Story of Race and Inheritance* (New York: The Three Rivers Press, 2004), at p. 429.
[934] Barack Obama, *Dreams from My Father,* p. 79.
[935] Barack Obama, *Dreams from My Father,* pp. 98–100.
[936] Barack Obama, *Dreams from My Father,* pp. 102–5.
[937] Barack Obama, *Dreams from My Father,* pp. 107–10.
[938] On the fictionalization, see David Maraniss, *Barack Obama: The Story* (New York: Simon & Schuster, 2012), pp. 371–373. Maraniss's biography also makes clear what Obama's autobiography does not, namely, the several of his sexual relationships, prior to his marriage, were with highly intelligent, white women. See Id., p. 420 ff. In fact, one of these women trenchantly observed to Obama that she felt separated from him by "the veil," id., p. 481, and sensitively urged upon him "an absolute conviction that his future lay down the road with a black woman," quoted at id., p. 497.
[939] Barack Obama, *Dreams from My Father,* p. 81.
[940] On Obama's ethical universalism, see David Maraniss, op. cit., p. 453.

images of the civil rights movement, which predated him, "became a kind of prayer for me, bolstering my spirits, channeling my emotions in a way that words never could."[941] Obama's biracial background had led some American blacks who met him when he came to the mainland to study to refer to him as "an Oreo."[942] For Obama, his choice to identify as black was very much an ethical choice made in light of what the American civil rights movement had meant to his mother and came to mean to him. It is not just that his mother was so much an expression of the civil rights movement in breaking the racist love laws by marrying the black man she loved and giving birth to his son. It was also that Martin Luther King Jr., through his discovery and brilliant use of a militant nonviolent voice, had found a moving and powerful resisting ethical voice that spoke to and energized not only the people of color and others he led into nonviolent resistance but had appeal and moral force for Americans generally. King himself described the nonviolent ethical voice of his movement as "disarming the opponent,"[943] calling to a deeper level of shared humanity and appealing to a sense of guilt over the divisions racism had allowed and sustained.

If patriarchy, as we have observed, often supports itself through a sense of shame and violence keyed to any real or imagined transgression of the gender binary, such shame shows its power by the ways in which it wars on human rationality, and rationalizes atrocity, as it did in fascist Germany and Japan. American patriarchy had supported our racism for a very long time. What King discovered and brilliantly expressed, as the great ethical prophet and preacher he was, was a way through nonviolent voice to appeal to the underlying sense of guilt that many Americans in the South and elsewhere had felt as well. When King speaks of "disarming the opponent," he is quite precisely describing the process by which a free ethical voice resists and exposes the violence of white racist patriarchy by appealing to an ethical voice that patriarchy had silenced by shaming it as unmanly. King's voice achieved its universalistic ethical appeal because he appealed both to deeper ethical values that Americans shared (including those of their Judaeo-Christianity) and to the constitutional principles

---

[941] Barack Obama, *Dreams from My Father*, p. 134.

[942] See David Maraniss, op. cit., quoted at p. 375.

[943] See Martin Luther King Jr., *A Testament of Hope: The Essential Writings of Martin Luther King Jr.*, ed. James M. Washington (San Francisco: Harper & Row, 1986), at p. 102.

of free speech and equal protection they also held in common. Unlike Obama, King very much had a father who was in his life and a patriarchal father at that, but he bridled at many of his father's choices as a minister. Indeed, King found his ethical voice not in relationship to his father but in relationship to the nonviolent Christianity of his mother and grandmother and in his understanding of Niebuhr and Gandhi. His resistance found its most immediately appreciative audience among courageous black women— including the women who began the Montgomery bus boycott even before King appeared on the scene.[944] Obama's mother was, by contrast, spiritual, not religious in a sectarian sense but, broadly speaking, a person rooted in the universalism of the ethics of care. As Obama put it, "[L]ike most of my values, I learned about empathy from her."[945]

Both King and Obama, as moral and political leaders, exemplify men who achieve their transformative ethical voices as men because they embrace a feminism that challenges the harms the gender binary and hierarchy inflict of men as well as women. King's nonviolence had the appeal and resonance it did because it released in him and others an ethical voice that arose from breaking the patriarchal link that required men to take up arms against injustice. And it was the force of truth that had brought Obama to national attention, his vote against the Iraq War had set him apart from his competitors for the Democratic party's nomination, and he was a self-identified feminist married to Michelle, a strong and outspoken and truly liberated woman, as free to be mom-in-chief as she had been to be Barack's boss and a hospital administrator. By the end of his presidency, Obama had come out in support of gay marriage.

Manhood was what the 2016 election was about. Although this couldn't be said directly, it was obvious once it became clear that despite all their talk about replacing Obamacare, when it came right down to it, the Republicans had no health-care policy. It was Obama himself they were determined to replace. After comparing the background and manhood of Trump and Obama, we can see why Trump himself and the Republicans who supported him were so infuriated by Obama, whose background and achievements so clearly challenged the gender binary

---

[944] See, for fuller discussion, David A. J. Richards, *Disarming Manhood*, pp. 131–180.

[945] Barack Obama, *The Audacity of Hope: Thoughts on Reclaiming the American Dream* (New York: Three Rivers Press, 2006), p. 66.

and hierarchy that Trump and the Republicans had supposed to be in the nature of things. Obama's election and presidency show this supposition to be clearly false, and Trump's election and presidency show how far they had to go, abandoning traditional Republican values and policies, to reverse or try to reverse the progress that had been made. There are now decidedly two alternative conceptions of manhood now available to us, one patriarchal, the other democratic. The case for choosing the more democratic conception no longer appeals only to prophetic American novels, however, ethically compelling and psychologically profound, but it is now very much on offer to American men from the example of both Barack Obama and Martin Luther King Jr. It is now at the center of our highly polarized democratic politics, and American men now need to be very clear that there is indeed a choice before them, and the compelling grounds both of personal happiness as well as ethics and democracy for them to embrace the democratic model. What are those grounds?

Reframing Democracy: Freeing Democracy from Patriarchy
From *Scarlet Letter* (1850) to *Phantom Thread* (2017)

I have tried to show in this book that men, many of them American, have resisted patriarchy though finding an ethical voice grounded in democratic justice. And their resistance was an expression of that free and equal voice—a voice that patriarchy had violently repressed and marginalized as not human because feminine or gay. I have tried to show their road to resistance in terms of the traumatic initiation of boys into patriarchy enforcing on them the gender binary and hierarchy, thus denying the parts of themselves, sometimes their deepest love that is regarded as feminine or girly or gay. I know this experience at firsthand and have come to think my experience is broadly shared among American men, gay and straight. I formulated this experience in terms of a secret self, a part of oneself, one's psyche, of which one speaks to no one, including those one loves because they also are caught up in patriarchy and are its enforcers. The defensive response of boys under patriarchy is their sense of a secret self where they can protect those parts of themselves that patriarchy forbids, as I did as young gay man at age sixteen to eighteen and turned to artists who showed me I was not alone, but my experience was broadly shared, I have come to think.

I began with Hawthorne and Melville, two prophetic American novelists whose astonishing artistic voices spoke more deeply of what democracy required, though one of them, Hawthorne, gave voice to a woman (Hester Prynne) and the other, Melville, to the voices of gay boys and men. And they show us as well, as Hawthorne does in the creation of Dimmesdale and Chillingworth, how patriarchy harms men— dimming their intelligence and chilling their hearts. And I have shown how Dickens, a straight man, resisted in the same way to give voice to the ways patriarchy unjustly harmed the most vulnerable of boys and men or girls and women. And the three gay artists—Henry James, Santayana, and James Baldwin—resist patriarchy as well and also give voice to powerful ethical criticism of American homophobia (Santayana) and racism and homophobia (Baldwin) and James Joyce to the criticism of ethnic and religious nationalism and Mark Twain to the criticism of American racism and Philip Roth to the criticism of anti-Semitism. Such artists resisting patriarchal manhood, includes great American movie directors, John Ford and Clint Eastwood. Ford is of particular interest to my argument as his secret self (homosexuality) was, so I argue, the voice of resisting patriarchy that we find in his art. And both Martin Luther King Jr. and Barack Obama clearly exemplify how a straight black man came through a resistance to patriarchy inspired by their antipatriarchal mothers to achieve the moral and political voices that advanced justice in the United States. In all these cases, these men worked from their experience as boys and young men and tell us about their own initiations into patriarchy, the moral injuries they suffered, and how they came to resist. They found their ethical voices precisely because they resisted the gender binary and hierarchy that denigrated such voices. They show us how men can and do resist patriarchy and how they are better, more just, because of their resistance. By resistance, they became more human.

Both Ruth Benedict, a cultural anthropologist, and James Gilligan, a psychiatrist, come, through their own stories of resistance to patriarchy to give voice to pathbreaking insights into patriarchy. Benedict thus showed the connections of patriarchy to both fascism and racism, and Gilligan to the roots of violence and the injustice of American criminal injustice, both its overcriminalization and its retributive institutions—the death penalty, racialized mass incarceration, solitary confinement, and prisons in general.

As I come to the end of my argument, I want to contrast two remarkable works of art, the 1850 novel, *The Scarlet Letter,* with which I began my argument, and the 2017 movie, *The Phantom Thread*, written and directed by Paul Thomas Anderson. The novel and the movie are separated by 167 years, and yet they both seem to me intimately connected, continuing a conversation by two married straight men, married with children, about the moral injuries patriarchy inflicts on men and how, through the love of women who resist patriarchy, they can come to resist. It shows the continuing strength and force of patriarchy in ostensibly democratic cultures that, just as *The Oresteia* (458 BCE) still speaks to us about patriarchy hiding in democracy (see chapter 2), these works speak to us of the same continuing problem, which is all too contemporary.

The Phantom Thread is a departure both in style and content from Anderson's seven earlier full-length films. These include *Hard Eight* (1996), *Boogie Nights* (1997), *Magnolia* (1999), *Punch Drunk Love* (2002), *There Will Be Blood* (2007), *The Master* (2012), and *Inherent Vice* (2014).

Almost all these movies feature young men and sometimes women traumatized by some kind of family abuse or loss. In *Hard Eight*, a young man first appears as quite lost, and an older man, a gambler, takes him under his wing and becomes a father figure to him; one learns later that the gambler (divorced and separated from his own children) had killed the boy's father and has now come to love and protect the boy he so damaged. At the end of the movie, the older man expresses to the boy his love. (The boy weeps.) The boy knows nothing of the murder of his real father. (Indeed, the older man murders a man who threatens to tell the boy.) The older man is protecting the only love he has ever known from shaming humiliation.

In *Boogie Nights*, a young man, abusively rejected by his parents, becomes a porno star (the movie centers on his enormous penis, which one actually sees at the end of the movie) connected emotionally to a porno movie director and his porno star wife/partner (who regards the boy as "her baby," though she has lost custody of her actual child.) Both of whom later take the boy in after he has been rejected by everyone else.

In *Magnolia*, a dying man had abandoned his dying wife and left his young son to care for her, traumatizing the boy who becomes a popular advocate of male patriarchal privilege, in effect, becoming the father who traumatized him. This narrative is counterpointed to that of a young boy on a popular American show, pitching adults against children in answering questions. The boy is abusively treated by both his father who insists the boy to go on when he does not want to any longer, as well as by the audience and leader of the show who will not honor his desire no longer to be a performing dog. The leader of the show has sexually abused his daughter in the past and who is now a drug addict. The intergenerational transmission of trauma—fathers to sons or to daughters—is the subject of the movie.

In *Punch Drunk Love*, a rather lost young man, long bullied by his sisters as a fag, encounters a young attractive women who, inexplicably, falls passionately in love with him and saves him from himself.

In *There Will Be Blood*, the darkest of these mostly quite dark movies, the villain at its center, played by Daniel Day-Lewis, is in the oil business and uses a young boy as "his son" (in fact, an orphan) and develops a fraught homoerotic love-hate relationship to a fanatical young minister, whom he later kills. The movie is based on the novel *Oil* by Upton Sinclair and is Anderson's most extreme portrait of American toxic masculinity and its patriarchal violence. It is painful to watch.

The Master centers on a homoerotic relationship between two straight men—a young traumatized and possibly psychotic young man who had served in the Pacific War against Japan and a cult leader (modeled probably on Elron Hubbard). The young man violently defends the leader from any criticism, and the leader, though married to a cold Lady Macbeth–like wife, is emotionally wrapped up in the young man, sharing alcohol and rough housing, and is quite needy of and even tender with the young man, though eventually the young man leaves him for a woman (perhaps, forming his own cult with her and others).[946] It is Anderson's closest study of cult-like contemporary patriarchal religion, rigidly resting on a strictly observed gender binary and hierarchy that leaves the patriarchs emotionally hollow in their all their rigidly hierarchical relationships both to men and women and emotionally needy for some relationship on more free and equal terms (in this case, to another man).

And *Inherent Vice* (adapted from the novel by Thomas Pynchon) is a rather narratively opaque treatment of a drug-addled detective and his off again, on again relationship to a young woman, who engages the detective to save her wealthy lover from being declared insane by his wife, and the wealthy lover settles for life in a cult-like home (which may or may not be an asylum).

Phantom Thread is a striking departure from the line of Anderson's earlier films. It is the only one of them in which a woman is at the center

---

[946] I am indebted for this point to Donald Levy.

of the narrative, and indeed the narrative ultimately is told from her point of view. All the other movies are largely centered on men, relationships between either older men as patriarchs to younger men or fathers to sons, bound in what Anderson regards as cult-like priestly hierarchies. There are almost no women in Anderson's darkest movie, *There Will Be Blood*, and women in the other movies are quite damaged women (a call girl in *Hard Eight*, a porno star in *Magnolia*, a sexually abused drug-dependent young woman in *Magnolia*, the coldly controlling wife in *The Master*, and a drug-dependent young woman in *Inherent Vice*). Sometimes in these movies, women save damaged men (*Punch Drunk Love*) or apparently save them (*Magnolia*); but in the former, her love is almost inexplicable and, in the latter, at best promissory (suggesting at the end of *Magnolia* some hope in a despairing world in which, at the end, ghastly toads rain down on Los Angeles, as punishment for its evils of child intergenerational child abuse).

Some of these earlier movies are cinematically astonishing (*Magnolia* is as close to polyphonic moviemaking as anything I have seen), and quite disturbing explorations of the American patriarchal heart of darkness (whether ruthless capitalism in *There Will Be Blood* or the perversions of American religion into cults led by men in *The Master*).

Phantom Thread is by comparison quite narratively direct for its close focus really on the relationships among the brother, his sister, and his lover and later wife (Alma). Unlike all the other movies, there is a powerful and intelligent women telling her story, and the quite patriarchally damaged man, whom she comes to love, comes finally to respond to her love. It is a movie about the difficulties of straight men in forming and sustaining real relationships to women and the steps women take in forming and sustaining relationships with such men. It is a major advance in Anderson's artistic voice dealing with how patriarchy harms men, and it does so because it so clearly portrays the role women can play in bringing men into loving relationships.

The Scarlet Letter and *Phantom Thread* are in conversation because they deal with the same subject matter, a man, Dimmesdale in *The Scarlet Letter,* and another, Reynolds Woodcock in *Phantom Thread,* morally crippled in his capacity for love by their initiations into patriarchy—Dimmesdale as a Puritan minister to a Christianity still uncritically patriarchal and Reynolds a coldly disassociated London dressmaker obsessed by his now-dead mother whose image, as he tells us, haunts him every day and holds him in the rigidly defined rituals of personal and creative life that she taught him. (He learned dressmaking from her.) In effect, his intimate voice does not express itself in any real relationships but only to a ghost who haunts him. In both cases, women fall in love with these men and have sex with them, but the women—Hester Prynne in *The Scarlet Letter* and Alma Elson in *Phantom Thread*—see clearly how crippled both men are in their capacity to love them—Dimmesdale, because maintaining allegiance to a patriarchal faith that condemns all forms of adultery, abandons Hester and her child, who must cope alone with the moral condemnation of the Puritan community Dimmesdale leads as its minister; Woodcock, because he treats Alma as yet another in his succession of women whom he uses and then abandons. In both cases, the women ask themselves: How can I bring such a man, with a secret self of great tenderness, emotional and moral intelligence, to reveal his love?

Women under patriarchy are, as I earlier argued (chapter 2), in a position to see patriarchal demands not as nature but what is said to be nature, and thus to question and resist its demands when they impose a barrier to their love. Hester Prynne in the novel comes very far in her resistance, her penetrating moral and political intelligence questioning the inconsistencies in the Puritan democratic challenge to monarchical absolutism—its failure to challenge its own absolutism, including matters of sexual ethics. Hester's remarkable freedom of mind sets her apart from everyone else in her community; she is quite alone except for her young daughter, Pearl, the child of her secret relationship with Dimmesdale. While she almost persuades Dimmesdale to acknowledge and act on their love and leave the community, the forces of patriarchy in Dimmesdale's psyche are too strong, and he again abandons her and dies.

Alma lives in a much less patriarchal world. Woodcock's sister, Cyril, who works closely with her brother and sees his demands, likes her and joins with and help her to understand and negotiate her brother's world. Alma starts as a marginal woman—a waitress yet strikingly someone who from the start sees Woodcock and recognizes him as a "hungry boy." The very name, Reynolds Woodcock, is worthy of comment; it is notable that this rigid man is surrounded by women—his dead mother; his sister and business partner; his lover, who serve for a time as his muse, with Alma ultimately becoming his wife and his associate in designing dresses; and the women he dresses (the countesses, princesses, society women, etc.). There is, in contrast to Anderson's other movies, no other man in the movie, except for a doctor who becomes Alma's ally and the person to whom she tells the story. Woodcock tells us early in the movie about the superstition that touching a wedding dress means one will never marry; their nanny, whom he and his sister called Black Death, would not help the sixteen-year-old Woodcock make the dress for his mother's second wedding. Cyril is not married, and neither is Woodcock; the superstition supposedly working out its black magic. It is a mark of the power of Alma's love later in the movie that though she touches the princesses' wedding dress as does Woodcook, they fall in love and marry. The phantom label sewn into the dress says Uncursed. It is Alma also who insists the Woodcock break with his fawning subservience to the wealthy women he dresses, urging him to take back his dress from a drunken woman unworthy of his art. Woodcock's ghosts have been exorcised, and the ghost of Woodcock's mother disappears as Alma in fact cares for him. Superstition has given way to experience.

Woodcock's world is tightly controlled by rituals (any sounds made by others at breakfast so disturb him as to ruin his day). His dressmaking never varies, and toward the end of the film, we are told clients are abandoning him. When Alma disturbs his routine by arranging a dinner alone with him (his sister, knowing her brother, warns her this will end badly) and serving him asparagus with butter when Woodcock likes it with oil and salt, he becomes paranoid, accusing her of trying to kill him and displaying a rage she had not seen before. Alma also sees that his compulsive and controlling working habits are followed by a need for a respite, as when at the beginning of the film, we see him driving to the country where his sister has encouraged him to go. She recognizes that men as gifted and sensitive as Woodcock protect their secret self by controlling everyone with whom they work and adhering to rituals that no one is allowed to question or disturb. As in the Cupid and Psyche myth, Alma (whose name means soul, as does Psyche) sees what Woodcock hides and discovers that, in fact (like Cupid), he is not a monster; he is a man in thrall to his idealized dead mother but also a hungry (vulnerable) boy. In the myth, it is when Psyche approaches the sleeping Cupid with a lamp that she sees the beauty and vulnerability he had hidden).[947] Both at the beginning and end of the movie, Woodcock is a "hungry boy." The lamp for Alma is her observant

---

[947]   On the Cupid and Psyche myth and its psychological significance for ethical resistance to patriarchy, see Carol Gilligan, *The Birth of Pleasure*. I am indebted for the analogy to Cupid and Psyche to Donald Levy.

emotional intelligence. With her love for Woodcock, she has come to understand, as lovers do, the boy in the man or the girl in the woman. Alma sees that she must act alone and realizes that, to break through Woodcock's armor, she must force him to let go control. She does so by making him ill (by poisoning him, short of killing him) so that he will, as she tells him at the end of the movie, be on his back, tender, helpless, and emotionally open to her—so he will allow her to care for him. As she does, and then she wants him strong again.

Alma researches poisonous mushrooms, and we see her walking in the woods and discovering the one she is looking for. Her going into nature suggests her search for the human nature that has been blocked by the culture that Woodcock embraced. As Alma comes to care for him in his illness, the image of Woodcock's dead mother, whom the movie had shown standing in Woodcock's bedroom in the wedding dress he made for her marriage to her second husband, disappears; the phantom thread to patriarchy has been cut. Woodcock falls in love with Alma, and they marry (Woodcock had earlier said he was a confirmed bachelor and would never marry), yet Woodcock still fails to acknowledge or encompass within himself her desire to play and for a life outside Woodcock's routines. (On New Year's Eve when he wants to work, she wants to go to an artists' ball.)

Thus she goes back into the woods again and we watch her gather the mushroom, administering it yet again, but now with Woodcock fully aware of what she is doing and why. It is significant that the antidote to Woodcock's toxic masculinity is itself a toxin, a poisonous mushroom. In the final scene, Reynolds watches Alma preparing the mushroom omelet and silently assents to it—he knows exactly what he is doing in taking the bite of that omelet: what he say is: "Kiss me before I get sick." The relationship is clearly consensual. Alma holds him in her arms, and then summons the attentive young doctor, allowing him to examine Woodcock to ensure that the poison will stay within viable bounds. It is Cyril who first brings in the doctor, who then becomes the person to whom Alma tells the story (her conversations with the doctor about her relationship with Reynolds begin and end the movie, and we realize that Anderson is telling this story from her point of view). Alma also makes a dress of which Woodcock's client approves, and is seen at the end working with him, becoming herself a couturier, something previously unthinkable. At the end of the movie, the couple are portrayed as having had a child, with the sister acting as a kind of godmother and the new family encompassing Alma's desire for fun as well as Reynold's passion for his work.

The role of Woodcock's sister, Cyril, in the narrative is important, as she comes to welcome Alma's joining her in taking care of her brother, who refers to his sister as "my so and so." We witness the growing alliance between women overcoming their initial suspicions; both of them love Reynolds, and in the end, they help one another in freeing him. The relationship of brother and sister has been important in my own life, but the movie shows something rarely disclosed, let alone talked about, namely, how difficult and powerful these relationships can be when both brother and sister come to choose forms of personal life, sometimes under the impact of love previously unimaginable that resist patriarchal conventions, in my own case and especially for my sister, at some personal cost. The sense of a common resistance and its benefits and costs, in a culture still highly patriarchal, deepens, if anything, such relationships, sustaining a relationship that remained vital even in the face of the losses and injuries patriarchy inflicts on those who resist. Care for the other, in light of this shared history, remains central for both brother and sister.

In a radio interview, Anderson explains that he and Daniel Day-Lewis, the actor who plays Woodcock, closely collaborated in making the movie. They are both straight men, married and with children, including sons. Their wives are from what we know about them, vibrant women; for example, Day-Lewis's wife is Rebecca Miller, an independent filmmaker and novelist who made a revelatory documentary of her father, the great American playwright Arthur Miller, "Arthur Miller: Artist" (2017). The documentary deals honestly with her father's three marriages, including the fraught second marriage to Marilyn Monroe, as well as his sometimes problematic relationships to his children (including a son with Down syndrome). Day-Lewis, as is his wont in preparing for the roles he takes on, studied the lives of designers and worked closely with the head of the costume department at New York City Ballet to learn the craft and the culture of dressmaking. Anderson says an experience of his inspired the movie, namely, when he fell ill with a bad flu, making it impossible for him to do what he usually did when ill, which was to "soldier through." This time he was so ill that he was on his back and needed his wife to care for him, and this led him to discover that such vulnerability nourished love. Of Alma's decision to use poison, Anderson said that Alma realized it would take "a gigantic and large act—big enough (for Reynolds) to feel dominated and cared about—that brings him back to his love for her." By being dominated, he means forced to let go of his need to be in control, to be the one who dominates others. Everyone in Woodcock's life is in his employ hierarchically, and he has no emotional room for anyone. Anderson cites the experience with his wife. It was only when he really needed her to take care of him that he could let her do so, and she told him, "I like you like this," and he thought, *Wouldn't it suit her to keep slowing me down for me not to be so compulsively busy?* For Anderson, Alma is the protagonist of the film; we are seeing the world through her eyes. The illness brought on by the mushroom is "creating an opening for women in his life to have him vulnerable and open."[948] Carol Gilligan calls such love of women for men "audacious love," a love which resists a gender hierarchy that harms both men and women and, though its very audacity, frees love.[949]

No one but two straight men, married and with children, could tell us what this movie tells us about the role women today play in new forms of love. I end with a discussion of *The Scarlet Letter* and *Phantom Thread* because these two works of art show how straight (and in both cases highly accomplished) men can and do come through the love of women to recognize how patriarchy morally injures them. These works also show us how difficult it is for men under patriarchy to resist its constrictions and what it takes for a woman to support their resistance. In both cases,

---

[948] See Terry Gross, "Oscar-Nominated *Phantom Thread*, Focuses on Fashion's Most Obsessive," interview of Paul Thomas Anderson, National Public Radio, January 23, 2018, https://www.npr.org/programs/fresh-air/2018/01/23/579990588/fresh-air-for-jan-23-2018-phantom-thread-director-paul-thomas. I am indebted to Carol Gilligan for bringing this interview to my attention and sharing with me her views on how to understand the movie and the interview. It was Carol who persuaded me that my initial distaste for the movie (I saw the movie long before she did) reflected more my own inexperience with straight relationships in marriage today than what the movie in fact shows about how far straight men as artists have come today in dealing with the continuing crippling role of patriarchal assumptions in heterosexual relationships. What I failed to see was the powerful voice of women in Anderson's narrative, quite unlike his previous movies. I only came to a sense of this when I studied Anderson's seven earlier movies in light of Carol's reading of *Phantom Thread*.

[949] See Carol Gilligan, "'In a Different Voice': Act II," *Los Angeles Review of Books*, at https://lareviewofbooks.org/article-in-a-different=voice-actII/

the cost to the men is the same: crippling their capacity to love, locking them in patriarchal rituals, which limit their creativity and constrain their ethical intelligence.

The argument of this book has now, I believe, shown the ethical and political harms to men whom patriarchy draws into supporting injustices including unjust wars and mass incarceration. Trump's election both confirms this dynamic and shows more starkly how patriarchy undermines and threatens American democracy. But the deeper harm is to men's capacity for love, which as *Phantom Thread* makes clear, is still very much with us 167 years after Hawthorne showed us this problem in American manhood in *The Scarlet Letter*. Hester Prynne very much walks among us, in larger numbers perhaps than ever before, hated and marginalized, as the election revealed, and Alma Elson is very much among us too, perceiving the injury men suffer and the need to resort to desperate remedies. The injury to personal love radiates out to the injury to empathize itself, as patriarchal men, notably Trump, create scapegoats and rationalize their religious intolerance, racism, sexism, and homophobia, along with the evils of caste and tribe.

We have already seen the part women can play in empowering men to resist patriarchy. We saw this in the role women, including his mother and grandmother, girlfriends and wife, played in Obama's resistance. And in our earlier discussion of the novels of Charles Dickens (chapter 3), Dickens shows us the crucial role of loving care for broken and ill men in bringing them back to life and love, including Betsey Trotwood's care of David in *David Copperfield*, as well as such care by men in Sam Weller of Mr. Pickwick in *Pickwick Papers*, Mark Tapley of Martin in *Martin Chuzzlewit*, perhaps most moving of all, Joe Gargery's care of Pip in *Great Expectations*.

There is hope surely in seeing how far Hawthorne and Anderson, straight men and artists, married with children, can come through the love of women resisting patriarchy—to see and acknowledge the crippling burdens the gender binary and hierarchy impose on men's psyches, disowning half of their humanity and thus living as half human, blind to what they have endured, and warring, as Trump wars, on challenges to patriarchy. There are more of these men today than ever before not enough, evidently, to defeat Trump but enough perhaps to tip the balance at this crucial moment in American history. The key to their doing so is, as Carol Gilligan and I argue in *Darkness Now Visible*, that they join women and gay men and others to see how the gender binary and hierarchy harm all of us and resist together. To do so, feminism must no longer be marginalized through the prism of patriarchy (as it was in Trump's politics), but it must be regarded as what it is, the most important emancipatory movement of our age to advance democratic equality in our personal and political lives. It has always been difficult for men under patriarchy to see feminism as it is, to see it not through a patriarchal lens but a democratic one. But the argument of this book shows that they can and have and are doing so. The groundswell of women's resistance in #MeToo and other resistance movements including as the initiators of Black Lives Matter is shifting tectonically our prism from patriarchy to democracy, and it is time for men in larger numbers to join that resistance.

We are indeed at a tipping point—a real choice between democracy and patriarchy. The choice after the election of 2016 could not be more evident or starker, as patriarchy under the pressure of this election came out of hiding and shamelessly displayed its populist appeal. Now that we see what the stakes are, our responsibilities of ethical resistance become more compelling than ever. And the heart of it is and must be resistance to patriarchy as a threat both to love and to democracy.

It is time now for American men across the gender spectrum to come forward and insist that patriarchy is not a marginal "feminist" issue of interest only to women and perhaps gay men but to all men, who are, I have come to think, patriarchy's most damaged victims and yet, paradoxically, remain among its advocates and enablers. Trump's victory makes this quite clear. Trump may himself be caught, even trapped, by the narcissism so central to his personality, but a man obsessed with winners cannot be expected easily to give up the strategy that elected him. That would require humility and self-knowledge and a lucid acceptance of one's own frailties, all of which Trump lacks. On the other hand, even he has sufficient improvisatory animal business intelligence not to regard a visibly self-destructive presidency—domestically and in foreign policy—as winning. That may be our best hope. We need, however, to ask ourselves as Americans how we can have come to the place we are at, and we have argued in this book what should unite us is that patriarchy now so visibly threatens our core democratic institutions and values. This book is written in part as a call to men to wake up.

My belief is that our psyches, even under the conditions of an American patriarchy now visible, are both alive and resilient, wanting to share with fellow citizens an honest sense of how we were drawn into complicity with

Trump and how we have come to resist. Resistance to Trump's victory shows that we have discovered in ourselves something both psychologically powerful and invisible, what Tolstoy found in himself and gave expression to in his portrayal of Karenin and what Tim O'Brien found in himself as, to his shame, he betrayed his conscience. What ethical courage for men like Tolstoy and O'Brien to come so far, discovering how their manhood had stood in the way of their humanity. Knowledge may lead to self-knowledge not only of our psyches but of our damaged and balkanized democracy, arising from our awareness of the endgame of patriarchy and what may be at hand, a community of free and equal people.

End of Text

BIBLIOGRAPHY

Ackroyd, Peter, Dickens (New York: HarperCollins, 1990).

Ackroyd, Peter, T.S. Eliot: a Life (New York: Simon and Schuster, 1984).

Adair, Douglass, Fame and the Founding Fathers (New York: Norton, 1974).

Aeschylus, The Oresteia translated by Robert Fagles (New York: Penguin, 1977).

Addams, Jane. Newer Ideals of Peace (Urbana: University of Illinois Press, 2007; originally published, 1906).

Adorno, Theodor W., Aesthetic Theory translated by Robert Hullot-Kentor (Minneapolis: University of Minnesota Press, 1997).

Adorno, Theodor W., Else Frenkel-Brunswick, Daniel J. Levinson and R. Nevitt Sanford, The Authoritarian Personality (New York: Harper & Row, 1950).

Adorno, Theodor W., Essays on Music (Berkeley: University of California Press, 2002).

Adorno, Theodor W., Minima Moralia: Reflections from a Damaged Life translated by E.F.N. Jephcott (London: Verso, 2005) (first published, 1951).

Adorno, Theodor W., Negative Dialectics translated by E.B. Ashton (New York: Continuum, 2007) (first published, 1966).

Allison, Graham. Destined for War (New York: Houghton Mifflin Harcourt, 2017).

Altemeyer, Bob, The Authoritarian Specter (Cambridge, Mass.: Harvard University Press, 1996).

Altemeyer, Bob, Rights-Wing Authoritarianism (Manitoba, Canada: The University of Manitoba Press, 1981).

Anesko, Michael Monopolizing the Master: Henry James and the Politics of Modern Literary Scholarship (Stanford: Stanford University Press, 2012).

Arendt, Hannah, The Origins of Totalitarianism (Orlando: A Harvest Book, 1976) (originally published 1950).

Auerbach, Erich, Mimesis: The Representation of Reality in Western Literature (Princeton: Princeton University Press, 2013).

Bailyn, Bernard, The Ideological Origins of theAmerican Revolution (Cambridge, Mass.: Harvard University Press, 1967).

Baldwin, James, Another Country (New York: Vintage International, 1990) (originally published, 1960).

Baldwin, James, Blues for Mister Charlie (New York: Vintage International, 1992).

Baldwin, James, Collected Essays edited by Toni Morrison (New York: The Library of America, 1998).

Baldwin, James, Early Novels and Stories Toni Morrison, ed. (New York: The Library of America, 1998).

Baldwin, James, Little Man Little Man: a Story of Childhood, written by James Baldwin and illustrated by Yoran Cazac (New York: The Dial Press, 1976).

Baldwin, James, Tell Me How Long the Train's Been Gone (New York: Dell, 1968).

Baldwin, James, The Amen Corner (New York: Vintage International, 1996).

Banner, Lois W., Intertwined Lives: Margaret Mead, Ruth Benedict, and Their Circle (New York: Vintage Books, 2003.

Banville, John, Mrs. Osmond (New York: Alfred A. Knopf, 2017).

Baradarajan, Tunku. "The Weekend Interview with Harvey Mansfield, Manhood in the Age of Trump," The Wall Street Journal, Saturday/ Sunday March 31-April 1, 2018, A13.

Barbu, Zevedei, Problems of Historical Psychology (New York: Grove Press, 1960).

Beckett, Samuel. Endgame (New York; Grove Press, 1958).

Bederman, Gail, Manliness and Civilization (Chicago: University of Chicago Press, 1995).

Benedict, Ruth, Patterns of Culture (Boston: A Mariner Book, 2005) (first published, 1934).

Benedict, Ruth, The Chrysanthemum and the Sword: Patterns of Japanese Culture (Boston: A Mariner Book, 2005) (first published, 1946).

Bethke Elshtain, Jean, Jane Addams and the Dream of American Democracy (New York: Basic Books, 2002).

Blechner, Mark J., Sex Changes: Transformations in Society and Psychoanalysis (New York: Routledge, 2009).

Blight, David W., Race and Reunion: The Civil War in American History (Cambridge, Mass.: Belknap Press of Harvard University Press, 2001).

Blumstein, Alfred et al., Deterrence and Incapacitation: Estimating the Effects of Criminal Sanctions on Crime Rates (ashington, D.C.: National Academy of Sciences, 1978).

Bourne, Randolph, The Radical Will: Selected Writings 1911-1918 Olaf Hansen, ed. (Berkeley: University of California Press, 1977; first published, 1916).

Bowers, Ron, Mark Twain: a Life (New York: Free Press, 2005).

Bowles, Nellie "The Prophet of the Patriarchs: If an overdose of female is our poison, Jordan Peterson preaches a masculine cure," New York Times, May 20, 2018, SundayStyles, pp. 1, 7,

Branum, Guy. "My Gay Voice," The New York Times, Sunday, July 29, 2018, p. SR7.

Braxton, Joanne M. and Maria I. Dierich, eds., Monuments of the Black Atlantic: Slavery and Memory (Munster: Lit Verlag, 2004).

Branch, Taylor, Parting the Waters: Martin Luther King and the Civil Rights Movement 1954-63 (London: Papermac, 1988).

Branch, Taylor, Pillar of Fire: America in the King Years 1963-65 (New York: Simon & Schuster, 1998).

Britten, Benjamin, War Requiem, Benjamin Britten conducting, on the London label, and available on CD, recorded in Kingsway Hall, London, January 1963.

Brooks, Peter, Henry James Goes to Paris (Princeton: Prince University Press, 2007).

Broyard, Bliss, One Drop: My Father's Hidden Life—a Story of Race and Family Secrets (New York: Back Bay Books, 2007).

Buruma, Ian The Wages of Guilt: Memories of War in Germany and Japan (New York: New York Review Book, 2015; originally published, 1994).

Carpenter, Humphrey, Benjamin Britten: a Biography (New York: Charles Scribner's Sons, 1992).

Caro, Robert A., The Years of Lyndon Johnson: The Passage of Power (New York: Vintage Books, 2012).

Carroll, James. An American Requiem: God, My Father, and the War that Came Between Us (Boston: Houghton Mifflin, 1996).

Carroll, James. Constantine's Sword: The Church and the Jews: A History (Boston: Houghton Mifflin, 2001).

Chapman, A.H., Harry Stack Sullivan: The Man and His Work (New York: G.P. Putnam's Sons, 1976).

Chu, Judy Y., When Boys Become Boys: Development, Relationships, and Masculinity (New York: New York University Press, 2014).

Collier-Thomas, Bettye and V.P. Franklin, eds., Sisters in the Struggle: African American Women in the Civil Rights-Black Power Movement (New York: New York University Press, 2001).

Conrad, Joseph, The Secret Sharer in Joseph Conrad, Heart of Darkness and The Secret Sharer (New York: Bantam Dell, 2004).

Cornell, Drucilla. Clint Eastwood and Issues of American Masculinity (New York: Fordham University Press, 2009).

Crain, Caleb. American Sympathy: Men, Friendship and Literature in the New Nation (New Haven: Yale University Press, 2001).

Crawford, Vicki L., Jacqueline Anne Rouse, and Barbara Woods, eds., Women in the Civil Rights Movement (Bloomington: Indiana University Press, 1993).

Creech, James. Closet Writing/Gay Readings (Chicago: University of Chicago Press, 1993).

Cronin, Brenda "Did Illicit Love Float 'Moby-Dick'?", The Wall Street Journal, Friday, May 27, 2016, at D3.

D'Antonio, Michael, The Truth About Trump (New York: Thomas Dunne Books, 2016).

Davis, Philip, The Transferred Life of George Eliot (Oxford: Oxford University Press, 2017).

Dassow Walls, Laura, Henry David Thoreau: A Life (Chicago: University of Chicago Press, 2017).

Dean, Michelle, Sharp: The Women Who Made an Art of Having an Opinion (New York: Grove Press, 2018)

De La Boetie, Etienne, Anti-Dictator translated by Harry Kurz (Mansfield Centre, Ct.: Martino Publishing, 2016).

Delbanco, Andrew. Melville: His World and Work (New York: Alfred A. Knopf, 2005).

Dickens, Charle, Barnaby Rudge edited by John Bowen (London: Penguin, 2003).

Dickens, Charles, Bleak House edited by Nicola Bradbury (London: Penguin, 1996).

Dickens, Charles, David Copperfield rev. ed. edited by Jeremy Tambling (London: Penguin, 2004) (first published, 1850).

Dickens, Charles, Dombey and Son edited by Andrew Sanders (Penguin: London, 2003).

Dickens, Charles, Hard Times edited by Kate Flint (London: Penguin, 2003) (first published, 1854).

Dickens, Charles, Great Expectations edited by Charlotte Mitchell (London: Penguin, 2003) (first published, 1860-61).

Dickens, Charles, Little Dorrit edited by Stephen Wall and Ellen Small (London: Penguin, 2003).

Dickens, Charles Martin Chuzzlewit edited by Patricia Ingham (London: Penguin, 1999) (first published, 1843-44).

Dickens, Charles, Nicholas Nickleby edited by Mark Ford (London: Penguin, 2003) (first published, 1839).

Dickens, Charles, Oliver Twist edited by Philip Horne (London: Penguin, 2002).

Dickens, Charles, Our Mutual Friend edited by Adrian Poole (London: Penguin, 1997).

Dickens, Charles, Pickwick Papers edited by Mark Wormald (London: Penguin, 2003) (first published, 1836-37).

Dickens, Charles, The Old Curiosity Shop edited by Norman Page (London: Penguin, 2000).

Dodds, E.R., The Greeks and the Irrational (Berkeley: University of California Press, 1959).

Douthat, Ross "God and Men and Jordan Peterson," The New York Times, Sunday, April 1, 2018, SR9

Duff, R.A., Punishment, Communication, and Community (Oxford: Oxford University Press, 2001).

Dunham, S. Ann, Surviving against the Odds: Village Industry in Indonesia edited by Aice G. Dewey and Nancy I Cooper (Durhan, N.C.: Duke University Press, 2009).

Edel, Leon, Henry James: The Untried Years: 1843-1870 (New York: Avon, 1953).

Edel, Leon, Henry James: The Conquest of London: 1870-1881 (New York: Avon, 1962).

Edel, Leon, Henry James: The Middle Years: 1882-1895 (New York: Avon 1962).

Edel, Leon, Henry James: The Treacherous Years: 1895-1901 (New York: Avon, 1969).

Edel, Leon, Henry James: The Master: 1901-1916 (New York: Avon, 1972).

Edgerton, Samuel Y. Jr., Pictures and Punishment: Art and Criminal Prosecution during the Florentin Renaissance (Ithaca: Cornell University Press, 1985).

Eliot, T.S., Collected Poems 1909-1962 (Orlando: Harcourt, 1968).

Eliot, T.S., his unpublished 1935 lecture, "The Christian in the Modern World," published as "Outside the catacombs," in The Times Literary Supplement, July 7, 2017, No. 5962, at pp. 16-18.

Eliot, T.S., After Strange Gods: A Primer of Modern Heresy (London: Faber and Faber, 1934).

Ellenberger, Henry F. The Discovery of the Unconscious: The History and Evolution of Dynamic Psychiatry (New York: BasicBooks, 1970).

Ellmann, Richard, James Joyce rev. ed. (Oxford: Oxford University Press, 1983).

Erasmus, Praise of Folly Betty Radice translation (London: Penguin, 1993).

Eribon, Didier, Insult and the Making of the Gay Self translated by Michael Lucey (Durhajm: Duke University Press, 2004).

Evans, Sara, Personal Politics: The Roots of Women's Liberation in the Civil Rights Movement and the New Left (New York: Vintage Books, 1980).

Farley, Margaret A., Just Love: A Framework fo Christian Sexual Ethics (New York: Continuum, 2006).

Faulkner, William, Novels 1936-1940 edited by Joseph Blotner, Noel Polk (New York: The Library of America, 1990; originally published, 1936).

Faulkner, William, Novels 1942-1954 edited by Joseph Blotner and Noel Polk (New York: The Library of America,1994).

Ferejohn, John and Frances McCall Rosenbluth, Forged Through Fire: War, Peace, and the Democratic Bargain (New York: Liveright, 2017).

Ferguson, Robert A., Inferno: An Anatomy of American Punishment (Cambridge, Mass.: Harvard University Press, 2014).

Fiedler, Leslie, "Come Back to the Raft Ag'in, Huck Honey," in A New Fiedler Reader (Amherst, N.Y.: Prometheus, 1999).

Fiedler, Leslie, Love and Death in the American Novel (New York: Criterion Books, 1960).

Fonagy, Peter Gyorgy Gergely, Elliot L. Jurist, Mary Target, Affect Regulation, Mentalization, and the Development of the Self (New York: Other Press, 2004).

Forman, Jr., James, Locking Up Our Own: Crime and Punishment in Black America (New York: Farrar, Straus and Giroux, 2017).

Foucault, Michel, Discipline and Punish: The Birth of the Prison System translated by Alan Sheridan (New York: Vintage Books, 1977).

Frame, Donald M. translator, The Complete Essays of Montaigne (Stanford: Stanford University Press, 1965).

Fromm, Erich, Escape From Freedom (New York: Henry Holt, 1965; first published, 1941).

Fussell, Paul, The Great War and Modern Memory (New York: Oxford Univeristy Press, 2000; originally published, 1975).

Garland, David, Peculiar Institution: America's Death Penalty in an Age of Abolition (Cambridge, Mass.: The Belknap Press of Harvard University Press, 2010).

Gay, Peter, Modernism: The Lure of Heresy From Baudelaire to Beckett and Beyond (New York: W.W. Norton, 2008).

Genesis 2:19, The New English Bible (Cambridge: Cambridge University Press, 1972).

Giddings, Paula, When and Where I Enter..The Impact of Black Woman on Race and Sex in America (New York: William Morrow and Company, 1984).

Gide, Andre, Corydon translated by Richard Howard (New York: Farrar, Straus Giroux, 1983) (original French edition, 1983).

Gide, Andre. Madeleine translated by Justin O'Brien (Chicago: Elephant Paperbacks, 1952).

Gilligan, Gilligan. "In a Different Voice': Act II," Los Angeles Review of Books, at https:// lareviewofbooks.org/article-in-a-different=voice-actII/

Gilligan, Carol, "Moral Injury and the Ethic of Care: Reframing the Conversation about Differences," Journal of Social Philosophy Vol. 45 No.1, Spring 2014, pp. 89-106.

Gilligan, Carol, The Birth of Pleasure: A New Map of Love (New York: Vintage, 2003).

Gilligan, Carol, Janie Victoria Ward, and Jill McLean Taylor, eds., Mapping the Moral Domain: A Contribution of Women's Thinking to Psychological Theory and Education (Cambridge, Mass.: Harvard University Press, 1988).

Gilligan, Carol, Nona Plessner Lyons, and Trudy Hanmer, eds., Making Connections: The Relational Worlds of Adolescent Girls at Emma Willard School (Cambridge, Mass.: Harvard University Press, 1990).

Gilligan, Carol, Annie G. Rogers, and Deborah Tolman (Eds.), Women, Girls, and Psychotherapy: Reframing Resistance (Haworth Press, 1991).

Gilligan, Carol and David A.J. Richards, Darkness Now Visible: Patriarchy's Resurgence and Feminist Resistance (Cambridge: Cambridge University Press, 2018).

Gilligan, Carol and David A.J Richards, The Deepening Darkness: Patriarchy, Resistance, and Democracy's Future (Cambridge: Cambridge University Press, 2009).

Gilligan, Carol and David A.J. Richards, The Deepening Darkness: Patriarchy's Resurgence and Feminist Resistance (Cambridge: Cambridge University Press, 2018).

Gilligan, Carol and Naomi Snider, Why Does Patriarchy Persist? (Cambridge, U.K.: Polity, 2018).

Gilligan, Carol and Naomi Snider, "The Loss of Pleasure, or Why We are Still Talking about Oedipus," Contemporary Psychoanalysis, 2017, Vol. 53, No. 2: 173-195.

Gilligan, James, Preventing Violence (New York: Thames & Hudson, 2001).

Gilligan, James, "Shame, Guilt, and Violence," Social Research Vol. 70 No. 4, 2003, pp. 1149-1140.

Gilligan, James, Violence: Reflections on a National Epidemic (New York: Vintage, 1997).

Gilligan, James, Violence in California Prisons: A Proposal for Research into Patterns and Cures (Sacramento: Diane Publishing Co. 2000, edited with an introduction by California State Senator Tom Hayden).

Gilligan, James, Why Some Politicians Are More Dangerous Than Others (Cambridge, U.K.: Polity, 2011).

Gilligan, James and Bandy Lee, "Beyond the Prison Paradigm: From Provoking Violence to Preventing It by Creating 'Anti-Prisons' (Residential Colleges and Therapeutic Communities", Ann. N.Y. Acad. Sci. 1036: 300-324 (2004).

Gilligan, James, "Terrorism, Nihilism, and Modernity: Analyzing the Dilemmas of Modernity," in Henri Parens and Stuart Twemlow, eds., The Future of Prejudice: Applications of Psychoanlaytic Understanding toward its Prevention (Lanham, Md.: Rowman & Littlefied, 2006), pp. 37-62.

Gilmore, David D. Manhood in the Making: Cultural Concepts of Masculinity (New Haven, Conn.: Yale University Press, 1990).

Gilmore, Michael T., "'Speak man!' Billy Budd in the Crucible of Reconstruction," American Literary History, Volume 21, Number 3, Fall 2009, pp. 492-517.

Goldberg, Michelle. "How the Online Left Fuels the Right," The New York Times, Sunday, May 13, 2018, p. SR11.

Goldsworthy, Adrian Pax Romana: War, Peace and Conquest in the Roman World (New Haven: Yale University Press, 2016).

Gombrich, Richard. What the Buddha Thought (London: Equinox, 2009).

Gorra, Michael, Portrait of a Novel: Henry James and the Making of an American Masterpiece (New York: Liverwright, 2012).

Greenblatt, Stephen and Peter G. Platt, <u>Shakespeare's Montaigne: The Florio Translation of the Essays: A Selection</u> (New York: New York Review Books, 2014).

Gross, Terry. "Oscar-Nominated 'Phantom Thread,' Focuses on Fashion's 'Most Obsessive,'" interview of Paul Thomas Anderson, National Public Radio, January 23, 2018, https://www.npr.org/programs/fresh-air/2018/01/23/579990588/fresh-air-for-jan-23-2018-phantom-thread-director-paul-thomas...

Grossman, Lt. Col. Dave, <u>On Killing: The Psychological Cost of Learning to Kill in War and Society</u> rev. ed. (New York: Back Bay Books, 2009; first published, 1995).

Haight, Roger. <u>Jesus: Symbol of God</u> (Maryknoll, N.Y.: Orbis, 2000).

Halberstam, David, <u>The Best and the Brightest</u> (New York: A Fawcett Book, 1992, originally published, 1969).

Haney, Craig and Philip Zimbardo, "The Past and Future of U.S. Prison Policy Twenty-Five Years After the Stanford Prison Experiment," <u>American Psychologist,</u> July 1998, vol. 53, no. 7, pp. 709-727.

Harris, Mark, <u>Five Came Back: A Story of Hollywood and the Second World War</u> (New York: Penguin, 2014).

Hart, H.L.A., <u>Punishment and Responsibility: Essays in the Philosophy of Law</u> Second Edition (Oxford: Oxford University Press, 2008).

Hartley, Jenny, <u>Charles Dickens: An Introduction</u> (Oxford: Oxford University Press, 2016).

Hazony, Yoram "Jordan Peterson and Conservatism's Rebirth," <u>The Wall Street Journal,</u> Saturday/Sunday, June 16-17, 2018, A13.

Hawthorne, Nathaniel. <u>The Scarlet Letter</u> (New York: Penguin, 1986).

Hawthorne, Nathaniel, Collected Novels (New York: The Library of America, 1983).

Hayford, Harrison editor, Herman Melville (New York: The Library of America, 1984).

Hedges, Chris, The Empire of Illusion: The End of Literacy and the Triumph of Spectacle (New York: Nation Books, 2009).

Hedges, Chris, War Is a Force that Gives Us Meaning (New York: Public Affairs, 2014, first published, 2002).

Herman, Judith Trauma and Recovery (New York: Basic Books, 1997).

Higgins, Charlotte. "The Guardian: The age of patriarchy: how an unfashionable idea became a rallying cry for feminism today," https://www.theguardian.com/news/2018/jun/22/the-age-of patriarchy-...le-idea-became-a rally-cry=for-feminism-tday?CMP+share_btn_link

Hirsch, Andrew von, Doing Justice: The Choice of Punishments (New York: Hill and Wang, 1976).

Hirsch, Andrew von, Censure and Sanctions (Oxford: Oxford University Press, 2003).

Hirsch, Andrew von, Past or Future Crimes: Deservedness and Dangerousness in the Sentencing of Criminals (Manchester: Manchester University Press, 1986).

Hoganson, Kristin L., Fighting for American Manhood: How Gender Politics Provoked the Spanish-American and Philippine-American Wars (New Haven: Yale University Press, 1998).

Hunsberger, Bruce E. and Bob Altemeyer, Atheists: A Groundbreaking Study of America's Nonbelievers (Amherst, New York: Prometheus Books, 2006).

Husak, Douglas N., Drugs and Rights (Cambridge, U.K.: Cambridge University Press, 1992).

Husak, Douglas N., Legalize this! The case for decriminalizing drugs (London: Verso, 2002).

Husak, Douglas N., Overcriminalization: The Limits of the Criminal Law (Oxford: Oxford University Press, 2008).

James, Henry, Autobiographies Philip Horne, editor (New York: The Library of America, 2016).

James, Henry, Complete Stories 1874-1884 William I. Vance, ed. (New York: The Library of America, 1990).

James, Henry, Complete Stories 1892-1898 David Bromwich and John Hollander, eds. (New York: The Library of America, 1996).

James, Henry, Literary Criticism Leon Edel, ed. (New York: The Library of America, 1984).

James, Henry, Novels 1880-1890 Daniel Mark Fogel, ed. (New York: The Library of America, 1989).

James, Henry, Novels 1881-1886 William T. Stafford, ed. (New York: The Library of America, 1985).

James, Henry, Novels 1896-1899 Myra Jehlen, ed. (New York: The Library of America, 2003).

James, Henry, Novels 1903-1911 Ross Posnock, ed. (New York: The Library of America, 2010).

James, Henry, Sr., The Nature of Evil: Considers in a Letter to the Rev. Edward Beecher, D.D. (New York: D. Appleton and Company, 1855).

James, Henry, Sr., <u>Substance and Shadow: Or, Morality and Religion in Their Relation to Life: An Essay Upon the Physics of Creation</u> (Boston: Ticknor and Fields, 1863).

James, William, <u>Writings 1902-1910</u> (New York: The Library of America, 1987).

James, William, <u>Writings 1878-1899</u> (New York: The Library of America, 1992).

James, William, <u>The Literary Remains of the Late Henry James</u> (Boston: James R. Osgood and Company, 1885).

James, William, <u>The Principles of Psychology</u> Vol. One (New York: Dover, 2015; originally published, 1890).

Jay, Martin, <u>Adorno</u> (Cambridge: Harvard University Press, 1984).

Jay, Martin, <u>The Dialectical Imagination: A History of the Frankfurt School and the Institute of Social Research, 1923-1950</u> (Berkeley: University of California Press, 1996) (first published, 1973).

Jay, Martin, <u>Reason After Its Eclipse: On Late Critical Theory</u> (Madison: University of Wisconsin Press, 2016).

Johnson, Edgar, <u>Charles Dickens: His Tragedy and Triumph</u> Volume Two (New York: Simon and Schuster, 1952).

Johnston, David Cay, <u>The Making of Donald Trump</u> (Brooklyn: Melville House, 2016).

Joyce, James, <u>A Portrait of the Artist as a Young Man</u> (New York: Penguin, 1992; first published, 1916).

Jozef Perelberg, Rosine ed., <u>Psychoanalytic Understanding of Violence and Suicide</u> (London: Routledge, 1999).

Julius, Anthony, Trials of the Diaspora: A History of Anti-Semitism in England (Oxford: Oxford University Press, 2010).

Julius, Anthony, T.S. Eliot, Anti-Semitism and Literary Form (Cambridge: Cambridge University Press, 1995).

Junger, Sebastian, Tribe: On Homecoming and Belonging (New York: Twelve, 2016).

Junger, Sebastian, War (New York: Twelve, 2010).

Kaiser, Walter Praisers of Folly (Cambridge, Mass.: Harvard University Pres, 1963).

Kakutani, Michiko, "When History Repeats," The New York Times, Sunday, July 15, 2018, SR 1, 4-5, at pp. 1 and 4.

Kant, Immanuel, Practical Philosophy translated and edited by Mary J. Gregor (Cambridge: Cambridge University Press, 1999).

Kazin, Michael, War Against War: The American Fight for Peace 1914-1918 (New York: Simon & Schuster, 2017).

Kenner, Hugh, The Pound Era (Berkeley: University of California Press, 1971).

Kenner, Hugh The Poems of Ezra Pound (Lincoln: University of Nebraska Press, 1985).

Kerlikowske, G., 2009 interview of John Erhlichman by G. Kerlikowske, heard in the documentary movie, 13th, directed by Ava DuVernay (2016).

Keynes, John Maynard, The Economic Consequences of the Peace (available at ReadaClassic.com 2010, originally published 1919).

Kildea, Paul. Benjamin Britten: A Life in the Twentieth Century (London: Allen Lane, 2013).

King, Jr.,Martin Luther, A Testament of Hope: The Essential Writings of Martin Luther King, Jr., edited by James M. Washington (San Francisco: Harper & Row, 1986).

Kinzer, Stephen, The True Flag: Theodore Roosevelt, Mark Twain, and the Birth of American Empire (New York: Henry Holt, 2017).

Kipling, Rudyard, The Collected Poems of Rudyard Kipling (London: Wordsworth, 1994).

Kipling, Rudyard, Something of Myself and Other Autobiographical Writings (Cambridge: Cambridge University Press, 2013).

Kohut, Heinz, The Analysis of the Self: A Systematic Approach to the Psychoanalytic Treatment of the Personality Disorders (Chicago: University of Chicago Press, 2009, originally published, 1971).

Kohut, Heinz The Restoration of the Self (New York: International Universities Press, 1977).

Kott, Jan. Shakespeare Our Contemporary translated by Boleslaw Taborski (New York: W.W. Norton, 1974).

Kramer, Matthew H., The Ethics of Capital Punishment: A Philosophical Investigation of Evil and Its Consequences (Cambridge, U.K.: Cambridge University Press, 2011).

Kranish, Michael and Marc Fisher, Trump Revealed: The Definitive Biography of the 45th President (New Yorik: Scribner, 2016).

Lawrence v. Texas 539 U.S. 558 (2003)

Lee, Bandy, The Dangerous Case of Donald Trump: 27 Psychiatrists and Mental Health Experts Assess a President (New York: A Thomas Dunne Book, 2017).

Leeming, David. James Baldwin: A Biography (New York: Knopf, 1994).

Levine, Robert S. and Samuel Otter, eds., <u>Frederick Douglass and Herman Melville: Essays in Relation</u> (Chapel Hill: The University of North Carolina Press, 2008).

Levmore, Saul and Martha C. Nussbaum, <u>American Guy: Masculinity in American Law and Literature</u> (Oxford: Oxford University Press, 2014).

Levy, Donald, <u>Freud Among the Philosophers: The Psychoanalytic Unconscious and Its Philosophical Critics</u> (New Haven: Yale University Press, 1996).

Lewis, Helen B. <u>Shame and Guilt in Neurosis</u> (New York: International Universities Press, 1971).

Lewis, R.W.B., <u>Edith Wharton: A Biography</u> (New York: Fromm International, 1985).

Lewis, Rhodri, <u>Hamlet and the Vision of Darkness</u> (Princeton: Princeton University Press, 2017).

Ling, Peter J. and Sharon Monteith, <u>Gender in the Civil Rights Movement</u> (New York: Garland Publishing, 1999).

Lippke, Richard L., <u>Rethinking Imprisonment</u> (Oxford: Oxford University Press, 2007).

<u>Loving v. Virginia</u>, 388 U.S. 1 (1967).

Manne, Kate "Reconsider the lobster: Jordan Peterson's failed antidote for 'toxic masculine despair," <u>The Times Literary Supplement,</u> May 25, 2018.

Manne, Kate, <u>Down Girls: The Logic of Misogyny</u> (New York: Oxford University Press, 2018).

Mansfield, Harvey C. <u>Manliness</u> (New Haven: Yale University Press, 2006).

Maraniss, David. <u>Barack Obama: The Story</u> (New York: Simon & Schuster, 2012).

Marcus, Steven <u>Dickens: From Pickwick to Dombey</u> (New York: W.W. Norton, 1986).

Marlantes, Karl. "The Bloody Pivot: Twenty-four days of nonstop urban battle that turned the tables in Vietnam," <u>The Wall Street Journal</u> Saturday/Sunday, June 3-4, 2017, C5,C6, at C6, reviewing Mark Bowden, <u>Hue 1968</u> (New York: Atlantic Monthly Press, 2017).

Martin, Robert K., <u>Hero, Captain, and Stranger: Male Friendship, Social Critique, and Literary Form in the Sea Novels of Herman Melville</u> (Chapel Hill: The University of North Carolina Press, 1986).

Massing, Michael, <u>Fatal Discort: Erasmus, Luther, and the Fight for the Western Mind</u> (New York: Harper, 2018).

McCarter, Jeremy, <u>Young Radicals: In the War for American Ideals</u> (New York: Random House, 2017).

McBride, Joseph. <u>Searching for John Ford</u> (Jackson: University Press of Mississippi, 2011).

McCarter, Jeremy. <u>Young Radicals: In the War for American Ideals</u> (New York: Random House, 2017).

McCormick, John <u>George Santayana: A Biography</u> (New Brunswick: Transaction, 2008).

McLean Taylor, Jill, Carol Gilligan, and Amy Sullivan, <u>Between Voice and Silence: Women and Girls, Race and Relationship</u> (Cambridge, Mass.: Harvard University Press, 1995).

Melville, Herman, <u>Moby-Dick</u> (New York: Penguin, 1992).

Melville, Herman <u>Moby-Dick or, The Whale</u> (New York: Penguin, 2003).

Melville, Herman. Billy Budd, Sailor and Selected Tales edited by Robert Milder (Oxford: Oxford University Press, 2009).

Merrell Lynd, Helen, Shame and the Search for Identity (London: Routledge, 2014; first published, 1958).

Mikel Brown, Lyn and Carol Gilligan, Meeting at the Crossroads: Women's Psychology and Girls' Development (Cambridge, Mass.: Harvard University Press, 1992 (paperback edition by Ballantine, New York, 1993).

Miller, Perry, The New England Mind: The Seventeenth Century (Cambridge, Mass.: Belknap Press of Harvard University Press, 1939).

Miller, Perry, The New England Mind: From Colony to Province (Cambridge, Mass.: Belknap Press of Harvard University Press, 1953).

Miller, Perry, The Life of the Mind in America (New York: Harcourt, Brace & World, 1965).

Modell, Arnold H., The Private Self (Cambridge, Mass.: Harvard University Press, 1993).

Moody, David A., Ezra Pound: Poet: Volume I The Young Genius 1885-1920 (Oxford: Oxford University Press, 2007).

Moody, David A., Ezra Pound: Poet Volume II The Epic Years 1921-1939 (Oxford: Oxford University Press, 2014).

Moody, David A., Ezra Pound: Poet Volume III The Tragic Years 1939-1972 (Oxford: Oxford University Press, 2015).

Morris, Edmund, The Rise of Theodore Roosevelt (New York: Random House, 1979).

Morris, Norval, The Future of Imprisonment (Chicago: University of Chicago Press, 1974).

Morrison, Andrew P. ed., Essential Papers on Narcissism (New York: New York University Press, 1986).

Mottley, Constance Baker. Equal Justice Under Law (New York: Farrar, Straus and Giroux, 1998)

Mounk, Yascha. The People vs. Democracy: Why Our Freedom Is in Danger and How to Save It (Cambridge, Mass.: Harvard University Press, 2018).

Nietzsche, Friedrich. On the Genealogy of Morals Douglas Smith trans. (Oxford: Oxford University Press, 1996).

Nussbaum, Martha C., Love's Knowledge: Essays on Philosophy and Literature (New York: Oxford University Press, 1990).

Nussbaum, Martha C., The Monarchy of Fear: A Philosopher Looks at Our Political Crisis (New York: Simon & Schuster, 2018).

Obama, Barack, The Audacity of Hope: Thoughts on Reclaiming the American Dream (New York: Three Rivers Press, 2006).

Obama, Barack, Dreams from My Father: A Story of Race and Inheritance (New York: The Three Rivers Press, 2004).

Obergefell v. Hodges, 135 S.Ct. 2584 (2015).

O'Brien, Tim, The Things They Carried (Boston: Mariner, 2009; originally published, 1990).

Olson, Lynne, Freedom's Daughters: The Unsung Heroines of the Civil Rights Movement from 1830 to 1970 (New York: Scribner, 2001).

Orwell, George. A Collection of Essays (New York: Harvest, 1981; originally published, 1946).

Parens, Henri, Alaf Mahfouz, Stuart W. Twemlow, and David E. Sharff, eds., The Future of Prejudice: Psychoanalysis and the Prevention of Prejudice (Lanham, Md.: Rowman & Littlefield, 2007).

Owen, Wilfrid, The Collected Poems of Wilfred Owen edited by C.D. Lewis (New York: New Directions Book, 1963) first published, 1920.

Parker, Hershel, Herman Melville: A Biography Volume 1, 1829-1851 (Baltimore: The Johns Hopkins University Press, 1996).

Parker, Hershel. Herman Melville: A Biography Volume 2, 1851-1891 (Baltimore: The Johns Hopkins University Press, 2002).

Paxton, Robert O., The Anatomy of Fascism (New York: Vintage Books, 2004).

Patterson, Orlando, The Rituals of Blood: Consequences of Slavery in Two American Centuries (Washington, D.C.: Civitas, 1998).

PBS American Experience, The Great War, aired on April 12, 2017

Perel, Esther, Mating in Captivity: Unlocking Erotic Intelligence (New York: Harper, 2007).

Perel, Esther, The State of Affairs: Rethinking Infidelity New York: HarperCollins, 2017).

Peterson, Jordan B. Maps of Meaning: The Architecture of Belief (New York: Routledge, 1999).

Peterson, Jordan B. 12 Rules for Life: An Antidote to Chaos (Toronto: Random House Canada, 2018).

Piers, Gerhart and Milton B. Singer, Shame and Guilt: a Psychoanalytic and Cultural Study (Springfield, Ill.: Charles C. Thomas, Publisher, 1953).

Plessy v. Ferguson 163 U.S. 537 (1896).

Powell, Neil. Benjamin Britten: A Life for Music (New York: Henry Holt and Company, 2013).

Pound, Ezra, Hugh Selwyn Mauberley (London: The Ovid Press, 1920).

Pound, Ezra, The Cantos of Ezra Pound (New York: New Directions, 1996).

Powers, Ron, Mark Twain: a Life (New York: Free Press, 2005).

Pozorski, Aimee, Roth and Trauma: The Problem of History in the Later Works (1995-2010) (New York: Bloomsbury, 2011).

Reichenbach, Hans, The Rise of Scientific Philosophy (Berkeley, Calif.: University of California Press, 1951).

Remnick, David The Bridge: The Life and Rise of Barack Obama (New York: Vintage, 2011).

Renehan Jr., Edward J., The Lion's Pride: Theodore Roosevelt and His Family in Peace and War (New York: Oxford University Press, 1998).

Richards, David A.J., A Theory of Reasons for Action (Oxford: Clarendon Press, 1971).

Richards, David A.J., Conscience and the Constitution: History, Theory, and Law of the Reconstruction Amendments (Princeton: Princeton University Press, 1993).

Richards, David A.J., Disarming Manhood: Roots of Ethical Resistance in Jesus, Garrison, Tolstoy, Gandhi, King, and Churchill (Athens, Ohio: Swallow Press, 2005).

Richards, David A.J., Foundations of American Constitutionalism (New York: Oxford University Press, 1989).

Richards, David A.J., Free Speech and the Politics of Identity (Oxford: Oxford University Press, 1999).

Richards, David A.J., Fundamentalism in American Religion and Law: Obama's Challenge to Patriarchy's Threat to Democracy (Cambridge: Cambridge University Press, 2013).

Richards, David A.J., Identity and the Case for Gay Rights (Chicago: University of Chicago Press, 1999).

Richards, David A.J., Italian American: The Racializing of an Ethnic Identity (New York: New York University Press, 1999).

Richards, David A.J., Patriarchal Religion, Sexuality, and Gender: A Critique of New Natural Law (with Nicholas C. Bamforth) (Cambridge: Cambridge University Press, 2008).

Richards, David A.J., Resisting Injustice and the Feminist Ethics of Care in the Age of Obama (New York: Routledge, 2013).

Richards, David A.J., Sex, Drugs, Death and the Law: An Essay on Human Rights and Overcriminalization (Totowa, N.J.: Rowman & Littlefield, 1982).

Richards, David A.J., The Case for Gay Rights: From Bowers to Lawrence and Beyond (Lawrence: University Press of Kansas, 2005).

Richards, David A.J., The Deepening Darkness: Patriarchy, Resistance, and Democracy's Future (with Carol Gilligan) (New York: Cambridge University Press, 2009).

Richards, David A.J., The Moral Criticism of Law (Encino: Dickenson, 1977).

Richards, David A.J., The Rise of Gay Rights and the Fall of the British Empire: Liberal Resistance and the Bloomsbury Group (New York: Cambridge University Press, 2013).

Richards, David A.J., The Sodomy Cases: Bowers v. Hardwick and Lawrence v Texas (Lawrence: University Press of Kansas 2009).

Richards, David A.J., Toleration and the Constitution (New York: Oxford University Press, 1986).

Richards, David A.J., Tragic Manhood and Democracy: Verdi's Voice and the Powers of Musical Art (Brighton, U.K.: Sussex Academic Press, 2004).

Richards, David A.J., Why Love Leads to Justice: Love Across the Boundaries (New York: Cambridge University Press, 2016).

Richards, David A.J., Women, Gays, and the Constitution: The Grounds for Feminism and Gay Rights in Culture and Law (Chicago: University of Chicago Press, 1998).

Richardson, Robert D., William James in the Maelstrom of American Modernism: A Biography (Boston: Mariner, 2006).

Ricks, Christopher, T.S. Eliot and Prejudice (Berkeley: University of California Press, 1988).

Robertson-Lorant, Laurie, Melville: A Biography (New York: Clarkson Potter, 1996).

Robinson, Paul H. and John M.Darley, "Does Criminal Law Deter? A Behavioural Science Investigation," Oxford Journal of Legal Studies, Vol. 24, No. 2 (2004).

Robnett, Belinda, How Long? How Long?: African-American Women in the Struggle for Civil Rights (New York: Oxford University Press, 1997).

Rorty, Richard. Essays on Heidegger and Others: Philosophical Papers (New York: Cambridge University Press, 1991).

Roth, Philip, The American Trilogy 1997-2000 edited by Ross Miller (New York: The Library of America, 2011).

Roth, Philip, Novels 2001-2007 edited by Ross Miller (New York: The Library of America, 2013).

Roth, Philip, <u>Novels & Stories 1959-1962</u> edited by Ross Miller (New York: The Library of America, 2005).

Roth, Philip, <u>Novels 1967-1972</u> edited by Ross Miller (New York: The Library of America, 2005).

Roth, Philip, <u>Novels & Other Narratives 1986-1991</u> edited by Ross Miller (New York: The Library of America, 2008).

Roth, Philip, <u>Novels 1993-1995</u> edited by Ross Miller (New York: The Library of America, 2010).

Roth Pierpont, Claudia, <u>Roth Unbound: A Writer and His Books</u> (New York: Farrar, Straus & Giroux, 2013).

Sadie, Stanley ed., <u>The New Grove Dictionary of Opera</u> Volume Two (London: Macmillan, 1992).

Saini, Angela. <u>Inferior: How Science Got Women Wrong—and the New Research That's Rewriting the Story</u> (Boston: Beacon Press, 2017).

Sanneh, Kelefa, "Sort Yourself Out, Bucko: The gospel of Jordan Peterson," <u>The New Yorker,</u> March 5, 2018, pp. 70-75.

Sartwell, Crispin. "Conversion Therapy Isn't the Cure for 'Toxic Masculinity,'" <u>The Wall Street Journal,</u> June 2-3, 2018, A15.

Santayana, George, <u>Dominations and Powers: Reflections on Liberty, Society and Government</u> (New York: Charles Scribner's Sons, 1951).

Santayana, George, <u>Scepticism and Animal Faith: Introduction to a System of Philosophy</u> (New York: Dover, 1955; originally published, 1923).

Santayana, George, <u>The Idea of Christ in the Gospels</u> (New York: Charles Scribner's Sons, 1946).

Santayana, George, <u>The Life of Reason Volume One Reason in Common Sense</u> (New York: Dover, 1980, originally published, 1905).

Santayana, George, The Life of Reason Volume Two Reason in Society (New York: Dover, 1980, originally published, 1905).

Santayana, George, The Life of Reason Volume Three Reason in Religion (New York: Collier, 1962, originally published, 1905).

Santayana, George, The Life of Reason Volume Four Reason in Art (New York: Dover, 1982, originally published 1905).

Santayana, George, The Life of Reason Volume Five Reason in Science (New York: Dover, 1983, originally published, 1906).

Santayana, George, The Genteel Tradition (Lincoln: University of Nebraska Press, 1998, originally published, 1967).

Santayana, George, The Last Puritan: A Memoir in the Form of a Novel critical edition co-edited by William G. Holzberger and Herman J. Saatkamp, Jr. with an Introduction by Irving Singer (Cambridge, Mass.: MIT Press, 1994) (originally published 1935).

Saunders Peirce, Charles in "Evolutionary Love," The Monist, Vol. 3, No. 2. (January, 1893), pp. 176-200, at p. 177.

Schickel, Richard. Clint Eastwood: a Biography (New York: Vintage, 1997).

Schoenberger, Nancy,Wayne and Ford: The Films, the Friendship, and the Forging of an American Hero (New York: Doubleday, 2017).

Schwartz, Sunny and David Boodell, Dreams from the Monster Factory (New York: Scribner, 2009).

Scott, Janny, A Singular Woman: The Untold Story of Barack Obama's Mother (New York: Riverhead Books, 2011).

Shapiro, James. A Year in the Life of William Shakespeare 1599 (New York: HarperPerennial, 2005).

Shatan, Chaim F., "Bogus Manhood, Bogus Honor: Surrender and Transfiguration in the United States Martin Corps," (1977) Psychoanalytic Review, 64(4): 585-610.

Shelden, Michael. Melville in Love: The Secret Life of Herman Melville and the Muse of Moby-Dick (New York: Harper Collins, 2016).

Shengold, Leonard. Soul Murder: The Effects of Child Abuse and Deprivations (New York: Fawcett Columbine, 1989).

Shakespeare, William, Troilus and Cressida in Shakespeare, Complete Works W.J. Craig ed. (London: Oxford University Press, 1966).

Shay, Jonathan, Achilles in Vietnam: Combat Trauma and the Undoing of Character (New York: Scribner, 1994).

Shengold, Leonard, Soul Murder: The Effects of Child Abuse and Deprivations (New York: Fawcett Columbine, 1989).

Showalter, Elaine. The Civil Wars of Julia Ward Howe: a Biography (New York: Simon & Schuster, 2016).

Siedentop, Larry, Inventing the Individual: The Origins of Western Liberalism (London: Allen Lane, 2015).

Snyder, Timothy. On Tyranny: Twenty Lessons From the Twentieth Century (New York: Tim Duggan Books, 2017).

Snyder, Timothy. The Road to Unfreedom: Russia, Europe, America (New York: Tim Duggan Books, 2018).

Stedman Jones, Gareth, Karl Marx: Greatness and Illusion (Cambridge, Mass.: The Belknap Press of Harvard University Press, 2016).

Steiker, Carol S. and Jordan M. Steiker, Courting Death: The Supreme Court and Capital Punishment (Cambridge, Mass.: Belknap Press of Harvard University Press, 2016).

Stephens, Bret, "Only Mass Deportation Can Save Us," The New York Times, Saturday, June 17, 2017, A23 (op-ed).

Stevens, Hugh. Henry James and Sexuality (Cambridge: Cambridge University Press, 1998).

Strouse, Jean, Alice James: A Biography (New York: New York Review Books, 2011).

Suggs, Jon-Christian. "Something About the Boy: Law, Ironic Comedy, and the Ideology of Agape in Billy Budd" (unpublished paper).

Swick Perry, Helen, Psychiatrist of America: The Life of Harry Stack Sullivan (Cambridge, Mass.: The Belknap Press of Harvard University Press, 1982).

The Last Puritan at https://en.wikipedia.org/wiki/The_Last_Puritan

Tierney, Brian The Idea of Natural Rights: Studies on Natural Rights, Natural Law, and Church Law 1150-1625 Grand Rapids, Michigan: William B. Eerdmans, 1970).

Thompson, Ann and Neil Taylor, ed., Hamlet: The Arden Shakespeare rev. ed. (London: Bloomsbury, 2016).

Thucydides, History of the Peloponnesian War Rex Warner translation (New York: Penguin. 1972).

Toibin, Colm, The Master (New York: Scribner, 2004).

Toibin, Colm, Marc Simpson, Declan Kiely, Henry James and American Painting (University Park, Pa.: Pennsylvania State University Press, 2017).

Townsend, Kim, Manhood at Harvard: William James and Others (New York: W.W. Norton, 1996).

Travis, Jeremy et al., The Growth of Incarceration in the United States: Exploring Causes and Consequences (Washington, D.C.: The National Academies Press, 2014).

Twain, Mark, Mississippi Writings (New York: The Library of America, 1982; originally published, 1884).

Valenti, Jessica, "Boys Need Feminists' Help Too," The New York Times Op-Ed Thursday July 26, 2018, A27.

Wake, Naoko, Private Practices: Harry Stack Sullivan, the Science of Homosexuality, and American Liberalism (New Brunswick, N.J.: Rutgers University Press, 2011).

Walzer, Michael, The Revolution of the Saints (Cambridge, Mass.: Harvard University Press, 1965).

Way, Niobe Deep Secrets: Boys' Friendships and the Crisis of Connection (Cambridge, Mass.: Harvard University Press, 2011).

Weisberg, Richard H. The Failure of the Word: The Protagonist as Lawyer in Modern Fiction (New Haven: Yale University Press, 1984).

West, Rebecca. Henry James (New York: Henry Holt, 1916).

Weinstein, Philip, Becoming Faulkner: The Art and Life of William Faulkner (Oxford: Oxford University Press, 2010).

Wineapple, Brenda. Hawthorne: A Life (New York: Random House, 2003).

Whitman, James Q., Harsh Justice: Criminal Punishment and the Widening Divide between America and Europe (Oxford: Oxford University Press, 2003).

Whitman, James Q., Hitler's American Model: The United States and the making of Nazi race law (Princeton: Princeton University Press, 2017).

Wolff, Michael, Fire and Furty: Inside the Trump White House p. 72 (London: Little, Brown, 2018).

Wood, Gordon S., The Creation of the American Republic, 1776-1787 (New York: Norton, 1969).

Woolf, Virginia. Three Guineas Jane Marcus edition (Orlando, Florida: Harvest, 2006) (originally published, 1938).

Woodhouse, A.S.P. ed., Puritanism and Liberty (London: Dent, 1938).

Wurmser Leon, The Mask of Shame (Northvale, New Jersey: Jason Aronson, 1984).

Wurmser, Leon The Hidden Dimension: Psychodynamics of Compulsive Drug Use (Northvale, New Jersey: Jason Aronson, 1995).

Young-Bruehl, Elisabeth Why Arendt Matters (New Haven, Conn.: Yale University Press, 2006).

Zimbardo, Philip, The Lucifer Effect (New York: Random House, 2007).

Zimring, Franklin E. and Gordon J. Hawkins, Deterrence (Chicago: University of Chicago Press, 1973).

INDEX

M

N

O

P